The World They Made Together

The World They Made Together

Black and White Values
in Eighteenth-Century
Virginia

MECHAL SOBEL

Princeton University Press, Princeton, New Jersey

Copyright © 1987 by Princeton University Press

Published by Princeton University Press, 41 William Street,
Princeton, New Jersey 08540
In the United Kingdom: Princeton University Press, Oxford

All Rights Reserved

Library of Congress Cataloging in Publication Data will be found
on the last printed page of this book

ISBN 0-691-04747-2
ISBN 0-691-00608-3 (pbk.)

First Princeton Paperback printing, 1989

This book has been composed in Linotron Trump

Frontispiece: Photographer Huestis Cook's son and nursemaid, 1868.
Cook Collection. Courtesy of the Valentine Museum, Richmond.

Clothbound editions of Princeton University Press books are printed
on acid-free paper, and binding materials are chosen for strength
and durability. Paperbacks, although satisfactory for personal collections,
are not usually suitable for library rebinding

Printed in the United States of America by Princeton University
Press, Princeton, New Jersey

9 8 7 6 5 4

For Zvi

with whom I have learned to redeem time past

Contents

Illustrations

Acknowledgments

I HAVE BEEN at work on the research for this volume for some years and have profited from the advice and help of many individuals. Herbert Klein and William Freedman read an early version of Part One and made significant suggestions. Allan Kulikoff and Ira Berlin read the entire manuscript and wrote extraordinary critiques that helped me revise the book. I owe them both a special debt of gratitude. Gary Nash read a late draft, and his astute criticism improved the volume substantially. Ronald Hoffman, a most generous colleague, gave judicious advice that I have deeply appreciated.

Living as I do, some 6,000 miles from Virginia, I have been dependent on many people for data, microfilm, photostats, and photographs. During a lengthy stay there, I very much appreciated the hospitality of the staffs and the outstanding resources of the Virginia Historical Society, the Virginia Baptist Historical Society, the Institute of Early American History and Culture, and the Colonial Williamsburg Foundation. Members of the staff of the Virginia State Library enabled me to obtain copies of important documents for study abroad. A grant from the Israel Academy of Sciences and Humanities made possible the purchase of microfilmed records, and the Research Authority of Haifa University generously provided funds to cover typing costs.

For permission to quote from manuscripts in their collections, I am most grateful to the Library of Congress, Washington, D.C.; the Massachusettes Historical Society, Boston; the Virginia Baptist Historical Society, Richmond; and the Virginia Historical Society, Richmond.

I would particularly like to thank Pat Almonrode, Fred Anderson, Yehoshua Arieli, Selma Aronson, William C. Beal, Richard R. Beeman, Dick Bruggeman, Reginald Butler, Edward A. Chappell, Paul I. Chestnut, Howson W. Cole, Douglas Deal, Helen Doherty, Michael Doran, Daphna Gentry, Harold B. Gill, Lucia S. Goodwin, Anne M. Hogg, William L. Hopkins, James H. Hutson, Judith S. Hynson, Arthur E. Imhof, John E. Ingram, Mary M. Ison, Gregory D. Jeane, Jon Kukla, Heinz Lubasz, Fritz J. Malval, Mark Mancall, Henry Miller, Michael Miller, Richard Newman, Michael L. Nicholls, James O'Malley, L. Eileen Parris, Darett B. Rutman, Vardite Selinger, Elliott Stonehill, Robert Strohm, Thad Tate, Keith Thomas, Robert Farris Thompson, Dell Upton, Charlotte Vardi, Marianna Weissman, David Wiener, Waverly Winfree, Francie Woltz, Gordon E. Wood, Michael Zuckerman, and Shomer Zwelling. Yoshiko Fukakusa was of great help in checking difficult bibliographical references. I am grateful to Genoveba Breitstein, who typed several versions of this work with skill, speed, and understanding. I also wish to give special thanks to my editor, Gail Ullman, who was very patient, supportive, and helpful, and to Cathie Brettschneider, whose fine editorial skills improved the manuscript.

My husband Zvi and my son Noam have both lived with this project for all the years I've been involved in it. They have probably learned more about Virginia and slavery than they wanted to know, but their willingness to listen and respond has been very important, and I learned a great deal from them. Certain interests of my older children—particularly Daniel's in the building of houses and Mindy's in spiritual traditions—have had their effect on me as well. To them all, my thanks.

It is not at all *pro forma* that I emphasize that no one who has read this work and/or helped me along the way agrees fully with the views presented here. In fact, fairly often I have come to opposite conclusions from those voiced by the very authorities I rely on for evidence, so that citations in the book often refer to those with whom I differ but whose evidence I have used. I'd like to ask their indulgence and to thank them too.

The World They Made Together

"It was like the garden of the Lord,
like the land of Egypt."

Genesis 13:10

Introduction

MANY YEARS ago, when I began to consider the First Great Awakening in the South, I was taken aback by the clear evidence of extensive racial interaction.[1] Nothing that I knew then about slavery explained how whites and blacks could have shared religious experiences in the eighteenth century. The more I studied the churches, and the more I found blacks and whites had been "together," the more I felt it likely that new questions had to be asked in relation to the period that preceded the revivals.[2]

I am now convinced that the Southern Awakenings were a climax to a long period of intensive racial interaction, and that as a result the culture of Americans—blacks and whites—was deeply affected by African values and perceptions. The interpenetration of Western and African values took place very early, beginning with the large-scale importation of Africans into the South in the last decades of the seventeenth century. In the eighteenth-century South, blacks and whites lived together in great intimacy, affecting each other in both small and large ways. They lived in the same houses as well as in separate houses that were more often similar than not; they did much the same work, often together; and they came to share their churches and their God. Their interaction was intense and continued over the lifetimes of most blacks and whites. In spite of a significant interpenetration of values between the two races, the whites were usually unaware of their own change in this process. Nevertheless, in perceptions of time, in esthetics, in approaches to ecstatic religious experience and to understanding the Holy Spirit, in ideas of the afterworld and of the proper ways to honor the spirits of the dead, African influence was deep and far-reaching.

This interpretation is based upon an analysis of the social history of eighteenth-century Virginia, the largest and most populous colony and home for a significant number of emigrants to virtually all the later settlements. In Virginia the racial balance was such that most whites were in both intensive and extensive contact with blacks. In 1700 some twenty-five percent of the population was already black; by mid-century sixty-six percent of the Tidewater area, the most heavily settled section, was black. This change was rapid and radical. Living through it, William Byrd II thought Virginia would become known by the name "New Guinea," and he and others came to fear the social results of the demographic transformation.[3] Even during

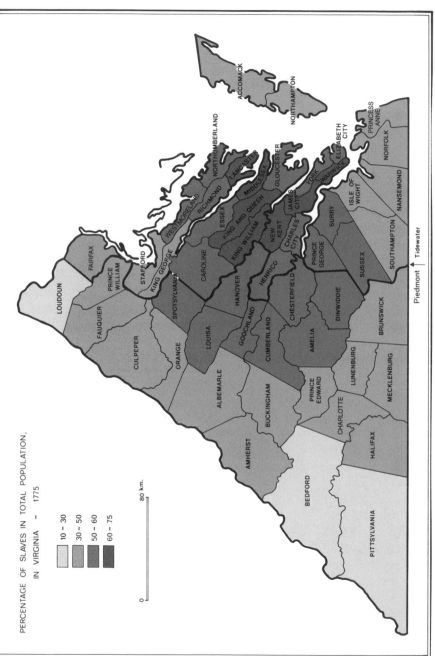

PERCENTAGE OF SLAVES IN TOTAL POPULATION,
IN VIRGINIA – 1775

10 – 30
30 – 50
50 – 60
60 – 75

0 ———— 80 km.

FIGURE 1. Virginia in 1775; blacks as a percentage of the population. The boundary between the Piedmont and the Tidewater is not a formal one, and many border counties are sometimes considered to be in the adjacent area. To the West of the Piedmont, slaves were less than 10 percent of the population. Based on maps in *The Atlas of Early American History: The Revolutionary Era, 1760-1790*, ed. Lester J. Cappon (Princeton

the dislocations of the Revolutionary period, the slave population continued to grow. By century's end most Tidewater counties had black populations above those of the prewar period; in the newer area of settlement, the Piedmont, the black population had risen enormously. Some counties were from sixty percent to seventy percent black, and all through the second half of the eighteenth century blacks represented over forty percent of the total population.[4] (See Figure 1.)

Whites in eighteenth-century Virginia found themselves not only in a biracial population but also in a biracial society. They worked with blacks, played with blacks, lived with blacks, and eventually prayed with blacks. Cultural interaction was not simply probable, it was virtually certain to have taken place.[5]

This interpretation is reinforced by an analysis of the cultures brought to America by the Africans and the English. Notwithstanding vast differences, both peoples brought preindustrial cultures to the New World in which there were far greater similarities with respect to modal attitudes and values than has generally been recognized. It was thus possible for many values and practices to meld or to reinforce one another, and this in fact did happen. In other areas where the cultures clashed, the process was more complex. It was not simply that the politically dominant racial group, the whites, maintained their traditions and imposed them on the blacks. On the contrary, the social–cultural interplay was such that both blacks and whites were crucially influenced by the traditions of the "other." As a result, a new culture emerged in the American South that was a mix of both African and English values.

The Africans coming to Virginia were a very mixed group, and analysis of their cultures raises the first set of significant problems. We more or less know the African ports from which the slave ships embarked, but the origins of their enslaved "passengers" are far more problematic. Well over 60,000 slaves were brought directly from Africa to Virginia, most arriving before 1740. The largest group was transported from the Bight of Biafra, a sizable number were sent from the Gold Coast, and a smaller number from Angola. Although most of Virginia's first-generation black population left Africa from these areas, a variety of ethnic groups were represented, among them Igbo, Tiv, Kongo, Fante, Asante, Ibibio, Fon, and others.[6]

But even though this study necessitates an analysis of African values, can and should these different ethnic groups be considered? Although the data now available on eighteenth-century Africa are far richer than what was known in the past, they remain problematic.

They are, in part, based upon the records of slave traders who visited the continent, the memories of slaves taken from there who recorded their recollections years later after exposure to other values, and accounts by missionaries and random travelers. However, in greater part, our ideas of eighteenth-century Africa are based on the works of twentieth-century anthropologists, who have often extrapolated past realities from later developments and/or relied on oral history.[7] Notwithstanding these limitations, there are by now myriad studies of African cultures and languages and extensive data on their traditions that, with the above caveats in mind, can and should be utilized for comparative purposes. Perhaps above all, it should be emphasized that these cultures, usually perceived as static, were in the process of gradual change before their contact with the West.[8]

The world views of many African peoples were introduced into Virginia, some similar to each other, some conflicting. On the surface, they appeared more divergent than they perhaps were. Divinities with different names were often of similar character. Mores and folkways, on the other hand, varied widely.[9] Most important, the diverse social structures, to which each world view had been integrally tied, remained behind. Sweeping change was inevitable. Africans of every class were brought over: rulers, caught in the "trade" or in wars; priests; traders; artisans; independent farmers; and those who had been slaves in Africa. Although traditional religious practitioners were occasionally singled out, America essentially leveled all Africans as slaves. However, in slavery a new process of value amalgamation and social distinction was begun.

By the third decade of the eighteenth century the Virginia slave population was more than reproducing itself. African-born slaves did remain an important part of the population until mid-century, when some thirty to thirty-five percent of all black adults in the colony were still "outlanders"; however their percentage declined rapidly after that point. Although over 13,000 Africans were brought in after 1750 and new arrivals could be found down through the trade's legal close in Virginia in 1778, by that time the black population had become an essentially American-born one.[10] With this population, a new Creole and Black-American culture was emerging, and that too must be analyzed.

The assessment of the values of the Europeans who came to Virginia presents a second set of problems. Scots, Scotch-Irish, Huguenots, and others certainly affected the Southern world view, but their influence has been assumed to have been of secondary importance and has not been considered separately in this assessment. The "vexed and troubled Englishmen" who brought mixed and changing values with them present problems in and of themselves. They were Puritans as well as Anglicans, and beneath these labels was often an amalgamated world view encompassing elements of an older value system.[11]

Ostensibly the Anglican world view dominated Virginia life and its institutions, with the Anglican Church the established church, and the church vestry carrying out civil and social regulations. This seeming dominance is deceptive; in actuality a wide range of values, including many that were closer to the medieval Catholic world view than to the new views of either Anglicans or Puritans, were brought into Virginia and continued to develop there. The social order, which approved and even facilitated physical dispersal (unlike settlement patterns in New England) as well as social separation of the "lower sort" from the "middling" and upper class groups, made possible the continuance of many of the old ways of thought and behavior.[12]

In eighteenth-century Virginia ethnic groups intermingled, the population grew, and soon came to be Virginian-born. Together with, and in part as a result of, these demographic changes, the social system was transformed. Specifically, the locus of population shifted westward, from the Tidewater to the Piedmont, and slavery replaced white servitude as the modal system of labor, affecting virtually all inhabitants.[13]

Recent research and analysis indicate that in the seventeenth century whites moving up the economic ladder had been very dependent on those below them.[14] They boarded former indentured servants or white newcomers in their small houses and rented or sold parcels of land to them. The capital thus gained enabled them to "move up," perhaps buying the services of another indentured white. With the fairly rapid shift to slavery, and the relative decline in new freed servants, poor and "middling" whites lost an important source of income, and the pattern of class development (and social interaction) was altered significantly.

The Piedmont, settled after these changes had begun, did not repeat seventeenth-century Tidewater history, with its early reliance on white servitude and the later rapid growth of a slaveowning elite. As this area was settled it moved relatively rapidly into widespread (but small-scale) slaveholding. A much more "middling" group of small-scale slaveowners dominated, many more individuals were slaveowners, and a higher percentage of the white population was working with blacks.[15]

Assessment of the values of this new slaveowning class poses one of the key problems addressed in this work. Although church records and some diaries and letters give us material recorded by "middling" and lower class people, there is no question but that these data are far more fragmentary than those from the elite. Even the rare extant diary of an indentured servant, that of John Harrower, is from the elite of the servant class, a tradesman turned teacher-tutor, and not from a field hand. In regard to both poor whites and blacks, much must be inferred from documents left by the white upper class. Although this entails great hazards, masters often inadvertently revealed a great deal about their slaves, servants, and neighbors, as well as themselves.[16] In some cases there is no contemporary comment on a point under discussion. At some risk, later evidence—clearly marked as such—has been introduced to extrapolate past events.

In Virginia, the world views of Africans, Englishmen, Afro-Americans, and Anglo-Americans underwent changes that at times seemed to leave the individual at the mercy of conflicting values. Yet out of these conflicts and interactions, functional and by and large coherent cultures emerged. In my assesment of this process Thomas Luckman's definition of a world view has proved of great value. According to Luckman, a world view is "an encompassing system of meaning in which socially relevant categories of time, space, causality and purpose are superordinated to more specific interpretive schemes in which reality is segmented."[17] He suggests that at the center of each world view there is (or should be) a congruent set of value discriminations relating to each of the four categories.[18]

Loosely following Luckman's categorization of the basic values in world views (discussed at greater length in Chapter 1), this book is organized in three separate sections dealing, respectively, with the following attitudes and their expression in social life:
1. attitudes toward time, especially as reflected in work behavior;
2. attitudes toward space and the natural world, as they affected settlement, building, and the naming of places and people; and
3. understandings of causality and purpose, examined in relation to explanations of death and the afterlife.

In each section African, English, Afro-American, and Anglo-American values, attitudes, and behavior are surveyed separately and in relation to each other.

Although this approach has structured comparisons and led to what

I believe are new insights, it does, however, present problems as well, especially regarding the analysis of institutions that affect values and are affected by them. Should an institution be considered repeatedly in regard to each value category? The family, for example, falls between categories and into all of them. It is discussed in part in the section on time, as family life regulated both daily activity and life-cycle events; it is discussed at length in relation to space, as the structure of houses and quarters affected family life, and the nature of families affected the building of houses and the patterns of settlement on the land. And finally, family is briefly discussed in the section on causality and purpose, as Africans, and later many Virginians, believed that life should be lived *for* kin, living and dead, because kin, it was believed, cause significant changes among the living and could, in fact, bring about death. (The institution of the church could also have been considered in all three sections, but it has been consolidated into the section on causality and purpose, violating the structure in strict terms but providing a far more coherent analysis than would have been possible otherwise.)

The problems in regard to evidence (the myriad peoples involved and the essentially oral traditions of both Africans and lower class whites), and the problems inherent in value analysis (especially the all-encompassing purview necessary—one that includes folklore, folk belief, folkways and mores, institutions, and noninstitutionalized behavior), are serious ones and can be resolved only in part. One problematic decision that had to be made with regard to evidence concerns the use of dialect reports found in eighteenth-century sources. While there is a history of the derisive reporting of back dialect by whites in order to make fun of and belittle Afro-Americans, there is also an important history of a rich and unique black language that evolved through pidgin and creole into black English. Recognizing both these developments, I have chosen to quote reports of dialect speech, both as evidence of whites' perceptions and values, and as data for the analysis of black language development.[19]

There is also the issue of the discrepancy between culture as lived and culture as analyzed. An individual, especially in times of great stress and change, often assimilates contradictory values and acts in noncoherent ways. Making "sense" of belief and behavior often does violence to its complex nature. Nevertheless, world views can be seen as incorporating great inconsistencies and yet as having an overall functional coherence.

Perhaps the most difficult problem involves the issue of causality.

Given the complex interaction of world views and the resultant cultural change, how can the historian assign weights to causal influences? Along with Maurice Mandelbaum and many others, I would maintain that in historical analysis causality should not rest on a "single factor" but rather should include all "those accompanying 'conditions' without which the event would not have occurred as it did and when it did." For Mandelbaum "the cause of an effect is the actual series of events that terminated in the specific effect."[20] However, although it is attractive, this seemingly clear formulation begs the issue. Historians do not often agree on the "actual series of events that terminated" in a particular outcome. Each historian's values and world view affect his or her vision and choice of both questions and data. This is particularly relevant to any issue involving blacks, who were "invisible" people for so long.[21] The Great Awakening in Virginia, for example, has been studied over a long period, and although blacks were known to have been present in large numbers at revival meetings, this fact was not seen as having affected the outcome. However, once the arrival of Africans in the South is *seen* as a relevant "event," and the question of possible African influence on colonial values and behavior is raised, then data long available do, I believe, support the interpretation of significant cultural impact. In the family, at work, and especially in the churches, the evidence of African influence is substantial. In other areas, the evidence is far more ambiguous and fragmentary; however, these cases generally show that changes occurred only after Africans came to Virginia, and that the changes did not occur in areas where there were no Africans. Probability and inference, as well as concern with artifacts and other evidence from the material culture, play a major role in this argument, as does ultimate acceptance of the view that important social change is overdetermined and causes sometimes conflicting.[22]

Notwithstanding all these problems and limitations, but with consciousness of them, I feel we must take the risks and hazard an analysis of the interrelation of the values of blacks and those of whites in the early period of their contact. In 1959, surveying the limited state of knowledge of African cultures, Herskovits and Bascom commented:

The historical component in culture, or in social institutions, cannot be rejected simply because written documentation is not available. The challenge of probing the past so as to understand the present remains. No problem disappears because we have imperfect or even in-

10

adequate means of solving it; if this were so, there would be little point to the study of either culture or social institutions, or to the whole of social science.[23]

Accepting this challenge, African Studies has come a long way since that relatively recent time. Many of the same problems of documentation and method plague the study of early American culture, and we have already seen that with similar levels of commitment and a willingness to take intellectual risks, remarkable new insights have been attained.[24]

In the recent past, enormous creative energy has gone into the study of American slavery, with major explorations of the extent to which African culture affected the culture of black Americans and with an almost totally new assessment of slave culture as Afro-American. Accompanying this new awareness of the African values brought into America, however, is an automatic assumption that white traditions influenced black ones. In this view, although the institution of slavery is seen as important, blacks are not generally treated as actors nor is their "divergent culture" seen as having had a wide-ranging effect on whites. Historians working in this area generally assume two social systems in America, one black and one white, and cultural divergence between slaves and masters.[25]

It is the thesis of this book that blacks, Africans and Afro-Americans, deeply influenced whites' perceptions, values, and identity, and that although two world views existed, there was a deep symbiotic relatedness that must be explored if we are to understand either or both of them.[26] This exploration raises many questions and suggests many possibilities and probabilities, but it also, I hope, establishes how thoroughly whites and blacks intermixed within the system of slavery and how extensive was the resulting cultural interaction.

I

Attitudes Toward Time and Work

1. World Views in England and West Africa

THOMAS LUCKMAN includes in his definition of a world view as "an encompassing system of meaning" the existence of an inner core, which he terms the sacred cosmos, an integrated mesh of central attitudes and values. Through the internalization of such a cosmos the potentially chaotic and frightening infinity of events "falls in place" and the life of the individual assumes purpose and direction.

The relationships between the world view, the individuals, and the social structure in a given culture are dialectical. In part, the world view "routinizes and stabilizes the individual's memory, thinking, conduct and perception."[2] However, the world view does more than provide "unthinking routine"; its structuring of significance provides a taxonomy, models, and goals in relation to which the individual must evaluate reality and choose action. The individual as participant becomes a coproducer, changing the world view by his or her action. Similarly, social institutions are products of the world view, but they also transform it. By stabilizing or emphasizing particular aspects of culture, institutions change the relative importance of these very aspects, leading to new responses.[3]

In times of unusual social change, normative processes are altered and individuals, institutions, and world views undergo change, but the nature of these developments is related to the character of the original values. Whether due to the Reformation, the new scientific discoveries, an ethic stimulated by expanding capitalism, or a combination of all these factors, world views appeared to be undergoing rapid transition in seventeenth-century England, a time when, as Christopher Hill has written, "the world turned upside down." Hill posits that by mid-century, "there was a great overturning, questioning, revaluing, of everything in England. Old institutions, old beliefs, old values came in question."[4]

New church affiliations became the outward sign of supposedly new values. Although some individuals remained Catholics, most became High Church or Low Church Anglicans, Puritans, Presbyterians, Baptists, Quakers, or other sectarians; many did not go to any church. The very poor and the young of all classes may have been outside the churches, as well as many others from all classes and age groups—in all perhaps some twenty percent of the population.[5]

Notwithstanding the wide range of creed and association, as well as nonassociation, there was, even among the affiliated, a great deal of inconsistency and incoherence. Small groups, with many new values, initiated institutional changes to which many other people were forced to adjust. For most people values changed far more slowly, and there is strong evidence that they retained a "medieval" outlook long after the English Reformation. This older world view emphasized the cyclical aspects of time and held in awe the power and charisma attached to particular places. An arational explanation of causality was still widely accepted, and it was believed that the purpose of humanity was to perpetuate the given social order.

Belief in the power of witches and wizards as well as of holy places, such as wells and even trees, had been integrally tied to the Catholic Church, whose ritual and calendar were associated with magical or holy people, places, and events. Although the Anglican Church formally abjured these practices, many Anglicans continued them. As Keith Thomas has shown, the Anglican Church itself often turned to "cunning" men and women to find thieves; Anglican ministers often ministered to the ill with all the old panoply of folk remedies, including charms and magic herbs; and the Anglican laity—as observed by Bernard Gilpin, a contemporary—practiced "idolatry, sorcery, charming, witchcrafts, [and] conjuring."[6]

Whereas reforming clergy changed ecclesiastical practices radically, the laity maintained traditional behavior wherever they remained in control. The formal rites at funerals, for example, were totally revised, and Puritan as well as High Church Anglican clergy eliminated most traditional aspects of memorials. With belief in purgatory denied, the fate of the dead was said to be sealed at death, and later prayers were not believed to change it. The funeral "served simply to dispose of the corpse."[7] For this purpose a short, simple burial service would "do" nicely and the elaborate medieval practices were dropped.

Catholic rites had been performed at the house, in a procession to church, in the church, in a procession to the place of burial, at the grave, and on the return from the cemetery. "In all, during these rites, twenty-six psalms and twenty-nine collects were said, and the Lord's Prayer was repeated seven times, apart from the service in church, which included another twenty-one psalms."[8] The Anglican Church reduced this ceremony to a relatively brief service in church, a procession, and a short committal ritual.

The laity did not follow this lead. The maintenance of traditional "rituals of eating and drinking and the distribution of gifts at the burial," all in the hands of congregants, "illustrate the survival of medieval attitudes and customs."[8] This important rite of passage was continued in as traditional a fashion as was possible, as were all other lay-controlled patterns of behavior, indicating the laity's maintenance of older values. Special times, special places, magical individuals, omens, and cures were all believed in.[10]

Although most English people still shared aspects of the traditional world view, at one and the same time a new, modern value system was emerging, and by the seventeenth century its parameters were clear: It was almost diametrically opposed to the medieval Catholic world view. Orientation to time can be seen as the key to the differences between them.

In the modern Western world view, time was eventually perceived as linear and irreversible. (However, it was still believed that there would be a last event, the second coming of Christ, that would take the world "out of time.") In this view, no value was attached to time: No time was better than any other and all time could be used for all activities.[11]

Place, concomitantly, was becoming divorced from time. The earth was seen as measurable and controllable: The landscape could be made and remade, new continents explored, and a "New World" settled.

The working conception of causality in this world view was very different from the medieval one: People were regarded as quasi-free agents. A chosen action was seen as having concomitant results. God, fate, and social position were not without significance, but emphasis fell on the individual person as the crucial causative agent functioning in a "clockwork" universe with independent laws. He or she had to study the world and learn how it functioned and what the causal connections were.[12]

The new understanding of the purpose of life was equally different: Change rather than repetition became the goal. Individuals were expected to become their better selves and develop not toward a traditional role but to a newer, purer (and more self-controlled) form. Change or evolution in individuals *and in society* became the overall dynamic goal of this world view, although here too the Christian belief in the messianic End of Days remained an outside limit.

The Puritan elite were perhaps the most coherent proponents of the new world view in the seventeenth century. They had come to see themselves as establishing God's new Zion in the new world and felt they were the leading part of an ongoing and unfolding tableau of purposeful change. Their recent past was of great significance, but the messianic end they were preparing for was of ultimate concern.[13] This helped them to see themselves as makers of history, who could take control of themselves and the world around them, and who should use the natural world and therefore study it and control it as well. Their use of time became central: They were hurrying to a new end.

Anglicans, with their calendar still tied to saints' days and the "cyclical remembrance and renewal of the most important events in the life" and death of Jesus, were in a transitional position.[14] Special times were still set apart, but there was a new concern with the rational use of time. Rationality, in general, was emphasized, and a new attitude toward causality and the purpose of life arose. However, Anglicans were generally less likely to see themselves as God-given instruments and to suggest that their history had cosmic significance. There was therefore less emphasis on self-control and control of the world around them. Nevertheless, the present rather than the past of the traditionalists was their chief concern, and the new attitude toward time, place, and causality affected many of them seriously.

Ironically, the West Africans who were brought to America, who are generally regarded as having been a heterogeneous group, may have brought with them a more closely shared set of perceptions. West Africans certainly didn't share one culture. Gods, family structures, economic pursuits, languages, folkways, and mores all differed widely. But they apparently did share a more basic world view that made possible the melding of one Afro-American culture under the impact of North American slavery. They shared understandings of spirit power, its nature and its possible control; of human beings and their purpose; and of time and its relation to space. The analysis of West African understandings of time, space, causality, and purpose brings us to an ideal world view that was articulated differently in many cultures but on a deeper level was widely shared by West Africans.[15]

In the traditional African value system the present was of chief importance, but its significance was weighed in terms of its continuation of traditions. The people of the present were evaluated in relation to their forefathers and the mythical-historical example they provided.[16]

Time past, when marked by notable events, was important time, remembered time. Time in which nothing worthy of note occurred was not worthy of being remembered. It did not exist in terms of space occupied on a calendar or in a record.

The future did not have the reality of the past and present. It would appear that the future was not envisioned in a Western sense. Traditional Africans did not look forward to radical change or to a messianic age, but rather they "remembered" the homes of forefathers, reestablished after death by their spirits and awaiting the souls of the living. Death was seen as a time of returning home, a spiritual journey into the past and not into the future. Present and future social life was expected to be a repetition of past forms.[17]

In this traditional African sacred cosmos, time was viewed as having a scale of value. There were good times and bad times, times that were favorable for a particular activity and times that were inauspicious for that special action. These particular events that were tied to time were also tied further to place. Events should and *have* occurred at particular places on the earth, places that were auspicious for and tied to the event.[18]

The events that once happened in particular places hallowed them. Gods and humans became tied to a place. Soil and bones, burial grounds and village locations, and even village plans were seen as holy. Streams and rocks harbor spirits, and certain places were particularly close to the gods. Soil and herbs growing in these places made charms efficacious. Place was thus sanctified and inextricably bound to time. The gods once lived in this (or another) particular place. It was theirs as the clan living there remained theirs. The gods could best be prayed to at particular places, and particular places were marked by them as "out of bounds" or dangerous for people.[19]

The attitude toward causality was also tied to the orientation to time. Traditional African peoples accepted the spirit power of the forefathers who lived in time past. Africans believed spirits and forefathers affected their destiny, although a spirit worker might use power to counteract power. People thus could and should act, but they were not viewed as free agents who could cause virtually any result. They were seen as subject to fate, but they could make contact with power or with an agent who had access to such power and who might affect fate. And since each individual was a member of a particular clan, his or her forefathers would have an interest in using their power for the clan's benefit. A person was not an individual acting alone, neither in present time nor in relation to past and future time. One's biological and social standing had cosmic significance.[20]

One's purpose was also an integral part of this world view. Traditional African cultures opposed change; in fact, overt innovation was anathema. Through rite and ritual the African strove for the goal of repeating the mythical past. Men and women were to become their fullest unified selves, but in this view selfhood was, as symbolized by the given names, a recreation of the forefathers. A grandchild carried a grandparent's essence as well as the same name. He or she was the grandparent's future, while the clan and the grandparent were the child's models. The child was to become the best of this given type in the given society. The overall orientation of this world view was cyclical: Time past was to be repeated.[21]

The quasi-medieval world view, retained in great part by the mass of Christians in England, was in some ways very like the traditional African world view. Both views apprehended time as cyclical, the present as of overwhelming interest with time past as important time, and slow rhythms as natural. They both accepted the sacredness of place and the arational nature of causality. They held the individual responsible for respecting taboos, rituals, and practitioners of magic. Both world views were essentially conservative.

These world views—the traditional African, the traditional Christian, and the modern Western world view—came into Virginia. The confluence between the traditional African and the traditional Christian led to an interpenetration of values, especially regarding attitudes toward time and place. African slow time, with its cyclical calendar geared to the agricultural year, was close to the English agricultural laborers' perception of time. Together, black and white laborers, who appeared lazy in the eyes of their masters, maintained their traditional view of proper response to time. Eventually, this view affected the sons and daughters of the elite, many of whose parents had had a more "modern" view of time and the world.

2. English and African Perceptions of Time

IN THE COMPLEX of values the perception of time is the most significant one. A culture's sense of time is the key to its nature, and for an individual a particular and developed sense of time is an "essential parameter of personality."[1] When the perception of time changes, all other values are affected; conflicts in world views are likely to center on conflicts in perception of time.

In seventeenth-century England time was still generally perceived as tied to its use or function, and not as an independent "system or method of measuring or reckoning." Clocks appeared on church towers and town halls and served both the church and urban workshops, but in a very inexact fashion. The old Catholic designations for times of prayer (some of which had been carried over into Anglican practice)—matins, at midnight or first cock-crow, followed directly by lauds, prime at sunrise, tierce at mid-morning, sext at mid-day, nones at mid-afternoon, vespers at close of day, and compline after the evening meal—were widely referred to and commonly understood to indicate set times.[2] Shorter periods of time took their names from church use as well, such as a short "pater noster whyle," or a "misrere whyle," but there was also the profane "pissing while."[3] In towns, bells rang at dawn and all through the day until curfew. Time was aural: its markings were heard and not read and the peeling of bells was an important part of communal life.[4] Bells called people to prayers, to markets, and to communal meetings, and informed them of fires, dangers, and deaths. (Some important parallels can be drawn with the functions of drums in African societies.)

However inexact, time was ordered in English churches and towns, and the society's use of church terms reflects the origins and continuing significance of keeping time. However, outside of the churches, most people did not need or want exactitude in relation to their daytime or their lifetime. This attitude toward time is reflected in the attitude toward birthdays: In pre-Restoration England, "the date of birth [was often] . . . 'prooved' by associating it with another outstanding event."[5] Although parish registers were kept from the early sixteenth century, most individuals after coming of age had as little need for their exact age as they had for exact time.[6] Life periods were marked by the individual's role and not by age. When large enough and strong enough, most people were set to work. The distinctions between age groups or life periods—childhood, youth, adulthood, and old age—were blurred, although patterned. "Life itself was commonly thought of as having a certain symmetry, a cycle from birth to death in which the prime of life was reached in the first years of marriage."[7]

Activities, both on a daily basis and in life periods, were "concurrently rather than sequentially organized," with any set time being seen in what has been termed a polychronic or encompassing fashion during which tasks on many levels might be undertaken.[8] This view is in contrast to the modern Western monochronic or vectoral perception of time, concomitant with which tasks are seen as developmental, one leading to another. Finishing one task is anticipated before starting the next. This holds true for daily life as well as for the life cycle. Education, for example, should be completed before work is begun and a family planned, and in each phase, work and leisure occupy separate periods in the day.

In the seventeenth century, sunrise and sunset governed much labor, and most workers were "servants" in husbandry or housewifery whose total time—and not hours per week—had been hired.

The English certainly knew the months of the year and counted years, but for the masses the cyclical agricultural clock was the crucial one, and it was tied to custom and belief, both Christian and pre-Christian. In England "it was usual to sow either when there was no moon or at a new moon. . . . Rams were put to ewes, setting of eggs put under the hen, and pigs killed, on the increase of the moon."[9] The English also widely believed there were lucky and unlucky days, following the continental belief in "Egyptian" or ill-omened days. However, different almanacs gave different advice and the individual often turned to religious custom for guidance.

Although church observances served as a reminder of time for farmers, magical power was clearly associated with these practices. Oats were to be planted when Genesis was read in Church, drilling was to be finished by Good Friday, and potatoes were to be planted after noon of that same day. "We sow our potatoes at the foot of the Cross" was a saying in South Devon. Keith Thomas notes that although the Catholic church had sought to combat this "magical" attitude, it had by its own calendar and its emphasis on saints' days "endowed every date in the year with some symbolic significance." There were good days for baptism, marriage, feasting, and fasting. Puritan attempts to eliminate these and other time-associated "superstitions" were not effective; in fact, the Puritan concern with Sunday rest was incorporated into the old system, and it too became an "unlucky" day on which to work or undertake certain ventures.[10]

Although time itself was most generally not regarded as an independent variable, and magical associations with particular times were still maintained well into the seventeenth and eighteenth centuries, there was, at the same time, a significant growth in the concern with measurement and use of time. Time was more generally "counted," radically improved time pieces were created, and redeeming time—using it "properly"—became the concern of the gentry, the masters, and the tradesmen, as well as the "religious."[11]

Upper class Anglicans were particularly concerned with the use of time. A preparatory school catechism advised young scholars to search their souls and ask themselves "How hast thou spent thy time, from thy childhood to this very moment?" [12] Bishop Thomas Ken, evaluating Lady Margaret Mainard's life in her funeral sermon, in 1682, gave her the highest praise: "Who is there can say, they ever saw her idle? no, she had always affairs to transact with Heaven, she was all her life long *numbering her days.*"[13]

English Puritans placed even more emphasis on counting days, hours, and minutes. Philip Henry repeatedly reminded himself: "Time is running into eternity. O, what wisdom it is to redeem it."[14] Believing that they were living near the end of days, and that at the Last Judgment they would each have to account for every second of their lives, Puritan journals and self-examinations focused on the use of time. Birthdays were noted, but both in England and in Massachusetts they became "occasions for solemn self-examination and humiliation."[15]

Puritans radically altered the English approach to proper usage of time. Each individual was to seek suitable, socially useful, and satisfying work in order to follow his or her "calling." Puritans still emphasized "strict accounting" in relation to time, but in shifting their concern away from asceticism and toward productive labor, and in coming to view the work of the husbandman, artisan, and tradesman as godly, they accomplished "a genuine transvaluation of values."[16]

Notwithstanding the functional use of his concern with time that was later made by an industrializing society, John Wesley came to his preoccupation with time out of concern for otherwordly salvation rather than through an emphasis on work in the world. It was Bishop Jeremy Taylor's *Rules for Holy Living and Dying* (1650–1651) that led him to "write down how I employed every Hour." As a result, Wesley knew that it was on May 24, 1738, "about a quarter before nine" in the evening, that God came to him. He demanded that every follower pay equal attention to every moment of every day so that they might be ready to "give a distinct account of the time and manner wherein they were saved from sin."[17]

In Wesley's view, the most important time was that spent in spiritual exercises, but he adjured his followers to "Be diligent, never be unemployed a moment, never be triflingly employed. . . . Be ashamed of nothing but sin: not of fetching wood, drawing water, if time permit; not of cleaning your own shoes or your neighbour's."[18] When he appealed to the poor at mass revival meetings, Wesley emphasized that they must live an ordered life, achieved through diligence, employment, and the control of their "sensual appetites."[19]

These Methodist values were in total congruence with the needs of the new workshops and the expanding economic ventures of the period. The gentry, the masters, the farmers, and the tradesmen were also demanding punctuality and ordered time. E. P. Thompson has made us all conscious of how slowly and incompletely and with how much difficulty this new discipline was imposed on the English workers. Traditional farmwork required a variety of skills so that both the independent farmer and his laborer had a relatively constant change of pace. Noting that "the work pattern was one of alternate bouts of intense labour and of idleness, whenever men were in control of their own working lives," Thompson suggests such a pattern may be "a natural human work-rhythm." Certainly the contemporary comments about English laborers indicate that they continued, or tried to continue, these irregular patterns when they became wage laborers.[20] In 1773 Arbuthnot said of rural laborers that "if you offer them work, they will tell you, that they must go to look up their sheep, cut furzes, get their cow out of the pound, or, perhaps, say they must take their horse to be shod, that he may carry them to a horse-race or cricket-match."[21]

The rural laborer on a year's contract, the "servant in husbandry," had always been pressured to conform to a day-plan of intense field labor from daybreak to nightfall, broken only for meals. After a day's work, he might be expected to "due some Husbandry office within doors till it be full eight a clock," and then he might yet have to attend to the cattle before retiring.[22] English servants in husbandry had traditionally responded to these unending demands on their time with a "deadened slowness" that had led manorial overseers to carry a stick. Down into the 1850s there were English farms worked by gangs and supervised by "gangers" holding and using whips.[23]

Ann Kussmaul's sensitive study of servants in husbandry recognizes they were widely viewed as "lazy" and cites on the one hand the doggerel of a servant:

> *I can sowe*
> *I can mowe*
> *an I can stacke*
> *And I can doe*
> *My master too*
> *When my master turns his back*

and on the other, the diary of an eighteenth-century master, William Marshall: "To read Marshall is to think that no challenge was greater than that of working with his servants without being tempted to throttle them."[24] This diary compares most interestingly with Landon Carter's Virginia diary: Workmen, black or white, were the enemy.[25] Manual labor was never considered choice labor, and it was not until after the Reformation that any positive merit was found in it. Lutheran and Calvinist "this-worldly asceticism" was very slow to be adopted by the working-class majority. It was not until the Methodist "Reformation" that the English widely accepted the view that work is a proper way of serving God. Even then servants in husbandry probably did *not* accept this ethic. Nevertheless, English farm owners in the seventeenth and eighteenth centuries were attempting to impose new time–work norms, much as the American slaveowners were to set norms for a full or half or quarter hand's task.[26]

While owners were making more precise demands, good workers seemed harder to get and were ostensibly behaving more inadequately. "The Farmers' Wives can get no Dairy Maids, their Husbands no Plowmen, and what's the matter?" asked Defoe. Contemporary commentators answered that the poor would not labor adequately by choice. They were lazy. Locke estimated 100,000 chose to beg or live on the Poor Rates in 1697. An anonymous commentator of 1681 was certain that the "Poor are so surly that most of them will not work at all, unless they might earn as much in two days as will keep them a week. And when they do work they will often mar what they do." The charge of "wanton idleness" was made on all sides: Dunning, Locke, Defoe, and Massie all found the English workmen wanting.[27]

What was wanting was the new attitude toward time shared by English Puritans and Anglican workshop and farm owners (as well as by some Virginia planters). English working men and women resisted the rationalization of their time. Saint Monday was their holy day and respected as widely as were daily breaks for tea and harder drink, time off for illness and family care, for fairs and horse-racing, and simply for idling.

In 1794, it was noted that "there was a practice which prevails . . . of giving them drink both forenoon and afternoon, be the work what it will; which is a ridiculous custom, and ought to be abolished without loss of time. What can be more absurd than to see a ploughman stopping his horse half an hour, in a cold winter day, to drink ale?"[28] Edmund Morgan suggests that at "best," in the most fertile grain-growing sections of the south and east of England, farmers engaged in an intensive agriculture that would have kept them and their laborers busy half the time.[29]

With a new interest in rationalizing agriculture and instituting industry, masters sought to end those old patterns that had served a social function in a society with serious underemployment. (Breaks had made the work fill more days, keeping a higher percentage of the poor under control, while irregular work shared out more widely the minimal wages available.)[30]

Interest in time in and of itself, and in regular and timed activity, had become both a church and a capitalist concern. The medieval church had needed to control time within the institution: the lives of the "religious" were regimented by fixed times of prayer. Most other medieval lives were regulated by their tasks and not by any set measures of time. The new world view sought to bring a new consciousness of time and a concomitant regimentation into the whole society. Work was to be done "by the clock" and could be done at any hour, in "shifts" and at night. The amount of work done in a set period of time assumed new significance, as masters sought to rationalize their operations. In the sixteenth and seventeenth centuries the working poor strongly resisted these changes. In widely embracing Methodism in the following century, English working people co-opted themselves to a school for modern values that, as E. P. Thompson has taught us, began to alter their orientations to time and work; but these changes came about after the great migrations to the new world.[31]

TRADITIONAL West African cultures shared a basic attitude toward time that was much like the traditional English attitude. They emphasized slow movement, patience, and waiting. The Tiv said, "In your patience is your soul," and most Africans apparently agreed.[32] But clearly, time was differentiated in Africa, and the particular work to be done usually established "the clock." For the Nuer, Evans-Pritchard found "The daily timepiece is the cattle clock, the round of pastoral tasks, and the time of day and the passage of time through a day are to Nuer primarily the succession of these tasks and their relation to one another."[33] The Nuer, the Tiv, and the Kaguro, whose time systems have been studied, did reckon time by the sun's position as well as by social activities. The Nuer began with the time of "very little light" (4:00–4:30), followed by "more light" (4:30–5:00), and some thirteen divisions of the day, so that in a sense they did recognize a natural clock. However, their use of time remained the paramount determinant: They talked about their time as correlated with their work, as "I will return at [the time of] milking." Similarly, the Tiv called dusk to about 10 P.M. "sitting together time," followed by the "time of the first sleep," "time of the second sleep," and the "time of the pre-dawn breeze."[34] There was then a recognition of periods of time but no calibration of time: There was no hour or minute. The Nuer periods were of varying duration, far smaller in the morning and graduating to "afternoon" encompassing roughly 3–6 P.M. As the periods corresponded with usage, rest time was far longer than cattle-feeding time. Time was not an independent variable; in fact, "there is no word for time in Nuer."[35]

Similarly, the passage of time over long periods was not measured. Nuer spoke of dry and rainy seasons as did the Kaguro and the Tiv, but long periods of time were not counted in years. They were "located" in relation to significant physical or social events, as in the time of a great flood, or a particular epidemic, or before the white man first came. Ages or birthdates were noted in the same way. They were associated with the agricultural clock and significant events. Many people also knew their ages by their age grades or age sets. In most ethnic groups, those born within a set period ranging from approximately two to ten years formed a group that shared activities and responsibilities. Most Igbo, for example, were in sets formed every two to three years and had three age grades: the elders, old men and women who wielded authority; a middle grade, responsible for communal work; and a children's grade, boys and girls who sang, danced, wrestled, and played together, often in ritual fashion. Below them were the infants, not yet in any class, and above them all the spirits who were elders now dead and believed to be in communication with the living elders.[36]

Genealogies were important, but they were not records. They were memories and myths of the forefathers who were to be prayed to and emulated. They were apparently accurate for some three generations, but earlier time was compressed. "There is only a dim 'long ago' which can be increased by saying 'long long ago.' "[37] The same vagueness was true of perceptions of the future. The Tiv referred to the future as literally "in front" of the present, and it too was usually measured by tomorrow or the tomorrow after tomorrow, or the next rainy or dry season. It had far less reality and importance than the past or present. The living community was the link that united the ancestors and the unborn "generations."[38]

Although there were important variations among African cultures in which months and days had names and meaning, this general presentism was universal, as was the correlation of social–physical events and notation of time. It should be emphasized, however, that most West African cultures knew a set rhythm of market days—every four, five, or seven days—that structured time. Further, agricultural events were generally tied to lunar calculations and were part of a yearly pattern if not part of a formal or recorded calendar.[39]

African Moslems did know and use the Moslem calendar, those influenced by Europeans were aware of and influenced by their calculations, and there were indigenous cultures that had yearly calendars and differing traditions. Olaudah Equiano, taken from Africa in the 1750s, reported that traditional religious practitioners "calculated our time, and foretold events, as their name imported, for we called them *Ah-affoe-way-cah*, which signifies calculators or yearly men, our year being called *Ah-affoe*."[40] Equiano's people, the Igbo, differed from most other West African groups in their attitudes toward work as well as time. Equiano proudly remembered a work ethic similar in one important respect to the Calvinists': it too laid emphasis on the universal need to work, although not as a calling or as redemption. It was simply the "way of the world."[41]

The Igbo and the Tiv traditionally valued hard work, but "work habits and attitudes in many African societies tend to be more consistent with the view that freedom from work is a prerogative of high status which must be publicly displayed to manifest one's social power."[42] African societies did stimulate marked competition for wealth, prestige, and power. Wealth was most often exhibited in tangible symbols of prestige—in conspicuous consumption or conspicuous possessions, including slaves. Attitudes toward responsibility for work were often differentiated by gender. In eighteenth-century Gambia, women did heavy and constant work while "The men were occupied for only about two months of the year, at seed time and harvest. . . . The men worked without respite at the customary times, when their whole existence might turn on their success, but for the rest of the year they hardly seemed even to bother to hunt or fish. . . . They lay . . . in the shade, smoking, gossiping, and playing a kind of

28

chess."[43] Freedom from work and leisure time for pleasurable public activities were generally important goals.

The institution of slavery, if not ubiquitous, was very much a part of most West African societies. It is believed that it expanded significantly in the period of the external trade to the West, but it was known widely before then and had grown markedly during the period of trade with the West Indies and South America, long before Virginia became a destination. Africans coming to Virginia knew the institution at home. Some had been slaves, others slaveowners or slave traders.[44]

Although virtually all Africans had some experience with slavery, slavery in the various ethnic groups had different parameters. In all, however, the first-generation slave was an outsider, a person without ties to and protection of kin. Whereas some groups allowed enslaved women (who were preferred slaves) and children to establish ties, in most groups it was the second generation that might hope for enmeshment in the social fabric. By and large, first-generation slaves were in a precarious position and could be sold or traded in times of need.

Africans brought their attitudes toward slaves and masters with them to Virginia, suggesting an important but totally unexplored issue. They had had experience with both "proper" slave behavior and the "rights" of slaves. Their expectations and reactions may well have been an important factor in shaping the character of American slavery. Africans also brought techniques and work customs to America. For example, both as slaves and as free people, West Africans often sang as they worked. Complex African rhythms accompanied work during the day as well as the celebrations at night, and these rhythms were brought to Virginia as well.[45] (See Figure 2.)

FIGURE 2. Early eighteenth-century Afro-Virginian drum. Sent from Virginia (probably by William Byrd) to Sir Hans Sloane, London, this 18"-cedar and deerskin drum is similar in design to Akan instruments. Photo courtesy of the British Museum.

3. Afro-American Attitudes

ROUGHT from Benin to Virginia in 1757 at age 12, Olaudah
Equiano (Gustavus Vassa) exhibited a very prescient awareness
of the controlling function of time and of clocks. On arrival, he
was given the task of fanning his master while he was asleep in his
bedroom.

*I indulged myself a great deal in looking about the room, which to me
appeared very fine and curious. The first object that engaged my attention was a watch which hung on the chimney, and was going. I
was quite surprised at the noise it made, and was afraid it would tell
the gentleman anything I might do amiss.*[1]

Use of time was at the heart of owners' criticism of slaves: they
wanted the slaves to change their perception of time and work.

Some slaves did radically alter their sense of time, especially those
in urban situations and those receiving Western education. (Equiano
himself developed a quasi-Puritan view.) Newly arrived Africans,
"outlandish" people, retained clearly African perceptions of time.
Sandy, who ran away from Thomas Wilson in 1768, indicated he was
a new arrival by telling the sheriff that he made "two crops for his
master" and that he had been a runaway for "two moons." Two new
slaves picked up in 1754 in Surry County "say they have been Ten
Moons from home."[2]

Nat Turner, a second-generation American, talked about time in a
mixed fashion. He attacked a slaveowner's house "about two hours in
the night," and he met with others "just before day"; but he did refer
to some events by clock time, as when he joined his friends for dinner
"about three o'clock."[3]

The group of Africans known as the *Amistad* rebels (who took over
the slave ship bringing them from Africa) exhibited an enormous
change in culture when they were out of Africa, and their changing
sense of time can be viewed as proof of this. When KA-LE wrote to John
Quincy Adams (their defender) in January of 1841, about halfway
through their experience, he noted, "Mendi people been in America 17
moons." By the time they were sent back to Africa, after more education and exposure to Western culture, his companion, Cinque, wrote
from aboard ship, one day before their Sierra Leone landing, "I very
glad. Two years gone." Moons had become years, at the same time as
many Western values had been superficially absorbed.[4]

The major educational thrust of those dealing with the *Amistad* rebels, as well as that of most white educators working with blacks, was to bring them to Christianity. However, in the eighteenth and nineteenth centuries Westerners still thought of *all* their values as Christian, and bringing someone to their faith essentially meant making them "Western." Eighteenth-century slaveowners expected Christian slaves to share their attitudes to time and work as well as to Christ.

Another *Amistad* captive confirms that this approach was operative in the 1840s. In a very interesting summary of what he had learned about the "Great God" in America, Banna lists: "he want all men to be good and love him   he Sent his Son into the world to Save us   from going down to held [sic], [and] *all men have Some work to do.*"[5]

Most Southern blacks did not absorb this Protestant ethic. Chastellux recognized that they saw the work that whites set them to as punishment and not as redemption.[6] They would have preferred to spend their time in other ways. Benjamin Franklin printed relevant slave "wisdom" that he noted was widely repeated:

Boccarorra (meaning the White men) make de black man workee, make de Horse workee, make de Ox workee, make ebery ting workee; only de Hog. He, de hog, no workee; he eat, he drink, he walk about, he go to sleep when he please, he libb like a Gentleman.[7]

Although this comment makes its point about the similarity of white gentlemen and pigs, nevertheless the black, too, wanted to eat, drink, sleep, and walk about "when he please." But slaves were constrained to do what their owners pleased, and this led to constant conflict.

All through the slave period visitors commented on the slowness of the slaves. Whites waited for everything—meals, horses, carriages, and completed tasks. Ebenezer Hazard, writing from Jamestown in June of 1777, noted:

Lodged at Taylor's, where the People speak very civilly, but the white People are too proud to do any Thing for a Traveller, & the Blacks so lazy, & slow in their Motions that he would have less Trouble in doing what he wanted done than in getting them to do it.[8]

Landon Carter was determined to root out "the Lazyness of our [black] People" in a systematic fashion through consistent and continued punishments. When "severe" whippings "day by day" did not increase his threshers' productivity, Carter came to recognize that they were working to some norm, but he was sure that outside agitators encouraged their dilatory pace.

[T]hey hear others don't thresh so much and the farmer from Mr. Wormeley's, I am certain, when he comes up is always inculcating this injury to me so that I must send the wench he comes after up to Bull run, for I see I shall do nothing here if he has opportunity of stealing up.

Carter recognized that a white person involved in a sexual relationship with a black partner was likely to have a social relationship as well. He discouraged the contact on this ground and continued to punish for laziness "by every method not barbarous that I can devise."[9]

Both Carter and Washington, like many other owners, selected slave overseers and entrusted them with management and responsibility. Both men came to feel they had made a mistake in their judgment, Carter expressing a sense of betrayal, as he came to see the very men he had chosen as "cursed villains." Their use of time as well as their work habits were at issue. For example, the carpenters (with their sons) had worked for a month on a tobacco house roof and had not finished. The crew, under a black overseer, began work well, but they slowed down radically. Carter intended to replace the black overseer but recognized this was not the solution to a far more basic problem: "I find it almost impossible to make a negro do his work well. No orders can engage it, no encouragement persuade it, nor no Punishment oblige it."[10]

Smyth, observing Virginia slaves in the 1780s, felt great sympathy for them, recognizing "the hardness of their fare, the severity of their labor, and the unkindness, ignominy, and often barbarity of their treatment," but he also suggested they were "extremely addicted" to sleep and often slept when set to work. In fact Smyth tells a wonderful tale "on himself," about how Richmond, his black servant, was instructed to bring his canoe to the opposite side of a peninsula while Smyth was proceeding to that spot overland. When Smyth arrived the canoe was not in sight. Assuming he would meet Richmond on the way, Smyth walked along the almost impassable shore calling his name. Many hours later, Smyth arrived "with my cloaths torn, my flesh lacerated and bleeding with briars and thorns, stung all over by poisonous insects, suffocated with thirst and heat, and fainting under fatigue" only to find Richmond "fast asleep in the canoe, exactly in the same spot where I had left him in the morning." Richmond proceeded to tell Smyth a tall, self-deprecating tale that so amused the white man, he forgave the black his "crime":

Kay massa (says he), you just leave me, me sit here, great fish jump up into de canoe; here he be, massa, fine fish, massa; me den very grad; den me sit very still, until another great fish jump into de canoe; but me fall asleep, massa, and no wake till you come; now, massa, me know me deserve flogging, cause if great fish did jump into de canoe, he see me asleep, den he jump out again, and I no catch him; so, massa, me willing now take good flogging.[11]

Smyth seemed to forgive Richmond both because he was won over by his humor and because he believed an African could not be held guilty for sleeping instead of working. Richmond, in telling this tale, had worked at turning the difficult situation around, and had succeeded.

Though they were often "addicted to sleep" in the daytime, blacks were quite active at night. "Nigger day-time" was a strange "contrary" term for slaves' nighttime, as a white contemporary explained, because blacks were "at leisure" at night.[12] As early as 1688 Governor Nicholson of Maryland noted that the slaves' "common practice on Saturday nights and Sundays, and on 2 or 3 days in Christmas, Easter and Whitsuntide is to go and see on another tho' at 30 or 40 miles distance. I have, several times both in Virginy and here met negros, both single and 6 or 7 in company in the night time."[13] All through the slave period this night traveling and celebration was noted, and patrols were in part created to control it. It remained, however, a widely followed pattern and wherever possible blacks met together after work. They made time for hunting, dancing, and religious meetings, using the nights for their own purposes.

Nights were also traditional times for celebrations in Africa. In eighteenth-century Gambia, for example, blacks "danced to the drums and also to the balafeu, all through the night and sometimes for as long as twenty-four hours."[14] Nighttime might well be dangerous time, when it was believed (in both Africa and America) that spirits were more likely to be encountered, but it could be used for celebration as well.[15]

Smyth has left us a detailed eyewitness report from the Virginia of the 1780s of nighttime activities very similar to those in Gambia. After work, he notes, a slave *instead of retiring to rest, as might naturally be concluded he would be glad to do, he generally sets out from home, and walks six or seven miles in the night, be the weather ever so sultry, to a negroe dance, in which he performs with astonishing agility, and the most vigorous exertions, keeping time and cadence, most exactly, with the music of a banjor (a large hollow instrument with three strings), and a quaqua (somewhat resembling a drum), until he exhausts himself.*[16]

A rare eighteenth-century autobiography of a slave, that of "Old Dick," who was living on Spencer Ball's plantation, Pohoke, in Fairfax County, was recorded by an English tutor, John Davis, who came to work on this plantation in the 1790s. This document, which seems to be in Dick's words, gives us unusual insights into an eighteenth-century Virginia slave's sense of time and place. "I was born at a plantation on the *Rappahannoc* River," Dick remembers. "It was the pulling of corn time, when 'Squire *Musgrove* was Governor of *Virginia.*"[17] Here Dick, an American, who was, as we shall see, "acculturated," indicates a very African attitude toward the calendar. His birthday was remembered in its relation both to the agricultural year and to an event of significance, but no exact date was known.

This African pattern was common among black Americans; nevertheless many blacks later blamed whites for "stealing" their birthdates as well as their birthrights. Frederick Douglass bitterly noted, "I do not remember to have ever met a slave who could tell of his birthday. They seldom come nearer to it than planting-time, harvest-time, cherry-time, spring-time, or fall-time." Douglass, seeing the white hold on the calendar as a power ploy, was certain that owners wanted "to keep their slaves thus ignorant."[18]

It was true that whites held this knowledge. Slave births were property records that were carefully kept. Most owners had ledgers for all their property, and in case after case these record books opened with listings of equine holdings. These horses were listed with their male and female progenitors carefully recorded. Generally, the pages directly following listed slave births, and here, in most cases, only mothers were recorded. It was true that a slave woman's offspring belonged to the owner of the mother's body. Thus if a slave woman's ownership was disputed, it was very important to know *her* children. If she were dower property, it was also essential. Recording of fathers was more common in the eighteenth century, but even in the nineteenth some owners did record fathers, and some white families did include the slave births in their family Bibles. But the norm was a ledger in which other property was listed as well, and where only black mothers were recorded.[19] There was without question much more than ownership involved in the owners' listing of mothers only. Slave marriage was often not respected and/or not truly recognized. The white record made a "fact" of this psychological and legal nonrecognition.

Blacks did not generally know their birthdates by the whites' calendar. Black Charles Davenport, who was "about 100" when the WPA interviewer asked his age, answered uncertainly: "Nobody knows my birthday, 'cause all my white folks is gone."[20] Most former slaves interviewed could not answer with "white accuracy." Israel Jefferson, when questioned in 1873, knew he was born "December 25—Christmas day in the morning." This was no doubt correct and was probably part of family lore, recounted each Christmas. But Jefferson was much more vague about the year, and in this case, given Thomas Jefferson's careful records, we can know what Israel Jefferson himself did not. Israel uncertainly suggested: "The year, I suppose, was 1797." Thomas Jefferson listed his birth as December 1800, and we can assume this was accurate.[21]

Birthdates were not important for most slaves in the eighteenth century: they were not indentured servants with a time to serve. What did it matter if a man was born in 1797 or 1800? In Africa people did not reckon time in years nor did they count their ages with any discrete numbers. Appearance, experience, and status were noted, although age groups or sets could establish a rough chronology. Crawling, walking, puberty, marriage, and the birth of a first child were significant markers in an individual's life. A man might say, "The Europeans came after I was circumcised, but before I married," and his social group would know approximately what time he was talking about.[22]

In America, as in Africa, blacks found events that had stories and therefore meaning attached to them worth remembering. Dick must have been told by his parents that he was born at the "pulling of corn time." Dick's parents were African, as he proudly recounted (taking the occasion to disparage mulattoes): "My father and mother both came over from *Guinea*." But he too remembered an inaccurate birth record: "Squire *Musgrove* was Governor of *Virginia*."[23] Not having his owner's records it is impossible to know with accuracy his birthdate. The tutor, John Davis, thought Dick was in his sixties in the 1790s. His autobiography informs us he had already had many experiences, was a skilled worker, and was looking for a wife when the Revolutionary War began. He may have been born anywhere between 1730 and 1750. No governor in the period—in fact, no governor of colonial Virginia—was called Musgrove. Did Gooch or Dinwiddie or Fauquier have a nickname or a plantation that had led Dick to call him "Squire Musgrove"? There were Musgroves in the colonial South, but none was a governor of Virginia. Dick remembered his owner's and his sons' names and other details of his life with seeming accuracy; perhaps a Musgrove was a local official.

Use of appropriate crops as the markers on a year's clock was, as we have noted, African, and it remained the usage of Afro-Americans. Samuel Scomp, a runaway who arrived in Philadelphia, reported he came "in watermelon and peach time."[24] Another runaway "left long about cotton chopping time." "Never thought about keeping dates," said a former slave. Remembering the white calendar and "reading" or "counting" clocks were not Afro-American traditions, although clearly those who sought to "make it" in the white world, such as Frederick Douglass, recognized that whites' perception of time was a key. After the Civil War, many blacks in Virginia, when asked their ages for records and in interviews, responded that the whites had burned the Bibles to deny them this knowledge. Although whites may have done this out of anger or spite, clearly it had not been blacks' custom to remember such years and dates. But white "ownership" of former slaves' birthdates seemed to become a symbol of what the whites had stolen.[25]

Life-cycle changes and significant events were remembered by blacks: "When the War broke out I had three little children." "I was a great big girl. . . . when the war ceasted." "I was a young man when the stars fell; and you know that was a long time ago."[26] A remarkable late-nineteenth-century Bible quilt made by Harriet Powers, born a slave in Georgia in 1837, records, along with Biblical cataclysms and promises of redemption, the "dark day of May 19, 1780," the "falling of the stars on Nov. 13, 1833, " and "cold Thursday, the 10th of February, 1895," when animals and people froze to death.[27] (See Figure 3, squares 2, 8, and 11.) Powers' quilt provides evidence that oral history kept these dates alive. Powers could not read but she knew of that "dark day" in 1780 and associated it with seven stars and a trumpet, New Testament symbols of Judgment Day. No doubt she had heard about it in sermons and/or stories.

Many whites too believed an eclipse to be a sign of the darkness to come. On May 29, 1778, the *Virginia Gazette* had warned of a coming eclipse of the sun. It was expected that "the darkness will be so great for near four minutes that the stars may be seen in the heavens, which will appear as they do at midnight." The notice was given so "that the ignorant may not be alarmed, and suppose it some dreadful omen, instead of what it really is."[28]

Many blacks had come to accept the Christian vision of the future insofar as it involved a cataclysmic end of time. Concern with future time in general, both personal and collective, began to change as blacks became Christians. In the process of having Christian visions they believed they had come to see and know the future and therefore accepted its existence in a new way. But in part, a heavenly future was assimilated into old understandings: Heaven was where forefathers, out of the past, waited for good Christians to come home. The past remained important time.[29]

If we return to Dick's narrative to analyze his concern with time, we find that he certainly focused on the past, but as a prolegomena to the present: "When I was old enough to work, I was put to look after the horses, and, when a boy, I would not have turned my back against the best negur at catching or backing the most vicious beast that ever grazed in a pasture."[30] Paralleling the preindustrial pattern in Europe, there was a proper time, when he was "old enough," that he was put to work. It was not at a "fixed" age, not at 5 or 7 or 13.[31] He apparently took great pride in his work and claimed great skill at a dangerous task. His abilities were recognized in that he was assigned to be his young master's groom. Tom Sutherland, the young master, was, in Dick's terms, "a trimmer." He changed Dick's life and his values. He introduced him to hard drinking, violent "wenching" among the black "Queens," and "he made me learn to play the Banger." While the black slave played, the white master danced a "Congo minuet" outperforming everyone else.

Tom Sutherland was killed by a slave "who found him overficious with his wife." When his younger Edinburgh-trained brother, Dr. John Sutherland, took over the plantation, he changed both its direction and the direction of Dick's life. Dick reported that he freed the elderly and gave them land. "He encouraged matrimony . . . by settling each couple in a log-house, on a wholesome patch of land." Dick's behavior also altered. He now sought a pure young woman and he wanted to settle down, but his old habits interfered. When he "bit off and swal-

FIGURE 3. (*Overleaf*) A black quilt as a historical record. Appliqué quilt, "The Creation of the Animals," by Harriet Powers, 1895-1898, records the eclipse on the "dark day of May 19, 1780." (See the top row, the second square from the left.) M. and M. Karolik Collection, courtesy of the Museum of Fine Arts, Boston.

lowed" the big toe of the rival for his beloved's affections, he was sold south to Savannah. There he was purchased by a tavern keeper and found his urban occupation far harsher than his plantation labor: "I was the only manservant in the tavern, and I did the work of half a dozen. I went to bed at midnight, and was up an hour before sun. I looked after the horses, waited at the table, and worked like a new negur."[32] Dick, who was proud he was all black, and proud of his African parents, who knew Congo minuets and Guinea love songs that his mother had taught him, saw this harsh work as the degrading work of "a new negur." He reports he drank heavily to help himself bear this burden. His spirit changed and was perhaps broken. With the outbreak of the war, he was sold and sold again, to twelve different masters, as he remembers it. "But I knowed I had to work, and one master to me was as good as another." Work had become the center of his life. War's end found him in Annapolis, "grown quite steady." Although he no doubt would have "matured" had he stayed on the Sutherland plantation, harsh work and insecurity had changed him significantly. The period of time he was on the Annapolis plantation is never given, but it was long enough for him to marry Hoga, have a large family with her, and see his owner, a "Squire Fielding," sell the children "directly they were strong enough to handle a hoe." When Hoga died, Dick married Dinah, a young tavern servant living twenty-five miles away, and had "some" children with her; becoming convinced of her infidelity, he later left her. (Dick notes that he had three wives and twelve children. His third wife, presumably at Ball's plantation, is not mentioned.)

Late in life Dick's fortune again took a bad turn, and his work patterns changed radically. Fielding went bankrupt, and Dick was auctioned off to a Squire Kegworth, and

put to work at the hoe. I was up an hour before the sun, and worked naked till after dark. I had no food but Homony, *and for fifteen months did not put a morsel of any meat in my mouth, but the flesh of a possum or a racoon that I killed in the woods. This was rather hard for an old man, but I knowed there was no help for it.*[33]

There was no help for it. For fifteen months (or moons) Dick was resigned to this work, but he did claim to have been "laying a plan to run away, and travel through the wilderness of *Kentucky*, when the old 'Squire died."

At this juncture Dick's fate altered remarkably. Notwithstanding his gray hair, and the signs that overseers had found him recalcitrant,

"Squire" Spencer Ball, son-in-law of Robert Carter, purchased him. "My back [was] covered with stripes, and I was lame of the left leg by the malice of an overseer who stuck a pitch fork into my ham." Ball probably assumed these marks were from his early days before he had "grown quite steady." Dick was openly grateful to Ball: "He has not a negur on the plantation that wishes him better than I: or a young man that would work for him with a more willing heart." For the first time since his youth, Dick felt at home and made plans for the future. "I don't doubt but I shall serve him these fifteen years to come." Dick claimed to have a large amount of work to do but did it willingly:

I do the work of Hinton, *of* Henry, *and* Jack, *without ever grumbling. I look after the cows, dig in the garden, beat out the flax, curry-comb the riding nag, cart all the wood, tote the wheat to the mill, and bring all the logs to the school-house.*[34]

In addition, he had built his own log house; cultivated his own corn and watermelons; and raised his own chickens, ducks, turkeys, and geese for sale. Dick's work was hard but clearly diversified, and he was probably on his own much of the time. It is likely he decided when to tote and when to dig, and if he was always busy, he also had real accomplishments and satisfactions. In his life he had significantly changed his attitude toward work. In his relatively fortunate position he could come to see work as self-satisfying and as a punishment.

There is ample evidence that many slaves' life cycles were parallel: As young children they felt "free"; old "enough," they were put to work and might well begin with pride in accomplishment and a sense of mastery. Youth often found them rebellious, breaking both black and white norms, and suffering for it by sale—providing owners with a good excuse for selling those whose sale would least upset family structure and childbirth patterns.[35] Harsh life experience matured them, and whereas some found their sense of self by opposing masters and slave-breakers (as did Frederick Douglass), others were "broken" in spirit or "adjusted fully" to the demands of harsh slave masters. Many, however, found a middle way, a mature acceptance of life's harsh reality, that gave them some pride in accomplishment and some self-respect.[36] When they reached old age they might well achieve a new stature in their own, in other blacks', and in whites' estimation. And this new position changed their attitude and their possibilities in regard to work. As Dick said of his own expertise: "I ought to know these things; I served my time to it."[37]

Landon Carter has left us with very detailed pictures of several of his slaves; the life of Jack Lubber, one of the black people he was intensely involved with, in some ways paralleled Dick's later development. Lubber had probably been born on a Carter estate. At any rate, he had spent many years on Carter's plantations and Carter had been directly involved with him. In the early phases of his life his pattern was very different from Dick's. Lubber was one of the slaves Carter had trusted and mistrusted. He had selected him as an overseer and then had been certain that he had lied, stolen, and allowed the other slaves to evade their "responsibilities." While he was an overseer Carter wrote, "Jack Lubber is a most lazy as well as stupid old fellow grown." He is "too easy with those people and too deceitful and careless himself."[38] When Jack Lubber was "retired," with but limited tasks assigned him in the fruit orchard, Carter's view of him altered radically.

I walkt out this evening to see how my very old and honest Slave Jack Lubber did to support life in his Extreme age; and I found him prudently working amongst his melon vines, both to divert the hours and indeed to keep nature stirring that indigestions might not hurry him off with great pain. I took notice of his Pea Vines a good store and askt him why he had not got them hilled; his answer was the Prudence of Experience, Master, they have not got age enough and it will hurt too young things to Coat them too closely with earth.[39]

In their joint old age Carter was ready to listen to Lubber and found both his use of time and his advice prudent.

As Lubber aged, Carter "aged" him even more. By 1774 he was writing that he had "suffered him to follow his own will now 9 or 10 years," although the diary records that he was still an overseer in 1770. Carter surveyed his slave's life, and as Lubber approached death Carter had nothing but praise for him: "As honest a human creature as could live, who to his last proved a faithful and a Profitable servant to his Master." Carter now "remembered" that in 1734 Lubber was foreman of his Mangorike field gang, but was aging and slowing down, and that in 1754 he made him overlooker of five hands at the Fork Quarter "in which service he so gratefully discharged his duty as to make me by his care alone larger crops of corn, tobacco, and Pease twice over than I had had by anyone . . . and besides shoats and piggs used by my house." Carter apparently forgot that he had earlier written that Lubber was "a Devil," "an old sun of a Bitch," a drinker, a cheat, and a liar. Carter claimed to have relieved Lubber of "abuse" from his own great-grandchildren, who were in his crew, and brought him and his wife, "our old midwife, to my henhouse at home, where I received until about 3 year ago the good effects of his care." He then allowed him " to live quite retired" for what turned out to be his last three years. "But ever active as his life has been he then became a vast progger in Catching fish, Beavers, Otters, Muskrats, and Minxes with his traps, a Constant church man in all good days," and he tended as well to his own garden. He died after getting a severe chill while trying to catch a minx that was destroying Carter's fowls.[40]

The longer Lubber had lived, the more Carter had valued him. In part this was due to Lubber's changed status and behavior. "A constant church man," he may have seemed to have had Christian values. On his own he was enormously active, and as an old man he had much more respect from other blacks. But it was also due to Carter's changing perception of Lubber because of his age. Slaveowners often perceived their elderly slaves as older than their own records should have informed them. In some cases slaves "aged" unnaturally from inventory to inventory; one year they were seventy, the following year they might well be seventy-five. By "ageing" a slave, the owner reduced the social distance between them and could allow himself to treat the black differently.[41]

Aged slaves were widely regarded as "fellow creatures" by white people, inasmuch as respecting them was not seen as dangerous to the master–slave system.[42] In fact, respecting them served the owner's interests, as they were often held responsible for order and stability in the slave community. Moreover, they often seemed to share the owner's attitude toward time and work. Charles Dabney's slaves assumed such shared values when, in 1769, they sent the oldest slave to air their grievances with their owner. They believed "a complaint from him would be listend to."[43] They, as their African parents, respected age and believed their owner would as well. Indeed, in the English tradition out of which Charles Dabney's family came, it was expected that "the old were to rule," although given the radical social change underway in England, and the widespread disdain for those over sixty, the reality fell far short of the old ideal.[44] In Virginia, blacks reinforced the old values of time, work, and respect for the elderly.

4. Shared English and African Experiences of Work

SERVING AS an indentured servant in Maryland in 1756 Elizabeth Sprigs, an Englishwoman, was sleeping on the ground and had few clothes and no shoes or socks. She was certain "many Negroes are better used," and indeed, some were. [1] Generally, however, when African slaves began to join English servants in the Chesapeake they did much the same work and were treated in much the same manner. "Servants and slaves worked together, drank together, often lived together . . . sharing the same rough life, the same hardships, the same abuse."[2]

Whites, women as well as men, "slaved" under overseers holding sticks, "workeing in the ground, carrying, or fetching of railes or loggs or the like things and beating at the morter."[3] They lived in quarters, were whipped for malingering, and were sold for offenses or when their masters died. They could expect to become free people, if they lived "long enough"; but as long as they were unfree laborers, their work and their lives were not very different from the Africans joining them.

Whereas in the seventeenth century and at the outset of the eighteenth most servants and slaves worked in the tobacco fields, by the third decade of the eighteenth century blacks were joining white artisans—carpenters, coopers, stonemasons, blacksmiths, miners, and tanners—working on plantations and in settlements. All these occupations kept blacks in close contact with white servants, laborers, and masters. Although most black women remained field hands, a small but growing number were employed in weaving, clothing production, dairying, and household and child care, keeping them in contact with skilled white workers, white families, and mistresses.[4]

The ruling white elite having had long experience with bound labor quickly recognized the dangers inherent in black and white interaction. They early sought to "separate dangerous free whites from dangerous slave blacks by a screen of racial contempt." In Bacon's Rebellion of 1676 the potential of joint activity of black and white "malcontents" was, in part, realized, and it seriously frightened many whites. Nathaniel Bacon and his officers appealed to servant and slave alike to "beare armes for the rebell parts, promising him his freedom if he would soe doe."[6] It was perhaps just this widely successful appeal to the indentured and enslaved that alienated masters and reduced Bacon's support.[7] Some ten percent of all Virginia's slaves, and perhaps seven percent of the servants, joined Bacon's army, and these slaves and servants, with potentially the most to gain from the rebellion—their freedom—and the least to lose, were the last to give in. A group of eighty black slaves and twenty white indentured servants, holdouts from a group of "about foure hundred English and Negroes in Armes" at Col. John West's house on the Pamunkey River, felt that the formal surrender by Bacon's "Chief Officers" on January 2, 1677, "had betray'd them." Indeed, notwithstanding promises to the contrary, the servants were punished as runaways and had to serve twice the time they had been "away." The slaves were returned to their masters.[8]

Almost immediately after the Rebellion was over, the ruling elite acted so as to degrade the black slaves and thereby separate poor blacks from poor whites. The Virginia slave code of 1680 and the subsequent laws regarding interracial sex were clearly part of this attempt. The 1680 statute certainly sought to protect masters when it legitimated the killing of slaves "leaving their master's property without permission" and "hiding or resisting capture after running away," as they had done in Bacon's Rebellion. However, when it became a crime for a black, whatever his or her status, to "lift a hand against a Christian," it was clearly part of the attempt to elevate the poorest whites. Guilt was to be proved by the oath of the [white Christian] party," and the punishment was thirty lashes on the bare back "well laid on."[9]

Ultimately, an ideology based on white superiority did divide poor whites from blacks; however, a very long history of black and white interaction preceded the marked separation of the nineteenth century. During the eighteenth century the upper class continued to work hard and long to make racism successful, passing ever harsher slave codes in 1705, 1723, and 1748. One of the main thrusts of these codes was to dishonor the blacks and thereby elevate the poor whites without actually having to give them anything. Marriage between the races and "miscegenation" became crimes (1691, 1705); it was decreed that no white Christian should be stripped to be beaten (1705); manumission became extremely difficult (1699, 1705); blacks could no longer testify against whites (1705); and free blacks were deprived of their right to vote (1723).[10]

Notwithstanding this onslaught, and the racism that did exist, the attempt to separate the two races was not as successful as early as has been assumed, as the black and white downtrodden continued to share work experiences and social experiences as well as repression at the hands of the elite. Because of these shared experiences they also shared certain reactions, needs, and values.

As suggested, the evidence strongly indicates that most whites in eighteenth-century Virginia lived in a black world of work. Slaveowning was widespread and grew more so over the course of the century. By 1740 over fifty percent of the heads of households in Middlesex County (in the Tidewater) owned slaves, most holding from one to five; in Lunenburg (in the Southside) over fifty-three percent owned slaves in 1769; and in Amelia (in the Piedmont) over seventy-seven percent owned slaves in 1778. Overall, both the number and percentage of slaveowning householders rose over the century, and there was marked acceleration in the last decades.[11] Although the mean population living at a quarter rose over this period, the majority of slaveowners still had under five slaves, and the vast majority under twenty. This means that all through the eighteenth century most white slaveowners were working as their own overseers, spending their days with their slaves.

Whites in the Tidewater area who were not slaveowners could rent slaves, a practice that was known quite early but became far more common in the last quarter of the century, and which then "made slave labor available to nearly all of the free whites" in the older areas of settlement where many planters were switching over to grain production and had "surplus" labor.[12]

Whites who were not slaveowners or renters were not out of daily contact with slaves. If whites were laborers, overseers, farm workers, or skilled craftsmen, they were probably working for other whites who were slaveowners. For all these owners, renters, overseers, and laborers, male and female, working with blacks was an integral part of their lives.

Each of George Washington's overseers, for example, was expected " to stay constantly on the Plantn. [sic] with his people" and to discourage white visitors.[13] At the same time as they were to be ever present, Washington wanted all his white workers to maintain their "distance" from the blacks, both psychological and physical. He wanted their housing to be sufficiently separate to mark their distinction as he feared whites would be "too much upon a level" with blacks if there were too much familiarity, but Washington insisted that overseers live in proximity to the quarters, and he himself put whites into slave houses and slaves into servants' quarters. Washington had become convinced that many of the whites working for him had not kept their distance and had become too much like the blacks. This particularly affected their work patterns and their use of time. Instructing a new manager, he

cautioned against an error which I have felt no small inconvenience from; and that is, that rather than persevere in doing things right themselves, and being at the trouble of making others do the like, they will fall into the slovenly mode of executing work which is practiced by those, among whom they are.

Whites "fell into the modes" practiced by the blacks. Washington leaves no doubt but that this is what he observed and felt he suffered from:

I have experienced this not only from European tradesmen, but from farmers also, who have come from England and none in a greater degree than Mr. Whiting, and one Bloxham, who preceeded him; and who, tho' perfectly acquainted with every part of a farmer's business; and peculiarly so . . . in the management and use of Oxen for the Cart or plow, double or single, with yokes or with harness; yet, finding it a little troublesome to instruct the Negros, and to compel them to practice of his *modes, he slided into theirs; and at length (which I adduce as a proof) instead of using proper flails for threshing the grain, I found my people at this work with hoop poles, and other things similar thereto.*[14]

The English overseer, like carpenters and other tradesmen, *"slided into"* African ways. Poles were used for threshing, carts and plows were allowed to deteriorate, and traditional African attitudes toward time were tolerated. Edward Kimber, visiting Maryland in 1736, observed that if "a new Negro . . . must be broke . . . You would really be surpriz'd at their Perseverance; let an hundred Men shew him how to hoe, or drive a Wheelbarrow, he'll still take the one by the Bottom, and the Other by the Wheel."[15] It is significant that Kimber viewed this behavior as due to "perseverance" or "Greatness of Soul" and not stupidity. Washington, too, recognized that slaves were successfully rejecting white ways, and that in doing so slaves were influencing their white "instructors." When Thomas Green was his "Overlooker of the Carpenters" in 1793, he observed that "although authority is given to him, he is too much upon a level with the Negroes to exert it from which cause, if no other every one works, or not, as they please,"[16] including Greene.

All through the period owners "obliged" overseers "to remain constantly with their people." This might mean they were with large groups of blacks—on William Byrd's estates the largest quarter housed seventy-nine—or with groups as small as three. Robert Rose had two quarters at each of which were one white man and three blacks.[17] These whites lived either adjacent to or together with the blacks at the quarters.[18] Under these circumstances interaction was constant and intensive.

Although the percentage of white field hands working with blacks was far higher at the outset of the century than at the close, all through the slave period blacks and whites planted and weeded and harvested together. In the last quarter of the seventeenth century James Revel, a white felon who was sold to "slave" with blacks in the fields of Rappahannock County, found himself with a group of five other whites and eighteen blacks. Revel's poetic lament attests to the fact that interrelationships were intimate:

> We and the Negroes both alike did fare,
> Of work and food we had an equal share . . . .

When desperately ill, he found:

> More pity the poor Negroe slaves bestowed
> Than my inhuman brutal master showed.[19]

In 1769 Washington was still hiring white day laborers at harvest time: Elijah Houghton, Thomas Williams, Thomas Pursel, John Pursel, and others worked for him and with blacks.[20]

Over the course of the century skilled white artisans trained blacks, so that by mid-century many of the master craftsmen in Virginia were slaves and fewer whites were on the plantations. In the 1730s Robert "King" Carter had twenty-six skilled workmen at his Great House: fifteen were white and eleven black. There were three carpenters, two white and one black; three tailors, two white and one black; one white blacksmith and one black; two white "sailors" and four black "sloopers." At the outlying Carter quarters there were eight other whites, as well as forty-two black foremen, nine black carpenters, five black coopers, nine black sawyers, and 190 black laborers. Certainly these eight whites worked and lived in a "black-dominated" world. The fifteen white servants at the Big House may have had white associates and friends, but all of them worked with blacks as well.[21] Nearly a century later, Thomas Jefferson relied almost exclusively on his black carpenters, joiners, blacksmiths, and painters, but they had originally worked with and been trained by whites, who were occasionally still called in.[22]

Every white working on a plantation worked with blacks, sometimes in surprising ways. John Harrower, Scottish indentured tutor on the Dangerfield Plantation at the time of the Revolution, hired a black to spin for him, so that he could sell what she produced. Caroline, a Dangerfield slave and the "wife" of the miller "on the next plantation," worked "nights or on Sunday," and Harrower paid her "three shillings the pound." Harrower also worked as a teacher in the black quarter. He "hade a small Congregation of Negroes, lear[n]ing their Catechism and hearing me read to them."[23] Dangerfield found he could make good use of Harrower's skills as a manager as well as overseer when the need arose.

The general pattern for whites working on plantations was that they were to work at their skill and to supervise and instruct blacks. In 1782 Robert Carter hired one Daniel Sullivan, an Irish weaver, to manage his plantation's weaving workshop. Sullivan worked with six black weavers, four black winders, all 14 to 16 years old, and one black woman, aged 65. Washington's smaller operation involved one white woman working with five "negro girls." George Mason hired a white man to be in charge of his black weavers and a white woman to oversee the black spinners. Jefferson hired white William Mclure to train his weavers, but after some two years, he felt they could work on their own.[24]

At Col. Spotswood's iron furnace the head founder was an Irishman, and some seven of those that "raised the ore" were white, but they worked with over 100 blacks on a 45,000-acre plantation.[25] This too was a common pattern.

Independent white artisans also had slave apprentices or assistants. For example, John Tayloe, builder, owned Ralph, a skilled stonemason, bringing Ralph with him to build in the countryside, as at Mt. Airy.[26] In 1793, George Washington was negotiating with a white master carpenter, who was going to bring four of his own slaves with him to Mount Vernon, where the white man was to be in charge of Washington's slave carpenters as well. The proffered contract stipulated: "That he will never be away from his people when they are at work and he is in health."[27]

The census of 1782 indicates that a large range of Virginia artisans owned slaves. In Richmond, three carpenters owned twenty-eight slaves; three chairmakers owned twelve; five tailors owned fourteen; two smiths owned seven; two silversmiths eight; a tanner, six. The number of slaves owned by each workman, as well as advertisements of slaves for sale and description of runaways, indicate that many of these slaves were skilled workmen rather than domestic servants.[28]

Africans came with skills from Africa, blacks learned trades from other blacks, and white artisans on plantations trained slaves. William Lee, for example, sent an indentured white blacksmith to his plantation in 1773, and ordered that "2 ingenious clever young Nigrae [*sic*] fellows [be] apprentices to him. "[29] There is, however, evidence that blacks, both slave and free, were formally apprenticed to white carpenters, joiners, and bricklayers.[30] Jefferson's slave, Isaac, recounted that for four years he was "bound prentice" to Jim Bringhouse, a white master tinsmith in Philadelphia.[31] George Washington suggested apprenticeship to whites for some of his freed slaves, and Robert Carter for his. The smaller number of young black people manumitted by the will of Thomas Flournoy of Powhatan County, in 1794, were also to be "bound out," the young men to mechanics, and the women to "some industrious person" to learn to "sew, spin and weave."[32] While Jefferson formally apprenticed Peter Hemings to a white chef in Paris, Jefferson's white carpenters, James Dinsmore, John Nielson, and others, trained his slaves in a less formal, but no less rigorous, fashion. (Slave John Hemings, their student, became a master craftsman.) Jefferson noted that "many [slaves] have been brought up to the handicraft arts, and from that circumstance have always been associated with the whites."[33] From that same circumstance, many whites were associated with the blacks.

On the larger plantations, these trained slaves trained others, often their sons or other family. John Hemings, who had become a master carpenter, trained his nephews. Jefferson's chef, Peter Hemings, trained another slave as a prerequisite to receiving his freedom. Landon Carter's carpenters, Tony, Guy, McGinnis, and Sammy, were training their sons.[34]

Given all these means of training, it is not surprising that black artisans became increasingly common in the last decades of the eighteenth century. White artisans, still working in Virginia, were working in an increasingly black world of work.

Other whites, too, had business relationships with slaves, both legal and illegal. Many blacks and whites worked out symbiotic relationships: blacks widely took plantation produce and exchanged it with poor whites for drink and hard goods. Poor whites were often dependent on this cheap source of provinder. Upper class whites knew this and were determined to separate them. Washington, for example, recognized that without "their connexion [sic] with my Negroes," local poor whites "would be unable to live upon the miserable land they occupy." He tried to buy out white tenant farmers whose influence he found pernicious, and to prevent his former carpenter's daughter from going into business as "it is to be feared her shop wd. be no more than a receptacle for stolen produce, [sic] by the Negroes." He knew of many shopkeepers "who support themselves by this kind of traffick."[35]

Evidence of black–white partnerships in crime is widely available. For example, in 1700, Francis Brown, a "negro" was apprehended along with the rest of a group of pirates, all white. All through the century, the writings of the elite as well as the court records of virtually every county provide evidence of black–white "trafficking" in stolen goods.[36] The confession of Roger Court Crotosse, servant to Col. John West of Accomac, suggests how natural it was for blacks and whites to take and share "stolen" food. Crotosse admitted to stealing, over the course of one year, turkeys, lambs, sheep, a sow, six pigs, and several hens, carrying them to a nearby swamp, or some outlying area, or a private spot, as the "shoomakers shop loft," and cooking and eating them. He shared in these activities with those around him, often with another white servant, John Fisher, but again and again with "a negro of his masters." Tony, Jack, and "Johny Negro" all shared his plunder, and Johny added potatoes that he seems to have had hidden in a cache under a board in the henhouse—a typical slave storage cellar.[37] During the Revolutionary War, interracial gangs, such as "Phillips," raided the Virginia countryside. Active until the summer of 1778, "Black and white members of the gang went on robbery expeditions together, and then hid from capture in the Dismal Swamp."[38]

Whites and blacks also had legal business relationships. Whites sold new and used clothing to blacks and found a ready market for inexpensive jewelry, trimmings, kerchiefs, and grog; blacks sold poultry, eggs, vegetables, and handicrafts to whites. (Slaves and indentured servants were generally given garden plots to till after work and on Sunday.) Robert Carter, for example, reported the case of Lancaster County slaves who traded their fowls for stools obtained from their overseer.[39]

A great many blacks were sailors or riverboatmen, working together with whites. Advertisements for runaways often expressed the fear that white sailors might have provided births for escaping black slaves. A law of 1784 stated that only one third of any ship's crew could be black, suggesting that crews had been, and perhaps continued to be, more black.[40] In 1774, Robert Carter had at least two blacks serving as masters of his schooners: William Lawrence on the *Harriet* and "Negro Ceasar," slave, in charge of the *Bear*.[41]

Whites were together with blacks in virtually all areas of work in eighteenth-century Virginia. While proximity is not proof of interaction and reciprocal influence, the revealing comments made by Washington suggest that some contemporaries saw that such a process was underway.[42]

In the eighteenth century the world of work structured the social world as well. Owners, overseers, indentured servants, and white artisans were living on the black plantation. Their daily contacts, and those of their families, had to include blacks. It has been noted that blacks and whites attended horse races and cock fights together, and occasionally danced and sang together. An investigation of family life will take us into myriad other areas, but work alone brings us to a formal, even ritual, celebration of the agricultural calendar that came to be a shared white and black holiday.

In England, the servant in husbandry, who, like the slave, was also harvesting someone else's crop, had expended enormous energy at the harvest and had celebrated with the most lavish feast of the year, the "Harvest Home" meal provided by the farm owner. Drink and special harvest songs, sports, games, and dancing were traditional.[43] The African, too, whether slave or servant or independent farmer, had generally celebrated the harvest with jubilant release. No wonder then that harvests were celebrated by both whites and blacks in the South. Compare Robert Shepherd's description of nineteenth-century American plantation practices with the traditional English Harvest Home and the West African fete:

Dem corn shuckin's was sure 'nough big times. When us got all de corn gathered up and put in great long piles, den de gettin' ready started. Why, dem womans cooked for days, and de mens would get de shoats ready to barbecue. Marster would send us out to get de slaves from de farms round about dere. De place was all lit up with light-wood knot torches and bonfires, and dere was 'citement a-plenty when all niggers get to singin' and shoutin' as dey made de shucks fly.[44]

In England, after the frantic work of harvesting was done,

the farmer came out, followed by his daughters and maids with jugs and bottles and mugs, and drinks were handed round amidst general congratulations. Then the farmer invited the men to his harvest home dinner, to be held in a few days' time. . . . And what a feast it was! Such a bustling in the farm-house kitchen for days beforehand; such a boiling of hams and roasting of sirloins; such a stacking of plum puddings. . . . By noon the whole parish had assembled.[45]

West Africans celebrated the harvest in rites similar to those of the English: The wealthy hosted, the whole population took part, and eating, drinking, singing, and dancing were integral parts of the celebration. Among the Tiv of northern Nigeria after the yam harvest, a "man of standing . . . kills a beast and broaches a pot of palm oil, which he devides amongst the women to cook, that men may come together and eat. The people are loud in their praises."[46] Among the Ohaffia Igbo of Nigeria, the yam is harvested October through December, the same months "when traditional merriment begins, when men take new wives . . . or perform *igbu ewu* ('killing of goats') a rite that precedes the giving of a daughter away in marriage."[47]

There is only fragmentary evidence that rites from African harvest festivals were observed in North America.[48] However, for both the English and the African farm worker, the harvest was a time of joy, a time to overeat, to drink, and to express feelings of personal and communal accomplishment and well-being. Physical expression was very important to both.

The congruence of English and African harvest celebrations makes it possible to understand how blacks, coming to white-owned and white-operated farms, would have joined in the celebration of Harvest Home with recognition of its meaning and would have made these celebrations their own, so that when white servants in husbandry became a minority, blacks continued the ostensibly old-English patterns.

Both whites and blacks came together again in the eighteenth-century revivals and in the nineteenth-century camp meetings that were often held after harvest in the fall, and which in part continued ancient harvest rituals.[49] They were communal outpourings of thanks and joy. Given the shared work experiences and harvest rituals that preceded these awakenings, their interracial nature is less surprising.

5. Anglo-American Attitudes

WRITING history in colonial Virginia, members of the white elite disregarded their own past. As Breen has emphasized, "the present state" of Virginia was the concern of Beverly, Byrd, Stith, and even Jefferson.[1] They saved few records, looked back to no great forefathers, and had no sense of decline since the first planting. On the contrary, they were by and large ashamed of Virginia's record but felt the colony could "turn around" and change its ways "now." They were presentists with hopes for the future. There was, however, a discordant note in these Virginians' presentism: They did look back to the classical past. If there was any past they wanted to claim it was that of Greece and Rome, as is reflected in the amount of time they invested in its study. In the primitive frontier society of 1622, George Sandys translated Ovid. In the first decades of the eighteenth century, William Byrd studied his Latin, Greek, and Hebrew daily; Thomas Jefferson recognized that it was still a "sublime luxury" to have been taught "to read the Latin and Greek authors in their original." Latin mottoes, names of houses and servants, and emblems for the colonies and later the new states all had symbolic value, as did the "classical" buildings of the new republic. It is important to try to understand their place in what was ostensibly a culture that accepted the presentist's view of time and that wrote history as if it were beginning now.[2]

Other white Virginians saw time differently. Although they did not write histories until after the religious revivals of the eighteenth century, when they did write, they wrote martyrologies and viewed their own local pasts as significant.[3]

The presentism of the elite did not mean that they took the passage of time lightly. On the contrary, William Byrd, Landon Carter, George Washington, Thomas Jefferson, and many others, all through the period, were concerned about time and the use of time. It was in fact one of their central concerns and signifies their early modern world view. They worried about how they themselves used their time, how their children made use of it, how other whites were occupied, and how their slaves used or "wasted" time. The elites' concern with time grew over the century, until it seemed to have had an almost frantic quality. By the close of the period, it was apparent they were fighting a losing battle with their children, their white servants, and their African slaves. Time in Virginia was slowing down rather than speeding up.

The evidence for this concern is provided by the slaveowners themselves. George Washington titled his diaries: "Where and How my Time is Spent," and the Rev. Robert Rose was moved to keep his diary, "Having frequently found the inconvenience of not keeping an account of the most prodigious [gift], Almighty God has intrusted with Man, Time."[4] William Byrd II had been adjured by his father to "Improve his time," and as an adult he kept an extraordinary daily diary that, like Washington's, records almost no reflection or introspection and no concern with past or future. His diary is written in a continuous present, preserving a record of the way he spent every minute and every hour. Byrd transmogrified the Puritan diary of spiritual hours— an accounting book of an individual's soul—into a "count" of his actions. He felt compelled to record whether he prayed or if he neglected to do so (occasionally noting he prayed with vigor); exactly what he ate and if he did not follow his eating rule (Dr. Cheyne's fairly rigid plan of one food at each meal with milk and grains predominating); what he read (and he clearly felt something was wrong if he did not read Greek, Latin, or Hebrew daily, whereas English, French, Dutch, and Italian could be added for entertainment); whom he saw on business and what was transacted; his social activities including all his sexual encounters; his exercise, his self-medication, and his defecatory patterns; his correspondence and his journeys; and a final checklist of his existential condition: health, thoughts, and humor, which were almost always "good." Here is the first entry of the earliest extant diary, which is fairly typical of his listings in this period:

Feb. 6, 1709. Rose at 7 o'clock and read neither Hebrew nor Greek. I said my prayers not till I came to church. I ate chocolate for breakfast. We went to church, from whence Mr. Anderson, Captain Stith and his wife, Captain F-c and Mistress Anne B-k-r came [with] us to dinner, who all went home in the evening. Daniel came from Falling Creek where all things were well and the sloop almost loaded. I said my prayers. I had good health, good thoughts, and good humor all day, thanks be [to God] Almighty. This day I learned that my sister Duke had miscarried.[5]

The day plans of Byrd and other elite slaveowners indicate how much of their time was spent with Africans and Afro-Americans. Besides living together in the Great Houses, these whites gave blacks instructions and criticism, heard complaints, meted out punishment, cared for the ill, and visited and "consulted with" the aged.

In Byrd's 1709–1712 diary we learn that he put bits in the mouths of failed runaways, tied up those who "pretended" to be sick, made a young man drink urine as punishment for soiling his bed, interfered in servants' sex lives, whipped with reason (stealing, idleness, poor cooking) and without reason but for "a hundred faults." He "played the fool" with women servants, accosting females both black and white. He shared twelfth-night drinks and cake with his servants, heard their stories, gave them gifts, allowed them to visit wives and families, as well as denied them favors and punished them. Blacks teased him, argued with him, negotiated with him, and above all, worked for him. Their patterns of work were his constant concern, and he spent much of his time with them, trying to control them.[6]

March 3, 1710. I rose at 7 o'clock and read a little in my common-place. I said a short prayer and ate milk for breakfast. We took a walk to the mill and then proceeded to the Falls where we ate some milk and pone. From hence we rode to Kensington where I reprimanded Robin for not looking after the cattle better. Here we went over the river to Burkland where things were in good order. Then we walked to [Byrd Park] where I had several of the negroes whipped for stealing the hogs [or hogsheads]. From hence we walked to Shokoe where things were in good condition. Then we went over the river again to the Falls and from thence to Falling Creek, where we ate venison for supper. I neglected to say my prayers but had good health, good thoughts, and good humor, thank God Almighty.[7]

Some thirty years later, still active, and still writing, Byrd ended *every* day with time spent talking to his black people. In fact, the phrase "I talked with my people" became a daily mantra.[8]

Most members of the Virginia elite spent several hours daily with their workers. When the Rev. Peter Fontaine of Westover Parish evaluated his day plan in 1749 he noted: "I . . . ride constantly every morning all over my plantation giving to my servants their several employments."[9]

Notwithstanding his many black and white overseers, Landon Carter devoted endless hours to overseeing his slaves directly. On June 19, 1770, he noted, "I visited my gangs three times this day, staying with them a couple of hours each time." Most days he visited them but once, but every day at home involved much contact with his slaves, and his diary includes more about these interactions than about anything else. (Over 149 slaves are written about by name, and many of the same individuals are written of repeatedly, and at great length.)[10] Much of the time Carter spent with his slaves was devoted to overseeing their use of time.

Washington, too, spent ordered time planning his plantation's work, supervising his supervisors, and observing his workers. Even when he was president, he apparently spent much time thinking of his black workers as many of his most detailed letters dealt with their use of time on his plantation. He demanded "regularity and punctuality" from himself and from all those around him, hoping that "in short everything would move like *clock work.*"[11]

At Monticello Thomas Jefferson installed an enormous clock in the entrance room that was both the symbol of his concern with time and the very real monitor of the families' days and hours. For Jefferson, time, via the clock, was the proper regulator of work. He designed this timepiece and referred to it as "the great clock," which became its proper name. The Great Clock dominated the Great House. It had two dials, one outside on the porch, and one inside, in the hall, and it was visible from the second-floor galleries as well. (See Figure 4.) The clock bell tolled on the hour, and it met Jefferson's specific requirement that the bell be loud enough to be "heard all over my farm." Intended to control the work routine of blacks and whites alike, the clock told the hours, minutes, and seconds and visually showed the day of the week in a graphic fashion. It controlled fourteen cannonballs rotating on bell wire, which dropped into place along the corner of the walls where the days were marked at appropriate intervals.[12]

Jefferson's passion for clocks well fit his passion for "keeping track of time" and not "losing any." He bought many clocks, came to know their workings well, and then designed clocks and oversaw their construction. It seems likely he and the family were never out of sight of a clock while in the Great House. His bedroom area had a tall handsome grandfather clock made by Thomas Voight of Philadelphia. Jefferson himself designed a double obelisk mantle clock, which may have been in his study, whereas "an elaborate gilt clock with a black and white enameled dial, featuring the figure of a woman representing France and a pillar supporting a globe," was probably in some more public part of the house. There was even a good clock in the kitchen, which was below and behind the main part of the house and out of the visual range of the Great Clock. Isaac Jefferson noted that his "Old Master" came to the kitchen regularly to wind it.[13]

Thomas Jefferson also carried a watch. When at home the last seventeen years of his life, he had a very set routine:

FIGURE 4. Thomas Jefferson's Great Clock. Placed in the entrance hallway at Monticello, its bell and seven-day calendar make time both aural and visual. Photo courtesy of the Thomas Jefferson Memorial Foundation, Inc.

My mornings are devoted to correspondence. From breakfast to dinner I am in my shops, my garden, or on horseback among my farms; from dinner to dark, I give to society and recreation with my neighbors and friends; and from candlelight to early bed-time I read.[14]

From 9 A.M. breakfast until dinner at "half after three o'clock" Jefferson was at his naillery, mills, or farms; in other words, in daily contact with his slaves for a set period of hours.

Jefferson sought to teach proper use of time to all the whites and blacks in his extended family. He advised his favorite grandson,

58

Thomas Jefferson Randolph, to take special care of "how your hours are distributed. For it is only by a methodical distribution of our hours, and a rigorous, inflexible observance of it that any steady progress can be made."[15] This had always been Jefferson's view. He had much earlier sought to control the way in which his 11-year-old daughter, Martha, used her "hours":

> With respect to the distribution of your time, the following is
>   what I should approve:
> From 8 to 10, practice music.
> From 10 to 1, dance one day and draw another.
> From 1 to 2, draw on the day you dance, and write a letter the
>   next day.
> From 3 to 4, read French.
> From 4 to 5, exercise yourself in music.
> From 5 to bedtime, read English, write, etc.[16]

Martha recognized that the way she used her time was a form of power that she held, and that she could satisfy or disturb her father by manipulating her own time. She made sparing use of this power. When she wrote him that she was not giving the "suggested" time to her studies, she could be fairly sure he would be upset and would respond.

His response to other concerns was not so predictable. On May 3, 1787, the possibility that some white sailors would be enslaved by North Africans moved Martha to speak out angrily about American slavery. "Good god have we not enough? I wish with all my soul that the poor negroes were all freed. It grieves my heart when I think that these our fellow creatures should be treated so teribly [sic] as they are by many of our country men."[17] Jefferson never commented on Martha's statement, but the letter that Martha received in return (which was actually written before he had gotten hers) synchronistically contains what well might have been Jefferson's reply. Without mentioning slavery, it indicates that to be without employment is the worst of situations and implies that a slave, being always employed, can be happy:

> ennui [is] the most dangerous poison of life. A mind always employed
> is always happy. This is the true secret, the grand recipe for felicity.
> The idle are the only wretched. . . .
> Be good and be industrious, and you will be what I shall most love
> in this world.[18]

Jefferson ostensibly believed happiness depended upon "contracting a habit of industry and activity." "Determine never to be idle," he advised Martha. "No person will have occasion to complain of the want of time who never loses any."[19] But it was not enough simply to be active: Activity should be regulated and follow clock time, not inclinations or whims.

Jefferson clearly recognized and was concerned with the many connections between use of time and slavery, as is indicated by one of his ritual acts. "[A]s each of his grand-daughters grew up and reached the age of twelve, Jefferson deemed that she had achieved the status of a young lady. Tradition states that he gave her on her birthday a personal servant, whom she was required to train, and a gold watch. Jefferson selected each of these watches carefully to fit the personality of the child."[20] What of the "servant"? Was she too selected to "fit the personality of the child"? Knowing Jefferson's concern with detail, I think we can be sure she was. Training a servant and using time properly were related activities, and both were seen as crucial to the "coming of age" of a young person. A woman who could not control "servants" was not an adequate woman, and a woman who did not use her time well or was idle would be wretched.

Martha absorbed these values. When competing with "Aunt Marks" for control of Monticello, she commented on this other woman's inability to control servants as a most significant flaw: "The servants have no sort of respect for her and take just what they please before her face."[21] Clearly Martha should be the one to take over Monticello, as she could take control of slaves. Indeed, Martha grew to be Thomas Jefferson's surrogate mate, running his enormous household to his liking, providing eleven grandchildren to fill it, and spending much of her time educating them. She was industrious and rarely complained of anything, although her own husband who became ill was absent much of the time. Martha Washington, too, though she did not share George's life and values in the same way that Martha Jefferson Randolph seemed to share her father's, saw herself as "steady as a clock, busy as a bee, and cheerful as a cricket."[22]

But many other Virginians seemed to fall far short of this clock-like ideal. Landon Carter involved himself in a lifelong war with his children over their improper use of time. He viewed his eldest son, Robert Wormley Carter, as an idler, a peripatetic wanderer, a drinker, and a "slave" to his passion for gaming. Carter also saw his overseers and slaves as lazy. He could try to keep them active and productive by means he could not use with his son, and he devoted much of his life to this purpose. The triangular relationship of Carter, his son, and his slaves became a key to family development. The son accused the father of brutalizing the slaves, and the father accused the son of stimulating their intransigence and even encouraging them to run away. The father wrote:

Is it not a Strange thing in a Son always complaining of his father's temper, to be so singularly Provoking as to encourage even his father's Servants, before his face to disobey him? No longer ago than last night when that hell born Coachman Ben was getting a pass to go to Capt. Ball's at which place he pretends he has a wife. I ordered the fellow to be sure to come to me at 10 o'clock this day. This Devil to his father said aloud, then the fellow need not go at all.[23]

Ben did go, and the clock betrayed him. When at eleven o'clock the next day Ben was not back, the elder Carter planned to whip him. His anger at his son was clearly involved, but the slave's attitude toward clock time and work was the ostensible issue.

Washington too had adjured his stepson to regulate his days from rising to lying down. Nothing was to be left to chance or spontaneous choice. The boy, John Parke Custis, was first "trained" at home and then sent to several private schools in hopes of inculcating discipline and the proper attitude to time and work. It was to no avail: He was considered "indolent."[24]

Contemporaries did not view Carter's son or Washington's stepson as exceptional. The stereotype of the indolent white Virginian was well established in the eighteenth century. In 1705, Robert Beverly had written of the "slothful indolence" of white Virginians. Byrd, echoing this view, gave as an example Cornelius Keith, whom he had encountered in his Virginia – North Carolina dividing-line expedition. Keith chose to live "in a Penn [rather] than [in] a House, with his Wife and 6 Children. . . . The Hovel they lay in had no Roof to cover those wretches from the Injurys of the Weather." When it was cold or raining, "the whole Family took refuge in a Fodder Stack." Keith could have worked in order to provide for his family but chose not to. He knew how to read and write and could make quernstones (handmill stones). Byrd held Keith in contempt, but at the same time, he envied him: "t'was almost worth while to be as poor as this Man was, to be as perfectly contented." Such ambivalence toward indolence was often voiced.[25]

The Rev. Peter Fontaine (1754) lamented the lazy nature of his contemporaries and praised those whites who taught their children to labor productively; but he too planned to leave each of his children slaves as well as land. Andrew Burnaby, visiting Virginia in the 1760s, found the general character of its inhabitants "indolent, easy, and good natured; extremely fond of society, and much given to convivial pleasures. . . . [T]hey seldom show any spirit of enterprize, or expose themselves willingly to fatigue." Nicholas Cresswell, visiting in the seventies, similarly judged "the inhabitants extremely indolent," but he liked them as well.[26]

This mixed view of white Virginians was widely held at the time of the Revolution. Writing to William Byrd III, Gen. Charles Lee pronounced this judgment on Byrd's son Otway and on all Virginians:

I can assure you he [Otway] is a lad of excellent parts, and I believe of the strictist honour. His only fault, or rather misfortune, is what is inherent in all the natives of the lower parts of America, I mean a certain degree of indolence, of listlessness, which I have laboured (and in great part succeeded) to conquer.[27]

When Thomas Anburey described the day-plan of the upper-class slaveowner in the last quarter of the century, it bore little resemblance to the way in which Byrd, Carter, Washington, or Jefferson reported spending their own days. He pictured a "lazy" mint-julep-drinking sot, so inebriated he had to be carried home from cockfights, horse races, or court days by his slaves. This stereotype was widely repeated, and there was virtually no dissenting voice or any debate over this "reality." Both locals and outsiders seemed to agree on the Virginians' attitude to time and work. Chastellux found the Virginians slothful, and Smyth, although he purchased a plantation and slaves and contemplated settling, found that "The customs and manner of living of most of the white inhabitants here, I must confess, did not a little surprise me; being inactive, languid, and enervating to the last degree."[28]

Contemporaries seemed to think that indolence was a Virginian development and sought local explanations. Burnaby suggested that the mild climate might be responsible, whereas Henry Hartwell, James Blair, and Edward Chilton (writing in the 1690s) concluded that because "the great labor about tobacco being only in summertime," Virginians "acquire great habits of idleness all the rest of the year."[29]

Ironically, it was Byrd, one of the great slaveowners of the first half of the eighteenth century, who was one of the first to point out that slaves "blow up the pride & ruin the industry of our white people, who seeing a rank of poor creatures below them detest work for fear it

62

shoud make them look like slaves."[30] This "insight" became the accepted explanation, echoed by Cresswell and Jefferson and many others. When Elkanah Watson, a young Connecticut businessman, went to Virginia in 1777, he too became convinced that slavery was the cause of the white people's laziness: "The influence of slavery upon southern habits, is peculiarly exhibited in the prevailing indolence of the people. It would seem as if the poor white man had almost rather starve than work, because the negro works."[31]

Having slaves in a society does demean physical labor, and this was certainly part of the explanation for Southerners' attitudes toward the use of time. However, many Anglo-Americans, helped by both African attitudes and slavery, were perpetuating an old English tradition of indolence.

6. Conclusions

IN EUGENE GENOVESE'S brilliant evaluation of slave values he emphasizes that Afro-Americans held a "rural, prebourgeois and especially preindustrial" work ethic. It is important to recognize that most Southern eighteenth-century Anglo-Americans also held a "rural, prebourgeois and especially preindustrial" work ethic that paralleled the black ethic in many respects.[1] Interaction between whites and blacks led to the interpenetration of these value systems and to the strengthening of both.

Most blacks and most whites came to Virginia with what looked like "lazy" attitudes to work. They were generally slow workers, who valued changes in the working pattern and holidays. Their "clocks" were work clocks, with both the day and the year tied to agriculture and not to a mechanical timepiece. Certain times had positive or negative valence for both peoples, and taboos and other traditions governed their use of time. Byrd's servant Sam, for example, would not work on Childermas or Holy Innocents' Day, as it was not a "fortunate" day to labor, and Byrd accepted this.[2]

Africans, as did Englishmen, widely respected the holders of wealth and expected them to be free from manual labor and to spend their time pleasurably. Both Englishmen and Africans also accepted status differentiation in society and the existence of "unfree" laborers. English indentured servants were not too far different from Igbo "pawns" who had sold themselves into servitude in order to gain funds, usually for a bride-price. Both could expect their servile status to extend for a limited number of years, and in fact only the English indentured servant could be sold from owner to owner.[3]

Many of both peoples had been dependent laborers in their home countries; most had not been independent entrepreneurs. Africans had known slavery; certainly some had been slaves in Africa, and others slaveowners. They may well have influenced whites' understanding of just what the slave's and the master's behavior should be. When Philip Fithian, tutor on Robert Carter's plantation, saw a slave prostrate himself on the ground before his master, he was not mimicking any English servant.

The humble posture in which the old Fellow placed himself before he began moved me. We were sitting in the passage, he sat himself down on the Floor clasp'd his Hands together, with his face directly to Mr. Carter, & then began his Narration—[4]

Although this body language disappeared, the attitude it expressed may have, in part, been retained.

Blacks and whites shared a history of servile service and of mixed respect for and antagonism to masters, and yet they often expressed pleasure in accomplishment. It is important to recognize that in both Africa and England the servile laborer might have had an ambivalent attitude toward his work. Both Africans and the English generally viewed physical labor as the "curse" of the poor, and in both societies it was widely felt that one should try to achieve a position in which such work did not have to be done. However, in both Africa and England there were other attitudes. Olaudah Equiano, writing of Benin in the early eighteenth century, claimed "we are all habituated to labor from our earliest years. Everyone contributes something to the common stock; and as we are unacquainted with idleness, we have no beggars."[5] However, although everyone should do something, not every moment of time was to be used for productive labor.

Many of the elite slaveowners had a divergent view of time and work. Their values were close to those of both the Anglican and the Puritan elite in England: Time was to be redeemed. Every moment was to be used productively. These people were free to choose how they would spend their own time, and many chose to use it to see that their unfree laborers were gainfully occupied. They therefore spent much of their own time with blacks, trying to influence them and being influenced by them.

In Virginia, the perception of time by blacks and whites of all classes changed. Over the course of the century some Virginians, including some slaves, obtained watches or clocks, but well over ninety percent of the population never had mechanical timepieces, and it is very likely that many of those who did regarded them as status symbols more than as mechanical regulators of their days.[6] On the contrary, there is evidence that whites "slided over" into black (and earlier English) attitudes toward time and work.

Members of the elite often found that their wives and children did not share their preoccupation with redeeming time. In 1710, Lucy Byrd, first wife of William Byrd II, had a dream that warned her of the implications of her changing values. A mother wisdom figure came to her and told her "the seasons were changed and time inverted" and that "several calamities would follow that confusion." Lucy may not have been aware that she herself was mixing African and English, traditional and modern, perceptions of time and work, but her husband did accuse her of not living up to "proper" norms, of being negligent and disorganized, and of not "improving" her time as he sought to improve his own.[7]

Byrd himself had a compulsion to fill every minute with recordable activity. He had a day plan (if not a life plan) that he imposed on each and every day. The African sense of time influenced him in that he felt he had to fight it every day of his life. When Byrd wrote his autobiography he suggested that he was torn by an inner "civil war" between laziness and diligence, between "inclinations and principles." This conflict can be seen as one between the African values he had absorbed from the blacks around him in his Virginia childhood and the Anglican values he had learned as a young man in England. At his English boarding school, Felsted, Byrd may well have sung a morning hymn like that sung daily at Winchester:

> *Thy precious time misspent, redeem,*
> *Each present day thy last esteem;*
> *Improve thy talent with due care,*
> *For the great day thyself prepare.*[9]

At home in Virginia, Byrd was like a king with black bondsmen and bondswomen serving him, making it more difficult and leaving him at times more anxious to redeem his own time.

Jefferson, born a year before Byrd died, was raised by acculturated slaves and sent to the Virginia College of William and Mary. He did not face an inner civil war, but he had a fixation on time, perhaps a reaction to the already well-established Southern slow time. He tried to force those around him to share his concern, and he did not limit his outreach to his own family. The University of Virginia, his final work of love, was dominated by another Jefferson great clock, mounted on the library's rotunda and attached to a massive bell to sound the hours. Jefferson requested that it be loud enough to be heard for two miles around. He intended the University to train the elite of Virginia in the proper use of time. Ironically, this clock became the chief target of the young University sharpshooters, the sons of the elite, who valued their skills with arms over Jefferson's concern with time.[10] They, as most Southerners, came to share an old Anglo-African attitude that appreciated slow or "cool" movement and pleasurable activity.[11]

This is not to suggest that black and white attitudes toward time were originally or became exactly the same. There were significant similarities and the possibility of confluence, but there were also significant differences. In an extraordinarily interesting analysis of data from Middlesex County, Darrett and Anita Rutman and Charles Wetherell have found that there were seasonal patterns to the begetting of children, and that blacks and whites differed in this basic area.[12] White births rose in January and February, peaked in March, and dropped significantly to a low in June, whereas black births peaked in May and remained high in June. What this difference means is not clear: Apparently some "inner" clock remained different and was probably tied to old English and African patterns. It is fascinating that these differences continued in a new intercultural context.

Although some private patterns of behavior clearly were different, the timing of celebrations was increasingly similar. Harvest festivals, Easter, and particularly Christmas became joint periods of communal celebration. At Christmas, slaves were generally given a real break from work and often traveled great distances to see families and to celebrate in communal groups.[13] Blacks and whites, who might share English Christmas puddings and drinks, also celebrated separately but at the same time.[14] For both, the Christmas period increasingly became a time for weddings.[15] A joint calendar and a shared attitude toward movement and pleasure led blacks and whites to share certain practices and understandings.

The shared Christian awakenings of the eighteenth century affected both black and white attitudes toward time, giving blacks a new Christian past and the expectation of a new future through Christian visions and giving whites a new appreciation of ecstatic experiences that took them out of time, making salvation rather than redemption of time of paramount importance.[16] Blacks in the South came to believe that if a figure in a dream moved quickly, it was a sign he or she was in hell, and if slowly, heaven was home.[17] Virginians, white and black, moving slowly, were at home.

II

Attitudes Toward Space and the
Natural World

7. African and English Attitudes

I N L O O K I N G at African concepts of space and the natural world we are faced with the same dilemma as with time, that of the myriad African peoples and their differing cultures. Nomads, hunters, agriculturalists, and fishermen clearly had different attitudes to land and specific places; but they all seem to have shared a special reverence for the natural world and a belief that spirit power inhabits it.[1]

Many Africans moved about a great deal. Nomadic tribes had their set routes, often extensive. But settled peoples moved, both out of necessity because of war or drought and out of choice, often picking up a whole community and reestablishing it. (The Tswana, a Bantu people, seemed to regard a village as having a life cycle, and when it became old it was left to decay and a totally new village was established.) Wives (or less frequently husbands) joined their spouses in different settlements; in some ethnic groups, age sets left to found new communities; at the death of some leaders the clans were rearranged; slaves were captured or sold; and children were raised by families other than those of their origin. Physical mobility was part and parcel of many Africans' lives.[2]

Nevertheless, most West Africans believed that individuals, families, clans, forefathers, and divinities were attached to place; and that rocks, trees, and rivers held power and could be the abode of gods. Above all, they believed the land itself could have power—spirit force. Among the agriculturalist Igbo, many of whom may have come to Virginia, the land "was worshipped and it was a hard taskmistress which, on provocation, could cause the harvests to fail and men to die prematurely—for the Igbo two of the worst disasters imaginable." Land was viewed both as having spirit power and as having jurisdiction over the most sacred restrictions. "It imposed innumerable laws and taboos to guide conduct between man and man and between man and itself. The transgression of any of these rules known as *omenala* [conduct sanctioned by the land], was promptly punished." Rules made by man (*Iwu*) were regarded as inferior to *omenala*.[3] Hunters, such as the Lele, were certain that the forest and the spirits that lived in it controlled their lives. At certain times they had to be quiet, to refrain from sexual activity, and to be cleansed ritually according to forest rules, or their hunts would be unsuccessful. Spirits, living in streams, were respected and feared.[4]

Town locations, town plans, house plans, and field layouts were all likely to have spiritual significance. In Akan towns seven quarters were set apart for seven clans that corresponded with the seven heavenly bodies that they believed ruled the world. Dogon towns, houses, and fields were all laid out with a correspondence to their cosmogony. Fields had to be farmed in a particular order and houses built in a special pattern, or the order of the universe would be upset and the crops would be affected.[5] The Igbo, and most other groups, had myths "validating" their claims to their land, while ancestral curses made particular places taboo for settlement. The Kikuyu avoided graves and battlefields. The Lango would not build on high places, believing the dangerous deity Jok to dwell on them.[6]

Most Africans built houses according to ritual requirements, and their location and structure had spiritual significance. The house was regarded as a place for the union of male and female, for work and for pleasure, and was often organized in terms of gender duality.[7] Sometimes invisible constructs, perhaps imaginary lines between houses, were of equal import. And although the carving of divinities on doorposts or the use of white paint might mark an explicit spiritual symbolism, much of the importance of structure and positioning was evident only to the initiated.

Meyer Fortes suggests that an African residence should be reguarded as a physical projection of the social organization of the family that lived in it.[8] The broader landscape of village or town reflected as well the wider social organization. Wives' rooms were around their husbands', sons' houses around their fathers', the village around the chiefs. (See Figure 32 in Chapter 9.) In some groups clan chieftains had two-story homes, whereas all others were one-story. Kings had palaces, their status obviously reflected in the physical structure.

Houses in West Africa were generally made of natural materials that decayed within a few years. They were repaired or rebuilt, or settlements were moved periodically. Houses were generally small. A basic unit of approximately 12 feet in length or diameter was the most widely accepted dimension. Much living was done outside the house, in compounds formed by many one-room houses. It was common to have separate houses for men, for women, for cooking, for storing grain, and so forth. Olaudah Equiano described his Igbo (Nigerian) home of the 1730s in great detail, indicating the social significance of the physical order:

In our buildings we study convenience rather than ornament. Each master of a family has a large square piece of ground, surrounded with a moat or fence, or enclosed with a wall made of red earth tempered, which, when dry, is as hard as brick. Within this, are his

72

houses to accommodate his family and slaves, which, if numerous, frequently present the appearance of a village. In the middle, stands the principal building, appropriated to the sole use of the master and consisting of two apartments; in one of which he sits in the day with his family, the other is left apart for the reception of his friends. He has besides these a distinct apartment in which he sleeps, together with his male children. On each side are the apartments of his wives, who have also their separate day and night houses. The habitations of the slaves and their families are distributed throughout the rest of the enclosure. These houses never exceed one storey in height; they are always built of wood, or stakes driven into the ground, crossed with wattles, and neatly plastered within and without. The roof is thatched with reeds. Our day houses are left open at the sides; but those in which we sleep are always covered and plastered in the inside, with a composition mixed with cow-dung, to keep off the different insects, which annoy us during the night. . . . Houses so constructed . . . require but little skill to erect them. Every man is a sufficient architect for the purpose. The whole neighborhood afford their unanimous assistance in building them, and in return receive and expect no other recompense than a feast.[9]

Although the circular hut is the shape most widely associated with African vernacular housing, the range of house forms or styles is and was quite extensive. Susan Denyer has condensed about a thousand recorded variations into thirty-two main types: four are variations of one-story round houses; several are two stories high; several are oval. There are the tent-like structures of nomadic peoples and several styles of caves or "dug ins." However surprising for Westerners who have tended to assume that the circular hut is normative, at least thirteen categories in Denyer's taxonomy are of square or rectangular houses. It is in West African "slave-exporting" coastal areas that "the rectangular gable-roofed hut is . . . characteristic. . . . We find it especially in the coastal areas of upper and lower Guinea, thus from the Bissago Islands, through Nigeria, down to the Congo estuary."[10] Many of the Africans coming to North America brought with them a tradition of building small, light rectangular cabins, with gable roofs. (See Figures 29–31, Chapter 9.)

West Africans "carried" their basic beliefs to Virginia as well. They brought the belief that spirit power could occupy natural places, and that particular individuals, through serving gods, could have access to this power. Divination was accepted by most West Africans as a means of learning the future, while magic and "witchcraft," although defined differently and seen as playing a different roll in the various West African societies, were used to effect a different future. Most diviners used special places in their divination, as the oracles at Aro Chukwu, which were important for "eating" large numbers of people who were actually sent into slavery. Natural materials were used in "witchcraft," as chicken bones for divination or blood, urine, and herbs in amulets. The natural world was seen as having "powers" to which the human world could gain ritual access.[11]

THE ENGLISH in the seventeenth century had a view of power connected to land, wells, and trees that was similar to that of Africans. It was widely believed that natural places could have charisma; their use was related to rites and taboos, both magical and religious. Catholic priests had blessed trees, wells, and land. Although Protestants knew that their church objected to both these beliefs and practices, they also widely knew they wanted to continue to propitiate guardian spirits.

In 1687 John Aubrey recorded how the people of Droitwich had learned the importance of continuing the ancient practice of praying at the local (salt) well.

This Custome is yearly observed at Droit-Wich in Worcestershire, where on the day of St. Richard the $\{{}^{Tutelar\ St.}_{Patron}\}$ of y^e Well (i.e.) salt-well, they keepe Holyday, dresse the well with green Boughes and flowers. One yeare . . . , in the Presbyterian times it was discontinued in the Civil-warres, and after that the spring $\{{}^{stop't,\ dried}_{shranke\ up}\}$ or dried up for some time. So afterwards they $\{{}^{revived}_{kept}\}$ their annuall custome (notwithstanding the power of y^e Parliament and soldiers), and the salt-water returned again and still continues.[12]

By the eighteenth century many such rites had been abandoned; however, there is evidence that similar practices were continued in towns in Derbyshire and in Nantwich until well past 1750. A magical spring was believed to come out of the ground in Warlingham whenever a "remarkable" event was in store: It was attested to before the Restoration in 1660, at the London Plague of 1665, and at the Revolution in 1688. Sacred trees were widely believed in, and in the West of England Aubrey reported they still "goe with their Wassel-bowle into the orchard and goe about the Trees to blesse them, and putt a piece of Tost upon the Rootes, in order to it." Wells and springs were "known" to have magical healing properties and were still visited. Land, trees, and water were still regarded as sacred and demanded special attention. Patron saints (or forefathers) were still addressed to help the living. The Droitwich well ceremony described above was addressed to a St. Richard. He was not a distant historical figure from the Jerusalem or Roman church but rather a local "forefather" remembered in the neighborhood, as Aubrey noted: "This St. Richard was a person of great estate in these parts, and a briske young fellow that would ride over hedge and ditch, and at length became a very devout man, and after his decease was canonized for a Saint."[13]

Keith Thomas has convincingly demonstrated that while the Protestant Church widely gave up the magical roles held by the Catholic Church, many of the people continued to believe that magic was potent, and that they needed means to control it. They continued to recognize spirits in wells, streams, trees, land, and houses, and they wanted ways to propitiate these spirits. Before the Civil Wars, Gospels had been read in the cornfields and at the springs; afterwards, some continued variants of their ancient customs, although some holy springs eventually became "health spas" and sacred trees parts of parks preserved for their "natural" beauty. The perambulation of Church parishes still involved blessing trees and physical locations with "magical" prayers.[14]

Most seventeenth- and eighteenth-century English people knew particular places intimately and valued them. They knew soils, streams, animal life, and weather in what seemed an almost intuitive way. Denys Thompson, who has collected much evidence of these old folkways, notes: "They observed the seasons proper for their varied pursuits almost as if they were going through some ritual."[15] This "almost" is too much of a caution: there *was* ritual in country living. Virtually every aspect of everyday life involved both special knowledge and ritual response. In addition to agricultural customs, there were "courting customs, childbirth customs, apprentice customs, customs to control or disapprove a neighbour's behaviour. The whole of life is Drama, an immense collection of things to *do* about it. Most are fixed: the topography sees to that."[16]

This fixed knowledge could come only from mothers, fathers, and grandparents who provided both knowledge of or beliefs about nature and proper ways of social response. A nineteenth-century wheelwright reminisced:

[T]he wheelwright buyer had to know . . . the soil the timber grew on. Age-long tradition helped him here. I, for instance, knew from my father's telling, and he perhaps from his father's, that the best beech

in the district came from such and such a quarter: that the very limbs from the elm in one park would yield good "stocks" (hubs for wheels); and that in a certain luxuriant valley the beautiful-looking oaks had grown too fast and when opened were too shaky to be used.[17]

Farmers were expected to know their land in the same ways carpenters knew their trees.

Most of the English also built very small and rude dwellings. Sixteen feet was the internalized norm that governed English building, and most cottages were either 16′ × 16′ or close to these dimensions with a single door or window on each side. Most English cottages had chimneys added in the sixteenth or early seventeenth centuries; until then smoke from the hearth had gone up through a hole in the roof. Earthen floors were still widely known, although by the seventeenth century many were filled in with boards or bricks. And although there was much improvement in lower class housing, the seventeenth century also saw the "mushrooming growth of bare cottages for the poor in country parishes." Whereas those who were better off had half-timbered or brick or stone houses, the poor still knew straw, thatch, or mud walls, thatch roofs, and mud floors. "Labouring families lived in poor one-room cottages for the most part."[18]

These English houses were often decorated with charms and mystically potent signs. Doorposts and witchposts to one side of the hearth were sometimes carved with fertility figures or other protective images. These openings were regarded as the danger points where witches could find access.[19] Although these doorposts and witchposts were on homes of the poor or "middling sort," the traditional English world view crossed class boundaries. Virtually everyone believed in part that time and place could be controlled by magic or arational means.

In spite of the development of more rational understandings of the world in the seventeenth and eighteenth centuries, these older ideas did not simply disappear. People in all classes continued to believe them through our period. In the eighteenth century many of the rich believed in ghosts, magic, witches, and charms. But the new views—the perception of the world as a clockwork universe functioning according to "natural laws" that could be scientifically investigated, wherein time and place were independent of charismatic power—were already important and seemed to appeal to people in certain eco-

76

nomic groups as well as to certain sects more than others. However, no one group had a monopoly on these ideas nor did any group hold them in a "pure" form. In the transitional seventeenth and eighteenth centuries, "rationalists" often held a panoply of "superstitious" ideas, and concepts we have come to see as magical were regarded as scientifically substantiated.[20]

Samuel Sewall's values might be used as an example of the mixed English world view of the period, giving us particular insight into views of the natural world. Although we think of Sewall as a Massachusetts Puritan, he was born and raised in England, and his values were English (Puritan) ones. As David D. Hall has shown, Sewall viewed natural phenomena as the "physical equivalents of moral and spiritual forces."[21] He was therefore concerned with rainbows, lightning, earthquakes, comets, dreams, diseases, and deaths as *omens* or prophecies. He regarded particular times and places as propitious and others as dangerous. Sewall consulted with a minister as to when to build his home. He saw coincidences as meaningful. He viewed many acts as magical and, for example, fasted not simply for its effect on his soul but as a ritual act that he believed had efficacy in and of itself. He believed in talismans and put pins into doorframes and wooden carvings of cherubim on gateposts. He regarded names as having magical properties. In all these beliefs, and in many more, he was continuing the arational traditions of the old world view. At the very same time he was a leading Puritan who believed in seeking one's calling and in changing one's self as well as the world.

William Byrd's satiric essay on English superstition serves to outline its extent: People went to witches, wizards, tea-leaf readers, and a vast panoply of other cult practitioners.[22] It had become fashionable to poke fun at some of these practices, as Byrd did, but that did *not* put a stop to them. Byrd himself went to an Old Abram for advice about his love life and his future success.[23] The upper class did become self-conscious about these beliefs, and it was often suggested that only the "rustic" or "rude" (i.e., the lower classes) held on to these values.[24] In actuality they pervaded world views at all levels.

It is more difficult to evaluate how deeply the new scientific outlook affected the lower classes. Certainly there was a large group of "scoffers" and doubters prior to the Reformation, and it is believed that this sector grew substantially during the critical periods of social and religious turmoil. To what extent they were directly affected by the new values is probably impossible to gauge, nor is agnosticism to be equated with rationality or vice versa. Many of the leading scientists were members of orthodox churches and were firm believers, and many of the illiterate poor laborers were unchurched scoffers.

MOST OF THE ENGLISH and the Africans of the seventeenth and eighteenth centuries held similar attitudes to the natural world. Belief in spirits was widespread, in both Africa and England, and the belief that certain individuals had esoteric knowledge and could contact, serve, or control spirits was also held in both societies.[25] In the traditional cultures of both peoples the natural world was seen as a place of mystery and hidden powers that had to be taken into account. Africans coming to America did not have a deviant rational tradition, but their view of the natural world was very close to the traditional view of most English people. Taboos were highly important; ritual acts were seen as having efficacy; holy places, holy times, and holy people could affect spirit or power. In this area of perceptions and values the possibility of confluence and melding was strong.

8. Black and White Visions in and of America

WHEN THE ENGLISH came to America they clearly brought their traditional understandings of the natural world with them.[1] God was turned to first, to bless journeys, but then magic workers were called on to ensure good winds, and amulets were obtained to protect them against evil spirits. William Byrd, writing to the English merchant, John Hamburg, in October of 1735, was "glad to hear your ship the Williamsburgh got home well, and that [Capt. Henry] Crane agreed with a witch at Hampton for a fair wind all the way." Witches at Hampton Roads, Virginia, and other British ports no doubt served many English mariners on their way to and from North America.[2]

John Harrower, a Scottish indentured servant, was on his way to Virginia in April of 1774 in the brigantine *Planter* when serious sickness began to spread among the servants and sailors. Their reaction to this dangerous situation confirms their belief in a magic tied to Christianity, which Harrower too seems to have accepted:

Thursday, 21st April 1774.
This morning a young lad, one of the servts. being very ill with the Fever and Ague, he begged me to apply to Mr. Jones the Chief Mate, and told me he cou'd give him something that would cure him; Mr. Jones first desired me to give him a womite and then wrote the following lines on a slip of paper and after folding it up gave it to me, to see it tyed up in the corner of his handkerchief or Cravat and wear it at his breast next to his skin with strick charge to him not to look at it himself nor let any other person see it or look at it untill he was got wel. The words are as follows.

> *When Jesus saw the Cross he trembled,*
> *The Jews said unto him why tremblest thou,*
> *You have neither got an Ague nor a fever.*
> *Jesus answered and said unto them*
> *I have neither got an Ague nor a fever,*
> *But whosoever keepeth my words shall*
> *neither have an Ague nor a fever.*[3]

Harrower came to a colony where belief in the occult was an integral part of everyday life before and, even more so, after Africans became a significant part of the population. However, unlike New England, only one witch case aroused wide interest in Virginia, namely, that of Grace Sherwood, prosecuted in Princess Anne County in 1705.[4] The handling of this case suggests a deep ambivalence about occult workers: Many people believed Sherwood was a witch, and yet they were unwilling to punish her. The case seems to reflect deep feelings of Virginians in regard to magic and the world around them and is worth looking at in detail.

In February and March of 1698 Princess Anne County Court considered three cases of defamation and slander, brought by James Sherwood and his wife Grace. They were suing Richard Capps, John and Jane Gisburne, and Anthony and Elizabeth Barnes, and brought some nine witnesses to court to attest that the defendants had all called Grace Sherwood a witch. The Gisburnes were charged with saying that she "bewitched their piggs to Death and bewitched their Cotton," and Elizabeth Barnes with claiming that "Grace came to her one night and rid her and went out of the key hole or crack of the door like a black Catt." The first case was settled out of court, but, notwithstanding the testimony of the nine witnesses, all of whom gave evidence "for James Sherwood," the juries found for the defendants and the last two cases were dismissed.[5]

By the fall of 1701, Grace Sherwood had neither the protection of James Sherwood nor anyone to stand with in court. She was a "Relict," and although she had a dwelling house, an "old bed," "a few old blankets," and "Seven old Cheres," it is clear she was left in a poor state. In the short inventory of her goods, virtually everything was labeled "old," including "one old poore mangy Scabby horse."[6]

In October of 1705, Grace Sherwood went back into court alone, suing Luke Hill and his wife Elizabeth, whom she charged "had Assaulted Brused Maimed & Barbarously Beaten" her. This time the charges were "proven" and the court awarded Sherwood twenty shillings damages and costs, but Sherwood was to pay dearly for this victory.[7]

On January 3, 1706, the Hill family retaliated, charging Grace Sherwood with witchcraft. The gentlemen justices "debated," required Hill to undertake to pay all costs, and finally decided to call "a Jury of women to decide." The sheriff empaneled twelve women, led by one Eliza Barnes as forewoman. (She may well have been the Elizabeth Barnes who was charged with stating that she had been "ridden" by Sherwood eight years earlier.) In March the twelve women reported to the court that "The Jury have sercath: [sic] Grace Sherwood & have found two things like *titts* with severall other spotts."[8] Sherwood was found to have what was then considered the most blatant outward sign of a witch, "some bigg [teat] or place upon their body, where he [the Devil] sucketh them."⁹ Notwithstanding this finding, the justices apparently did not act, leading Luke Hill to petition the General Court in Williamsburg. The General Court turned to the Attorney General for his opinion, and Attorney General Stevens Thompson sent the case back to the local Princess Anne County Court, pointing out that they had not charged her "with any particular act." He suggested they reinvestigate, and if there were grounds, make exact charges and then send Sherwood to Williamsburg to be tried by the General Court.¹⁰

In response (in May of 1706) the local court ordered that "Graces house & all suspicious places" be searched "carfully for all Images & such like things," but now not one of the women that was called would serve on an investigative jury, notwithstanding the fact that the court threatened the women with being charged with contempt and "the utmost severeity of the law." The court became "doubtfull that they should not get" a single woman to serve, and it abandoned the procedure. Perhaps the women were afraid of Sherwood's powers, or it is possible they wanted her to remain in the community. Strangely, not one word of Sherwood is recorded in the lengthy transcript, where it is noted only that she had "little or nothing to say."¹¹ The gentlemen justices then decided to try the water ordeal, the second major method of "witch-prooving" used in seventeenth-century England. In 1597, King James I explained that "God hath appoynted (for a super-natural signe of the monstrous impietie of Witches) that the water shall refuse to receive them in her bosom, that have shaken off the sacred water of Baptism."¹² If Sherwood floated, it would convict her of being a witch, and if she drowned, she would be considered innocent. Most interestingly, we are told that Sherwood underwent this trial *"by her own consent."* Apparently she was so confident of her powers that she assumed she could win in what appeared an impossible situation. Events seemed to prove this the case. Whereas the justices had earlier shown their feelings toward Sherwood by acts of omission, they now made a permanent record of their unusual concern for the defendant. "The weather being very rainy & bad soe yt. possibly it might endanger her health it is therefore ordr." that the ducking be postponed, and further decreed that "boats & men" should be present at the examination "alwayes having care of her life to pe.serve [*sic*] her from drowning."¹³

Grace Sherwood was bound, dunked into deep water, and yet was seen "swimming . . . contrary to custom." A great crowd had come down to the Ferry at Jno. Harper's plantation (it was later to be known as Witch Duck) and saw this remarkable occurrence. At this point "five antient weamen" did agree to reinspect her body. They found "two things like titts on her private parts of a Black Coller," and declared "that she is not like them: nor noe other woman that they knew of."[14] The court decided to put her in jail until a "future tryall." With her witch's marks confirmed and her having floated, it would seem likely she would have been condemned and executed. However, this was not the case. Very little is known about further developments, but it would appear that no other trial occurred. Sherwood was not sent to Williamsburg, and no final disposition of her case was made. She may have been "loosely confined" to the jail for some time, but later in life she apparently lived perfectly freely; when she died in 1740, she left a son her estate of 145 acres, a house, cattle, and some possessions.[15]

Grace Sherwood became a fairly positive figure in Princess Anne County folklore. She was credited with the ability to sail to England in an eggshell; the power to make suitors ardent; control over some aspects of nature, so that she could, among other acts, spoil the milk of an enemy's cows, bring about the death of pigs, or "bewitch cotton"; and general magical wisdom. She was known to have broken with custom by wearing men's clothing, and to have been contentious, seemingly alienated from two of her own sons as well as from others. But she clearly was known to have had wide powers that were not particularly malevolent; for example, she was said to have brought rosemary to Virginia. Sherwood seems to have mixed the traditions of English white witches and black witches. She performed both good and bad deeds, and although some certainly wanted to get rid of her, others, apparently the majority, seem to have either accepted her or been highly ambivalent.[16]

The county justices believed that the physical sign of a "titt" was proof that a woman was a witch. They knew what other evidence they should look for: "Images and such like things," and they apparently knew where to look, that is, where she was reputed to work. They accepted the dunking test as a real test, but even after she failed it, they *did not want to harm Grace Sherwood.*

In the 1970s a small bottle filled with pins was found buried some three miles from the Princess Anne Court site. In England, such small jars filled with urine and pins, buried upside down, were known as "witch jars" and were believed to "send back" curses to their originators. Finding such a bottle in Sherwood's neighborhood may link it to her, but aspects of the Sherwood case, as well as the widespread belief in the occult, suggest that other workers may also have been in the area.[17]

Magic was still widely accepted in the society from which Virginians had come. In seventeeth-century England Robert Burton had claimed "sourcerers are too common. Cunning men, wizards, and white witches . . . [are] in every village."[18] It appears likely that English migrants to Virginia accepted occult workers as a matter of course, and it is probable that some witches and wizards made the journey to the South as well. At least three individuals were hanged as witches on ships coming to the Chesapeake; at least one of these three had confessed to practicing witchcraft. Virginians were apparently always loath to prosecute suspected witches and even raised legal questions about one of these executions at sea.[19]

There were no witch hunts in Virginia, although there is ample evidence that people believed that cunning men and women were active.[20] Between 1626 and 1705, only eight individuals were charged with witchcraft. Of these eight, only one, William Harding, was found guilty and punished, whereas three were fully exonerated.[21] There were another ten cases in which individuals who were called witches by neighbors brought suits for slander against their accusers (as Grace Sherwood had). In these and other court cases there is evidence of a wide range of magical beliefs: A Virginian giving a court deposition in this period felt it was legitimate to "ascribe his poor hunting to the spell of another (1626), hold that only the horseshoe over his door protected his sick wife from the evil intentions of a neighbor woman . . . (1671), could attribute to a witch the death of his pigs and withering of his cotton (1698), and . . . insist that 'to his thoughts, apprehension or best Knowledge' two witches 'had rid him along the Seaside & home to his own house' (again 1698)."[22]

There is other evidence of interest in and use of magic: In the seventeeth century leading Virginians had a considerable range of occult literature in their libraries. Although fewer books of this sort were purchased in the eighteenth century, that may be due to the decline in English publishing in this area rather than to any decline in Virginians' interest.[23]

There were others who believed that objects they owned protected them from death. William Buckingham, who had shot a black man whom he accused of whipping his horse, claimed: "that his dealings were . . . with the devil and that he was (as the saying is) powder proof and that by the virtue which he always carried about him, no man could make a bullet hurt him."[24]

John Craig, a Scottish Presbyterian minister who settled in Augusta County in 1740, recorded that he went into a trance when his child was born. This child soon died. Shortly afterwards his farm animals were the only ones in a common herd to die, and he suspected malevolence. His neighbors, in turn, suspected him of using "charms" to try to discover the guilty; nevertheless none of those involved turned to the legal authorities.[25]

In 1736, George Webb had reminded Virginia magistrates that they were obliged, by "the colony's own laws," to try settlers for practicing witchcraft, for using occult techniques to find lost goods, and for provoking "unlawful love."[26] Clearly he believed the occult techniques were being used, and that magistrates as well as citizens were not eager to resort to legal measures to control their use.

Good Christians accepted what we call magic, and most did not see it as a competing system. To be in league with the Devil was, after all, within Christian understandings. But Christians did not view all magic as deviltry. God had given men and women powers as well—the power of tongues, of healing, of visions, and of esoteric knowledge. Although a great deal of "Catholic" magic was abjured, especially in rote form, the sectarians welcomed individuals with God-given gifts, and Baptists and Quakers as well as Puritans and Anglicans harbored arational views.[27]

The world view of William Byrd compares most interestingly with that of Samuel Sewall. Like Sewall, he spent time in England as a young man, but Byrd was born in Virginia and lived there, on a slave plantation, for his first six or seven most formative years. In part, his world view should be seen as a Virginia value system. Byrd too believed in the prophetic validity of dreams and omens. He saw these as portents of future developments, particularly of deaths in his black and white family. "As sometimes dreams have been true," he worried when he dreamed that his wife, his daughter, and he himself had died. He saw a "flaming sword in the sky" and "a shining cloud exactly in the shape of a dart" over his plantation and was sure they portended some evil that he or his family would suffer. This "afterwards came to pass in the death of several of my negroes after a very unusual manner."[28]

Byrd went to fortunetellers, and he welcomed the ministrations of witches for "good winds." He too regarded ritual as having a magical efficacy in and of itself, and he ritualized his "profane" time. There was a time to pray, a time to dance (or exercise), a time to read, a time to work, and a time to "talk to my people." His eating patterns too were rigid and ritualized, and about the only thing truly random in his days was his fornication. And with all this, Byrd was a proper Anglican of the Latitudinarian school, a follower of Tillotson, seemingly a reasonable and "rational" modern man.[29] In actuality he was very much a believer in magic and conjur along with God and Christ, and it is likely he "talked to his people" about matters of this sort as well.[30]

While white Virginians believed that witches could assure good winds, talismans could protect health, and occult practitioners could bring positive reactions from lovers, some of them seemed to regard the land itself, Virginia, as having magical powers. The imagined Virginia of the early years had the qualities of a vision experience: it was virginal and pure, a Garden of Eden. Even those who had actually been there saw its verdant lushness as extraordinary. "We have discovered the main to be the goodliest soil under the cope of heaven," wrote Ralph Lane from Roanoke Island in September of 1585, "abounding" with fruit trees, grapes, wheat, flax, cane sugar, corn, and apothecary drugs. "[B]eing inhabited with English, no realm in Christendom were comparable to it."[31] His glowing report, published by Hakluyt, led poet Michael Drayton to sing of "VIRGINIA, Earth's Only Paradise," where harvests were to be made without "toyle," and nature provided "Fowle, Vinison and Fish . . . All greater than your Wish."[32]

Given the extraordinarily harsh vicissitudes of seventeenth-century Southern life, it might have been expected that this early vision would have died, but it did not die entirely. The dream of the Garden of Eden survived a century of great hardships: much sickness, a high death rate, many broken families, extensive white servitude and suffering, a civil war (Bacon's Rebellion), and a long economic depression in the last third of the century. Although most whites in this century lived in small rude cabins, on small clearings, without hedges or gardens or flowers, nevertheless some retained the Edenic image. The rising expectations and promise of eighteenth-century life, tied to the expansion of slavery, revitalized and refreshed this dream, and a limited number of whites saw a new vision and a reality of Eden in what Lewis P. Simpson has called "The Garden of the Chattel."[33]

In 1705, Robert Beverly experienced "an ecstatic and sensuous vision of the paradisaical garden in Virginia," symbolized by the actual garden of William Byrd: "Have you pleasures in a Garden?" he asked; he answered that he himself was surprised that "All things thrive in it," in particular the scarlet, green, and gold "Humming Bird, which revels among the Flowers, and licks off the Dew and Honey from their tender Leaves." In the honeysuckle covering Byrd's "Summer-House," "ten or a dozen of these beautiful Creatures together . . . sported about me so familiarly, that with their little Wings they often fann'd my Face."[34] Beverly had probably spent much time courting William Byrd's eldest daughter, Ursula, in this garden. They were married in 1697, and her death in 1698 may well have influenced his seraphic imagery; but in writing of the garden as Edenic he was drawing on a widely shared image.

Not everyone, however, found Virginia a Garden of Eden. In fact, Beverly's wife, Ursula, had been sent to England at the age of four because her parents felt "shee could learn nothing good here, in a great family of Negro's."[35] She had probably returned to Virginia only a year or two before her marriage. When Ursula left Virginia (c. 1684), the Byrds had been living in rude frontier conditions at the falls of the James River. The Byrd garden—Beverly's Eden—was developed only after 1688, when the Byrd family moved downriver to Westover and built a Big House. The Big House and its garden became the symbol of their selves, one with which they could forge an affective bond.[36] It was part and parcel of a new plantation style of living, new to the Byrds, and essentially new to Virginia. The new summerhouse covered with honeysuckle may well have been a thatched hut built by Africans (over 100 of whom had been purchased by Byrd). It was probably as big as the small stone house Byrd had inherited on his uncle's estate at the falls in 1662.[37]

The new plantations seemed to realize another aspect of the old Edenic dream: Blacks had been placed in the imagined Eden long before Virginia was settled with African slaves. A map of paradise with a black accompanying Adam and Eve was published by Samuel Purchas in the first decades of the seventeenth century, and blacks had been envisioned in Solomon's gardens, as well as in the afterworld. (See Figure 5.) By the opening of the eighteenth century there was a "Paradise" in Virginia. Richard Lee had named his Gloucester County land Paradise plantation, and there were Africans working there.[38]

The Edenic dream, with blacks in it, became very important to William Byrd II, but he came to it slowly and with great difficulty. He was born in 1674, and his father sent him away from Virginia at a young age. He grew up in England, becoming a London gentleman committed to the pubs, coffeehouses, gambling houses, theaters, and bawdy houses of the world's greatest city. He briefly attempted to live in Vir-

FIGURE 5. A black in paradise. The "Paradisus" map in Samuel Purchas, *Purchas His Pilgrimes*, Book 2. London, 1625. Courtesy of The Henry E. Huntington Library.

ginia in 1699 and returned again in 1705, when he stayed for a decade. During this stay in Virginia, Byrd very significantly turned to translating the "Song of Songs" from Hebrew to English.[39] His own situation as a white king figure with black concubines was parallel to that of the white lover in the Biblical song. There, the Bride sings,

I am black, but comely, O ye daughters of Jerusalem as the tents of Kedar, as the curtains of Solomon. Look not upon me, because I am black, because the sun hath looked upon me. . . . My beloved is white and ruddy, the chiefest among ten thousand. 1.5; 5.10

87

Byrd no doubt took pleasure in the Biblically sanctioned eroticism of this book, and we can be fairly certain he was conscious of the parallel: In a rare evaluative diary entry he then noted, "Everybody respected me like a King."[40]

In 1726, Byrd, returning again to Virginia, this time to stay, replaced his image of a Solomonic garden of ecstasy with a patriarchal garden of industrious work. His new vision equated the Garden with a mechanical clock:

Like one of the patriarchs, I have my flocks and my herds, my bondmen, and bond-women. . . . I must take care to keep all my people to their duty, to set all the springs in motion, and to make everyone draw his equal share to carry the machine forward. . . . [W]e sit securely under our vines, and our fig-trees without any danger to our property.[41]

Byrd tried to transfer his dream of the Garden into a new reality. He traveled at this time over miles of uncharted wilderness to plot the boundary of Virginia, and this journey took on deep psychological significance for him. He felt he tested himself and the land and conquered both. He came out in control of himself, of those around him, and of the land itself. Byrd obtained 20,000 acres of land located at the western terminus of this journey (at the junction of the Dan and Irvine rivers on the Virginia – North Carolina border), and he called this land "Eden." (See Byrd's map, Figure 6.) Beverly's descriptions of Virginia were fittingly used to advertise Byrd's paradise, on which he promised to settle at least 100 white families. (A shipload of Swiss settlers on their way to Eden foundered in a storm, and most drowned.)[42]

Byrd was able to maintain his dream of a Biblical garden until 1736, when, perhaps due to a combination of personal depression, colonial difficulties, and reports of brutal racial violence in the West Indies, he brought another image to consciousness. He drew a new dream picture, or nightmare, of Virginia as a "New Guinea" peopled by desperate rebellious "Ethiopians" who would "tinge our rivers as wide as they are with blood"; idle poor whites who would rather steal than work; and masters forced to be inhuman "furies" in order to control the vast numbers of black slaves.[43]

Neither Byrd's dream nor his nightmare was realized. Slaves certainly were not bondmen and bondwomen, and Byrd was not a Biblical patriarch; but he did establish black and white clans that continue to be important in Virginia to this day. His own son, William Byrd III, however, lost faith in both the dream and himself and took his own

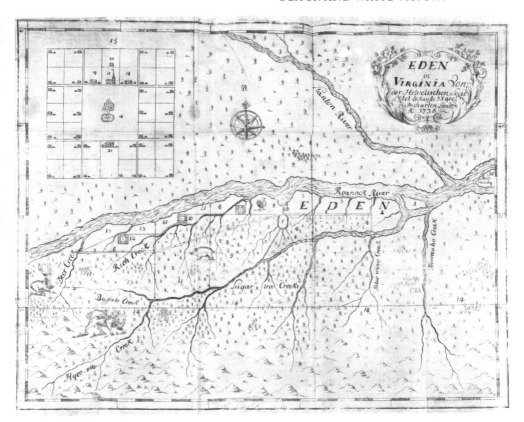

FIGURE 6. Map of "Eden in Virginia." A projected urban and rural paradise from *New-gefundenes Eden*, 1737, attributed to William Byrd. Courtesy of the John Carter Brown Library at Brown University.

life. A black Byrd, Sam Byrd, Jr. (a slave named for his free black father), was an important recruiter for the Gabriel Insurrection in Richmond in 1800. However, "rivers of blood" did not flow, and slavery did not end then.[44] The dream of the Garden of the Chattel was not a family possession and was not lost in Byrd's disillusion or through slave rebellion. Although held by a minority, it was an important stream in white Southern thought through the whole slave period and provided for some a Biblical legitimation for slavery and a dream future. After the end of slavery, the lost garden, the loss of paradise, was a proper image for the defeated South.

The Edenic image was important for a small group, but even among the elite it was not universal. Washington and Jefferson, for example, never wrote of their plantations in these terms, although Washington did refer to his "vine and fig tree," suggesting his home fulfilled the Biblical promise. However, both these men shared another attitude toward the natural world that was important among their class: they wanted to control it. They wanted fields neat and hedges straight, in an artificial landscape that can be interpreted as a secular transformation of the Edenic myth: All will be perfect under human control.

When Jefferson set out to build Monticello he had his workmen change the mountain. Working with hand tools, they cut off its top, making a large level area for his "stage." The plan of his garden indicates the kind of order and control he sought:

March 31, [1774].
laid off ground to be levelled for a future garden. the upper side is 44.f. below the upper edge of the Round-about and parallel thereto. it is 668 feet long, 80.f. wide, and at each end form a triangle; rectangular & isosceles, of which the legs are 80.f. & the hypotenuse 113.feet.[45]

The plantations and gardens of the elite were in stark contrast to most Virginia farms, where disorder seemed to reign. The archaeological digs at Kingsmill plantation suggest that at farms and quarters garbage was rather randomly disposed of, that large puddles collected near these houses, and that pigs probably rooted in them freely.[46] Most Virginians were not living in a beautiful garden, and they had probably come to Virginia with a relatively realistic, rather than a dream, image. More reality-oriented, their needs were symbolically served by the contemporary maps of Virginia that were popular. These maps were concrete two-dimensional representations of a new land that could now be "known" by those contemplating settlement. The maps showed that the Chesapeake had endless seacoast and navigable rivers. The myriad Indian towns named and placed by Captain John Smith on his Virginia map in 1606 "proved" the potential of the land: it had supported a settled populace.[47] When printed, Smith's map was dominated by a large-scale drawing of a well-proportioned Susquehanna Indian, carrying a tomahawk, a bow, arrows, and a wild boar on his back. Based on John White's eyewitness drawings, the Indian was long-haired and muscled and wore amulets and leather dress. A drawing of chief Powhatan's home flanked the map on the opposite side. The illustrations suggested Virginia was populated by a settled and healthy, if primitive, people who were hunters. Their physical appearance was not overly strange to English eyes. (See Figure 7.)

FIGURE 7. Indians and Indian place names. These people and places were different but comprehensible, as depicted in a detail from John Smith's map of "Virginia," 1612. Courtesy of the British Library.

Indians still symbolized the Chesapeake on Augustine Herrman's important map of Virginia and Maryland of 1673, which was very widely disseminated and copied. These Indians were already more idealized figures, and there was far less detail of dress and weaponry. Indians were no longer the exotic natives met in the new Eden. They were being reduced to a symbol of the past. (See Figure 8.)

By 1753, when Joshua Fry and Peter Jefferson's excellent map of the "settled parts" of Virginia and Maryland was published, there were no Indians on it and relatively few Indian place names.[48] The prominent cartouche was designed by an English artist, Francis Hayman, one of the first designers of historical prints who no doubt sought to be accurate, but had never visited the New World. The drawing showed four blacks and four whites, literally representing the Virginia population, which was thought to be fifty percent black by 1750. The four

FIGURE 8. Idealized Indians, as depicted in a detail from Augustine Herrman's map of "Virginia and Maryland," 1673. Photo courtesy of the John Carter Brown Library at Brown University.

whites pictured were a trader, a bookkeeper checking cargo, and two gentlemen clients dressed as proper Englishmen in a London climate would be. The four blacks were clearly African slaves, dressed in diaper-like loincloths, three hard at work preparing tobacco casks for shipment, with at least one a cooper, tightening the end of a tobacco hogshead. One black, although dressed as the others, was serving the whites wine and pineapple, the symbols of hospitality in colonial Virginia. (See Figure 9.)

This map informed Englishmen that notwithstanding the numerous African people in Virginia, who looked different (smaller as well as black) and were near-naked (far less dressed than the Indians had been in John White's drawings), or who were "infantilized" by their diaper-like garments, white Virginians could continue to look like and function as if they were Englishmen. This one picture presents a new image of Virginia: a tobacco-producing slave society that was prosperous and a good place for Englishmen. The changes in the place names on the map indicate the vast changes that had taken place since Smith's map was made. Powhatan Flu had become the James River,

FIGURE 9. Cartouche from "The Map of Virginia" by Joshua Fry and Peter
Jefferson, 1753. Blacks and whites were illustrated in their "proper places."
Courtesy of Princeton University Press.

and many of the Indian towns were now English settlements known
by English names. There was, however, still a Manakin Town; a Tap-
pahonock Marsh; Chukatuck, Warrasqueak, and Chipaki rivers; and
Namezem and Winipomask creeks. These were colorful Indian names
in an English world of Norfolk, Jamestown, and King and Queen
County.

Virginia was never called New Guinea, and the Fry-Jefferson map
mentions no place names that can be identified as Afro-American.
There were some names in current usage that never appeared on a
map. For example, two of the farms owned by John Wayles, and later
the property of his son-in-law Thomas Jefferson, were called
"Guinea" and "Angola." Angola Creek in Cumberland has preserved
this name. There was a road in Middlesex County known as the Negro
Road, and places were often known locally by the names of the blacks
occupying them, as Aunt Millie's Spring, or Jacko's or Nero's Quarter.

Later settlements of free blacks were sometimes called New Guinea, Freetown, or Affriky Town, but these too were local realities, not mapped areas to be made known to the world.[49]

In the southside, where the "middling" and the poor determined many place names, "Terrible Creek," "Difficult Creek," and "Fucking Creek" confirm that these settlers had less than romantic attitudes toward the land.[50] The acrimonious land disputes that filled the court dockets and land "perambulation," an important communal ritual in which the boundaries of each property were marked every four years, further indicate popular white attitudes to land.[51] There is no evidence that perambulations retained rites of a religious nature, as parish perambulations in England had. Although Virginia perambulators marked trees and drank copiously, these acts, although ritualized, were secular. This, and the legal evidence, suggests that land was generally viewed as a commodity, and we know it was often rapaciously sought and literally fought over.[52]

However, some poor whites did begin to "dream" of a new future, tied to land ownership, after they came to Virginia. John Harrower, for example, had come to Virginia as a place of last resort. "Reduced to the last shilling," unable to pay his debts, and unable to find work in England, he felt "obliged to engage to go to Virginia for four years." Harrower was very quickly won over to this new "pleace"; notwithstanding the fact that he was in an unfree status as an indentured servant, he felt himself "verry pleasantly situated on the Banks of the River Rappahannock." He soon wrote to his wife of his hopes to make her "a Virginian Lady among the woods of America," which he already found "more pleasant than the roaring of the raging seas round abo't Zetland," his old home.[53] The new place was a garden in the woods, with more blacks, he claimed, than could be counted.

Our Family consists of the Coll. his Lady & four Children a housekeeper an overseer and myself all white. But how many blacks young and old the Lord only knows for I belive there is about thirty that works every day in the field besides the servants about the house; such as Gardner, livery men, and pages, Cooks, washer & dresser, sewster and waiting girle.[54]

Harrower died before his indenture was up. The high death rate in the colonial Chesapeake no doubt ended many dreams and influenced many of those who lived to have a harsher view of life's realities.[55]

As suggested, some Virginians, poor as well as rich, had come to the

new land with Edenic dreams. Hakluyt had reprinted Ralph Lane's description of Virginia's perfection in a promotional tract, and it had apparently had some effect in England.[56] When developers sought to at-
tract Swiss yeomen to Byrd's lands, they too used the image of the
"New-Found Eden" and expected it to have symbolic significance. (In
Beverly's words, Virginia was described as "the best place on earth."[57])
Some settlers lost their dream images in Virginia, whereas others actually developed dreams while there. For most settlers, however, the
magical and symbolic meanings attached to land competed with and
apparently most often lost out to economic concerns. Nevertheless,
many white Virginians did retain deep emotional attachments to
place, and the Edenic dream remained a reality and a cultural "re-
source." Perhaps only a minority were generally moved by it; however, in the revivals of the Great Awakening, many more came to see
Virginia as a potential Garden of Eden and tried to change their lives
so that they might realize it.[58]

LONG AFTER the Civil War, a former slave remarked, "I been here a
long time, and I ain't tired of staying." Blacks had been in the South a
long time, and although many moved about a great deal after the war,
most stayed not too far from "the old home place." It was home to
them too in a very significant way.[59] However, slaves in Virginia were
outside the system of landownership. They were on the land, tilled
the land, and were generally given private gardens to cultivate to sup-
plement their own food, but the land did not "belong" to them legally.

Spiritual ownership of the land was, as it were, another question.
Blacks had a strong attachment to place in Africa without private
ownership of land. We know that after arrival some tried to return to
Africa. In May of 1771, "Step" and "Lucy," not long in Virginia, ran
off with a group of slaves "being persuaded that they could find the
Way back to their own Country."[60]

Some newly arrived slaves did try to establish African-style villages
in Virginia, but they did not succeed. This was the experience of a
group of some fifteen who, in 1729, ran off from a new plantation on
the James River, to "the fastness of the neighbouring Mountains," and
were planning a new "settlement" when they were recaptured.[61]

In the few eighteenth-century black memoirs extant there is some
evidence of early slave reactions to the land. Equiano and Job longed
for their homelands, as no doubt most slaves did.[62] Some small
shadow of that longing for Africa must have come through to Thomas

Jefferson. His *Virginia Almanack for 1771* includes an "Inscription for An African Slave" in Jefferson's hand. Not having been identified as the work of any published writer, it is assumed to have been written by Jefferson. In any event, he thought the sentiment worthy of note:

INSCRIPTION FOR AN AFRICAN SLAVE
Shores there are, bless'd shores for us remain,
And favor'd isles with golden fruitage crown's
Where tufted flow'rets paint the verdant plain,
Where ev'ry breeze shall med'cine every wound.
There the stern tyrant that embitters life,
Shall vainly suppliant, spread his asking hand;
There shall we view the billow's raging strife,
Aid the kind breast, and waft his boat to land.[63]

On arrival, Africans in America believed that after death their spirits would return to the traditional spirit abode near their homelands. As blacks became Christian, heaven became the new collective homeland of all blacks: *all* their forefathers were expected to be there, and all members of families could plan on meeting there. Reuben Madison, born in Virginia in 1781, went through severe trials after his wife was sold away from him, but he found consolation as he had the very real "hope of meeting her and my children again in the Kingdom of God, when we should never be separated." George Pleasant or Hobbs, sold south to Tennessee, wrote to his wife Agnes Hobbs, back on the "family" farm in Virginia, "In heaven lets meet when will I am determnid to nuver stope praying, not in this earth. . . . In glory there weel meet to part no more forever. So my dear wife I hope to meet you In paradase to prase god forever."[64] This is *not* to suggest that blacks lost their special attachment to land, trees, rocks, and water. On the contrary, blacks continued to develop very deep attachments to place and to communicate these to whites as well. Virginia relatively quickly became home, and it may well have been that blacks played a significant part in stabilizing and rooting the extended black–white plantation families there.

Blacks in Virginia recognized spirits in trees, rocks, rivers, and houses. They knew that magic workers could have special control over the spirits or that magic could lodge evil spirits in their own houses, animals, pots, tools, or food. Spirits could make them move at will, and objects often "acted" malevolently due to the spirit activating them. "Ha'nts kin te'k enny fo'm, w'ite folks, even a brickbat, block, chair er anything."[65] Blacks in the South told of pots running

FIGURE 10. A Virginia bottle tree. A contemporary drawing of a black's house and tree, seen some thirty miles south of Richmond. This tradition is similar to one from the Congo "for protecting the household through invocation of the dead." Courtesy of Robert Farris Thompson.

away, "a swamp going to sleep and having bad dreams," and trees being holy or evil. Trees were widely named, and the names were assumed to affect their character: A tree, named after a large person, was believed likely to grow to be large.[66]

The West African pattern of placing shiny objects in trees, perhaps as an invitation to spirits to come down and guard against evil, can still be found in Virginia, where glass bottles are now used.[67] (See Figure 10.)

Certainly not every white child baptized trees or knew of bottle trees, but many of them spent time in their early childhood with black children playing in fields and woods, hunting and fishing, sharing lore and "superstition." Whites and blacks, both believing that power resided in natural objects, both accepting "magical" explanations and magic workers, could expect that the others knew something worth knowing or fearing.[68] Spirit power was potent, allied as it was to

97

knowledge (and control) of nature and its healing and poisoning potential. Available evidence suggests that throughout the slave period a melding of black and white understandings of magic and spirit power was underway. We will never be able to document the exact interaction, but several areas of contact suggest possibilities.

Whites coming to the New World did *not* have a rich folklore about snakes, although they certainly figured in Biblical story and myth and had significant symbolic meaning. But it was in America that whites heard the tales of snakes "charming" animals and people, and snake lore was essentially a new development for them. Bartram, Byrd, Walduck, and others wrote down facts and fancies; the people told tales.[69]

Blacks came to America with a rich folklore about snakes. Snakes were believed to embody spirits, and spirit workers came with snakeskins, if not live snakes, which were collected in the South. Extensive rituals governed their care and "honor"; voodoo based on Dahomean practices recognized the god Damballa-wedo in the snake. The snake was "mounted" by the voodoo Queen, and she was "penetrated" by the God.[70]

When whites in America developed a new concern with snakes, those who wrote about the issue wrote only of Indian knowledge and folklore; blacks were not mentioned by John Lederer, Benjamin Bartram, or William Byrd. But it seems highly unlikely that Lederer, traveling in Virginia and South Carolina, and Byrd, living in Virginia and talking with his people daily, would not have talked with them about snakes. When Byrd collected a live Virginia rattlesnake for the Royal Society, it was likely to have been a black that collected it for him. Whites were not ready to give any "credit" to blacks in terms of ideas or values, but they were sharing them nevertheless.[71]

In most areas of such lore, both the English and the Africans had similar ideas. Both believed in eternal souls and in the possibility of spirit journeys, in ways that were both different and yet similar. Ghosts and the "living dead" were not exactly the same, but people apparently assumed the same reality was apprehended. In the process, the concepts did come closer to each other. Blacks and whites had concepts of both positive rootwork and malevolent witchcraft that were similar and could be melded. Africans had not believed in the Devil, but many African deities had evil and dangerous inclinations, and it was believed witches could use their power harmfully.[72]

Both peoples, for example, had ideas about power in rocks and stones. In England it had been believed that certain stones could cause evil, that a curse could be buried "on" a stone, and that other stones cured diseases, helped lovers, or made a man potent.[73] In Africa, among the Dawoyo for example, stones were believed to "cause everything from toothache to dysentery."[74] Both the afflicted and those who did not want to be afflicted paid fees to a stone's guardian. In Virginia some mix of ideas *may* have occurred. There are "documented" madstones that "took out madness" and were known to be in use in the 1740s.[75]

When it came to artificial charms, whites widely used amulets or sigils and recognized blacks' ability to make "hands" as well as potions and poisons.[76] Whites both feared this ability and yet respected blacks' esoteric knowledge. Whites passed laws against blacks' "doctoring" or conjuring and prosecuted poisoners, but they did occasionally go to black doctors and no doubt went to black witches and magic workers as well.[77] More information was probably exchanged in informal ways during daily contact, especially when blacks cared for ill whites or whites took care of blacks. White midwives and doctors were often hired to treat blacks, while masters and mistresses widely prescribed for and treated slave ills.[78] Many whites regarded themselves as very knowledgeable about the care of illnesses, but they were nevertheless interested in the knowledge of others less educated than themselves. John Custis, for example, who prided himself on his "diligent" study of "phisick" for more than forty years, was open to experimentation, and when "a woman that came from England" used "mountain flax" to relieve a "Negro Distemper" that he himself had, he was ready to try it.[79] It seems likely he would have been willing to try a remedy his slaves knew about as well. Lt. Gov. Gooch pressured the black slave Pawpaw until he revealed the roots and barks he used to cure yaws in his successful practice. In payment, in 1729, Gooch bought Pawpaw's freedom from his owner, Francis Littlepage, but insisted that Pawpaw remain in contact with Gooch as he wanted him to reveal "some other secrets he has for expelling poison, and the cure of other diseases."[80] Gooch clearly respected his knowledge and ability.

In Virginia black spirit workers continued practices of spirit possession, whereby they were filled with the spirit they served when in trance. Before blacks were Christians, most whites viewed these practices as "Devil-Dances" and were certain the practitioners were in league with Satan.[81] But then, they accepted that many whites were as well. Later, blacks and whites shared Christian vision experiences that were both similar and yet very different.[82]

9. Sharing Space Inside the Little House

BLACKS AND WHITES, sharing ideas about nature, were sharing occupation of the same place under similar conditions. In the seventeenth- and eighteenth-century Chesapeake most whites and blacks lived in rude wooden houses of like construction and size. Their physical world was remarkably similar.

The Great House had appeared early in Virginia, but very few whites lived in a "castle" or even a four-room house. In the first third of the eighteenth century, when the Great Houses of the first generation of large plantation owners proliferated, perhaps some fifteen or twenty were scattered over the countryside. The vast majority of the 84,000 whites and the 36,500 blacks in Virginia in 1730 apparently lived in one- or two-room wooden houses with rude lofts, wooden chimneys, and earthen or wooden floors. This remained the case through most of the eighteenth century. It was only in the last third of the eighteenth and primarily in the nineteenth century that significant numbers of whites moved into more permanent and larger quarters. Blacks then remained in what became known as slave cabins—quarters that had once been basic housing for most of the population.[1]

The basic similarity of black and white housing has been established through archaeological research, recorded house descriptions, and the analysis of the wills and inventories of eighteenth-century Virginians. In Lancaster, for example, "relatively few houses who[se] contents were inventoried between 1710 and 1740 were described as larger than a single room."[2] Probate inventories from 1721 to 1730 indicate that "twenty-seven to thirty-four of Virginia's wealthiest descendants had lived in houses with two ground-floor rooms, while two lived in houses with only one main room."[3] The late-seventeenth-century "mansion" of Robert "King" Carter, Corotoman, in the Northern Neck, for example, was probably a one-and-a-half-story house, with two rooms downstairs and two up.[4] What Carter and the wealthier population generally had by this time was a complex of small buildings, many of them not very different from the slave cabin.

When John Fontaine visited Robert Beverly's 6,000-acre plantation in November of 1715, he was struck by the simplicity of the Beverly Park house: "This man lives well, but has nothing in or about his house but just what is necessary, tho' rich. He hath good beds in his house but no curtains and instead of cane chairs he hath stools made of wood."[5] Much later in the century Thomas Jefferson's sister and her husband, Dabney Carr, were living in a small wooden house; the first house Jefferson himself built at Monticello, the one he brought his bride to, was an 18′ × 18′ "box." (See Figure 11.) Jefferson seemed to have a contradictory two-sided ideal of the perfect space. At Monticello he built himself an open, light-filled innovative stage, on a grand scale, but had a smaller house in Bedford as a retreat, and a tiny separate room for meditation in the garden at Monticello. He noted that Carr, "with a table, a half dozen chairs, and one or two servants," was "the happiest man in the universe."[6]

Most of the white population, not having any choice in the matter, lived in small "square" houses all their lives, and their possessions remained simple and limited, much like those of the slaves. In the third decade of the century one John Pines, a white freehold in Lancaster County, owned a poor nag, a cupboard, a cedar chest, two tables, and five chairs, all together worth no more than twelve pounds, nineteen shillings. "He and his family slept on the floor on old bedding,"[7] much as the slaves around him did. William Byrd, traveling in Virginia in this period, wrote of being "pigged lovingly together" when he shared floor space with eight other white people in a one-room house.[8] George Washington, surveying in the Northern Neck in 1749/1750, found whites competing for the best floor space. Each night he "lay down before the fire upon a Little Hay Straw Fodder or bairskin which ever is to be had with Man Wife and Children like a Parcel of Dogs or Catts & happy's he that gets the Birth nearest the fire." He and his hosts did not remove their clothing "but lay and sleep in them like a Negro."[9]

FIGURE 11. Jefferson's Small House. Jefferson's first home at Monticello, 1770, embodied Jefferson's small-house ideal. It became the "South Pavillion" once the mansion was built. Photo courtesy of the Thomas Jefferson Memorial Foundation, Inc.

These "primitive" practices and limited possessions were not very different from those of the poor in England or those of the blacks in Africa and in Virginia. The poor Cornish cottage in the eighteenth century contained "a rude table," benches, and stools. "The children sat on blocks of wood. For the rest there were a few earthenware cups, saucers and basins, some wooden or tin plates, an iron crock for boiling and a kettle or baker."[10]

Of Igbo possessions, Equiano wrote: "The walls and floors . . . of these [houses] are generally covered with mats. Our beds consist of a platform, raised three or four feet from the ground, on which are laid skins, and different parts of a spongy tree, called plantain. Our covering is calico or muslin. . . . The usual seats are a few logs of wood; but we have benches . . . ; these compose the greater part of our household furniture."[11]

A Henrico County slave cabin was inventoried just prior to the turn of the century (1697) and it had "several chairs and a bed, an iron kettle weighing fifteen pounds, a brass kettle, an iron pot, a pair of pot racks, a pot hook, a frying-pan, and a beer barrel."[12] This was more than most slaves or poor whites then had in their cabins. It was very common for slaves and whites to have no more than the "1 iron pot with pot hookes" and "1 old fryin pan" that Robert Dudley's mulatto woman took with her to her new slave cabin in 1701.[13]

The material standard of living was not static. Acquisition of amenities by the "middling sort" increased significantly in the first half of the century and continued rising more moderately throughout the period. By 1750, white people were much more likely to have "coarse ceramics, bed and table linens, chamber pots, warming pans, and some means of interior lighting," items that approximately two-thirds of the white Chesapeake population had not had in 1715. However, on the one hand, material possessions were still quite limited, and on the other, slaves too could more easily purchase or barter for these now more readily available items.[14]

Devereux Jarratt, for example, the son of a fairly substantial slave-owning and landowning family, left home in 1752 to seek his fortune, taking his "all," which was no more than a slave might well have owned: "a pair of coarse breeches, one or two oznaburgs shirts, a pair of shoes and stockings, an old felt hat, a bear skin *coat*." This list can be matched by many of those in advertisements for runaway slaves, with perhaps his bearskin coat the only unusual item, but still one that a slave might have obtained. That very year, in advertising for a 25-year-old runaway slave sawyer named Tom, John Mecom of Isle of Wight County noted he "had on when he went away, a dark brown

Halfthick Jacket and Breeches, an Oznabrig shirt, a Felt Hat, white Yarn Stockings, and a Pair of double-channel'd Pumps: He took with him a brown Holland Coat, a white Linen Shirt, and a Pair of blue mix'd Stockings," while Jemmy, an "Eboe," ran away wearing a worn bearskin coat. Jarratt apparently was conscious of how ordinary his possessions were and sought some mark of distinction as he set out to begin a new life as a teacher. "And that I might appear something more than common, in a strange place, and be counted somebody, I got me an old wig, which, perhaps being cast off by the master, had become the property of his slave, and from the slave it was conveyed to me."[15]

Notwithstanding the continuous upward trend in whites' material possessions, as late as the Revolutionary period some thirty percent of the white population of the Tidewater owned "no land, no slaves and a few farm animals."[16] These whites, and an even higher percentage of those in the Piedmont, including most of the "middling sort," were likely to be living in small one- or two-room houses, similar in size to slave housing.[17] François Chastellux, in Virginia in 1780, observed this phenomenon and was deeply disturbed at "the state of poverty in which a great number of white people live in Virginia. . . . [A]mong [the] . . . rich plantations where the Negro alone is wretched, one often finds miserable huts inhabited by whites, whose wan looks and ragged garments bespeak poverty."[18]

In addition to its small size and poor quality, Virginia's rural housing elicited comments about its village-like character. Houses, both big and small, were generally surrounded by outbuildings that Benjamin Latrobe described in 1796 as appearing "to follow the dwelling house as a litter of pigs their mother."[19] A century earlier, in 1687, this pattern was already apparent and elicited comment from Durand de Dauphine:

Whatever their rank, and I know not why, they build only two rooms with some closets on the ground floor, and two rooms in the attic above; but they build several like this, according to their means. They also build a separate kitchen, a separate house for the Christian slaves, one for the negro slaves, and several to dry the tobacco, so that when you come to the home of a person of some means, you think you are entering a fairly large village.[20]

Important new evidence has been found to support this view that most whites lived in small houses, and that the "well off" lived in complexes of similar small buildings. Michael L. Nicholls has located and analyzed an unusual 1785 survey of housing in Halifax County, in the southwestern part of the state, where "middling" settlers predominated. When Congress asked for information about inhabitants and property, one surveyor, James Bates, assumed they wanted house size and construction details. He recorded the existence of 1,002 structures serving 239 families, of whom twenty-seven did not have their own homes. In giving us the particulars of 211 homes, he provided a uniquely detailed picture of this eighteenth-century landscape.[21]

Bates termed sixty-seven homes "cabins" and did not give any further details. Clearly this word denoted a particular dwelling, probably a one-room log cabin, possibly with a loft. Of the 181 houses he does detail, three-quarters were either 16' × 20', 16' × 16', or 16' × 12'. Larger houses were most often 16' × 24'; the largest 28' × 42', and the smallest 8' × 8'. Over seventy-five percent of the people were living in one-room log or plank houses of less than 320 square feet. The 211 small homes were surrounded by 791 outbuildings: barns, shed, smokehouses, corncribs, chicken houses, and so forth.

Over fifty percent of the householders surveyed by Bates owned slaves, and almost all these slaveowners were in one- or two-room houses, together with an average of four additional family members. Their slaves lived in equally cramped quarters. Most slaves apparently lived in lofts, barns, kitchens, or small cabins. At the nine quarters specifically identified in Bates's inventory, the buildings "appear quite similar to the homes of the area's white families in size and construction."[22]

Although Halifax was in the western part of the state, it would appear that housing all over Virginia was similar. The extraordinary archaeological research done at Kingsmill plantation, near Williamsburg, and William Kelso's analysis of these data, reveal both the village-like appearance of this large plantation and the range of housing built for both blacks and whites. (See map of Kingsmill, Figure 12.) The eighteenth-century Kingsmill properties had substantial Big Houses made of brick: the Bray's manor at Littletown, circa 1700–1781, one and a half stories high, 53' × 29', and the Burwell family's Kingsmill mansion, circa 1724–1820, two stories high, each floor 61' × 40'. This mansion was flanked by two brick dependencies (22' × 45') that housed slaves along with the kitchen and plantation offices and created a symmetrically ordered Big House complex. (See photo of extant dependencies, Figure 13.) There was also a two-room home on the property (42' × 19') that was apparently first used by whites and then by blacks, communal slave quarters (40' × 18' and 28' × 20'), as well as a large range of other wooden, earthfast buildings in three separate quarters. One quarter was stretched out along Quartermaster Road, the main road passing Kingsmill's Big House and connecting Williamsburg with Burwell's Ferry Landing. Two other quarters were to the north and east, the second near the second Big House incorporated into the Burwell plantation.[23] These wooden buildings ranged in size from a 40' × 18' two-room building with a 12' × 36' lean-to to an 8' × 8' structure. When the Kingsmill properties were put up for sale by the Burwell family in the 1780s, they were appropriately advertised as having "every necessary outhouse."[24]

In the Kingsmill pattern, the brick Great House with a well and brick "offices" (kitchen, dairy, laundry, and storehouse) were symmetrically arranged on a prominent bluff, with extensive formal landscaping, whereas virtually all the wooden, earthfast structures were apparently randomly strung out along a road—their placement restricted only by the location of spring water for the slave dwellings, some quarter mile down the road, with large "puddles" and waste disposal areas nearby. This pattern was probably repeated at other large plantations in the early eighteenth century.[25] On the poorer farms, where most slaves lived, lofts, kitchens, and small cabins housed the black population, and both blacks and whites lived amidst disorder.

By the last decades of the century a new trend toward overall order and symmetricality affected many of the larger plantations. George Washington, for example, reorganized his slave housing in 1793, taking a great deal of time, trouble, and expense to have the outlying slave houses and cabins moved and refit. They were reorganized in rigid lines or streets, "a uniform shape in a convenient place," as he described it. The "convenient place" was along a straight fence, opposite the overseer's house at each outlying farm.[26] At Muddy Hole farm, however, where Davy, a slave, was the overseer, the slaves remained in small cabins, randomly situated among the trees. (See Washington's map and "slave row" housing, Figures 14 and 15.)

Washington's slaves lived in a wide range of housing. At the Big

FIGURE 12. (Overleaf) Williamsburg and Environs, 1781. Recent archaeological research confirms that this eighteenth-century map by Nicholas Desandrouin accurately charts the formal cluster of Big House and dependency buildings, and the Kingsmill quarter, stretched along Quartermaster Road between Burwell's Ferry and Williamsburg. It is very likely that the other houses depicted here existed as shown. Most of the quarters, as at Blair's and Porce's, were not symmetrically aligned; however, at New Quarter on Queen's Creek and at several other locations, three buildings can be found in line opposite a fourth, possibly the overseer's. Map no. 51, Rochambeau Collection, courtesy of the Library of Congress.

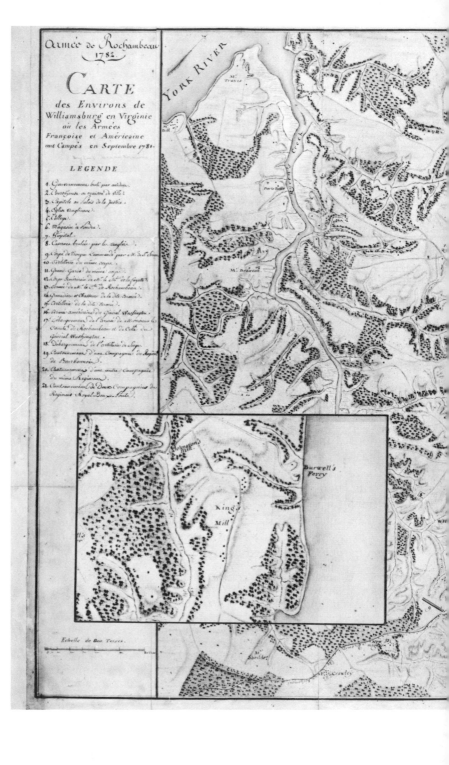

JAME'S RIVER

FIGURE 13. Two Kingsmill "Offices." These two once-elegant mid-eighteenth-century brick service buildings housed slaves and "offices," including the kitchen, pantry, and scullery. Constructed of Flemish bond brick, with fine interior chimneys, they had two rooms on each floor, approximately 22' × 22' each. Built flanking the Big House (no longer standing), they created a courtyard that housed a formal garden. Photo courtesy of the Library of Congress.

House, circa 1785, he built what he called the Greenhouse Quarters. These were two immense halls, each 20' × 70.5', flanking a central greenhouse room that gave these quarters a substantial Big House look from the outside, belying the fact that unlike his family mansion, these "mansion" quarters housed some ninety slaves.[27] Other slaves lived in cabins, some near the mansion but most of them at the four outlying farms. These were built by the occupants themselves out of locally available logs, with the interstices "daubed and filled in."[28] But even at the quarters, groups of slaves lived in larger, carpenter-built houses of scantling, plank, and shingles. Analyses of the black families on Washington's plantation indicate that most married couples were living at separate locations, and these larger houses may

FIGURE 14. An original survey and plot of Mt. Vernon and neighboring estates, by
George Washington, December 1793. This map includes a rare notation of slave
and overseer's homes. On the enlarged section, lower left, showing Union Farm,
note the neat lineup of five buildings (which housed 36 slaves) opposite the white
overseer's house, in contrast to the tiny cabins in the woods at Muddy Hole,
lower right, where Davy, a black, was overseer of 41 slaves. Photo courtesy of The
Henry E. Huntington Library.

FIGURE 15. Black row housing in "Goose Alley" on the Hampton Grounds, 1880. This is the straight-line style that was popular by the close of the eighteenth century. Photo courtesy of the Hampton University Archives.

well have accommodated mixed related and unrelated groups. Similarly at Philip Ludwell Lee's plantation, it would appear that groups of eight to twenty-four slaves were communally housed in one- or two-room structures.[29]

White homes, too, in the seventeenth and first half of the eighteenth centuries, often housed "motley crews" of relatives, inlaws, stepchildren, boarders, servants, and slaves; but by the late eighteenth century, these homes had by and large come to house more stable nuclear families. Black patterns changed over this time as well. As blacks married and established families, the small cabin came to be the modal form. Earlier, most blacks probably had lived in kitchens, lofts, sheds, and houses in communal arrangements, although the very small slave hut was known at the outset of the slave period as well.[30] "[T]he first thing to be done," advised a Southerner to prospective planters in 1710, "is after having cutt down a few Trees, to split

110

Palisades or Clapboards and therewith make small Houses or Huts to shelter the slaves."[31] Such small cabins could, of course, house a mixed group rather than a family. I. F. Smyth, in Virginia in 1774, slept one night in what he described as a small "wretched and miserable" one-room hut, with one bed and no other furniture. A white overseer and five or six slaves lived here together, isolated by over five miles of wilderness in each direction.[32]

The slave, Old Dick, had reported that his young owner, Dr. Sutherland, encouraged slave couples to live in separate cabins, and this may well have been representative of a process underway with both blacks and whites moving slaves toward family homes. Dick himself was very pleased when Spencer Ball "allowed me to build a log-house, and take in a patch of land where I raise corn and water *Melions*. I keep chickens and ducks, turkeys and geese."[33] John Davis, the schoolmaster on this plantation, living himself in a small log house, described Dick's home in some detail:

Dick's *log-hut was not unpleasantly situated. He had built it near a spring of clear water, and defended it from the sun by an awning of boughs. It was in Mr.* Ball's *peach-orchard. A cock that never strayed from his cabin served him instead of a time-keeper; and a dog that lay always before his door was an equivalent for a lock.*[34]

Whites certainly played a role in blacks' use of space. They wanted their homes small, cheap, and generally near one another, although Dick and many others were living apart. Jefferson is known to have ordered his overseer to build the Negro houses close together so that "the fewer nurses may serve & that the children may be more easily attended to by the superannuated women." He, as many other slaveowners, selected sites for slave houses. For example, he wrote his overseer in Bedford County, Joel Yancey, "Maria having now a child, I promised her a house to be built this winter, be so good as to have it done. place it along the garden fence on the road Eastward from Hannah's house."[35] Jefferson's promise was clearly given in response to a black's request, dependent on her family status. Maria was Hannah's sister. They no doubt *wanted* houses next to each other. The overseer is being ordered to do what the slave wanted. Slaves also wanted small proximate housing: it fit their own inner language of building and space. And slaves probably wanted small cabins for each family: it now fit their social needs.

At Jefferson's quarters after the turn of the century it would appear women, both with husbands and without, had cabins. He wrote his overseer, Jeremiah A. Goodman, that "Several of the negro women complain that their houses want repair badly. this should be attended to every winter. for the present winter, repair, of preference those of women who have no husbands to do it for them."[36]

When slaveowners built slave quarters or barracks for house slaves, sometimes what seems to have been a black inner language influenced them. Jefferson seems to have built his servant quarters with the 12-foot African protoform in mind. He described Mulberry Row, just below the Great House at Monticello, as including "a servants' house 20½ f. by 12 f. of wood, with a wooden chimney, & earth floor," three servants houses 12' × 14', with wooden chimneys and earthen floors; one 12' × 20½'; a joiner's shed 12½' × 25', and a stable 12 × 105½. Only the washhouse was 16.5' × 16.5'.[37]

Houses that were 12-feet square, or close to that size, dotted the countryside, sometimes used for white although most often for black homes.[38] (See Figures 16, 17, 18, 19.) Sometimes the very same building served blacks and whites serially. In 1770, Landon Carter recorded that "Guy and the Carpenters gone to build Jamy and Jugg a 12 foot house, then to new fit their house and remove it for Doleman to live in." Here, Carter's black carpenters were building a 12' × 12' house for a black couple, but they were also refitting a similar former slave cabin for John Doleman, white overseer at Fork Quarter, who had a wife and child. "The Carpenters removed Jugg's house as far as Doleman chose to have it from the spring."[39] Doleman, like the slaves, did not have a well: springs served slaves and probably most whites in the eighteenth century.

One feature does seem to distinguish eighteenth-century slave housing from that of whites: earthen root cellars, often wood-lined, dug near the chimneys, and generally later backfilled with debris,

FIGURE 16. Blacks and their cabin, Virginia, 1897. The construction of the cabin and chimney was similar to slave homes as described in the late eighteenth century. Photo courtesy of the Virginia Historical Society.

have been found in slave quarters at Kingsmill and Monticello.[40] In the large communal buildings at Kingsmill, up to eighteen backfilled cellars have been found. (Kelso posits that they were used for private food storage and perhaps filled with the bones of animals taken without the plantation owner's knowledge.) The presence of these cellars at most Kingsmill buildings has led to the assumption that they were occupied by slaves. This has made it difficult to identify the white overseer's home. What seems likely is that here, as at Carter's plantation and at Washington's, whites occupied buildings that had been slave quarters, indicating important inner values in relation to shared space. Black and white housing had been much the same and was interchangeable. (See illustration of overseer's house, Figure 20.) But this situation was itself changing, and by the end of the eighteenth century, whites were more likely to be in larger houses and/or to want to mark their distinction from slaves. In the 1790s Washington's two black overseers at Muddy Hole and Dogue Run farms each had houses 16' × 20', one room up and one down. At the other farms the white overseers' homes were of similar construction—scantling, plank, and shingles—but considerably larger. At Union farm the house had two rooms below, each 16' × 18', one room above, and a separate kitchen shed.[41]

During most of the eighteenth century, if the poor or "middling" white was in a house larger than the small slave cabin, it was only slightly larger, and although a much higher percentage of the white houses appeared to be frame dwellings, many of these were log houses covered with boards.[42]

We now know that white and black cabins as well as most of the houses of the white planters were built by essentially the same methods of construction. Inasmuch as almost all early Chesapeake housing decayed and disappeared, it was not known that it was of an extremely simple or "primitive" type of construction, no longer widely used for housing in seventeenth-century England, although still known then as an easy and economical means of building impermanent barns and sheds. Archaeological research has now shown these buildings were virtually all earthfast, with their "framing members . . . standing or lying directly on the ground or erected in post-holes." The available evidence has been summarized and analyzed in a comprehensive fashion by Cary Carson, Norman F. Barka, William M. Kelso, Gary Wheeler Stone, and Dell Upton, making it clear that earthfast building was ubiquitous in early Virginia.[43] Carson et al. posit a three-phase ideal history for Virginia housebuilding: Each family would build a

113

FIGURE 17. Virginia blacks and their cabin, mid-nineteenth century. This chimney construction allowing for ease of separation from the house in case of fire, was a seventeenth- and eighteenth-century tradition. Heustis Cook Collection. Photo courtesy of The Valentine Museum, Richmond, Virginia.

FIGURE 18. A double quarter and occupants in Gloucester, Virginia, in the 1880s. Many Chesapeake slaves lived in similar homes in the eighteenth century. Photo courtesy of the Hampton University Archives.

hut, then if possible a house, using the hut or cabin for a kitchen or service area. Finally, a substantial home might be built, utilizing non-earth-bound technologies. They cite the example of John Mercer, an English merchant, who squatted in an abandoned hut on his arrival at Marlborough, Virginia, in 1726. In 1730, "he built a frame house with wooden chimneys and sixteen years after that a permanent dwelling, a fine brick mansion."[44] However, although most whites moved from hut to house, many stayed put in very small, earthfast houses, or replaced them with new but similar structures. The third ideal phase was reached by relatively few.

The most common house, so common it was soon called the "Virginia House" throughout the Chesapeake, was a composite of forms and techniques that Carson and Upton emphasize were known in England (but were not dominant) *together with what have been recognized as local innovations*, which aimed to get a small, essentially

115

FIGURE 19. Servants' quarters near the Big House at Bremo, Fluvanna County. Quarters near the Big Houses were almost always of better construction than those on outlying farms. Photo courtesy of the Library of Congress.

temporary house built quickly and cheaply. Corners were literally cut and the buildings made lighter and far simpler to construct. Corner posts set into the ground obviated foundations and skilled stonework. Roofs were lightened and complicated joinery avoided as "clapboards [were] nailed directly to the rafters [which] lent an entire roof frame

FIGURE 20. A late-eighteenth-century overseer's house at Eyre Hall, Northampton County. Originally approximately one third smaller, this house was very close to a small slave house in overall dimensions and was similar in construction to the best slave houses built near substantial Big Houses. Photo courtesy of the Library of Congress.

most of the longitudinal rigidity it needed."[45] Floors may well have been earthen and chimneys wooden. By the eighteenth century, frame buildings on blocks came to be increasingly common, but the hole-set structures were known down through the slave period, and many of the simplified techniques were carried over into the later building. Siding often hid logs, and blocks were used to prop up decaying post-hole structures.

The modal white house and the modal black house shared this technology: Both were originally earthfast, and both came to be largely of frame or of log-pen construction. Both were also built to a standard plan in the mind if not on paper: "square, [with] . . . one central opening per wall; a front door, a rear window, a window on one end, a chimney on the other."[46] (At the outset these chimneys were generally wood and mud; by the end of the eighteenth century many whites and some blacks had brick chimneys.)

Whites most often built this box 16' × 20', whereas blacks more often built it 12' × 12' or 12' × 16'. Over time, whites either added on or built as if they were adding on other units. Henry Glassie's innovative study of vernacular houses in middle Virginia has led him to find a deep structure in the "language" of this building. There were apparently visions of this basic unit and basic ways of manipulating and combining these units. Without articulating them, builders followed set patterns and set rules for generating change based on these patterns. Glassie concludes that "a repetitious structuring of repetitious elements well expressed [the Virginian's] . . . intention for order." This house was a "rigidly disciplined" artificial object, with no intrinsic ties to its location or to its materials. An inner vision shaped it in the same way, whether it was made of planks, logs, or brick.[47] (See Figures 21 and 22.)

Thomas Jefferson had recognized (but disparaged) this limited language of building:

The private buildings are very rarely constructed of stone or brick, much the greatest portion being of scantling and boards, plastered with lime. It is impossible to devise things more ugly, uncomfortable, and happily more perishable. There are two or three plans, on one of which, according to its size, most of the houses in the State are built. The poorest people build huts of logs, laid horizontally in pens, stopping the interstices with mud. These are warmer in winter, and cooler in summer, than the more expensive construction of scantling and plank.[48]

FIGURE 21. (*at left*) The Lesser-Dabney House. Probably built for Samuel Dabney (1752-1798). This was then considered an "elegant" home. Reprinted with the permission of Henry Glassie from *Folk Housing in Middle Virginia* (Knoxville, Tenn., 1975).

FIGURE 22. (*at right*) The Parrish House, Louisa County. Fairly typical of mid-eighteenth-century white housing, this house of sawed logs, roughly 18' × 20', was divided into two rooms (8' × 18' and 12' × 18'), and had a loft overhead as well as a shed off the chimney end. Reprinted with the permission of Henry Glassie from *Folk Housing in Middle Virginia* (Knoxville, Tenn., 1975).

The first plan was a simple box, square or oblong, an X house. Glassie found that the most common expansion of the simple rectangular X house was a three-room structure that he calls the XY_3X combination, where Y_3 is approximately half of X. (For example, one such house had rooms of 15 feet deep by 15', 7 ½', and 15'.)

$$15' \quad \boxed{\begin{array}{c|c|c} X & Y_3 & X \end{array}} \quad 15'$$
$$15' \quad 7\frac{1}{2}' \quad 15'$$

This XY_3X structure is also the underlying pattern of what is commonly called the "dogtrot" house, a plan very common across the South. The dogtrot is a "one story house, composed of two equal units separated by a broad open central hall and joined by a common roof," already known as an "old-fashioned Virginia double-house" in the eighteenth century.[49]

Earthfast simplified houses were being built in Virginia long before

118

Africans arrived in large numbers, but the radical lightening of the frame and the vast expansion of the repetitive forms apparently occurred in the last quarter of the seventeenth century and during the early eighteenth, coinciding with the vast growth of the African and Afro-American population. Although simplification of English wood-building techniques occurred in New England as well, this radical and even revolutionary lightening of the frame occurred *only in the South*. Clearly, physical limitations were not the cause, as wood, and especially heavy beams, were readily available. In addition, it took more work to cut the timber into lighter pieces, although less skill to raise a house when virtually all pieces were from the same standard lumber. What was involved was a revolution in perception. (See Figures 23, 24, and 25.)

Dell Upton, in a careful analysis and comparison of wood building all along the eastern coast, concludes that "the most extreme instance of reductionism and adaptability in the New World occurred in the Chesapeake region. There the original English form was so distorted as to be unrecognizable." The Virginia frame of 1700 went a long way toward the simplification and standardization of the balloon frame of the nineteenth century. Where "the traditional Anglo-American frame was a three-dimensional enclosure, the Chesapeake frame consisted of two parallel long walls, braced at the corners and at the partitions and connected by joists across their tops." Standard 10-foot bays and 4 × 8- and 3 × 4-inch parts "were the rule." "The dimensioning of timbers according to their relative structural load and the complex, multidirectional joints that characterized New England carpentry . . . were not used in the South."[50]

It seems probable that Africans contributed significantly to this tradition and were responsible for what Upton, Carson, and others have recognized as the local "Southern" innovations that were fused with English traditions. Africans widely used earthfast methods of construction, light pole siding, and roofs in which the beams were light and the covering was a structural element. Floors were hard-packed earth, exteriors shingled, and interiors plastered. Remember Equiano's description of building methods in the Ika district on the Niger River: Houses "are always built of wood, or stakes driven into the ground, crossed with wattles, and neatly plastered within and without. The roof is thatched with reeds."[51] The saddleback or gable roof was widely known in Africa. "Saddleback roofs nearly always rested on wall plates supported on forked uprights within the walls. The ridge pole was sometimes supported by upright poles but usually

FIGURE 23. Kongo Granaries, African post-hole construction as found in Angola, about 1910. Photograph reproduced by permission of Heinemann Educational Books, Ltd., London, © 1978, from *African Traditional Architecture*, by Susan Denyer.

FIGURE 24. (*at left*) Virginia post-hole construction. Acquinton glebe in King William County, late nineteenth century. Compare with Kongo Granary, Figure 23. Photograph by Dell Upton, courtesy of the Virginia Historic Landmarks Commission.

rested between the gable ends. Tie beams were only occasionally used."[52] Early gable roofs on Virginia houses did use tie beams, but in the radical lightening of the frame, these were eliminated. Roof coverings in Virginia were often structural elements, much as thatch was in Africa.[53] (See Figures 26–31.)

There was a widely known African house form wherein separate houses were covered with a continuous roof. Although these were often round houses and surrounded an open impluvium or an open court (as built by the Diola in Senegal, the Manjak and Papeis in Guinea Bissau, and the Guro and Gagu of the Ivory Coast), other peoples built to a rectangular plan, using a continuous roof (the Bini, Yoruba, and Ekoi of Nigeria). In effect, buildings were being combined under one roof with a passageway between them, as in the Southern "dogtrot." (The tripartite dogtrot form, with one roof bridging two outer buildings, was known in Africa, as were passages that connected two single-room houses.)[54]

Africans generally had separate houses for cooking and storing food. They had long found that this kept their houses "cool and sweet" as Beverly commented about the Virginia pattern in 1705: "All their drugeries of cookery, washing, dairies, etc. are performed in offices detached from the dwelling houses which by this means are kept cool and sweet."[55]

FIGURE 25. (*at left*) Exposed simplified Virginia construction. This example of eighteenth-century standardized framing is at the Powell House, Isle of Wight County. Photograph by Dell Upton, courtesy of the Virginia Historic Landmarks Commission.

FIGURE 26. (*at right*) Roof construction: England. This is a queens post roof truss from Ford's Farm, Tilehurst, Berkshire, England, 1645, illustrating the comparative complexity of construction and the varying sizes of supports then in use. Courtesy of the Royal Commission on the Historical Monuments of England.

FIGURE 27. (*at top*) Roof construction: Africa. A house under construction, Bolobo, Zaire, about 1910, illustrating the uniform, lightweight, and simple construction. Photograph reproduced by permission of Heinemann Educational Books, Ltd., London, © 1978, from *African Traditional Architecture*, by Susan Denyer.

FIGURE 28. (*at bottom*) Roof construction: Virginia. Southern house being dismantled, reveals roof's simplified structure, very similar to an African roof. Photo courtesy of James O'Malley.

FIGURE 29. Igbo House, Oratto area, southeastern Nigeria, about 1925. Note the rough plank construction, similar to many Virginia buildings. Photograph reproduced by permission of Heinemann Educational Books, Ltd., London, © 1978, from *African Traditional Architecture*, by Susan Denyer.

FIGURE 30. (*at left*) Kongo House, Angola, about 1910. Note size comparable to eighteenth-century white and black homes. Photograph reproduced by permission of Heinemann Educational Books, Ltd., London, © 1978, from *African Traditional Architecture*, by Susan Denyer.

FIGURE 31. (*at right*) Ngongo House, Zaire, about 1910. Note the single opening per side, a pattern followed by Virginians. Reproduced by permission of Heinemann Educational Books, Ltd., London, © 1978, from *African Traditional Architecture*, by Susan Denyer.

There is increasing evidence of African influence on other American homes. John Michael Vlach, in a very careful study of the shotgun house in Louisiana, Haiti, and among the Yoruba in Nigeria, reached the conclusion that Africans brought this house plan with them and built it in the Islands and in North America.[56] The shotgun is a narrow house roughly 12' × 20', divided internally into two or three rooms, one opening directly into the other. (See diagram, left.) It changed somewhat over time and place: the door was shifted to the far end, a porch was added, and the building methods used in America were essentially European. But the plan of the house, once

123

thought to have evolved solely from somewhat similar Indian dwellings, was clearly related to African home styles. (See diagram, right.)
This house form was widely used for slave quarters and was later
adopted by poor whites as well and became a popular form whose
roots were not known.

In evaluating the Louisiana shotgun houses, provenance can be
fairly well established. In Virginia the problem is more difficult. Although white contemporaries could not possibly know it, the one-
room English house was, in certain basic ways, so like many one-
room African houses that the sharing in Virginia cannot be assigned
weights. Nevertheless, it is *likely*, not just possible, that the African
aesthetic (as well as African skills) played a significant role in the new
world.

Notwithstanding the Yoruba shotgun style, Africans generally
thought in terms of single rooms. Compounds consisted of groups of
single rooms, each with its own entrance. The compound grew with
need—each time a wife joined, a room would be added and perhaps an
additional granary as well. The inner language was one of separate
units, X and parts of X, added to each other in an ordered pattern. The
inner language of the Virginia building seems to be related to this African style more than to the English, where inner space (the old open
hall) was often divided up rather than added to. Compounds in Virginia were more like African compounds and quarters much like
wives' quarters, in a chief's compound, than they were like an English
farm.[57] (See Figure 32.) Perhaps most important in this evaluation is
the fact that *African houses were by and large very light construc-
tions*. Frameworks were most often of wood, bamboo, or palm fronds.
Walls were made of split bamboo, palms, raffia, or cleft wood. Mud
plaster might cover the outside or inside or both. Simple repetitive
forms were used throughout Africa, as they were in Virginia.[58]

Blacks built houses all across the South, both in terms of time and
place. First-generation African builders as well as American-born
white-trained "master" builders put up houses for both blacks and
whites. Robert Carter sought an African builder who was "an Artist"
who "underst[ood] building mud Walls."[59] Pisé buildings were put up
at Bremo and Four-Mile Tree plantations, and Washington advocated
building with mud.[60] But most houses were scantling and plank or log,
and blacks were building them from the seventeenth century on.
White builders too, who worked with blacks, in part "slided into"
black ways.

Obviously African-style buildings were rarely seen. The health spa

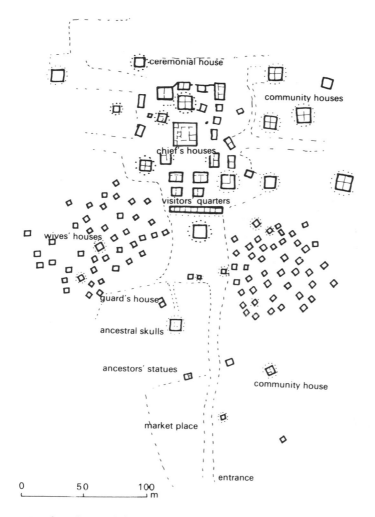

ceremonial house

community houses

chief's houses

visitors' quarters

wives' houses

community houses

guard's house

ancestral skulls

ancestors' statues

community house

market place

entrance

| 0 | 50 | 100 m |

FIGURE 32. Plan of a Bamileke chief's "house." Batoutam, Cameroon, about 1960.
In some African societies, as well as in colonial Virginia, a Great House was
surrounded by dependencies of a substantial nature, whereas most of the
population lived in small huts or cabins. Drawing reproduced by permission of
Heinemann Educational Books, Ltd., London, © 1978, from *African Traditional
Architecture*, by Susan Denyer.

at Warm Springs was described as a "little bush village" in the eighteenth century, and the conical roofs that topped many small African huts seem to have reappeared on innumerable Virginia outbuildings, built with English techniques.[61] (See Figure 33.) However, in most buildings the influences were more indirect, more subtle, and far more important.

FIGURE 33. A conical roof in Virginia. A wood shingle roof on a 12' × 12' locust powderhouse at Greenway Court, Clarke County, built for Thomas, Lord Fairfax, c. 1750. The building's shape was very like an African hut, whereas the building methods were English. Photo courtesy of the Library of Congress.

10. Sharing Space Inside the Big House

W HEN A VIRGINIAN wanted to mark his success, he did so by conspicuously abandoning the small house form. The mark of success all over the South, and later in the Midwest, became a two-story house, the I house, clearly set off from the slave and "poor-white" cabin. Often these I houses were only one-room deep, four-room houses (two on two), but they were viewed as substantial houses when compared with one-story cabins. In Africa this high-level status was generally reserved for chiefs, and their houses were readily identifiable by scale. Both the Africans and the English recognized the "Great House" as belonging to a man of substance. The association was such that slaves (and probably poor whites) came to call slaveowners' homes Great or Big Houses no matter how small they actually were. Ironically, the I house was sometimes a simple dogtrot house with an added second story. A new outer "skin" covering the whole would hide its origins.[1]

Appearances and titles meant a great deal to both blacks and whites. The dogtrot with a second story "became" a Great House, and the slaveowner's home was a "Great House" whatever its size. A man's self grew with his status, and his house should have reflected this. If it did not, it would be "made to," in title if not in reality.[2]

There were, however, a limited number of mansions, enormous both in size and significance. It has been estimated that there were a dozen mansions built in Virginia "in the 1720s and 1730s, in the first wave, and more than two dozen in a second wave between 1750 and 1776."[3] These buildings played an important symbolic role, and their white inhabitants, the rulers of Virginia, played an important political and social role. But these houses were also occupied by blacks, who, although owned by whites, were very much a part of the black–white family system that became normative in the eighteenth century and was affecting whites in every aspect of their lives. (See Figures 34 and 35.)

R. D. Laing has defined the family as a "system comprising persons in relationship." He suggests a three-pronged analysis of (1) the politics of these interrelationships, (2) the family history (or the history of these interrelationships over time), and (3) the internalized fantasy system that can develop.[4] Blacks and whites were, by this definition as well as by their own usage, in one family. They were in a "system

FIGURE 34. The Big House and dependencies at Green Hill, Campbell County. A classic eighteenth-century "town-like" configuration built by Samuel Pannill, beginning in 1797. Photo courtesy of the Library of Congress.

comprising people in relationship." The two most extensive diary records of the eighteenth-century South, those of Byrd and Carter, prove what is suggested in virtually every smaller fragment extant: blacks were part and parcel of family relations and were actors on the family stage. Their relationships with whites affected not only themselves but also the interrelationships among the whites—husband and wife, father and son, and siblings. All relationships in a slaveowning household involved slaves, and the day-to-day interaction built up the fam-

ily history. The reality and history of these black–white families produced the "fantasy system" in which relationships in the family were internalized and provided a model for other intrapersonal relations.

The Great Houses were the setting for these mixed-race families. Given names, they represented the owners' appearance to the world, as the eighteenth-century slaveowners consciously recognized. Landon Carter's Sabine Hall, described as "an airy and elegant Georgian structure high on a hill that looked southward over six gardened terraces to the Rappahannock River three miles below," may have been designed by architect Richard Taliaferro. Nevertheless, Carter clearly saw it as an extension of his self and suggested by its name his identification with Horace who sought to retreat from the snares of worldly competition to his "Sabine vale."[5] Its importance to Carter can be guaged by the fact that it was only when Carter was in serious decline, readying himself for death, that he was ready to give up control of the house's shape and form. On July 2, 1772, he noted that work had begun "to make the alteration in my house which My son desires may be done. As I am soon in all Probability to leave the world, I have consented to it."[6]

Carter's home played an important role in his dreams, giving us some insight into its unconscious meanings. Carter wanted to believe that his home, the household he had established, was crucially important to his son, his slaves, and even to his forefathers. On the day that he had a serious falling out with his son, Carter dreamed of "entertaining many dead People" in his Great House. His son might reject him, but important people from the past gave him the honor that was his due.[7]

Notwithstanding this ongoing conflict, Carter's son chose to remain in his father's house, and Landon Carter knew this was important. Robert Wormley Carter chose to have his children reared in the Great House, with the black family that had reared him, and to wait

FIGURE 35. Slave quarters at Green Hill. Built in the early nineteenth century, this fairly typical slave house was 14' × 20', 1 ½ stories high, and framed with 3" × 4" stud walls and rafters, covered with clapboards. The exterior and the roof have been recovered, but the "board and batten" door is the original one. Photo courtesy of the Library of Congress.

for the time when he could begin to alter the house to suit his own image.

An incident that reveals a good deal more about this house's significance occurred in April of 1773. A severe thunderclap struck Sabine Hall with "a noise . . . resembling more the mighty burst of a bomb than anything else." Traveling down through the house, from roof to upper room, through Carter's chamber, along the Piazza, through the outer schoolroom and the Common building, breaking windows as it went, the lightning struck at least four people, three of them black. Tom, a slave, appeared dead, but he responded to Carter's lengthy ministrations of bellows, vomits, clysters, and emulsions. Here is Carter's rendering of the scene for posterity:

Reader, whoever thou art, picture to yourself this dismal sum. Grandchildren many, though unhurt, with every sorrowful countenance, though ignorant of the consequences, Yet crying with Concern. A mother calling but for her babies though in her company, and going from place to place to be safe, through some confused expectation; and Poor slaves crowding round and following their master, as if protection only came from him, and yet quite void of senses enough to assist me. [8]

Carter saw himself as stable in the center of all this turmoil, and he felt certain that his acts had restored Tom's life. Nevertheless he believed that it was ultimately the Great House, although hit, that had protected him and his extended family, for if they had "gone out then without a special Protection, we must have been . . . destroyed." Carter did not know that Africans often abandoned a house or even a settlement hit by lightning. They saw it as a bad omen, or a defilement. His "reading" of this incident was totally different from the interpretation they were likely to have reached. [9]

Carter's house remained the symbol of shelter for himself and, he thought, for his blacks. When, at the outset of the Revolution, a group of his slaves ran away in response to the promise of freedom proclaimed by Lord Dunmore, Carter was deeply disturbed, and his dream life reflected this attack on his security and his home.

July 25, 1776. A strange dream this day about these runaway people. One of them I dreamt awakened me; and appeared most wretchedly meager and wan. He told me of their great sorrow, that all of them had been wounded by the minutemen, had hid themselves in a cave they had dug and had lived ever since on what roots they could grab-

ble and he had come to ask if I would endeavor to get them pardoned, should they come in, for they knew they should be hanged for what they had done. I replied a good deal. . . . I can't conceive how this dream came into my brain sleeping, and I don't remember to have collected so much of a dream as I have done of this these many years. It seems my daughter Judy dreamt much of them too last night.[10]

Clearly both Landon and Judy Carter, and one must suspect many other whites, were deeply shaken by the fact that some 800 Virginia blacks had "run-away" to freedom. Carter set this disturbing world to right in his dream by viewing the blacks as utterly lost without him and their plantation home. They were reduced to eating weeds and living in primitive dugout caves. In the dream, unlike the reality, they begged him to take them back into the family. In actuality it was a black man named Moses who led them to their freedom, and although most of them may have died from the rampant illness among the freedmen, no one returned begging.[11]

Although Carter may have had personal problems that magnified his sense of home as retreat and protection, other Southern gentlemen also became concerned with both the exteriors and interiors of their houses in ways that make fairly obvious their symbolic significance. The Great House was like a temple to the clan leader: a high place, symbolically if not actually, that was generally situated by great waters that gave access to great ships from far places. Thomas Jefferson's house and his relation to it provide perhaps the best possible example of this development. As noted, the very top of Monticello, little mountain, was leveled by Jefferson for his house. Some six months of difficult labor were necessary before any building could begin. The Great House had to be on the summit, above everything around it, looking down on Charlottesville, and the court, the church, and later the university. (Jefferson sacrificed proximity to water for this height.) The house became his passion: He built and rebuilt it over a period of some forty years (1769–1809). It was to be (and has become, after a long period of neglect) his permanent monument. Jefferson, as well as his black family, is buried on its grounds, and there at his request stands the obelisk that records his great deeds.[12]

Houses and blacks were mixed together in Jefferson's conscious and unconscious mind from his earliest youth. His first recorded memory was of being carried by a black slave (on a pillow) from his parents' simple house, Shadwell, to Tuckahoe on the James. Jefferson did not grow up in his own house but in that of the far richer William Randolph, where his father and mother served as foster parents to the orphaned Randolph children.[13] His father was not their guardian, and the property was never his. The elder Jefferson was more like a general overseer (the plantation had fourteen of them), although he was never called such. He had volunteered to rear these children in their home, on their property, among their slaves. It seems likely that the young Jefferson was conscious of this arrangement. He certainly was passionately committed to having a Great House of his own design and on his own land at the earliest possible time. He chose the hill and had begun building long before his marriage.

Although Jefferson hired white master carpenters, slaves built Monticello, and slaves lived there with him whenever he was there. They cared for it, and his retreat at Natural Bridge, when he was gone. They were, in fact, there always. They were waiting for him there in December of 1789, when he returned from his lengthy stay in France. They welcomed him as though he had returned from the dead, as though he was a risen god. "Wild with joy" on hearing of his return, they had been given the day off and awaited his arrival. Martha, who came home with him, gives us this account of the heady event:

The negroes discovered the approach of the carriage as soon as it reached Shadwell, [four miles from Monticello] and such a scene I never witnessed in my life. They collected in crowds around it, and almost drew it up the mountain by hand. The shouting, etc., had been sufficiently obstreperous before, but the moment it arrived at the top it reached the climax. When the door of the carriage was opened, they received him in their arms and bore him to the house, crowding around and kissing his hands and feet—some blubbering and crying—others laughing. It seemed impossible to satisfy their anxiety to touch and kiss the very earth which bore him.

The black family preserved this day in their folklore and magnified it. Jefferson's great-granddaughter, Sarah N. Randolph, heard about it from former slaves who had been there:

I have had it from the lips of old family servants who were present as children on the occasion, that the horses were actually "unhitched," and the vehicle drawn by the strong black arms up to the foot of the lawn in front of the door at Monticello.[14]

Sarah N. Randolph believed the black version of the event to be the correct one and held that Martha's memory "may have failed her." Here we have a fine example of how blacks kept family history, made it their own, and returned it to the next white generation. Blacks played a very important role in preserving, magnifying, and disseminating family history. Their own ideas of kin and kinship responsibility permeated this heritage.

All the Great Houses were built by slaves and needed slaves to run them. Moreover, slaves lived in them and with all the elite white families. Early-seventeenth-century Virginia houses had already moved toward segregating servants to separate areas, and servants' "quarters" were often actually separate houses before blacks arrived in great numbers.[15] In the Great Houses servants were needed at close hand. They had constantly to clean, cook, and serve, and even if kitchens and wash houses, stables and quarters, were separated from the Great House, the blacks that cared for the children and mistress, as well as the waiters, butlers, and doormen, all had to be in and around the whites. Even the revolving "serving" doors on Jefferson's dining room could not keep blacks out, unless he and other whites were actually to serve and clear at table. Blacks were in white houses, both those of the elite and certainly those of the poor, where they often lived or spent a great deal of time.[16]

Virginians, born and reared with this pattern of interracial proximity, rarely commented on it when the interaction went smoothly, although later a few noted how hard it was for them to be served by whites in the North.[17] Reports of problems sometimes provide evidence of the racial reality. The marital troubles of Jones and Anne Irwin, for example, let us "into" their house. When the Irwins recorded a "separation" agreement at the York County Court of March 20, 1727, Jones agreed that Anne should "have half of the dwelling house to live in," some land to have worked by slaves, cash, beef, corn, wool, "syder," and milk, but he adjured his wife: "You shall from this time quit all command and Authority you have over me or any of the servants." As proof of how ever-present these servants were, Mrs. Irwin was forbidden to complain to Mr. Irwin of any servant's offense, unless she put "locks upon her doors and keep them locked when you are not present."[18]

In another revealing incident, when Mrs. Priscilla Dawson died while she and her daughter were visiting the Dangerfields, John Harrower noted, "This Night [March 10, 1775] the young Ladys Mama died her[e] and none knew it until the morning notwithstanding her Daughter and a Niger waiting maid was in the room all night."[19]

Northerners or foreigners visiting the South, highly conscious of the differences in life style, have left us important recorded evidence of black–white intimacy. These outsiders expressed great shock at seeing white men *and women* go among the "animal-like" naked blacks on board slave ships, picking and "poking." But "undress" was

apparently not simply a shipboard phenomenon. Too many northerners and Europeans commented on it for it to be fiction. On the other
hand, we know runaway male slaves were "covered" with osnaburg or
linen shirts, or kersey jackets, "dossil" great coats, breeches, trousers,
leather aprons, stockings, and shoes, while a slave woman might be
dressed, as one was, in "a striped red, white and yellow calimanco
gown, a short white linen sack, petticoat of the same, a pair of stays
with fringed blue riband, a large pair of silver buckles, and [a] . . . pair
of silver bobs."[20] Although many slaves had ragged and torn clothing,
slaves certainly did not generally go about naked. What may have
been different were the ages at which it was considered proper to
"cover" children, as well as black "body language," which may have
seemed suggestive or revealing to outsiders. Most of the comments
about slave undress deal with young black people, 10 or 12 years old,
whose clothes did not "hide their nakedness" and went about thus
"amongst their master's children" or served at table. They were probably wearing long shirts; or shifts, revealing boys' genitals and young
women's breasts. Northerners and Englishmen were clearly
shocked.[21]

The homes of white Virginians were different from English homes,
and different values were being transmitted to the young. It is possible
that William Byrd I had this in mind when he wrote that his children
"could learn nothing good here in a great family of negro's."[22] Young
whites often spent time with blacks. If they were from the upper class,
they had possibly been nursed by a black and were probably daily
cared for by blacks. When in July of 1728, Thomas Jones wrote his ailing wife in England about the care her infants in Virginia were receiving, he spent much time describing the slaves' and the children's interaction:

> I have bought some Negro's this year and Keep a Girl here that
> promises both in Temper & Capacity to make a Good Servant. She is
> very good natur'd, & tractable, lively and handy among the Chil-
> dren. Tom keeps to his old Maid Daphne and is grown very fond of
> her calling upon Da, Da, in all his extremities. The 'tother tends upon
> Dolly and will make a much better dry Nurse than Daphne.[23]

Tom's and Dolly's mother, Ann Cook Pratt Jones, was away from
home, but such nursing would have continued after her return. The
Jones's household had black nurses, but not a "mammy": No black
woman had been put in charge of all the children, nor of any other aspect of household management. In fact, Jones was finding the household unmanageable and wanted his wife to hire an Englishwoman as

overseer for the household affairs. She, much like the overseer in the fields, was slated to spend her time overseeing the blacks, that is, with the blacks.

Many Southern homes were motherless temporarily or permanently, and by mid-century many were without white supervision. Landon Carter, widowed, complained, "I have none but Negroes to tend ny children" and worried that they were fed too much heavy food, such as young blacks ate. (He notes his children did not have as much exercise as the slave children, and he thought that as a result the "loads of gross food" made the white children sick.)[24] Blacks continued to care for the next generation, Carter's grandchildren, even though his daughter-in-law was very much a part of the household. In fact, fear of the loss of these caretakers was one of the reasons his son cited for staying on in the strife-torn household.

Wetnursing by new Africans may not have been common, but by mid-century, when a high percentage of the adult slaves were Virginian born, it was not considered improper for blacks to nurse the children of the elite. Outsiders, such as Jonathan Boucher (1759), thought the practice "a monstrous Fault," and Philip Vickers Fithian (1773) seemed shocked to learn that "wenches" had suckled several of Robert Carter's children; but elite Virginians had come to accept this as a matter of course.[25] Thomas Jefferson, in recounting to his daughter the family history, noted that when, as an infant, she had been quite ill, she had recovered "by recurrence to a good breast of milk." He suggested that his ill granddaughter Anne might respond to the same treatment, but he cautioned "if a breast of milk is to be tried . . . I [trust] it should however be some other than your own."[26] That this "other" was black in both cases Jefferson did not mention nor did he have to. Both he and his daughter would have assumed it should be. (See frontispiece and Figure 36.)

In 1795, Martha Jefferson felt compelled to leave several of her children at Monticello while she traveled extensively with her ailing husband. Clearly slaves were taking daily care of the children then, as they did when she was at home. Thomas Jefferson's overseer later reported that

Ursula was Mrs. Randolph's nurse. She was a big, fat woman. She took charge of all the children that were not in school. If there was any switching to be done, she always did it. She used to be down at my house a great deal with those children. . . . They were all very much attached to their nurse. They always called her "Mammy."[27]

136

FIGURE 36. White children, black nursemaid. Gov. Spotswood's grandchildren cared for by a barefoot young black woman: Alexander Spotswood Payne and his brother, John Robert Dandridge Payne, with their nurse, 1790-1800. Oil on canvas. Gift of Miss Dorothy Payne. Virginia Museum of Fine Arts.

In a sensitive assessment of the mammy as culture arbiter, Eugene Genovese notes:

It was they who imparted the speech of the quarters to the children of the Big House, who introduced them to black folklore, who taught them to love black music, and who helped bend their Christianity in the folkish direction the black preachers were taking it.[28]

In 1736, Edward Kimber, a young British "Gentleman" on an American tour, recognized this aspect of blacks' influence on whites; but he criticized Virginia parents for allowing it, suggesting that there was "one thing they are very faulty in, with regard to their Children, which is, that when young, they suffer them too much to prowl among the young Negroes, which insensibly causes them to imbibe their Manners and broken Speech."[29]

Virginians were not too likely to comment on this interaction, unless something went wrong. They were all "imbibing" black "manners and speech" and not conscious of the changes, and/or were unwilling to analyze the process in which they were involved.[30] When, on rare occasions, a Southern critic mentioned these developments, it was usually when some personal animus was involved. After William Byrd III separated from his first wife, his mother, Maria Taylor Byrd, was very critical of her daughter-in-law's behavior. She was certain her granddaughter was being neglected by her white mother, and this led her to an unusual comment on the child's black companions. Writing of then 6-year-old Elizabeth, Maria Taylor Byrd commented caustically (1760):

I am greatly disturbed at the education of the little lady at Belvidere who's mamma ly's in bed till noon & her chief time is spent with servants & Negro children her play fellows, from whom she has learnt a dreadfull collection of words, & is intollerably passionate. She was at play with a girl, who I order'd to call somebody to me, which made her so extremely angerry that she curs'd me in the bitterness of her heart & wished me in heaven. I do assure you I was scared & could hardly forbare whipping her: but as I could not tell how much that might be resented I forbore.[31]

Mrs. Byrd knew that "to wish her in heaven" was to wish her dead. Blacks often played on the meaning of words, and in their terminology "to pray for someone" could mean to pray for their death.[32]

White children did often spend a lot of time with blacks, who were their playmates as well as their servants. Letitia Burwell, who grew up in the antebellum period at Botetourt Court in Mecklenburg County, a plantation with over 100 slaves, recalled that "my mother and grandmother were almost always talking over the wants of the negroes—what medicine should be sent, whom they should visit, who needed new shoes, clothes or blankets." Letitia went with them on their rounds.[33]

Even those children in the schoolroom with a white tutor might spend much of their time with blacks. John Harrower's journal indicates how peripatetic was his students' attendance, how much less likely girls were to be students, and that when they were, they were taught on the weekends only. The rest of their time might well involve them with blacks, playing or learning homemaking arts.[34] The Carter children, both boys and girls, studied with Philip Fithian from 7:00 to 8:00 and from 9:30 to 12:00. But from noon till dinner at 3:00

they were out on their own. Fithian noted that "Harry is either in the Kitchen, or at the Blacksmiths, or Carpenters Shops," in other words, with the slaves.[35]

Martha Washington was, according to her husband, very attached to two young black women. She taught them embroidery and sewing, her major occupation, and for several years they sat working together daily. Certainly the Custis grandchildren, growing up with Martha and George, must have known these black women very well. Oney Judge, one of these slave women, had been under Mrs. Washington's tutelage since the age of 12. Notwithstanding her special status, or maybe because of it and the constant supervision that went with it, she ran away with a young Frenchman. In September 1796, Washington learned that she was in Portsmouth, New Hampshire, and unsuccessfully tried to recover her, pleading Mrs. Washington's particular attachment. (Flexner claims Washington felt that Martha reared these two slaves "almost . . . as if they were her own children.") Some fifty years later, when an interview with Oney Judge Staines was published in the *Liberator*, she still harbored strong anger against the Washingtons, whom she did not regard as foster mother and foster father. She resented the fact that they had never taught her to read or write; she accused George of being a Sabbath desecrator, playing cards and drinking wine on Sundays; and she was sure he had been prepared to take her back to slavery by force. Warned, she had hidden and remained free.

Washington had wanted her back, and given the steps he seemed willing to take, it would appear that much more than just a question of property was at stake. Mrs. Washington was emotionally involved with this young woman, but although George was seeking her as a stepfather might a runaway stepdaughter, he was ready to treat her as property at one and the same time.[36] (See Figures 37 and 38.)

The family interrelationships at Monticello were both much clearer and much more clouded. As is well known, the Jefferson white and black families were, in part, related by blood as well as fictively. Sally Hemings, whether she was Jefferson's mistress or his favorite nephew's concubine, was *in* the white family long before she bore children. Daughter of Betty Hemings and John Wayles, she was Martha Wayles Jefferson's half sister and Thomas Jefferson's sister-in-law. The other Hemings-Wayles were all related to the Jeffersons as well.[37]

In the Jefferson-Randolph-Hemings household, Ursula, who was Great George and Ursula's granddaughter and was married to Wormley Hemings, was Mammy, while Sally Hemings's half brother, John,

FIGURE 37. "A Family Group." A painting by Charles Phillips, Virginia, c. 1745.
Photo courtesy of the Colonial Williamsburg Foundation.

was called "Daddy." (John was Betty Hemings's child, but he was born
after John Wayles had died, and his father was one of Jefferson's white
carpenters, John Nelson.) The white children were very attached to
"Daddy" John, visiting him often in the carpentry shop, and receiving
miniature woodwork from him. Jupiter, Jefferson's body servant, was
called "Uncle Juba" and was very close to the children as well. When
writing to his daughter, Mary T. Eppes, in 1779, Jefferson noted that
"Ellen [her niece] gives her love to you. She always counts you as the
object of affection after her mama and uckin [Uncle] Juba."[38] She put
Juba before her father, her grandfather, and all whites except her
mother. This Uncle Jupiter had been with Jefferson at William and
Mary and had traveled with him when he was a young lawyer on cir-

cuit. He had been in his household when he married, when his children were born, and when his wife died. He knew the sons-in-law and the grandchildren. He was clearly "in the family" until his death in 1800, a death that Martha blamed on a black doctor's medicines.[39]

Monticello was very much a black and white household. The eleven Randolph children grew up not only with Mammy Ursula, Daddy John, and Uncle Jupiter, but with "black" aunts Betty Brown, Sally, Critta, Betty Hemings, and Nance, and Uncles Bob, James, Peter, and Martin. Most of the extended Hemings family were around them, working much on their own, and several of Great George and (old) Ursula's children were there as well. Nine of Sally's and Betty Brown's children were also on the mountain and were certainly the white grandchildren's playmates. Although Jefferson rarely wrote any comment on this situation, he did comment on his other grandson's companions: "Francis (Eppes) enjoys as high health and spirits as possible. He wants only a society which could rub off what he contracts from the gross companions with whom he of necessity associates."[40]

Martha Jefferson Randolph was also circumspect about what she wrote about servants, especially about the Hemingses, but she was very eager to get her sons into boarding schools and was clearly happier with their progress there than at home.[41] Martha certainly remembered her children's mammy, but the only memorial she left of her was recorded in French by a French visitor to Monticello. Eugène A. Vail, interested in a wide range of American culture, stayed at the Jefferson house in the course of a grand tour and interviewed Martha and the Jefferson black family. He devoted a chapter in his 1841 book to "Black Literature," but what he published were the words and reminiscences of Martha Randolph and her slaves.[42] Vail heard the slaves sing a lament for Thomas Mann Randolph, Sr. (Martha's father-in-law) and recorded it. In it, the slaves familiarly referred to their old master as Tom, and Isaac Jefferson records that they generally called him "Tuckahoe Tom."

> At the time that Colonel Tom lived and prospered
> There was joy and prosperity at Tukahoe
> Now that Tom is dead for ever
> There is no more happiness, alas, for us at Tukahoe.

Vail noted that this verse was followed by a guttural, perhaps African, refrain he could not commit to paper.

Vail recorded two of Mammy Ursula's folktales and commented that the children always expected each story to be told and each song

FIGURE 38. General George Washington and his slave, William Lee, as painted by John Trumbull. Lee, with Washington during the war, remained his slave until Washington's death, when he was willed his freedom and a $30 per year annuity. Photo courtesy of the Metropolitan Museum of Art.

to be sung in exactly the same manner every time. They had become a part of the family tradition, and they were retold to Vail with great emotion. The Devil's song was sung rapidly and in a staccato fashion, whereas his intended victim's song was slow and plaintive. The barking of dogs and the chopping of an axe were all acted out. Although one story involved the Devil, Vail commented that this Devil seemed to have the character of an "African Forest Spirit," and that it was he rather than God who could bring death. It was the Good Mistress in this story, who, with the protection of supernatural dogs, cut the Devil in pieces. This Mistress "Diah" called her dogs with an African-style incantation that the mammy sang, and that Martha and all her children knew very well.[43]

The blacks and whites at Monticello were in one interacting family group, but notwithstanding the large number of interrelated blacks, many black families were broken and in many cases the Big House had "only fragments of families—sibling and cousin relations." Norton, Gutman, and Berlin suggest this fragmentation "may reflect a

142

common familial pattern among privileged bondspeople."[44] Blacks at many of the Big Houses were apparently cut off from their families and could visit them only at holiday time. But others had family close by, if not at the house. George Washington's complaints about the proximity of blacks who were not "in the House" indicate their presence:

There are a great number of Negro children at the Quarters belonging to the house people; but they have Always been forbid (except two or 3 young ones belonging to the Cook, and the Mulatto fellow Frank in the house, her husband; both of whom live in the Kitchen) from coming within the Gates of the Inclosures of the Yards, Gardens & ct; that they may not be breaking the Shrubs, and doing other mischief; but I believe they are often in there notwithstanding: but if they could be broke of this practice it would be very agreeable to me, as they have no business within.[45]

Big House blacks were often with their children, who came there against orders; and white children in the Big House were with "approved" black playmates, like Bett Brown's and Sally Hemings's children, or with those who simply came there.

On the other hand, it is likely that blacks who were cut off from their familes of origin by the "call" to serve in the Big House (a coveted role) forged deeper ties to their white families, who became fictive kin. Henry St. George Tucker took a young boy, Bob, from his family home in Williamsburg to serve as his manservant as he, too, left home to start his career as a lawyer in Winchester. Bob left his mother, sister, and extended family back in Williamsburg and, no doubt, the home he had been born in. The move uprooted and disturbed Bob leading him to try to build an immediate attachment to his new master; Bob's emotional state, in turn, deeply affected his white owner.

—I enclose a short note from Bob to his mother. Poor little fellow! I was much affected at an incident last night. I was waked from a very sound sleep by a most piteous lamentation. I found it was Bob. I called several times before he waked. "What is the matter Bob?," "I was dreaming about my mammy Sir!!!" cried he in a melancholy still distressed tone: "Gracious God!" thought I, "how ought not I to feel, who regarded this child as insensible when compared to those of our complexion." In truth our thoughts had been straying the same way.

How finely woven, how delicately sensible must be those bonds of natural affection which equally adorn the civilized and savage. The American and African—nay the man and the brute! I declare I know not a situation in which I have been lately placed that touched me so nearly as that incident I have just related.[46]

Henry St. George Tucker clearly *was* touched deeply and even saw himself sharing emotions with a black; but he had to draw back, even as he was making these comments, and remind himself that the African was a "brute."

By the following month Henry was describing Bob as "very docile and good-tempered" without any reminders to himself of his "brutish" nature.

His simplicity and affectionate temper have awakened my sensibility more than once. . . . I was detained at Court this week longer than I expected. When I returned I found him as usual sitting on the steps waiting for me. The tears came into his eyes and with the most artless freedom he cried: "I am mighty glad to see you, Sir, tho' you've been gone so short a time. I couldn't have been gladder to see anybody but my mammy and my sister."[47]

Henry St. George Tucker's sympathy was again deeply aroused. "Poor fellow, thought I, and is it not then cruel to part you from those friends." Tucker quickly legitimated the parting that he was responsible for, and most significantly, his legitimation now tried to make of Bob a spiritual equal. He wrote, "Yet must we all do our duty in that state of life to which it has pleased God to call us:—and am not I too separated from all my friends!" The fact that the white had made the decision to leave Williamsburg whereas the black had not must have been obvious to Tucker, but he saw them both as following their calling.

Henry St. George Tucker, it should be noted, came from a family that sympathized with slaves, both in individual cases and in regard to their plight as a people. His father, to whom these letters were addressed, had fought for blacks' rights in the courts, submitted a manumission plan to the lawmakers, and expressed a general sense of guilt at their situation. But it took the love of a young black boy to break down the stereotype the son had maintained about the savage African.[48]

On rare occasions whites acknowledged the "strong" and "lasting" attachments they formed for blacks living with them in their homes and families. One white petitioner, turning to the government for approval of manumission as was required after 1806, pleaded love as the basis. Here the white woman petitioner clearly regarded herself as the fictive kin of the black:

Your petitioner, Mary Austin, of Hanover County, begs leave to represent to the General Assembly that she is possessed of a Negro women aged about fifteen years named Amanda. That the said Amanda, whilst an infant, had her mother taken away from her and was affected with a long and painful illness, during which time your petitioner from motives of duty and humanity nursed her. That your petitioner during her attentions to the said Amanda formed, perhaps unfortunately, a strong and from its continuance, it seems, a lasting attachment for her. And it is now the inclination and intention of your petitioner to endeavour to form in the said Amanda till the age of eighteen habits of industry and virtue.[49]

Mary Austin begged the lawmakers to secure her "happiness" and clearly was willing to express and make public her motherly love for Amanda.

The opposite emotion, one of anger and resentment, was also often aroused in interracial contacts, but these negative emotions indicate how intimate the contact was. The fragments of Sally Cary Fairfax's diary, written in 1772 when the young girl was perhaps 11 years old, indicate that blacks figured in almost every aspect of her daily life. (Sally was living with her parents at Toulston plantation, Fairfax County, and wrote of Belvoir plantation, her grandparents' home, as well as of Mt. Vernon, whose proprietor, "Collo. Washington," was a good friend of her father's.)

On friday, the 3d of Janna, that vile man Adam at night killed a poor cat, of rage, because she eat a bit of meat out of his hand & scratched it. A vile wretch of new negrows, if he was mine I would cut him to pieces, a son of a gun, a nice negrow, he should be kild himself by rites.[50]

"I would cut him to pieces, a son of a gun." A world of anger is wrapped up in those words, no doubt displaced from many other areas of her life. The only anger expressed in Sally's diary is expressed against "Vile Adam."

Sally was usually concerned with parties and guests, with clothes and "neclasses," but she was already ready to criticize the work patterns of the "servants": "On thursday the 2d of Jan., 1772, Margery went to washing, & brought all the things in ready done, on thursday the 9th of the same month. I think she was a great while about them, a whole week if you will believe me, reader." Yet this same angry and critical child could feel deep sympathy for a slave, in this case possibly a runaway being taken back, with punishment awaiting him, as Sally's terse comment suggests: "On friday, the 10th of Jan, in the morning came here danny genens, overseer for taff, & taff went away accordingly, poor taff, I pity him, indeed reader."[51]

Sally closed this section of her diary with a note that Adam, of cat-murder fame, had "cut down a cherry tree." No doubt there were people in the family who reacted strongly to this incident (they certainly did not think it a Washington-like act), but this time Sally's attention was diverted by the birth of a red and white calf, and Adam's evil act was simply noted.

In the small fragment of Sally Cary Fairfax's diary that has been preserved out of a total of seventeen entries covering Christmas 1771 and the first month of 1772, slaves figure in six "memorable" events. Sally's emotions varied from the anger and annoyance to the pity we have seen, but they also included the simple recognition of the slaves' presence as when "Margery mended my quilt very good." Certainly all the daily routine interactions were not recorded, but there were enough unusual events involving whites with blacks to leave no doubt but that interaction was intimate and significant for both.

Black and white interaction involved both sexes and every age group. Lucinda Lee Orr, a young woman being "courted" by several young men in 1782, nevertheless still played pranks together with her black maid.

I have undrest myself, and Libby is going to comb my hair. Milly and Miss Leland are gone in the Garden. I propose to Libby to go and frighten them: she agrees, and we are going to put it in execution. . . . We scared them a good deal. Milly screamed pretty lustily.[52]

In the diary kept by the mature widow, Martha Dangerfield Bland Blodget, in 1795–1796, while she was in charge at Cawson plantation, in Prince George County, Virginia, almost every second item relates to the slaves, indicating how intertwined their lives were.[53]

Outsiders sometimes thought the blacks were too much present. Chastellux, visiting Virginia between 1780 and 1782, thought white babies were given enough parental attention but was afraid the older offspring were neglected by their parents; he related this to the "great number of slaves at hand to wait on them and their children."[54] Blacks were holding white babies, giving them their first and most significant eye and body contact. They were physically caring for them and teaching them their first words. They were responding to them "in all their extremities" and spending much time with them as they grew, especially in their times of play and joy. Blacks were clearly talking to, singing to, and deeply influencing white children. They were their mammies, aunts, uncles, and playmates, as well as their servants. Their presence and influence were both physical and spiritual.

Blacks and whites continued to interact all through their lives, but this first period of intimacy probably had a lifelong effect on whites' values and identity. There is some evidence from the life of William Byrd II of how deeply black bodies and perhaps black attitudes toward sexuality affected him. Although Byrd grew up in England, he had been born in Virginia and had spent his first six or seven years there. In later life, when he wrote of sexual urges, he used images that indicate he associated sex with naked black bodies.[55] When he did return to Virginia, he showed no hesitancy in approaching black women. He recorded that on Oct. 21, 1711, "At night [at Col. Harrison's] I asked a negro girl to kiss me," and on Dec. 9, 1720, "I felt the breasts of the Negro girl which she resisted a little."[56] Byrd not only felt lust for black women, he appreciated black beauty. When on his way west into the wilderness in 1728, he recorded that he and his companions "took a walk into the Woods, and call'd at a Cottage where a Dark Angel Surpriz'd us with her Charms. Her Complexion was a deep Copper, so that her fine Shape & regular Features made her appear like a Statue en Bronze done by a masterly hand."[57] However, other, more lusty images of black women were in his unconscious, and in his commonplace book (adjacent to classical wisdom sayings) he recorded gross jokes about blacks and white together.[58]

Byrd did try to impose on his servants a different moral code from the one he followed, for they were clearly engaging in interracial sex as well, but what he objected to was their adultery. On June 17, 1710, "I caused [Tom] L-s-n to be whipped for beating his wife and Jenny was whipped for being his whore." Tom and his wife were white and Jenny was black. In this and other cases, it would be difficult to judge Byrd's servants' race from his recorded reactions. They appear to have been much the same toward blacks and whites. He punished servants, slaves, and relatives, including his niece, nephew, and wife. He sexually approached both black and white women. Sexual contact in this extended family was part of its life, and Byrd, slaves, and white servants all played a role in it. Byrd recorded:

I threatened Anaka with a whipping if she did not confess the intrigue between Daniel and Nurse, but she prevented by a confession. I chided Nurse severely about it, but she denied, with an impudent face, protesting that Daniel only lay on the bed for the sake of the child.[59]

Anaka was black whereas Daniel, the nurse, and the child being cared for in the midst of the intrigue were white.

Lucy Byrd, William's wife, punished both white and black servants, but her most violent attacks seem to have been reserved for black slaves, and a black seems to have been the only one who returned her violence with violence. The whole "family" got into this act. Lucy Byrd had once "caused little Jenny to be burned with a hot iron." Some six months later Lucy Byrd and Jenny "had a great quarrel" that apparently involved a serious physical fight in which the mistress "got the worst but at last by the help of the family Jenny was overcome and soundly whipped." In this incident, as in myriad others, blacks and whites interacted both publicly and privately. They fought, made alliances, and plotted revenge. "The family," black and white, helped (and hindered) each other. A year after this fight in which the family subdued Jenny, Byrd reported, "I had a terrible quarrel with my wife concerning Jenny that I took away from her when she was beating her with the tongs. She lifted up her hands to strike me but forebore to do it. She gave me abundance of bad words and endeavored to strangle herself, but I believe in jest only. However after acting a mad woman a long time she was passive again."[60] Byrd was defending a black woman from his wife and was ready to anger his wife seriously over this issue. Jenny was clearly a part of their family and was affecting their marital relations.

Sexual innuendo and sexual action were very much a part of Big House life. The intimate details of Robert Carter's family, made famous through Philip Vickers Fithian's journal, suggest how openly the young talked of sex, liaisons, and fecundity. In March of 1774, Carter's oldest son, Ben, age 18, was challenged by his younger brother: "It is reported that two Sundays ago you took Sukey (a young likely Negro Girl maid to Mrs. Carter's youngest son) into your stable, and there for a considerable time lock'd yourselves together!" A half year later (September 1774) the whole Big House was upset by a break-in that Fithian records may have been to "commit fornication with *Sukey*, (a plump, sleek, likely Negro Girl about sixteen)." The family suspected Ben, who retaliated by casting aspersions on others' "con-

148

SPACE INSIDE THE BIG HOUSE

stitutions" and the offspring they might have. Even Fithian, the proper Presbyterian New Englander, had come to see Sukey as a "plump, sleek" and "likely" girl. He, too, came to suspect Ben but found this thought very "unwelcome" and "so Base." What is most important is that, as Philip Greven has noted, he and other members of this family thought it likely that Ben had tried to enter the nursery, where younger siblings and the white housekeeper were also sleeping, in order to be with Sukey.[61]

Interracial sex had accompanied interracial relations from the outset, both inside and outside the Big House, and had involved white women as well as white men. Cases of illegitimate mulatto children, born to white women, appear in virtually all the church and county court records, although their number declines in the eighteenth century.[62] Only rarely was a case of violence recorded. In 1681, white Katherine Watkins, wife of a Quaker farmer in Henrico County, accused a mulatto slave, John (Jack) Long, of raping her. Her description of events indicates that she and other whites were drinking and socializing with blacks. The judges (among them was William Byrd I), knowing this to be true and apparently treating the case as they might the charge of rape brought against a white man, explored the possibility that Mrs. Watkins had enticed the black man. At the trial one John Aust (white) deposed that he had been present and seen Katherine Watkins kiss John Long; that he had heard her tell him that he was "as well come as any of My owne Children" at her house; and that after drinking many cups of whiskey with the black and white group, she had lifted another black's shirt and commented, "Dirke thou wilt have a good long thing." She threw still another black on the bed, kissed him, "and putt her hand into his Codpiece." The deponent then saw Katherine follow John/Jack into a sideroom, at which point he left, leaving Mrs. Watkins with the group of black men. Apparently social intimacy was acceptable, but just as clearly, certain bounds had been overstepped.[63]

Black reactions to white–black sexual relationships were rarely expressed directly. Old Dick tells us that young Thomas Sutherland was murdered by a slave, whose wife he had apparently taken with violence. Sutherland was reputed to have been

mighty ficious when he got among the negur wenches. He used to say that a likely negur wench was fit to be a Queen; and I forget how many Queens he had among the girls on the plantations. . . . The young 'Squire did not live long. He was for a short life and a merry

*one. He was killed by a drunken negur man, who found him over-fi-
cious with his wife. The negur man was hanged alive upon a gibbet.
It was the middle of summer; the sun was full upon him; the negur
lolled out his tongue, his eyes seemed starting from their sockets, and
for three long days his only cry was Water! Water! Water!*[64]

Assuming this story was true, it must have had a deep effect on all the
blacks and whites in this family.

White John Davis, the Englishman who recorded Dick's history
while living on Spencer Ball's plantation, commented that on the Sabbath the black

*girls never failed to put on their garment of gladness, their bracelets,
and chains, rings and earrings, and deck themselves bravely to allure
the eyes of the white men. Nor are they often unsuccessful; for as the
arrow of a strong archer cannot be turned aside, so the glance of a
lively negro girl cannot be resisted.*[65]

Davis intimates he had been "taken" and did not see himself as a
taker.

Joel Williamson maintains that colonial Virginia "supported conditions nearly ideal for the proliferation of a large mulatto population." Unique in its large numbers of both blacks and whites in close
association, early Virginia also had many more white men than
women, and these factors, together with the low social and unpro-
tected legal status of the blacks, "set up powerful forces for miscegenation." Given the extreme intimacy of Virginia blacks and whites,
Williamson concludes that large-scale "miscegenation was not only
possible, it was probable." Moreover, although many relationships
were transitory, "a highly significant number (of whites) established
long-running relationships with a single mulatto woman."[66]

Long-term interracial relationships were likely to have an effect on
both partners, as well as on their households and all the children in
them, black, white, and mulatto. John Custis probably had such a
long-term relationship with Alice, a slave he owned.[67] Custis's marriage to Frances Parke (Lucy Byrd's sister) had been a troubled one.
The Custises had come to the point where they would not talk to each
other: They sent messages via a black go-between, although they had
apparently tried "to end . . . all animostys and unkindness" between
them, going so far as to register an agreement regulating her behavior
and his financial obligations in court in 1714. Frances died in March
of 1715, but John harbored such bitter memories of her that when

writing his will in 1743, he insisted that his tombstone should include the statement that he had "yet lived but seven years which was the space of time he kept a Batchelors House at Arlington on the Eastern Shoar."[68]

Although Custis certainly did not memorialize on his tombstone his relationship with Alice, he did devote more than half his will to "my Negro boy Christoforo John otherwise called Jack born of the body of my slave Alice." Jack was clearly an important member of his family and an important part of the Big House life, and Custis's will was written to try to ensure that he would retain this position after Custis's death. Houses and housing played an important role in his plans.

I hereby Strictly require that as Soon as possible after my decease my Equitor build on the Said Land I bought of James Morris Situate near the head of Queens Creek in the County of York for the use of the said John otherwise called Jack a handsome Strong and convenient dwelling house according to the Dimensions I Shall direct and a plan thereof drawn by my said friend John Blair Esquire and that it be completely finished within Side and without.[69]

The dimensions of John/Jack's house are not given, but it clearly was not to be a one-room or a two-room cabin, as the detailed furnishings that John Custis took care to provide well indicate:

When the House is completely finished it is my will that the same be furnished with One Dozen high Russia Leather Chairs One Dozen Low Russia Chairs a Russia Leather Couch good and Strong three Good Feather Beds and Bedsteads and furniture and two good Black Walnut Tables.

Evaluating Chesapeake life styles, Gloria Main adjures us: "Count their chairs . . . and you will be able to predict a family's position on the ladder of importance in their community."[70] With two dozen chairs John/Jack would have ranked very high up the ladder, but in his case appearances would have been deceiving. Chairs did not make the man, but his father knew what the proper symbols were. He was leaving him a dreamed-of Big House as the most important step in trying to ensure his future status.

There is strong evidence that John/Jack was involved in the politics of this family and may well have been his father's favorite. In 1749, when Daniel Custis sought his father's blessing for his proposed marriage to Martha Dandridge, he apparently had good reason to believe

151

his father opposed the union. One of Daniel's friends, a J. Power, went to sound out the elder Custis. Most significant, Power felt that a special gift to young mulatto Jack would predispose the father to look with more favor on his legitimate son. Daniel's friend chose to give an expensive and symbolically significant present to young Jack, claiming it came from Daniel. He rushed to tell Daniel of this act, writing, "Hurry down immediately for fear he should change the strong inclination he has to your marrying directly. I stayed with him all night, and presented Jack with my little Jack's horse, bridle, and saddle, in your name, which was taken as a singular favor."[71]

John Custis had apparently provided a white nurse (probably Mrs. Anne Moody) for his mulatto son, had ostensibly manumitted him, and had left him property. When he died in 1749, his will stipulated that the legitimate son should care for him until he should reach age 20. That very year, son Daniel married Martha, and John/Jack may have already been listed as a slave in his father's estate, where a Jack, age 12, "fore feet 10 inches high," was among the slaves that became Daniel's property.[72]

Jack certainly stayed with Martha and Daniel Custis for many years. In fact, Jack was still in Martha's family after Daniel Custis's death in 1757, and remained there when she married George Washington in 1759. He was apparently treated as a special and trusted family servant. It is unlikely that this was what his father had in mind for him, but he did remain in the family until 1760, and it is likely that the Custis children (Washington's charges) knew him well.[73]

One of the witnesses to the land transaction for the mulatto child's property was George Wythe, lawyer, teacher, and Thomas Jefferson's mentor. Wythe later had a mulatto child in his household—Michael Brown—who was also raised in a bifurcated environment. Michael was no doubt much influenced by Wythe's values and was being tutored in Greek and Latin and all the proper classical subjects; but the woman responsible for his upbringing was a black housekeeper, Lydia Broadnax. Mulatto Michael Brown apparently behaved in the manner expected of a young white man. A white who knew the family well noted, "He had caught the suavity of his Master's Manners." Brown might have joined Jefferson's household had he not been poisoned by Wythe's white nephew, apparently jealous of Brown's status as heir to Wythe's estate and perhaps ashamed of his public position. Wythe's will had recommended Brown to Jefferson's "patronage," and after the boy's death Jefferson wrote that he was very saddened not to have had charge of him.[74]

Whites who wanted to leave Big House homes for mulattoes or blacks were often unsuccessful. In 1728, John Davis wrote his last will and testament providing his "Negro Woman Betty" with her freedom, possession of her own two children, and the Davis plantation, all to be hers on the decease of his wife who was very much alive. Mrs. Davis outlived John and successfully contested his will. When she died a year later, black Betty, age 30, and her boys, 18 and 14, appeared as part of Mrs. Davis's estate. They remained slaves in a slave cabin. Perhaps if John Davis had not tried to leave them his Big House and lands, the court would not so readily have denied them their freedom. Betty and children had also been promised they were to have their freedom when the white wife should die, a disturbing promise in a slave society where everyone feared death could be "brought on" by blacks if it was desirable. Davis's dying wish was denied.[75]

George Washington's last will and testament also promised his slaves freedom after his wife's death. This was certainly an aggressive act toward his wife. Indeed, she found that she could not live with the fear of their taking her life and decided to free them within one year of his death. As his feelings for Martha may have been ambivalent, perhaps his unconscious last wish was fulfilled.[76]

Some fifty years after Betty (Davis) was denied her freedom and her home, John Barr willed his slave Rachel and her (probably their) daughter, Rachel Jr., their freedom. Leaving twenty-five acres of land and adequate funds "in trust" with his brother Zacheriah, he asked him to supervise the building of a house for Rachel. Zacheriah, although the recipient of other slaves and much property, did not fulfill the trust placed in him. He chose to try to sell both Rachels. The blacks, with the aid of a protective white family, and the intervention of Justice of the Peace Thomas Ludlow Lee, were saved from sale, and in June of 1777, the Virginia legislature passed a bill emancipating the elder Rachel and allowed her to hold property.[77]

Although many blacks were freed in the last decades of the century, most slaves were not given their freedom or willed any property. The number of slaves actually grew, and most continued to live in contact with whites. Those in and around the Big Houses (and in the little white houses) had the most intimate contact and affected whites in all aspects of their lives.[78] The Big House, symbol of white supremacy, was home for a black and white family.

11. Naming the Inhabitants

ALTHOUGH THE AFRICANS and the English did not know it, there were some very close parallels in their attitudes toward names and family. In both locales there were variant traditions. Both had patterns of naming children for parents or grandparents; both had traditions of naming with prime concern for the meaning or connotation of the name; both had rites of passage associated with namings and involving "baptisms" with water; and both had traditions that suggested that the day of the week the child was born affected his or her character.[1]

What has come down as an English nursery rhyme clearly reflects earlier folk belief:

> Monday's child is fair of face,
> Tuesday's child is full of grace,
> Wednesday's child is full of woe,
> Thursday's child has far to go,
> Friday's child is loving and giving,
> Saturday's child works hard for a living,
> But the child that is born on the Sabbath Day,
> Is bonny, and blithe, and good, and gay.

The Asante too believed that dependent upon the day one is born, a different type of *Kra* or soul enters the body and gives the individual a "disposition" to a particular type of character. They singled out Monday's and Wednesday's children as particularly directed by their birth, and serendipitously they too believed Monday's children are "quiet, retiring and peaceful, whereas Wednesday's children are "quick tempered, aggressive and trouble-makers."[2]

The practice of naming children after grandparents, to honor them, was widely followed in both England and Africa. In Africa there was the conscious recognition that this was to fulfill obligations to spirits and to invite them, as it were, to inhabit or help the new namesake. Among the Kikuyo

tribal custom requires that a married couple should have at least four children, two male and two female. The first male is regarded as perpetuating the existence of the man's father, the second as perpetuating that of the woman's father. The first and second female children fulfill the same ritual duty to the souls of their grandmothers on both sides. The children are given names of the persons whose soul they represent.[3]

154

The English, it would seem, often named first sons for fathers, but if the son was the child of a first son, he was, as it were, named for his grandfather too. Some, however, chose the grandfather's name by choice. There were apparently no hard and fast rules that had to be followed.

Some names were chosen in both societies for their connotative or denotative meanings. Before the Reformation, the English widely named their children for Catholic saints. George Stewart has found that after the Reformation (in the 1540s) some eighty-four percent of baptismal names were still of religious origin, with John the most common name.[4] For women, saints' names such as Agnes, Katherine, and Margaret remained popular, along with the New Testament names, Elizabeth, Mary, Joan, and Anne. Here again, as with lay rituals, it is clear that we have signs of "a strong tradition and an essential conservatism," further evidence of the quasi-Catholic or traditional value system.

By the time Jamestown was settled, the names of post-Biblical saints were used less often, and Old Testament names were on the rise; apparently it was in Massachusetts that a revolution in choice of name came about. There Catholic and old Norman names virtually "disappeared" and Biblical names came to account for ninety percent of all male names, some fifty percent from the Old Testament and forty from the New. The Old Testament rose as a source of women's names as well, accounting for close to half; but this pattern had begun abroad.[5]

Unlike Massachusetts, Virginia retained the old English tradition. A very small pool of names accounted for over fifty percent of all white Virginia names.[6] For men, they were John, William, Thomas, and Richard, but after 1700, Richard was replaced by James, a strong indication of Scotch-Irish presence. For white women, there was similarly a very limited traditional pool, with Catholic saints' names, which were virtually never used in New England, always important in Virginia, whereas the Old Testament names so important in Puritan communities were rarely used. In Virginia, Mary, Elizabeth, Ann, and Sarah accounted for most women's names, but (saints) Catherine, Margaret, and Winifred remained in use along with Alice and Barbara. (Among the men, too, an occasional St. George, as in the Tucker family, marks a radical difference from the Puritan practice.) Although the names chosen by white Virginians remained the same as those chosen by the English of the seventeenth century, there was a significant change in pattern over time. In the seventeenth century, some fifty percent of boys were given their father's name, whereas only perhaps ten to fifteen percent were given the first name of their paternal grandfather. By the eighteenth century, most white first sons were named for their paternal grandparent, with second sons often given their father's name. Daughters' names, too, followed this changing pattern.[7]

Blacks, whose African traditions had often involved naming children for all four grandparents, and who had rarely used parents' names for offspring, began to follow what seems to be the eighteenth-century Virginia "white" pattern, with many named for grandparents along with many a first or second son named for his father.[8] It is likely indeed that whites were influencing blacks to name sons after their fathers, although blacks may have been motivated to do this in order to announce and record parenthood.[9] At the same time the possibility should be considered that blacks may well have influenced whites in the direction of naming first children after grandparents. It was the "proper" form of respect and honor, and as we have noted, African patterns of honor seem to have affected plantation families.

At least one slaveowner chose to name his four children for their four grandparents' families, much as an African would. Robert Carter (1774–1805), son of Charles Carter of Shirley, married Mary Nelson in 1796, and they named their first son Hill. The father explained in a testamentary letter that this was "in memory of ancestors on your Grand Father Carter's side," although he did *not* choose his own father's name, Charles. Their second child was a daughter, and they called her Anne "after your Grand Mother Carter." Lucy followed, "after your Grand Mother Nelson," and Thomas "after your Grand Father Nelson." Having two boys and two girls, in mixed order, made everything work out very neatly, and the four siblings had four old family names from both sides of the family, with the father's family honored first, although the grandfather himself was pointedly excluded.[10]

There were other African patterns that are important to note in terms of new-world developments. Many Africans had more than one name. Among the Bakongo, for example, "an individual is not necessarily known by the same name to everybody. When he takes a new name and a new role he does not thereby drop other names and roles."[11] Some names were "secret" and perhaps known only to child and parents; some were given at initiation, at puberty and/or when joining secret societies. A person, generally believed to have more than one soul, could have several names and reveal different parts of himself or herself on different occasions.[12] It is possible this pattern helped slaves to accept the names the master gave them in the Big House while they retained names of their choice or nicknames in the black community. Many certainly had two or more names.[13]

New Africans in America were by and large given names by their owners.[14] Orlando Patterson views this act as one of the initiatory rituals undergone by a new slave in virtually every slaveowning society that, he believes, "give symbolic expression to the slave's social death and new status."[15] Freud recognized that "A man's name is a principal component of his personality, perhaps even a portion of his soul."[16] Slavers in Africa gave slaves new names, although they knew that plantation owners would repeat this demeaning practice. Significantly, in 1787, James Arnold, a surgeon on the slaver, the *Ruby*, recorded that "The first slave that was traded for, after the brig anchored at the Island of Bimbe, was a girl of about fifteen who was promptly named Eve, for it was usual on slave ships to give the names of Adam and Eve to the first man and woman brought on board."[17]

Robert "King" Carter, dealing with shiploads of new Africans, adjured his steward in 1685: "I hope you will take care that the Negroes both men and women I sent you up last always go by the names we gave them." He felt "sure we repeated them so often . . . that everyone knew their names and would readily answer to them."[18]

Numerous advertisements for "new Negroes" who spoke no English but had English names indicate that "naming" was one of the first acts a new owner undertook. Scymour Powell, for example, advertised in August 1752, for a runaway boy, "about 14 or 15 Years of age," who had come to Virginia that very summer. Powell noted, "He can't speak English, but will answer to the Name of York very readily."[19]

White owners chose names of three distinct types: Most male names were chosen from the same limited pool used by parents for their white sons, but diminutives or nicknames became the blacks' proper names. Thus the most popular slave names were, it seems, Jack and Will, clearly the John and William that were the top two for whites. For girls and women, the pattern was more complex, but Elizabeth became Betty, Catherine became Kate, Susanna became Sue, and perhaps Moll stood in, as it were, for Mary.[20]

Both black men and black women, however, had names that whites rarely ever did. Among them were the second group of names apparently given by whites—place names, perhaps important to the owner, or significant in regard to the ship that brought the slave. London, Glasgow, York, Bristol, Edinburgh, and Barbary were the names of blacks in eighteenth-century Virginia.[21]

The third distinct group was that of demeaning classical names: Cesar, Hercules, Baccus, and Hannibal all appear on the slave property lists. When Thomas Jones's house was served by Venus, Pallas, Daphne, and Mercury, all black slaves, it is clear he chose the names and it is likely he recognized both the irony and the degradation involved. He was participating in a very old tradition, wherein classical names had early become a humiliating badge of servility.[22]

There was a fourth group of slave names, a small number of clearly African names, either retained by Africans or given to children born in America. In the same year (1728) that the Jones household had its Venus, Pallas, Daphne, and Mercury, the inventory of the Edmund Curtis estate revealed he had Coffee (Friday), Cage (perhaps Cudjo or Monday), Kalf, Quarthe (perhaps from Quao or Thursday), and Piecah, among his seventeen slaves. The Curtis slaves showed the broad range of possibilities: five (above) with names probably derived from African names; two with classical and demeaning slave names, Nero and Pompea; and ten, including seven children, who had names very similar to those of the whites around them: Hannah, Margery, Peggy, Rachel, Nell, and two Janes. However, not all the young were being Anglicized: Quarthe and Piecah were young girls.[23]

By 1775, families such as that of Robert Cobbs already had an Old Hannibal and a Young Hannibal; but it was much more common to find Old Frank and Young Frank, Will and Will Junior, Daniel and Daniel Junior, and similar differentiations between fathers and sons or grandsons. As Gutman has suggested, this indicates that most slaves were giving their children English names but leaving open the possibility that they were following African patterns of naming.[24]

Although only a small number of slaves retained or were given African names in Virginia, the importance of African names lies not only in their number.[25] It is significant simply that some African names were known to both blacks and whites in Virginia, and that some children born there were so named. In the second half of the century, Margery and Moody, slaves of Francis Jerdone (a Scotsman settled in Louisa County), had three children they called Sam, Rose, and Sukey, and then, in 1766, they chose to call their fourth child Mingo. Their fifth, born in 1768, they named Maria, but in 1771, they chose the very African-sounding name of Comba for their sixth child. They, and one assumes the Jerdones, accepted a mix of very African and very English names.[26]

Other African names seem to appear randomly, decreasing in incidence over the century. "Thursday," "Saturday," and "Sunday" were christened at Christ Church prior to 1704. Coffee, Quash, Phebe, Quamana, Wolk, Eno, Quaco, Codjo, Abba, and Cuba all were names of slaves in eighteenth-century Virginia.[27] The fact that Lorenzo Turner found a high percentage of African words used as names in the Georgia Sea Islands, many of them secret or family names, suggests the possibility that this had more widely been the case in Virginia in the eighteenth century, although Virginia slaves never experienced the near-isolation of the so-called "Gullah."[28]

Virginia slaves did, however, have their own names, many of them not secret. In the advertisements for runaways, owner after owner wrote of "aliases" that their slaves went by, and they cautioned that the slave might well change his or her name. They sought "Joe, alias Josiah Sally," "Bob" who calls himself "Edmund Tamar," "Jupiter alias Gibb," "Pysant [Italian?] alias Vincent," "Bob alias Kit," "Hankey alias Hagai Sexton," this last a woman indicating one of the different ways blacks used white names.[29]

Notwithstanding the fact that most whites did not acknowledge that blacks had surnames, many slaves adopted them and they were, on occasion, referred to by whites. "John Denmera a Negro belonging to John Lear" presented a freedom petition to the Council in 1711. Thomas Swan, negro, ran away from Anthony Armistead in 1703, and a hue and cry were issued for his apprehension. The status of "John Darling which belonged to Peter Bowdoin" was discussed by the Council in 1740. An inventory of John Carter's estate made in 1750 lists Tom Tucker and Charles Evans among the slaves, as well as Mingo, Mendor, Dinor, Old Abba, and Old Ebo (the last four being women). However, in most records English names predominated, and most slaves seem to have been known by their owner's family name, as Jefferson's Isaac, who later called himself Isaac Jefferson.[30] There is evidence that many of the black runaways, as well as the blacks joining churches, had surnames that, although they may have been those of a previous "master," were not the same as their present owner's name. Philip Alexander advertised for a Robert Fanwick; Samuel Apperson for a Jon Bibbin; Robert and Mary Burwell for a Jack Dismal; Edward Carter for "a likely Negro man, who calls himself John Cellars." Indeed, Gutman maintains that although whites may not have used them, by the 1780s, most slaves had surnames.[31]

When blacks adopted the English names given them as their own, they often shortened and changed their pronunciation. Isaac Jefferson, for example, called his mother Usley or Usler, although Jefferson records her name as Ursula. She "may have derived her name from Ursula Byrd of Westover," who was named for her English aunt.[32] Ursula Jefferson's granddaughter was in turn named for her grandmother, and the name was then in both black and white family traditions.

To a limited degree blacks could make names their own and were probably increasingly free to choose their offsprings' names, as we find them beginning to use more Old Testament names than the whites around them did; but some owners were still ready to force ironic shame on their slaves. Cain, who "had a large scar over one of his eyes," was likely to have known the Biblical story and unlikely to have kept this name after he ran away.[33] Africans, like Puritans, did not believe evil names should be given: They were believed to influence character development.[34] Blacks later took first names such as Jesus, Christian, or Moses, and surnames such as Baptist or Freeman, indicating their continued concern with a name's meaning. They were apparently ready to accept some names that whites thought ridiculous, such as King George, Queen Esther, or General (the name of a slave with both feet amputated), perhaps believing that some power came to them from these names. Personal honor and dignity were primary African values, and slaves sought to maintain names consummate with their own self-images. Virginian-born George called himself George America, and perhaps the name helped him to forge a character that could run away and make enough "trouble" to be outlawed, so that his owner, Thomas Watkins, offered five pounds "to any person that will kill and destroy him," and only forty shillings "if taken alive."[35]

In a similar advertisement for an outlawed runaway, one John Brown announced that if his slave Peter was "brought home alive" he would pay thirty shillings, but if someone would kill him and his fellow runaway and "bring me their heads," he would pay ten pounds apiece.[36] Brown's use of the term home is significant. If alive, Peter should be "brought home." Whites regarded slaves as at home on their plantation, and as part of their families. The term family was used much as the English had, when they talked of apprentices and servants-in-husbandry as part of their families. The master of an English family had control over those in it, and although the family was undergoing change they were still expected to show the master honor and obeisance. (Africans too regarded the head of a family or clan as having great status and deserving much honor.)[37]

English servants, both in the house and in husbandry, were not allowed to marry without their master's approval. In seventeenth-century Virginia, indentured servants were also forbidden to marry, and

160

female servants had their indentures extended if they bore children out of wedlock. When Africans began to come into the society and slavery for life became a reality, the civil authorities floundered at first in their handling of interracial sex and marriage. In the famous act of 1662, the Virginia assembly decided both that any child born of a slave was also a slave and that in the case of fornication between a "Christian" and a "Negro," the Christian was to pay twice the normal fine. The process of trying to separate whites and blacks was underway, but it apparently was *not* clear to the Burgesses that they had the right to declare any marriage illegal. They did go further in the post-Bacon's Rebellion atmosphere of 1691. They passed an act indicating what they then thought the limit of their prerogatives:

[What]soever English or other white man or woman, bond or free, shall intermarry with a Negro, mulatto or Indian man or woman, bond or free, he shall within three months be banished from this dominion forever.[38]

Blacks and whites apparently did continue to marry, as petitions were circulated in Surry, Prince George, and Accomac counties, protesting this practice; in 1705, a harsh law reaffirmed the official intention to prevent "abominable mixture and spurious issue."[39]

Whereas mixed marriages were strenuously objected to, slave marriages were simply not recognized by the civil authorities, although most churches did come to accept the legitimacy of the marriages of Christian slaves. At the outset, slave children were probably a burden and not welcomed in the work-oriented and hard-pressed community. It eventually became apparent that slave reproduction was ultimately profitable, and that black slavery was a seemingly permanent addition to the society and needed regularization. At approximately the same time slaves, having reached a more normal balance of the sexes, began to form more relatively stable marriage arrangements. Because of these developments, many more whites began to recognize black couples as married.[41]

In John Brown's 1767 advertisement for his slave Peter he recognized his family status and history: Peter, Brown notes, who ran away from Norfolk, "has a wife at Little Town, and a father at Mr. Philip Burt's quarter near the half-way house between Williamsburg and York; he formerly belonged to Parson Fontaine, and I bought him of Doctor James Carter."[42] Peter's mother may have once been at Fontaine's, his father was at Burt's, and his wife at Little Town, while Peter had been in Norfolk. "Broad" wives, abroad or away from the hus-

161

band's domicile, were very common, and clearly these were the only possible matches for the large population living on farms with small numbers of other blacks. Family homes were impossible for them, even if their owners recognized their unions, although it became customary to allow visits by husband mid-week and Sunday, and many slaves took other occasions as well.

Although the percentage of slaves that married continued to rise over the course of the eighteenth century, white recognition and or honoring of these unions may have declined toward the end of the century. A comparison of the Carter and Jerdone records, among others, suggests this.

Robert "King" Carter (1663–1732), massive importer and owner of more slaves than any other single individual in Virginia, certainly recognized the slave family as an established institution by the time he wrote his will. He left "George the cooper, and his wife and children," "the cook wench Priss her husband Old Robin and her children," "Tom Gubey and his wife and children" (and David his brother), and "Negroe Frank, the carpenter, and his wife and children. . . ." At his house there were four black couples with seven children; one father and one mother with one child each; an old woman; six young laborers; and nine older children outside of families. All of his quarters had couples with children as the modal type, as well as numerous single adults.[43]

The records of Francis Jerdone, a Scotsman who settled in Virginia in 1740, establishing four or five successful plantations, including Jerdone Castle in Louisa County, seem to present a stark contrast. Jerdone kept a "slave book," as did most Virginia slaveowners, in which he recorded births by mother alone and literally mixed in his slave holdings with his records of horse purchases. However, in 1770, when he chose to record the fifty-five slaves "on the plantation where he livith," he recorded them by families: "Old Adam, his wife and 3 children," Calabar, his wife Moll and four children, Aaron and Winney, and eight children [G]opher and his two children. Out of fifty-five slaves, Jerdone listed five two-parent families with a total of nineteen children; one father with two children; two mothers with a total of three children; and one couple without children. Jerdone clearly recognized marriages, even where there were no offspring.[44]

When Francis Jerdone died in 1771, and his widow, Sarah Macon Jerdone, took over the plantation management and the records, the slave family disappeared from all Jerdone documents. Henceforth children were always recorded as the sons or daughters of their mother, and no fathers were mentioned.

Most late-eighteenth- and early-nineteenth-century plantation records list only mothers and children, although a minority of church records, account books, and especially Bibles record black families' fathers as well as mothers. The Joshua Skinner family Bible (1783–1835), one of many similar Bible records still extant, records "Ishmael Son of Dave and Hannah was Born August the 25th 1793" and "Dave Negro Boy Son of Dave and [Choc] was Born April the 14th 1791." Between 1783 and 1835, Skinner recorded forty-one black births (ten in the eighteenth century), and in all but four cases both father and mother were listed.[45] Landon Carter most often referred to children as their father's: Gardner Johnny's stout boy, Toney's son Toney; Nat, son of Nassau; Johnny's girl; George's boy George; Manuel's Harry, Billy, Will, Peg, and "Manuel's Sarah." Even an infant was recognized as "A sucking child of Talbot's."[46] Robert Carter's famous manumission of 422 slaves, begun in 1791, was done in full recognition of family existence. It was to be staggered over time, and couples were to be freed together.[47]

Analysis of the plantations toward the end of the century indicates that planters who recognized slave marriages did not necessarily house couples together. Evidence of this has been found at Jefferson's and Washington's farms, where in the 1790s only nineteen couples seem to have been living together, whereas another twenty-one couples were divided by their work assignments. Children too were often separated from parents, even when owned by the same "master."[48] It is possible that to some extent this pattern, which suited owners' needs, loosely fit a black acceptance of the appropriateness of women and children being housed separately.

Disrespect for black marriages and families may have helped some whites find acceptable the sales that divided black couples and children, and it served to reinforce the image of blacks as morally unequal to whites, making the "peculiar institution" seem appropriate to "their" peculiar differences.

In the eighteenth century, blacks were generally talked of as "family" by their white owners. At the opening of the century Byrd wrote that three in the "family" were killed by Indians; in 1776, Jefferson recorded the "Number of souls in my family" and it was twenty-six free and eighty-three slave.[49] The slave was coopted into the master's "family" much as the indentured servant before him had been. However, unlike most servants, slaves came to have wives and children.

Although they could not be regarded as proper heads of families, this change in status may have helped a slaveowner begin to consider his slaves as separate from his "family," which was coming to mean his close relations.

In the Baptist and Methodist churches, blacks, together with whites, found a possibility of renewing baptismal patterns, having their names recorded, and having their marriages honored.[50] It was there that they were once again called brother and sister in a new black and white Christian family and became members in restricted societies that had rites, rituals, taboos, and charisma.

12. Conclusions

L IKE ADAM in the Garden of the Lord, elite Virginians wanted to name everything around them: their land, their homes, and their black "chattels." They wanted control over what was, on occasion, envisioned as a Land of Eden. However, both the land and its inhabitants often imposed their intransigent wills.[1]

Most white Virginians, as most other white settlers in the New World, had an "essentially proprietary and exploitative attitude" toward land, and many were ready to move on, repeatedly, to look for "the main chance."[2] In 1774, Governor Dunmore noted that "Americans . . . will remove as their avidity and restlessness invite them. They acquire no attachment to Place: But wandering about seems engrafted to their nature."[3] In this, as in other crucial assessments, Dunmore erred. Mixed with this modern perspective, in which land is a means to an end (primarily financial profit, status, and power), was a far more traditional attitude in which land was seen as having God-given powers of its own. Some Virginians formed deep attachments to special places. Jefferson wrote of Monticello: "I am happy nowhere else and in no other society." He found rational explanations for his deep attachment, but it is clear it had a mystical element: "All my wishes end, where I hope my days will, at Monticello. Too many scenes of happiness mingle themselves with all the recollections of my native woods and field to suffer them to be supplanted in my affections by any other."[4]

Old English and African attitudes toward the holiness of particular places, and the magical power inherent both in them and in spirit-workers, reinforced each other and gave root doctors, cunning men and women, and even witches an acceptable role to play.

Such cultural interaction was underway in many areas. The small simple houses of most blacks and whites provide an example of this process that affected the use of space and the landscape. As suggested, an almost "balloon"-style framing, lightweight posts, and ultrasimple roofs were used extensively in Virginia from about 1700 on and influenced subsequent building throughout the South and West. Africans generally built lightweight, uniform structures. Africans also thought in terms of compounds of many single-room houses, separate kitchens and workrooms, clustered around Great Houses of chiefs. When additional space was needed, additional rooms were built. Enclosed housing was of a small module. As Glassie has so brilliantly shown,

Virginia builders internalized a transactional language of building based on small units and their combination.

Most blacks and most whites were living in such small and similar houses. Their views of space and its use were in part shared, although blacks were more likely to be living in "community"—in quarters with other blacks and generally some whites. Whites living in the countryside were often more isolated than blacks. John Davis, in Virginia at the close of the century, recounts that when he was traveling to a settlement called Frying Pan, he stopped a white boy and inquired how far he yet had to go. The boy replied: "You be in the pan now." The Pan was four log huts and a meeting house, near Newgate. Spencer Ball's plantation, Pohoke, eight miles away, where Davis was working, had many more houses (and people) than Frying Pan.[5]

Unlike the small houses and most of the so-called Big Houses, which were often small houses in disguise, a very small percentage of slaveowner homes were actually mansions built in an English tradition. The family life inside these houses, however, was uniquely Southern: Blacks and whites were inside them sharing in new Afro-English traditions and creating new joint families, as well as separate ones.

By mid-century blacks and whites were in one family, by blood and by adoption, all over Virginia. They were interacting in ordinary times and at times of celebration. Elkanah Watson, a New Englander experimenting with life in the South, wrote a rare and important description of a public celebration when, in the summer of 1787, he traveled together with a member of the local elite to Hampton County, Virginia, to attend a cockfight:

We reached the ground, about ten o'clock the next morning. The roads, as we approached the scene, were alive with carriages, horses, and pedestrians, black and white, hastening to the point of attraction. Several houses formed a spacious square, in the centre of which was arranged a large cock-pit; surrounded by many genteel people, promiscuously mingled with the vulgar and debased.[6]

Blacks and whites together were "the vulgar and the debased." They were betting, shouting, and fighting with each other, but they were also likely to hunt, dance, and "play" together.

Blacks and whites often shared in amusements. When blacks danced at night, whites are known to have attended. Isaac Jefferson, slave at Monticello, reported that Randolph Jefferson, Thomas's brother, "used to come out among black people, play the fiddle and dance half the night."⁷ When the Northern tutor, Fithian, found his teenage white students dancing with the slaves, he was disturbed; but Southern whites may have been more comfortable with the practice than he was. On Sunday, January 30, 1774, Fithian recorded:

*This Evening the Negroes collected themselves into the School-Room, & began to play the Fiddle, & dance. . . . Ben & Harry were of the company—Harry was dancing with his Coat off—I dispersed them however immediately.*⁸

Dick's master, Sutherland, danced his "Congo minuets" with black "Queens."⁹ Slave-style "Negro jig" dances became a closing feature at white cotillions, paralleling the parodies of white dances done by the slaves. In 1776, an observer of these jigs "borrowed . . . from the Negroes" and danced by whites, suggested they were "without any method or regularity." What he apparently meant was that they were spontaneous and emotional:

*[A] gentleman and lady stand up, and dance about the room, one of them retiring, the other pursuing, then perhaps meeting, in an irregular fantastical manner. After some time, another lady gets up, and then the first lady must sit down, she being, as they term it, cut out. . . . The gentlemen perform in the same manner.*¹⁰

Black musicians played at the white dances, and reciprocal influence was underway here, with black "rhythm" influencing whites.

Rites of passage often involved racially mixed groups. Blacks and whites were together at births and christenings, weddings, deaths, and funerals. Interaction in the churches is a separate story, but within the family, religious rites often brought racially mixed groups together. Slaveowner John Williams routinely noted in his journal for July 23, 1771: "I had all my family given up to the Lord by prayer, the children, black and white, particularly by laying on of hands."¹¹ This routine "sharing" in the family was perhaps the most significant of all.

Landon Carter's diary provides extensive evidence of the reality of the black–white "family" as defined by R. D. Laing: of black–white family politics, of joint family history, and of an internalized "fantasy system." Carter had long and intimate relations with blacks, whom he originally trusted, trained, nursed when sick, and clearly relied upon. He came to see himself as their mentor, their teacher, and even their savior, rescuing them from the gallows or, in his dreams, from barbarism. But "they" all became "ingrates," and he saw them as returning his goodness with evil: ruining his property, drinking to excess, and abandoning him. His slaves, Manuel and Nassau, both filled this role of "foster son" and both rejected Carter and eventually ran away.

When Nassau was away from Landon Carter "on a Drunk," Carter decided to sell him and wrote: "I have been learning to do without him and though it has been but very badly yet I can bear it and will." But Carter could not bear this loss easily. Nassau was an old family member—Nassau's father had belonged to Landon's father, and Nassau's son Nat was Landon's as well. Landon Carter threatened to sell Nassau, outlawed him, and saw him run off to Dunmore, but he apparently took him back into the family after each and every episode.[12]

Carter's anger at his slaves contributed to his anger at his son's life style, and his anger at his son's rejection of him became mixed with his jealousy of black's family relations as well. All were involved in a complex reality and "fantasy system."

After the close of slavery, Letitia Burwell, whose great-grandfather had come from Kingsmill and established Botetourt Court in Mecklenburg County, retained an Edenic image of the plantation past: altruistic masters, contented slaves, white cabins, and beautiful gardens. Notwithstanding these mythical aspects, her memories suggest much that is important in relation to both whites' and blacks' sense of place, identity, and family. Virtually all of Burwell's early memories involved blacks. Were she to have excluded them from her autobiography, she would virtually have had no past and no identity. Burwell did try to convince her readers, and herself, that black slaves were dependent on whites and could not function without them, but she succeeded in demonstrating that *she* was dependent on blacks and could not function without *them*: "Confined exclusively to a Virginia plantation during my earliest childhood, I believed the world one vast plantation bounded by negro quarters."[13]

III

Causality and Purpose

13. African and English Explanations of Death and the Afterlife

A FRICANS widely believed that humans were originally immortal. Many myths suggest that God sent two messages to earth: a fast animal carried the message of life and a slow one the message of death. In all cases, a particular act on the part of the fast-moving animal upset what seems to have been the apparent intention of God. In one tale it was told that the dog carrying the message of life stopped to gorge itself on food, and thus the slow-moving toad "won the race" and brought death to humankind. In this tale, as in many others, death appears to have come by accident, perhaps by the "unthinking" act of some animal, but not because of any individual's act. God, of course, arranged the race, but the implication is that the animals had free will.[1] However, "African mythology explains the world by reference to symbolic oppositions and polarities that serve to categorize complex social and moral relationships."[2] Perhaps we should understand the dog/toad polarity as symbols for human personalities and learn that the self-serving individual bears the guilt for death.

There is a second and very different African tradition, this one much like the Biblical one, in which it is told "that God forbade the first people to eat either a certain fruit, or eggs, or animals." When they ate this forbidden food, "death came to them."[3] The similarities with the Biblical tale of Adam and Eve are such that many West Africans, encountering the Christian Bible, thought they recognized an old story of their own.

Neither the similarities of this myth of origins nor the differences of the first conception account for the ensuing radical difference in understanding. John Mbiti explains that

Even though people believe that death came into the world at a very early date in the history of mankind, they believe also that every time a person dies this death is "caused." There are several ways in which it is caused. . . . People believe sorcery, witchcraft and evil magic cause death. . . . Spirits may be blamed. [And] . . . Curses, broken taboos or oaths are sometimes believed to cause deaths.[4]

Africans believed that *every* death had a cause involving human beings, and that every death should be explained: Who is the sorcerer involved? Who used evil magic? Who called on spirit power? Perhaps the person who died had broken a taboo, and this had caused punishment. But although this was held possible, it was seen as far more likely that someone else cursed the dead one or sent a "poison" or an evil spirit. (Mbiti notes that "It is sometimes believed that God may call old people to leave this life," but he emphasizes that such an understanding is "rare, and only in a few societies is such a belief entertained."[5])

In virtually all cases, diseases and accidents that were the ostensible causes of death were seen as brought about by agents, human or spiritual. The living were seen as having a moral responsibility to find the *primary cause* of each death. On hearing of a death, Africans often said, "An enemy hath done this thing." Then, much as police investigating a murder or doctors conducting an autopsy in Western society, the proper authorities sought out the causal agent. Igbo, after covering a grave, spoke to the spirit of the dead one: "Follow and . . . kill . . . the one who killed you." In many ethnic groups a "corpse," a symbolic representation of the dead person, made with nails and hair from the body, was carried around the village. "The bearers often say that they are moved against their will and they may stop and point at some person as guilty."[6]

African religion, popularly thought of as nonrational, can be seen as "a very pragmatic technique for understanding, predicting, and controlling" events.[7] African perceptions of death place a type of control in human hands. If individual deaths are caused by individuals, the social welfare of the society is served by finding those responsible. The "murderers" may be those violating social norms and causing social disorder; or personal anger or animus may have "caused" harm. The punishment of the guilty (and the group catharsis undergone in the process) no doubt fulfills deep needs in the society, as has been suggested in the literature dealing with witch hunts both in Africa and in the West.[8]

The seventeenth-century English were concerned about the cause of death as well. Their Biblical "myth" also suggested that human beings were originally immortal. When the Christian asked, "How has death gained its empire over us?" the answer found in the story of Adam and Eve, like the second (less popular) African tradition, placed all the responsibility on human shoulders. In the interpretation shared by seventeenth-century English Protestants, "The answer is quick and definite: death happened, damnation happened because man through sin rejected the gift of life which God had given him.

Man killed himself, as it were." Death was the punishment for original sin.[9]

There were less definite answers to other questions raised by death: Who or what caused each individual death? Why does death come when and as it does? Does the life of the individual bear any causal relation to death?

The English in this period did believe human beings could cause other humans' deaths. Jews were believed to bring the plague. Malevolent spirits were believed to cause illness, and witches could control these spirits. The medical records of *maleficium* indicate how widely held these beliefs were: Keith Thomas has found "over 120 cases of suspected witchcraft in Richard Napier's casebooks (1600–1634) and over 50 in those of William Lilly (1644–1666)." Most of the English executions for witchcraft took place between 1550 and 1675. The English were then ready to believe human agencies were involved in their ills. "The land is full of witches," said Lord Chief Justice Anderson in 1602. "They abound in all places." The effect of their curses and evil magic was widely believed in.[10]

It is not fully clear what people believed about the relation of sin to death. It was often believed that "others" died for one's sins. The deaths of wives, children, and servants were seen as a punishment for their master. But an individual could die as a punishment for his or her own sins, although it was widely recognized that the pure and innocent often died young. Of what sin was the babe in arms guilty? In the end, life and death were accepted as the gifts of God. "*Unto this God the Lord belong the issues of death* . . . and all our periods and transitions in this life, are so many passages from death to death." The dying John Donne (1572–1631), preaching what was virtually his own funeral sermon, maintained that "Our critical day is not the very day of our death, but the whole course of our life." Yet he had no assurance of what awaited him, only mystical faith grounded in the death of Jesus, which he described in agonizing detail. Christ

gave up the ghost: and as God breathed a soul into the first Adam, so the second Adam breathed his soul into God, into the hands of God. There we leave you, in that blessed dependency, to hang upon him, that hangs upon the cross. There bathe in his tears, there suck at his wounds, and lie down in peace in his grave, till he vouchsafe you a resurrection, and an ascension into that kingdom which he hath purchased for you, with the inestimable price of his incorruptible blood.[11]

The English Protestant view left the individual in a far more unre-
solved state than did the African. God knew human fate, and in fact
many believed it was predestined. Sin was the cause of death, but it
was the original sin: "In Adam's fall, sinned we all," as English and
later American children learned with their alphabet. But sins of the
individual, or of some malevolent force working for the Devil, might
well play a role in any individual's death. There was no ritual to find
the cause and no communal catharsis to heal the wounds, other than
the grief at the funeral or the "letting go" at the wake, and there was
little security about "life" after death.

African beliefs about afterlife varied, but virtually all Africans believed that the spirit or spirits in men and women lived on after
death.[12] They lived in some realm, perhaps in the earth, or on it, or
nearby. (Very rarely were they believed to be in the sky.) In the afterlife, "Life continues more or less the same . . . as it did in this world."
However, that world is the better place, the real "home," where forefathers live on. Dying is "going home."[13]

The funeral is the rite of entry into the world of the dead. "The more
lavish the burial rites observed on his behalf, the more confident is he
of a fitting reception into the underworld of spirits." With a proper
burial, the spirit "goes over" into its new realm without difficulty.
Again, moral acts are not immediately involved, unless one focuses
on the moral responsibility of those still alive to provide the proper
burial service, or the proper life lived by the dying person—proper in
the sense that he or she married and had offspring to guarantee the
proper funeral and the carrying on of tradition.[14]

There are two relatively limited areas in Africa, in Nigeria and
Ghana, where "some people believe that the dead appear before God
to receive their judgment depending on what they have done with
their lives." The good are believed to go to the good homeland of the
forefathers, the bad to a realm of "misery," but "eventually God takes
pity on them," and they too go "home."[15]

Although all this sounds positive, African ideas of the afterlife were
not always so reassuring. Not everyone could expect to live with the
spirits, and there were many complicating factors. An ancestor was
one who had lived to a great age. Babies and young people were read
out of the immortal realm, and thus early death was a disaster. All
sorts of "dishonorable deaths" ruled out participation in the next
world, such as deaths due to certain diseases, accidents, physical abnormalities, and abnormalities in behavior. The "ancestor" was one

who had lived "in conformity with the rules of society," had physical and moral integrity, and had achieved the wisdom of age.[16]

In all, in order to join the forefathers, an individual had to have been an integral member of the society, not a deviant or an outsider in any way. Slaves were outsiders. They were not generally buried with free men, and memorials were not set up to house their souls. Among the Igbo, for example, slaves' bodies were dumped into the bush. It was not expected that they would be in the land of spirits.[17]

The seventeenth-century English Protestant did not believe sacred rites or the passage of time would ensure arrival in heaven. Although the reality of purgatory was now rejected, and the Church maintained that masses could have no effect, belief in hell remained very powerful; in a sense the Protestant was far less able to secure ritual help or assurance in regard to the future than the Catholic was. "The misery of a bad Christian is altogether insupportable," taught Thomas Ken (1637–1709), Bishop of Bath and Wells. "He has Christ for his enemy, the devil for his father, and hell, with all its miseries, and torments, and despair, which are all eternal for his doom." The church Catechism spoke of Christ coming "to judge the quick and the dead." Ken's explanation was according to tradition: "All the dead shall be waked out of their graves . . . [and] all shall rise with the same bodies they had on earth." At the resurrection

Thou wilt re-collect their scattered dust into the same form again; that our souls shall be reunited to our bodies; . . . that the bodies of the wicked shall be fitted for torment, and the bodies of the saints changed in quality, and made glorified bodies, immortal and incorruptible, fitted for heaven, and eternally to love and enjoy Thee.[18]

The catechism told of the resurrection of the body at the End of Days, but there was the expectation that at death the soul immediately traveled to hell or to heaven. Thus, when in 1682, Ken sang the praises of a saintly parishioner, Lady Margaret Mainard, he envisioned her as already in God's bosom. He described her holy life and death and concluded that "her Soul was set at liberty, and on the wings of Angels, took a direct, and vigorous flight to its native Country Heaven from whence it first flew down."

There then we must leave her, in the bosom of her heavenly Bridegroom, where, how radiant her Crown is, how ecstatic her Joy, how high exalted she is in degrees of glory, is impossible to be described,

175

for neither eye hath seen, nor ear heard, nor has it entered into the heart of man, to be conceived, the good things, which God hath prepared for those that love him, *of all which she is now partaker.*[19]

Here Ken echoed both Luther and Calvin: Heaven would be joy, but its nature could not be known.[20]

Sin in life may not have been the immediate cause of death, but the place of afterlife, heaven or hell, was seen as related to the individual's moral actions. There was no simple formula or assurance, however. God could save the worst sinner, and good acts did *not* guarantee the salvation of any soul. Salvation was not to be assured in any simple fashion, although God was seen as choosing his elect in eternity. "The grace of God in the adoption of the elect is unchangeable," wrote Perkins, "and he that is the child of God can never fall away wholly or finally."[21] But the Church of England was less clear than the Puritans about designating the children of God. The elect were to go to heaven, but who were these children of God? Ken seemed certain about Lady Margaret Mainard, but how could one know about oneself? And what of the others? Hell was to be the abode of the fallen in perpetuity.

These understandings of death gave meaning to life. African religions that appeared so spirit-centered can be viewed as, in essence, human-centered.[22] The individual's goal is self-perfection, to be made whole or to achieve "oneheartedness." Marriage, wherein male and female complement one another and expand the kinship relationships that establish order; parenthood, which makes the individual part of the ongoing generations; and a "mastery of divinity," wherein ritual and/or ecstasy can restore life, lead to wholeness. But the basic means to wholeness is "mastery of the self." "An African's esteem for someone is a function of his ability to dominate his passions, emotions, behavior, and actions." The world to come is vouchsafed to one who has mastered himself and become whole in this life.[23]

In the sixteenth and seventeenth centuries, an English Protestant would not have said that he or she was using spiritual forces to become a fuller person. Such an individual might well have held that one would become a better person through a spiritual life, but the goal was ostensibly to serve God's will—even if the person suffered—and not one's own benefit on earth. Thomas Cranmer (1489–1556) held that we are called to "repentance, hope, love, dread, and the fear of God" in order "to serve him in all good deeds, obeying his commandments . . . , to seek in all things his glory and honour, *not our sensual pleasures and vain-glory.*"[24]

176

In the seventeenth century, John Donne (1572–1631) would still emphasize the painful choices to be made in order to live the Christian life.:

Take heed where you place your treasure: for it concerns you much, where your heart be placed; and, where your treasure is, there will your heart be also. *And then opens this symbolical . . . Y, into two horns, two beams, two branches; one broader, but on the left-hand, denoting the treasures of this world; the other narrower, but on the right-hand, treasure laid up for the world to come. Be sure ye turn the right way: for,* where your treasure is, there will you heart be also.[25]

An individual's fate was dependent upon duality: He or she was to choose one path, the narrower and harder one, and not seek to unite holiness and a pleasant life.

A radical shift in Christian understandings of life's purpose was, however, underway, and it is a shift that marks the modern world view. Again, the Puritans came to hold the new view in perhaps its purest form. They turned from shunning the world to hallowing it. It was Calvin's understanding of calling that informed the new view: Each individual was believed to have a God-given proper role in the world, and in serving God *in the world*, a person would become his or her own best self. This was indeed a reformation of old values.[26]

Anglican values also changed and came to embrace the world more positively. John Tillotson (1630–1694), an enormously popular and influential churchman, maintained that "Religion and obedience to the Laws of God, do likewise conduce to the happiness of particular persons, both in respect of this world, and the other." Tillotson claimed that proper religious practices promoted good health, increased estates, and led a person to an "established reputation."[27] Success was in and of itself a proper goal; religion was good for success and success was good for religion. Men and women were still seen as having an eternal life, but God's demands were in no way in conflict with the "good life" on earth. The goal or purpose of human existence seems to have become rather suddenly that of living the good life, now and forever. Seeking eternity was no longer seen as in conflict with earthly delight.

14. The Awakening to the Spirit in Virginia

JOHN TILLOTSON was very popular among the elite in early eighteenth-century Virginia, much as he was in England. (William Byrd II, for example, read his sermons of a Sunday.) This popularity is not surprising, as Tillotson advocated a "sweet reasonableness" and a painless adaptation to the world as it is, which did indeed suit the established church and the elite that supported it.[1] When George Whitefield arrived in the South, he took Tillotson to be the symbol of the weakness of Southern Anglicanism and attacked him ferociously.[2]

Virginia had experienced a period of religious extremism that had affected early life in the colony, but by the opening of the eighteenth century the church controlled very limited aspects of Virginians' lives.[3] The established church was run by the elite (through the institution of the vestry) and for the elite.[4] Church attendance was in great part a social affair, with business conducted prior to the formal proceedings, and "social-lunching" together an important postchurch activity. All these activities for the upper class were ritualized; the lower classes, although welcome to sit in the back or in the balcony of the church, were marginal to its life. Even Devereux Jarratt, who was fairly well off, maintained that he felt he was one of the "simple folk" and, as a result of his self-perception and attitude toward class, would not have thought to talk with a minister. "We were accustomed to look upon, what were called *gentle folks*, as beings of a superior order."[5] Although baptized, Jarratt certainly would not have gone to a minister for spiritual advice or counseling. Many poor whites never went to church, were *not* married by ministers, and were not baptized. And although a growing number of blacks born in Virginia were being baptized, most of the slaves were not baptized either.[6]

Byrd, who was a vestry man at Westover Parish, attended church fairly often: forty-five percent of the time when he first returned to Virginia, but in the last period of his life even he went only twenty-nine percent of the Sundays.[7] In 1724, Rev. Peter Fontaine had reported that in this parish (which was some 30 miles long and had 233 families) he conducted services at three separate churches, in rotation. He estimated that twenty-five communicants took the sacrament of the Lord's Supper at each church three times a year. Nevertheless he claimed two thirds of his parishioners attended services. Although this may have been true at Byrd's well-appointed parish church, with its "good Communion plate, large silver Bason instead of a font, decent Communion Linen, Surplice, a Velvet carpet, cushion, and pulpit cloth," it is unlikely that as high a percentage came to his other churches, which symbolically exhibited their class status by having few of these ritual objects.[8]

There is much evidence that class was a vital factor in attendance at Southern church services, and that in general attendance was far lower than that in the middle colonies or in the Northeast.[9] At Bruton Parish in Williamsburg, Commissary James Blair could honestly state, "On Sunday morning we have full congregations"; but even here it is unlikely that all the 110 families in his ten-mile-square area participated. Alexander Forbes at the Isle of Wight Church reported that "a small proportion" of his 700 parishioners attended, and Thomas Dell revealed that "scarce one third of the parishioners" came to church in Hungar's Parish in Northampton. At Henrico Parish, on the James, there were some 400 families and "sometimes 100 or 200 attend" church. However, no more than twenty took communion at any one time, and the minister acknowledged "the people are not so observant of Devout postures as could be wished."[10] He was clearly understating a very general "case." As the Rev. John Lang lamented, the people were "supinely ignorant in the very principles of Religion, and very debauch't in Morals." Significantly, Lang saw this ignorance reflected in the parishioners' lack of proper preparation for death.

I have already with Terror observed some upon a death bed, others on a sick bed though requiring to have the holy Sacrament of the Supper administer'd; So wofully [sic] ignorant, that upon examination and tryall they could not rehearse the Articles of Our Christian Faith, nor the Lord's prayer and Commandments, nor give any solid account of the nature and use of the holy Sacrament. Others offer to come to the Lord's table on Christmas day, whom I discovered to live in incest as Married persons: these are very trying instances and very deplorable blindness.[11]

Writing in the 1720s, Hugh Jones confirmed these reports of "vice, profaneness and immorality," irreverence, ignorance, and neglect of baptism.

For want of confirmation persons are admitted to the Holy Sacrament with mean and blind Knowledge, and poor notions of the divine mysteries of the Supper of the Lord. . . .
Ministers are often obliged to bury in orchards, and preach funeral sermons in houses, where they also generally marry and christen; and as for weddings there is no regard to the time of the day nor the season of the year.[12]

Holy places as well as holy times were being altered radically.

The world view of the poor masses was not that of Byrd or of the elite, and it was likely to have shown even greater evidence of pre-Reformation beliefs but in a now incoherent mix with new values. Even though they violated them, the masses retained earlier ideas of time and place, medieval conceptions of causality involving the Devil and spirits, and Catholic and early Protestant attitudes toward purpose, demanding denial and "world-shunning." Religious practices waned, and the Catholic Church's sanction and control over these ideas were gone, but the old emphasis on sin and hell remained potent.

After 1750, spiritual revival was widespread in Virginia. It began in response to the needs of the lower class, to their conflicts in values, and to their longings for coherence. Almost invariably, when it came, *it came when and where whites were in extensive and intensive contact with blacks.* Awakenings in Virginia were a shared black and white phenomenon, in which each world view stimulated, permeated, and invigorated the other. For over half a century blacks and whites shared spiritual experiences, and the effect was deep and lasting in both communities. Virtually all eighteenth-century Baptist and Methodist churches were mixed churches, in which blacks sometimes preached to whites and in which whites and blacks witnessed together, shouted together, and shared ecstatic experiences at "dry" and wet christenings, meetings, and burials. A long period of intensive mass interaction ensued.[13]

In the nineteenth century, black and white churches were to go essentially separate ways, but the joint experience of the eighteenth century altered the world views of each. They emerged far more coherent than at the outset of the experience, with their understandings of death and afterlife changed as a result.

The new religious experiences of the Great Awakening of the mid-eighteenth century took place either outside or in very small church buildings, which in themselves were symbolically significant. As Rhys Isaac has so well demonstrated, the churches of the Anglican es-

FIGURE 39. Rehoboth Methodist Church, Monroe County, (West) Virginia, 1785. A log church, much like the slave and poorer white homes, this structure still stands, now preserved as a historic building. Photo reprinted with permission of Hastings House Publishing Co., © 1963, from *The Colonial Houses of Worship in America*, by H. W. Rose.

tablishment made a statement through their shape and form: with their grand size and fine orderly finish, most were reflections of the elites' self-image.[14] Blacks *and poor whites* did not feel welcome there. The small wooden churches of the new sects invited the poor to a new homecoming. Most of the rough new meetinghouses of Baptist and later Methodist congregations were very like the simple cabins of both whites and blacks. They were small, plain wooden structures, often earthfast, built of logs or planks, with few doors or windows. (See Figure 39.) Methodists, in fact, often used windowless barns.[15]

Blacks were at the early meetings in fields, barns, and small wooden churches, and contemporary whites understood their appeal. The Rev. Samuel Davies, commenting in 1757, recognized blacks' spiritual confusion and existential need: "Many of them only seem to desire to be, they know not what: they feel themselves uneasy in their *present* condition, and therefore desire a *change*."[16] From the outset, blacks warmed up many revival proceedings. They "desired a change," recognized spirit and spirit power, and were ready to participate in ceremonies of rebirth and renewal. Ecstasy and spirit travels were an integral part of their tradition, and blacks welcomed this first appeal to their participation.[17]

Their participation deeply affected George Whitefield and the mood of his revival. His journal reported their emotional participation in his meetings; by 1740, he was ready to oppose the strongly held local aversion to conversionary efforts, acquiesced to by most Anglican ministers, and to challenge slaveholders publicly. His challenge was not based on abstract rights but on experience: "As I lately passed through your provinces, I was touched with a fellow-feeling of the miseries of the poor negroes."[18] Negroes attended his meetings, pressed into his room, and touched his person. They began to experience rebirth and to receive the right hand of fellowship. In response, Whitefield specifically challenged whites in Virginia to reconsider their views of blacks and of themselves:

Think you, your children are in any way better by nature than the poor negroes? No! In no wise! Blacks are just as much, and no more, conceived and born in sin, as white men are; and both, if born and bred up here, I am persuaded, are naturally capable of the same improvement. And as for the grown negroes, I am apt to think, that whenever the Gospel is preached with power among them, many will be brought effectually home to God.[19]

Perhaps Whitefield too had thought himself better by nature than the negroes. Now he knew he was not.

Whitefield rejoiced with the black converts and apparently came to new insights and found new strength. He took on the slave masters in this major attack (reprinted by Franklin and many colonial presses), coupling it with his charges against Tillotson, and warned the Southerners, "Although I pray God the slaves may never be permitted to get the upper hand, yet should such a thing be permitted by Providence, all good men must acknowledge the judgement would be just."[20]

Whitefield met with blacks wherever he went. He went *to* them when he visited plantations: "I went, as my usual custom is, among the negroes belonging to the house." Slaves flocked to hear him wherever he preached. He became convinced God would show them a particular providence. "God will highly favour them," he wrote in his journal, "to wipe off their reproach, and shew that He is no respector of persons." He now began to add a special address to "the poor negroes" at the end of every sermon, promising that Christ Jesus "will wash you in his own blood." "Shew them, O Shew them," he cried, "the necessity of being deeply wounded before they can be capable of healing by Jesus Christ." In a radical turnabout, he bid the Christian slaves *"to pray for me."*[21] His was a call for both deep ritual involvement and reciprocal aid. Blacks who had been ready for a new birth responded immediately and emotionally.

Whitefield's success with blacks became an important part of his followers' folklore. His ardent supporter, William Seward, recorded in his journal that a black servant, requested to mimic Whitefield at a club, refused and instead preached, " 'I speak the truth in Christ; I lie not; except you repent you will all be damned!!' This unexpected speech broke up the club, which has not met since." Seward too found "one Negroe brought to Jesus Christ is peculiarly sweet to my soul."[22]

John Marrant, the black missionary whose autobiography later made famous his conversion by Whitefield, was "struck to the ground and lay both speechless and senseless near half an hour" in response to a Whitefield sermon. He felt challenged by the call to "Prepare to meet thy God, O Israel." Whitefield came to him personally and told him, "Jesus Christ has got thee at last."[23]

Whitefield's sermons were simple and repetitive and very powerful. He graphically pictured damnation and hell, with its eternal fires melting every bone, and the inner experience of the Holy Spirit, which he claimed he had felt and now sought for his audience. His audiences, both blacks and whites, were alternately agitated and soothed, and many "melted" in their midst: they had an experience with spirit, often marked by tears, moans, and fainting.[24]

"Black countenances, eagerly attentive to every word they heard, and some of them washed with tears," played an important role in the emotional response that met Samuel Davies's preaching. In the late 1740s this Presbyterian became minister to seven churches in Hanover County and soon became "the primary instrument in the Great Awakening throughout the entire colony." Davies appealed to the blacks, they responded, and he too was apparently affected by the interaction. By 1757, some 300 were attending each Sunday service, and he had baptized 150. Baptism was given only

after they had been Catechumens for some time, and given credible evidence, not only of their acquaintance with the important doctrines of the Christian Religion, but also of a deep sense of these things upon their spirits, and a life of the strictest Morality and Piety. As they are not sufficiently polished to dissemble with a good grace, they express the sensations of their minds so much in the language of simple nature, and with such genuine indications of Sincerity, that it is impossible to suspect the possession of some of them, especially when attested by a regular behaviour in common life.[25]

Davies recorded the direct influences of blacks on his own spiritual life:

March 2, 1756. Sundry of them [the Negroes] have lodged all night in my kitchen; and, sometimes, when I have awaked about two or three a-clock in the morning, a torrent of sacred harmony poured into my chamber, and carried my mind away to Heaven. In this seraphic exercise, some of them spend almost the whole night.[26]

He came to believe that "the *Negroes* above all the human species that ever I knew, have an ear for Music, and a kind of extatic [sic] delight in Psalmody." He spent much time teaching blacks to read the Bible and listening to their songs and prayers. He expected that the "*poor African Slaves* will be made the Lord's free men."[27] (See Figure 40.)

Davies's colleague, John Wright, of Cumberland County, reported that "one hundred and thirty persons got under very hopeful religious impressions, among whom were about twenty Ethiopians who spoke to me about their souls concerns." Wright was "transported" by the "exercises [sic] of the most savage boy of them."[28]

Classes to teach slaves to read the Bible became acceptable in Hanover in the 1750s. Rev. John Todd, who had some 600 slaves in his three Hanover County churches, claimed that by 1760, "hundreds of *Negroes* beside *white* people, can read and spell, who a few years since did not Know one letter."

The poor Slaves are now commonly engaged in learning to read; some of them can read the Bible, others can only spell; and some are just learning their letters. —But there is a general alteration among them for the better. The sacred hours of the Sabbath, that used to be spent in frolicking, dancing, and other profane courses, are now employed in attending upon public ordinances, in learning to read at home, or in praying together, and singing the praises of GOD and the Lamb.[29]

With "joy," Todd noted that at the communal table "these poor *Africans*" were "not like frozen formalists," and they did not rise "with dry eyes."[30]

The diary of James Gordon, an Irish Presbyterian who had settled on

FIGURE 40. Slaves with books. This picture, from the 1850s, was possibly taken after a prayer meeting. Note the presence of white children. Photo courtesy of the New York Historical Society.

a substantial plantation in Lancaster County in 1738, and was a member of one of John Todd's congregations, confirms that in 1759, "religion seems to increase among us." He was referring to a small new congregation that had just grown to fifty-three members. Blacks were already members, and many more were to join. Gordon himself played a role in this excitement and in its interracial aspects, and on at least one occasion he "read a sermon to the negroes." Blacks here sometimes met separately, as they had in Davies's and Todd's other congregations, but they were often together with whites. When in late September of 1759 there was a prolonged meeting (probably at Harvest Home time), Gordon simply recorded, "Our negroes have attended Sermons these four days." In May of 1760, Gordon attended "a pretty large company of the common people and negroes, but very few gentlemen. The gentlemen that even incline to come are afraid of being laughed at."[31]

This Presbyterian revival was in the Northern Neck, a section in which the Anglican Church was in a most "lamentable state of decline."[32] The lower classes there, blacks and whites, were "ripe" for harvesting together. Although Davies addressed an appeal to slaveowners to educate "all of their family members," including slaves, he did not have to appeal to his congregants, mostly "common people," to accept blacks in their midst. They were already doing so.

Gordon estimated that from seventy to eighty blacks attended the 1760 Christmas service, and when Whitefield came through Virginia in 1762, so many blacks and whites came, there was not nearly enough room for all to sit in the chamber. "September 4, 1762. Mr. Whitefield preached to a crowded house. Mr. Whitefield was obliged to make the negroes go out to make room for the white people. Several, white and black, could not get room."[33] Although these Presbyterians *were* accepting blacks and were sharing experiences with them, there was no question about who came first. They sat together inside until there was no more room, and then the blacks had to rise to make room for whites, although they joined other whites standing at the windows.

Gordon's diary suggests the very common involvement he had with his slaves. He too cared for them, was cared for by them, and eventually became disillusioned with their work patterns. On June 2, 1760, he lamented, "Went about the plantation, found everything amiss almost; the things of this life much disquiet me, my people are so careless." Whether they were careless or not, Gordon did not come to hate his black family, as Landon Carter did, and the spiritual life of his people continued to interest him. He kept track of their market value as slaves, but he also shared in their religious experiences. On February 24, 1762, he noted, "Frank, a daughter of Betsy and old Jack, died. A few hours before, she told her mother she was dying and hoped to see her in heaven." James Gordon no doubt believed that he too would meet them both there.[34]

Davies had drawn the picture of their joint salvation very graphically:

—And O! When all these warriors meet at length from every corner of the earth, and, as it were, pass in review before their General in the fields of heaven, with their robes washed in his blood, with palms of victory in their hands and crowns of glory on their heads, all dressed in uniform with garments of salvation, what a glorious army will they make! and how will they cause heaven to ring with shouts of joy and triumph![35]

Gordon shared his spiritual life with poor whites and with slaves. He had apparently taken Davies's admonition to slaveholders very much to heart.

What are you! What being of mighty importance are you! Is not another as dear to himself as you are to yourself! Are not his rights as sacred and inviolable as yours! How come you to be entitled to an exemption from the common laws of human nature! Be it known to you, you are as firmly bound by them as any of our species.[36]

While Whitefield's enthusiasm had begun a revival in 1740, and Davies's Presbyterian awakening affected a limited number in the Northern Neck in the 1750s, it was the Separate Baptists under the leadership of Shubal Stearns who sparked an extraordinary awakening that affected the masses over a much longer period. Stearns, a New Englander who had been deeply influenced by Whitefield but had become a Baptist, journeyed South to do "the Lord's work," living at Opequon Creek and Cacapon, in Berkeley and Hampshire Counties, (West) Virginia, from the summer of 1754 until the summer of 1755. In the fall of 1755, he established himself at Sandy Creek, North Carolina, and from there influenced, and was influenced by, the developments in Virginia. Stearns had come from Connecticut with a small band of about fifteen devoted followers. In Virginia and South Carolina he soon had hundreds and then thousands of active believers, many missionaries in the field. Clearly the "chemistry" of the interaction had been important. He found a large black and white population very receptive to his message and his medium.[37]

Stearns called for personal and communal experience, commitment, and ritual. He was concerned with each and every soul, demanded dedication, and promised personal salvation as well as a rich communal life. He offered a coherent world view with rich personal and communal rewards. His demands were high, encompassing virtually all of an individual's life, but his promises were exciting, both in their means and in their ends.[38]

Stearns proposed replacing the aristocratically run institution of the "other," the Anglican Church, with a consesus community of equals. A Baptist church is its members. No outside body can dictate any aspect of policy or belief. A church calls a person to preach and makes that person a "preacher" by virtue of that call, not by education or outside authority. All the poor white and black members would be brothers and sisters in Christ in this consensus-run community of equals. Each individual should have an equal voice, as together they would establish discipline and judge one another. The church was to be made up of the regenerate: those whom God had saved and who had experienced God's "precious dealing with their souls" in ways they could recount to others. This experience of being "born again" was central and was a sign of the spiritual equality of the highest and lowest. A slave could certainly experience saving grace, even when his owner had not. And all those who were saved could be assured of life everlasting: God in heaven awaited the lambs, all the same and all equal.[39]

Stearns's fellowship replaced the formal baptism of infants with the highly emotional testimony and often ecstatic immersion of those old enough to recognize and recount their experience with spirit. They replaced the learning of the catechism with the yearning for ecstatic spiritual experience, and the celebration of the Lord's Supper at Christmas, Easter, and Whitsunday with very frequent "love feasts" when the bread and wine were brought to the people. As Donald Mathews has noted, the Separate Baptists emphasized physical contact. Babies were dry christened; adults were held while they went under water and often while they "shouted" for joy. After baptism there was the "laying on of hands," when the preacher prayed for the candidate, and the extending of "the right hand of fellowship" to the new brother or sister. The brethren washed each other's feet, anointed the ill with "holy oil," and gave each other the "kiss of charity." At all services they sang vigorously and most often found that some of their number experienced spiritual "travels" or ecstasy that had them shouting and moving.[40]

Stearns and his small congregation formally introduced this polity to Virginia. The almost immediate response and excitement it generated, and the long-term growth that ensued, suggest that the Virginians wanted and needed an all-encompassing emotional and spiritual experience. They needed to take control of their own lives, to impose limits and taboos, and to share both discipline and ecstatic experience with their neighbors, thereby creating a new community.

Blacks and whites were together in virtually every new congregation in Virginia. In this, the Baptist phase, and later in the 1770s and 1780s when the Methodists instituted many of the same or similar practices, racially mixed groups responded, and no participant seems to have questioned seriously the propriety of these "promiscuous" gatherings. White and black, male and female, new converts created new churches.[41]

The Baptist excitement began as a mixed black–white phenomenon, and whites who had lifetimes of intimate association with blacks did not regard it as strange that this new religious experience was a shared one. Blacks were singing and shouting and "having a Christ" right along with whites. In fact, from the outset, it was recognized that their emotional response and spiritual sensitivity helped whites to "come through."

Baptist churches really were independent and were somewhat different from each other in practice. The records that have come down to us seem to reflect such differences in relation to black–white interaction. Some forty Virginia Baptist Church record books are extant from the eighteenth century.[42] Virtually all the records indicate that both blacks and whites were members, in widely varying proportions, such as the 150 blacks and 50 whites in the Burruss or Carmel Church in Caroline County in 1800, or the reverse relationship of 71 blacks and 126 whites in the Buck Marsh or Berryville Church in Clarke County in 1772–1788. There were only 26 white men in this second congregation, whereas there were 40 black men.[43] Generally, black men represented a much larger percentage of the churched blacks than white men did of the churched whites.

Although many blacks began to hold informal all-black meetings on their plantations, a few of the early formal churches were all black as well, such as the Williamsburg "African" Church of Gowan Pamphlet, 1776, and the church on William Byrd III's plantation in Lunenburg County, begun in the late 1750s, in the wake of a revival conducted by whites William Murphey and Philip Mulkey, who organized the mixed Dan River Church. There was an independent "Negro Baptist Church" in King and Queen County by 1782, and in 1788 the Davenport congregation in Petersburg was "mostly people of color" but did have "a few white members." By 1803 it had become the Church of the Lord Jesus Christ (later Gillfield Church), and there were no white congregants.[44] Blacks, on the other hand, were in virtually all eighteenth-century Baptist churches, and in most they were usually a very large block.

Churches followed very different patterns of registering their black members: Some never noted color, some occasionally did, and others had separate listings of slaves from the outset.[45] The Water Lick Baptist Church in Shenandoah County was founded in 1787 by a group of Baptists that left a church at South River. They were already experienced in the faith. Seven men and nine women signed the original covenant; the sixth man was Negro Joseph and the seventh Negro Daniel, and the ninth woman was Negro Jeanny. Clearly, as at Gordon's Presbyterian meeting, they were the last among equals, but they were definitely recognized in this egalitarian church that gave women the vote in 1787. Blacks appear regularly in the church records. There we learn that Brother Daniel was a slave "intrusted with the management of his quarter upon the river" and that he was suspected of theft because he sold some meat. Daniel's own spiritual growth as a result of this incident seems apparent from the record. At first he denied the fact that he sold the meat, but then, in "owning" his own sin (of lying) he found new strength:

Bro. Thos. Buck entered a complaint against Br. Daniel (negro) for uttering a falsity about selling some bacon. Br. Daniel (a slave to Mr. Peter Catlett and intrusted with the management of his quarter upon the river) sold a few pounds of bacon and being questioned therefor by some of the members denied it. But in a short time returned to the same person owned the fact and the crime of uttering a falsity in denying it, with such evident marks of repentance as gave full satisfaction to those members withal informing them that what he sold was his own property given him by his master for his own private use. That he sold it in pity to the buyer. That his denial was owing to his fear his master might be displeased with him as he had given him meat to use and not to sell.[46]

As was usual, the church appointed a committee to investigate, and in this case they went to Daniel's owner, Peter Catlett, who was not a member of their church. They reported back that Catlett thought Daniel had "done nothing but what he thought just." Daniel was *not* cowed or broken by this incident. On the contrary he immediately "appointed meetings for the public exhortation of negroes," an act that met with a mixed reaction. Daniel was clearly an "actor" in this scene. A slave, he voluntarily chose to contribute to the church fund, although only heads of households were expected to do so. His opinions were also heard, and although we do not have the details, later, when he showed "partiality in the church," it was "a cause for distress" and dissension, and the community tried to work up a consensus.[47]

Blacks and whites in one congregation had to be at peace with one another, or "in fellowship." Disagreements had to be aired, and forgiveness extended, by all parties. Daniel's is not a unique case. Blacks appear in these church records as individuals, and their interaction with whites can be documented. Again, there is no doubt but that black opinions were being heard and counted in many matters, not only in defense of charges made against them.

Blacks were part of the covenanting "inner group" that formed many of the churches, signing the covenants with their white brothers and sisters. Of the 74 original members at the Dan River Church, 11 were black. Of the 158 who were in the Hartwood Church at its origin in 1771, 24 were black. Lower Banister, organized in July of 1798, then had 31 whites and 11 blacks. The church that Robert Carter and Hannah Ludwell Lee Corbin joined, the Morattico Church, had more blacks in it than whites, including 29 of Carter's own slaves. In the church they were his equals, able to bring criticism of their master as the proper "business" of the church.[48]

Slaves *did* bring criticism of whites to communal sessions. It was not simply an abstract right, although it is most likely that they were careful and concerned in their use of this privilege. The slaveowner could simply leave the church and continue or intensify his behavior. (He could not join another Baptist church without a letter of dismissal showing that he was not under censure.) It should be emphasized that in William Warren Sweet's term, Baptist and later Methodist churches were "courts" for their members. All issues of behavior and misbehavior were to be brought before them. They dealt with issues between whites and whites, blacks and blacks, and *whites and blacks*. They concerned themselves with relations between wives and husbands (condemning wife beating) and parents and children (demanding that parents instruct children and servants in proper behavior), and they condemned "immoral acts" in everyone.[49]

In Virginia, in the last third of the eighteenth century, Baptists found a large range of activities immoral, strictly delimiting proper behavior. It was immoral to play the violin or banjo or sing worldly songs or to dance, to dress "gaudily," to go to horse races, to bet, to drink to excess, to swear, to talk spitefully, or to disturb the consensus in a church family. In 1785, "Joseph Dinry was deeply cencured [*sic*] for whipping his wife." The Broad Run Church found his behavior

An action in or esteem, not a little scandalous For a husband to beat his wife, we judge to be a practice contrary both to Scripture & Reason; to the law & the Gospel. And as such, not to be once named among Christians. Not to be tolerated in the Church of Christ, on any pretense whatever.[50]

In 1780, the Upper King and Queen County Church took

into consideration the many superfluous forms and modes of Dressing, and condemned the Following, viz. Cock't hatts, curl'd and powdered hair, also tied hair by manr [sic] likewise two stocks the one white and the other Black at the same time. Gold to be worn by none—High Crown'd Caps—Rolls—Necklaces, Ruffles, Stays & Stomagers.[51]

Upper King and Queen excommunicated Davise's Jack (a slave) and

agreed that any member who takes the liberty to go to a horse race or any other such unnecessary, unprofitable and sinful Assemblies or Gatherings of People are Directed to come to the next succeeding church meeting and there to be answerable to the church for such conduct.[52]

Excommunication was the usual punishment for violation of clear-cut taboos. Sinners could return, exhibit contrition, and ask for reinstatement, but until then they could not participate in the life of the church or the community, nor could they be buried by the church or expect God to welcome them to heaven.

Blacks and whites were widely excluded for these same faults. White Henry Watkins was excommunicated "for playing the violin and associating in the company of wicked men," and "Negro Jedia" for "stealing from a brother." Blacks as well as whites used these church forums to settle disputes among themselves. In 1799, George and Ben brought a dispute to the Buck Marsh meeting over how much money had changed hands between them (to buy potatoes) and who had called whom a liar. There was "a black sister wishing the advice of the Church in a certain [matter] on her mind [about] Marrying a man who has formally had a wife." One Brother Ned brought charges "against Sister Sarah (servant to Wm. Larue) that Sarah had taken some Meat from her Master which he conceiv'd was not honestly come by." The church investigated and decided the charges were due to the animosity Ned held against Sarah and "that it proceeded from other matters which happen'd Between them some time before."[53]

Whites brought very much the same range of issues for discussion, although the blacks' concern with their own monogamy (and the whites' concern with black monogamy) was a major issue.

Sexual behavior played an important role in the new morality of these church families. Fornication and adultery were anathema, and the church set out to counter the laxity of social norms in Virginia, in which black–white interaction had played a role. Blacks were adjured to marry other blacks, to regard their marriages as permanent, and to refrain from sex prior to marriage, outside of marriage, and/or with whites. Whites were given the same admonitions and adjured to refrain from sex with blacks. Their power and position as owners and overseers was recognized as a very dangerous one.

In 1799, "Theo Coleman's Guice [was] Excommunicated for keeping two wives." The next year Guice was accepted back "by repentance," which no doubt included his putting aside one wife. Mulatto Charles, on the other hand, was excommunicated for "putting away" his one wife.[54] Divorce was not allowed for whites or blacks (except if one partner was guilty of adultery), nor was a white (slaveowner) allowed to "separate" (a euphemism for selling) a slave from his marriage partner. In Upper King and Queen Church they made this plain: "Query: Is it agreeable to scripture for any member to part man & wife? Answer: No. And any member who Shall be guilty of such crimes shall be dealt with by the church for such crimes [sic] misconduct."[55] The Buck Marsh Church reached a similar conclusion in 1791, holding both slaves and slaveowners accountable: They then embarked on a serious evaluation of their black members' marital lives and charged many blacks with "sinfull parting from their spouces" with both whites and blacks bringing charges.[56]

Whites were also widely censured for sexual misconduct. In 1795, Occoquan Church excluded two white women, one for being "previously married" and the other for "a disorderly way of life." Both blacks and whites were commonly charged with "adultery," but only black "Dunn's Peggy [was] excommunicated for keeping a White man as husband unlawfully."[57]

Although "disobedience and Aggrevation" to a master were recognized as cause to excommunicate Negro Nemney, and "Negro Lemon was excommunicated for lying and disobedience to his master," charges involving blacks and whites usually revolved around thefts by the black slaves, violence of the white slaveowners, or sexual misbehavior of both races.[58]

Thefts, as we have seen, were simple cases. Investigative committees were established, often including blacks, and their findings were discussed by the whole church. Consensus was sought, and there was no question but that when a slave "took" something from a master, it was theft. Negro Isaac was "reported" to have taken a "horse, bridle and saddle" belonging to one James Mason. Isaac had already been "tryed for the offense" by his owner and by the Justices of the Peace for Northumberland County. Nevertheless his church, Morattico, concluded that it would investigate the charge, and if they thought it were "true," he would be excommunicated.[59]

Violence to slaves involved questions of both fact and theory. The church had to establish not only what the master had done but what he had a right to do. In June of 1772, the Meherrin Church discussed the question, "Is it Lawful to punish our servants by burning them & in any case whatsoever?" They resolved the issue with a unanimous "No" and immediately moved to suspend Brother Charles Cook "for burning one of his Negroes." In July, Cook, who owned three slaves and at least 150 acres of land, came to a small business meeting to "acknowledge his sin in unlawfully burning one of his Negroes." He was requested to appear before the whole congregation, blacks and whites together, "to give the Church satisfaction." This incident appears to have been traumatic for Charles Cook. There is no evidence of his having had any call to preach prior to his punishment, but by September of 1772, Cook was preaching. Several of his own slaves joined the church, perhaps due to his conversionary efforts. By June of 1775, the church called this former slave burner "Our beloved Charles Cook," as he was "unanimously chosen as a Teaching Elder" for the Sandy Creek branch, a congregation with a very large black membership. In 1777, Cook was given a commission to "Itinerate" or preach around the countryside where, once again, blacks were an important part of his audience. Cook's interaction with blacks and the church had apparently changed his values and his life: From a slaveburner he had become virtually a missionary to the blacks.[60]

Cook's church, Meherrin Church, also moved further in its concern with black welfare. In May of 1773, they considered

Whether it is lawful for a Bro. or Sister to whip or beat one of their servants or children, members of the Church, before the method that Christ has prefered [sic] & laid down in the 18th Mathew, Solved No. [By a] Majority.

194

The eighteenth verse in Matthew calls for a private verbal confrontation with a wrongdoer and then, if necessary, criticism by a group. The final punishment suggested is shunning:

Moreover if thy brother shall trespass against thee, go and tell him his fault between thee and him alone: if he shall hear thee, thou hast gained thy brother. But if he will not hear thee, then take thee with one or two more, that in the mouth of two or three witnesses every word may be established. And if he shall neglect to hear the church, let him be unto thee as a heathen man and a publican.

Slaveowners did bring charges against their slaves in church, whereas blacks made more sparing use of this forum. Charges against whites could backfire, but they could also play a role even if proved false. "Negro Abigel, belonging to Brother Hunton," was excommunicated "for slandering & false accusing her Master to other Brethern [*sic*] and then denying it before the Church."[61]

In 1772, Sister Rebekah Johnson of the Meherrin Church was accused "by two of the Black Brethren of the sin of anger and unchristian language, also [of] offering something like parting of a black Bro. & Sister (Man and Wife)." She "own'd . . . part of their allegations" and "seem'd penitent," but the blacks would not accept this. Their charges were apparently far more extensive than what she "own'd." The church appointed a committee of four whites *and two blacks* (Brothers Dick and Sam) to interview all those concerned. The committee succeeded in establishing peace, and although no details were recorded, Sister Rebekah Johnson and Sister Esther (her servant) gave each other the right hand of fellowship. Although we cannot know what happened to Estis, the black husband involved, it appears most likely he was sold away, and that Esther had to make her peace with this, perhaps recognizing that Joseph Johnson, husband and master (and not a church member), was responsible.[62]

Brother Sherwood Walton, an active member of the Meherrin Church in the 1770s, was accused of sin by one of his slaves who was not a member of the church. There ensued a fascinating story, recorded in great detail by the church clerk, that indicates above all else how ready the white brethren were to believe that their brother in good standing (who served on disciplinary committees) could himself be guilty of a sexual sin, as well as to what lengths a slave would go to besmirch a master's "good name."

September 1775. Bro. Sherwood Walton accused by some of the Brethren for being guilty of, or at least offering the Act of uncleaness to a Mulatto Girl of his own—The circumstances are as follows. 1st the Girl proved with Child. She often hinted to his Daughters that her Master was the Father of it (if she was with child). Upon that he took to correct her for it, she found him in it, and declared she believed he was the father of it, if any one was; Tho she knew not that any person had carnal knowledge of her but supposed it might be done while she was asleep but that she knew of his coming & offering such things at times to her. This she affirmed, and would not relinquish at the expense of being well drubbed for it several times, this was prov'd to us. At the time of her extremity in childbearing she was charged by the Midwives then to own the truth & clear her Master, if clear, and as her extremity was more than common they told her it might be a judgement of God upon her, and that she might die; but all could not prevail upon her—she confidently affirmed what she had said she then said, but behold when the child was born, it proved to be a remarkable black child, a Negro without any doubt proved by the Midwives & other people who saw the child which gave satisfaction to all the church but 4 . . . [listed by name]. Some of the Brethren neighbours declared her to be of a remarkable wicked Temper & disposition, & did believe she accused him in order to revenge (inso) [?] that it was proved he was always very severe to her & upon closely questioning him, Bro. Walton, he denied the fact, 2 of the Brethren relinquish'd their scruples . . . the other 2 yet [held out].[63]

The last two individuals who objected to reinstating Walton were "worked on" to bring the community back into harmony, and finally, some time after the black baby was born, all those attending church offered Walton the right hand of fellowship. (One sister, Old Sister Rivers, absolutely refused and absented herself from meetings.)

Walton's slave woman had used the church and church rules to put Walton through a great deal of distress. His behavior had been investigated, his violence to his slaves exposed, and his morals seriously questioned. His daughters had heard the charges as had his neighbors and, in fact, the whole community. Although he was exonerated of "fathering" her child, he certainly emerged with a different public image from what he had before.

Charges against other slaveowners were upheld by Baptist churches: Nero, a slave, charged his owner, John Lawrence, with "misconduct," and the South Quay Church expelled Lawrence. James

Johnson was excommunicated by the Black Creek Church as were a Brother Tines and his wife for "using Barbarity toward their Slaves."[64] If the white brother or sister remained strong in the faith and wanted to return, as Lawrence and Cook did, the church could serve as a moral guardian of a black's human rights. But in other cases, as in those of Johnson and Tines, there is no record of white contrition, and it is certainly possible that the punished slaves were punished even more barbarously after these incidents. Other whites in the churches, however, were affected by the bravery and courage of these blacks and were brought to a new consciousness of the realities of slavery.

Slavery per se began to be an issue in the Baptist churches. Again, it was not ideology but the reality of contact and shared spiritual lives that brought whites to this changed perception. Now, too, they had a view of themselves as moral agents, living in a godly way, and criticizing their own behavior. Church after church asked, "Is it a Rituous [sic] thing for a Christian to hold or cause any of the human race to be held in slavery?" After serious consideration they answered, "Unrighteous!!" It is important to emphasize that inasmuch as consensus had been worked up, this was the church as a whole speaking. These were not leadership decisions or a bowing to directives from above.[65]

As whites and blacks shared church life, more whites came to see the institution of slavery as evil. John Poindexter, a successful slave-owner who originally was enraged by his wife's 1788 conversion to the Baptists, was himself converted and rebaptized in 1790. He began to preach in 1791, and soon became very popular, establishing churches and converting hundreds. He himself was also "converted" in regard to slavery. In 1797, he called for prayers for

the Poor Slaves, who are groaning under grevious oppression in this part of the Lord's Vineyard; I have been an advocate for Slavery, but thanks be to God, My Eyes have been Opened to see the impropriety of it, and I long for the Happy times to Come, when the Church of Christ shall loose the Bands of Wickedness, undo the Heavy burdens, and let the oppressed go free, that her light may Spring forth in the Morning—and her Righteousness go before her—[66]

Many other Baptists were moved to recognize the unrighteousness of slavery.[67] David Barrow, born in 1753 to a farm family in Brunswick County, was "reborn" in 1770. He preached successfully at Mill Swamp Church, Isle of Wight, 1774; fought in the Revolution; and returned to Virginia to preach to growing numbers. In 1784, he freed his slaves, feeling "The Spirit of the Lord is upon me . . . to preach deliverance [emancipation] to the captives."[68]

Robert Carter, one of the few of the top elite to join the Baptists in this period (1777), had become a Swedenborgian by the time he began to free his slaves in 1791, but Leland and other Baptists had influenced him deeply. He too had come to see slaveowning as a sin.[69] Most white Baptists, however, continued to live with slaves, as owners, managers, or neighbors, and most black Baptists continued to be slaves.

New Baptist John Self, Landon Carter's overseer at his Rings Neck plantation, stayed at his job so that he might do God's work, as Carter recorded:

News just came John Self at Rings Neck turned a Baptist, and only waits to convert my people. He had two brethren Preachers and two other with him; and says he cannot serve God and Mammon, has just been made a Christian by dipping, and would not continue in my business but to convert my people.[70]

Although Self and Poindexter continued to live with slaves and slavery, out of moral responsibility, their shared new faith probably helped some new black Baptists to find the inner strength to risk running away. Owners certainly seemed to think this was so. It was noted that Runaway Hannah "pretends much to the religion the Negroes of late have practiced," and George Noble felt constrained to describe his former slave, Jupiter, "alias Gibb," as having scars on his back from a recent whipping at Sussex courthouse, "having been tried there for stirring up the Negroes to an insurrection, being a great Newlight preacher." In other words, it was his preaching of the word that stirred rebellion both in him and in his audience.[71]

In 1789, the sheriff of King William County complained to the governor that blacks and whites were meeting together, often until two or three in the morning, and that the whites had prevented the patrollers from carrying out their duty by throwing them out of the window of the meeting house. That they were willing to defy the law indicates how important it was to those whites to have blacks at their meetings.[72]

Baptist preacher John Williams (1747–1795), who owned twenty-two slaves, kept a journal of his journey to churches, outdoor meetings, and "revivals" held in the summer of 1771, when hundreds generally came; it was reported that from four to five thousand had assembled for the largest meeting. Christians were "shouting," there was "a good deal of exercise among the people," and Williams found

198

himself with "some liberty and a feeling sense of souls." It is particularly interesting that he did not fear the Devil but spirits.

There were "six preaching gifts among us," he recounts.

I immediately seem'd to have the greatest impression I have ever had, though did not know from what spirit, therefore, waited some time for some of the rest. All seem'd to be backward which made me conclude mine was from God, but He only Knows whether it was. I was so constrained I could not forbear. I got up & sung & preached to the people from Revelations, 21st chap. & 7th & 8th verses.[73]

These chapters in the Bible deal with salvation and with hellfire in graphic terms; they may have seemed particularly addressed to both the Afro-American and the unchurched white Virginian, given their references to "sorcerers and idolators."

That same summer William Lee adjured his overseer to try to keep his slaves from having contact with the "New Light Preachers" who "have put most of my ~~people~~ [sic] Negroes crazy with their new Light and their new Jerusalem."[74] But Lee, and other owners frightened by the new developments, did not succeed in stopping blacks from attending the mass meetings.

At these meetings blacks shared spiritual experiences with whites. Here, as at baptisms and at funerals, blacks had ecstatic vision experiences and recounted "God's precious dealing with their souls." The conversion experience was seen as an experience with death and ecstasy—the hellfire and balm that Whitefield, Williams, and Davies had brought news of. Blacks and whites both knew that to come to Christ was to *die* to the old life, as the old self, and to be reborn in a new spiritual growth. The baptism experience was graphically one of death, of going under the waters, where only the spirit can find nourishment, and rebirth in ecstasy. Whites and blacks were regularly baptized together and "came through" shouting and singing at the same time.[75]

Blacks began recounting their experiences by placing their spiritual journeys in a matrix of African time. One former slave reported, "One day while in the field plowing I heard a voice." Another heard God when "I was about grown." "When the voice first spoke to me I was in the cotton patch." "After I got married," God struck. This voice had to be "checked out" or validated, and it was a sign of just how important white time was becoming that God occasionally brought the magical knowledge of whites' reckoning of age as the gift-proof of true prophecy. A little girl was told "O ye generation of vipers, who had warned you to flee from the wrath to come? My little one, you are now eight years old. Go and ask the Lord to have mercy on your dying soul." The mother accepted the vision as a true one because it gave her daughter white calendar-wisdom.[76]

Blacks regarded this God as a "time God," but this meant a God who came in his own time and who let everyone know that he could not be hurried. He came in visions at his own will and taught patience. "I saw, as it were, a ladder. It was more like a pole with rungs on it let down from heaven, and it reached from heaven to earth." Man had to climb this ladder, slowly.

These black visions converted white Christian concern with the end of days into visions of time past and of forefathers. In vision travels blacks traveled to heaven and saw God as well as their mothers and fathers and other dead relations. The reality of forefathers' power, believed in by Africans, was reinforced by these "Christian" vision travels. And in the visions, time past was seen as part of the present and of the future.

> I wonder where's my dear mother
> She's been gone so long
> I think I hear her shouting
> Around the Throne of God.

Heaven was home and blacks sang: "I'm going there to see my mother'n, fathr'n," and family. And they "visited" them there from time to time in ecstatic trances.[77]

In these visions blacks also saw new fictive kin: Jacob, Moses, Gabriel, and Jesus were met with and talked to. They became common ancestors, new generations in the genealogical tables, regarded as common to whites and blacks alike. In accepting Christianity, Jacob, Moses, Daniel, Gabriel, and Jesus became spiritual forefathers, as they did in Africa. "When Tiv encountered Europeans and heard the creation story, they immediately accepted 'Adam and Ife' as part of their cosmic doctrine."[78]

For Africans, the "living are reflections of the dead and vice versa." Similarly, American black Christians compared themselves to Adam in his marital troubles with Eve, and to Jonah, who tried to evade responsibility and God's call. They expected to "wrassle" the Lord like Jacob and to find a Moses to lead them from slavery. When black mourners lay moaning on the floor, waiting for the spirit to come to them, the Christians around them sang:

Rassal Jacob, rassal as you did in the days of old
Gonna rassal all night till broad day light
And ask God to bless my soul.[79]

In these vision tales blacks recounted that when they were converted they had to die. God struck them dead:

On Thursday Morning, the sun was shining bright, I was chopping corn in the garden, when a voice "hollered" and said, "Oh, Nancy, you got to die and can't live." I started to run because it scared me but I got weak and felt myself dying from my feet to my head. . . . I cried, "I am dying; I am dying; I am dying. Lord, have mercy on my soul." As quick as a flash I felt a change.[80]

After seeing hell, heaven, and God, Nancy Williams, a slave in Virginia, recounted that she "started to shouting in the spirit and haven't stopped yet. I died the sinner death and ain't got to die no more. I am fixed up for the building." Black after black was called by name and then "was killed dead to sin and made alive again in Jesus Christ." The dying and death were experienced as very real. When God struck Nancy Williams, she claimed her owner was ready to have her buried. She was "put on de bench whar dey laid out de daid."[81] The ensuing trip down to the fires of hell and up to the white glory of heaven—where a true home, a "building," awaited and where eternal life would really be lived—was also very real. Slaves believed they had truly been to these places. They had seen and felt the fires of hell, and their inner essence, part of their being or one of their souls, had been taken on a perilous journey, through trials, up to heaven. The "little me" that was in the "big me," the little Mary in the big Mary, had been taken by a spirit guide to the blazing white of God's throne. There,

I was told that I was one of the elected children and that I would live as long as God lives. I rejoice every day of my life for I know that I have another home—a house not made with human hands. A building is waiting for me way back in eternal glory and I have no need to fear.[82]

Black vision experiences repeated these themes over and over. God knew the sinner by name—the name used in baptism and on the church books. Miles, Patience, Peter, James, Esther, Quamina, Clocy, Anika, Moses, Fanny, Aggy, Bristol, they are all "called by name." God knows their inner essence and they have an eternal name that symbolizes it. No slaveowner could take away or change this name.

201

These people knew that their souls came from God and would return to God, much as Africans believed that their souls were from spirit and would return to spirit. These black Baptists believed that God *killed them dead.* Encounters with God were not mild or gentle affairs. God struck them down, gave them harsh spiritual experiences, and only then brought them to a rebirth.

Consider the parallels of the slave experiences with this description of the experience of an Azande woman-diviner in Africa as recorded by E. E. Evans-Pritchard:

Nambua said that, "she died and . . . [her co-villagers] dug a grave for her and everyone wailed. Her soul went forth and appeared at the place of ghosts. She was just looking about when all her [deceased] relatives collected and made a circle around her. It was her mother who said to her, 'What have you come here for? Get up and go whence you came. Go away quickly.' She departed from amongst these people and her eyes at once opened. Everyone ceased wailing and she began immediately to wake from death and recovered completely."[83]

Similarly at the initiation of a medium along the Lulua, BaSonge, or BaLuba of Zaire, the initiate is also "believed to have been dead, to have traveled to the land of the Souls, and to have then returned to life."[84]

In Africa most mediums had died and been reborn during their initiations. In addition, most young people had also undergone initiations into "manhood" and "womanhood," and these near-universal ceremonies also involved a symbolic rebirth. Africans had wide experience both with symbolic death and rebirth as well as with ecstatic joy. A high percentage of African ethnic groups followed ritual that aroused religious ecstasy, although only special mediums served the gods directly.[85]

Afro-American Christianity gave every individual the opportunity to die and be reborn. It amalgamated African understandings of death and spirit travel to the world of forefathers, with Christian visions of God and heaven. Every Christian could find a "home" with God and with kin. Jacob would be there, and Moses, and Jesus, and grandmothers, grandfathers, wives, husbands, and children. A building was waiting, a Big House for all the saved.

The new Christianity changed the African linkage of close kin and unique afterworld, which had excluded the stranger and the slave from the afterlife of an ethnic group, to a linkage of all Christians to one Heaven. In Africa, even a married couple might expect to be separated after death. The Igbo, for example, sent a wife's body, and presumably her soul, to stay with her father's clan.[86] Now all God's children could expect to be in the Christian heaven; certainly status as a slave was not a barrier. On the contrary, "the last would be first." The cause of death and the age of the deceased would not keep an individual out. A slave, beaten to death, could expect to view his master in hell while he was in heaven. Black understandings of immortal places as well as time, while maintaining important continuities with African values, had altered significantly.

Whites too changed their values and understandings. They became more "open" to ecstasy and spiritual life, ready and willing to have "experience," and to share their experience with others. They opened themselves to communal criticism, something Africans may have had more experience with, among co-wives, secret society members, and at the chief's court. And they came to accept death as the gateway to the continuation of the vision world they had already experienced, where their families awaited them, rather than as a terrifying unknown.

15. The Later Fruits of the Great Awakening

I N THE WAKE of the Baptist revivals a wave of excitement went through the Virginia Anglican Church and flowed into its "daughter," the Methodist movement. In 1775 and 1776, Robert Williams, George Shadford, Thomas Rankin, and Devereux Jarratt led extremely emotional religious meetings, and excitement spread into Amelia, Dinwiddie, Brunswick, Sussex, Prince George, Lunenburg, and Mecklenburg counties.[1]

These leaders were in the old church, but their methods were very new and much like those of the Baptists. They succeeded in appealing to the "common people" with many blacks among them. Robert Williams is reported to have stood on the Norfolk courthouse steps, sung a hymn, knelt in prayer, and preached to the "disorderly crowed" that was always there on court days.[2] As they called meetings, large numbers began to come to hear them, and they stayed to participate, singing, praying, and taking the sacrament. Jarratt wrote of a meeting that lasted "all night and till two hours after sunrise."[3] Rankin and Jarratt traveled together, and Rankin's journal records that at times hundreds of blacks attended their meetings. It is no wonder that here too participants, such as Henry Lee, recorded extraordinary emotions.

I have been at meetings where the whole congregation would be bathed in tears; and sometimes their cries would be so loud that the preacher's voice could not be heard. Some would be seized with a trembling, and in a few moments drop on the floor as if they were dead; while others were embracing each other with streaming eyes, and all were lost in wonder, love, and praise.[4]

Blacks and whites together were dying and being reborn in very African-style celebrations. "It is common with us," wrote a Sussex County preacher in 1776, "for men and women to fall down as dead under an exhortation."[5]

At one such meeting, Rankin himself had a religious experience such as he had never had before, not even at the Wesley-led revivals in which he had participated in England. While he was preaching at a protracted meeting at Boisseau's Chapel, south of Petersburg, on Sunday, June 30, 1776, Rankin and "the people were overcome with the presence of the Lord God of Israel."

[S]uch a time as this I never, never, beheld. Numbers were calling out aloud for mercy, and many were mightily praising God their Saviour; while others were in an agony, for full redemption in the blood of Jesus! Soon, very soon, my voice was drowned amidst the pleasing sounds of prayer and praise.[6]

Rankin noted that "almost every one" of the black people there was "upon their knees; some for themselves, and others for their distressed companions."

When at White's Chapel, Virginia, the following Sunday, July 7, 1776, Rankin met with a congregation of 400 to 500:

I preached from Ezekiel's vision of the dry bones: "And there was a great shaking." I was obliged to stop again and again, and beg of the people to compose themselves. But they could not: some on their knees, and some on their faces, were crying mightily to God all the time I was preaching. Hundreds of Negroes were among them, with the tears streaming down their faces.[7]

Again and again, spirit was felt in Rankin's meetings, and he knew that the blacks had played an important role. His descriptions always couple excitement and black presence, although a causal role is not formally assigned. At Petersburg he wrote, "such power descended that hundreds fell to the ground, and the house seemed to shake with the presence of God. The chapel was full of white and black, and many were without that could not get in."[8]

The Methodists welcomed these times of great excitement, but they were also prepared for the slack times between revivals. Organization was their forte. The growth of Methodist societies within the Anglican Church was strongly supported by both Rankin and Jarratt who viewed early Methodism as a renewal movement within the Anglican Church. Blacks and whites were organized into societies, classes, and bands. A band was a group of from five to ten, classes were twelve or more, who met weekly with a leader and functioned much as a therapy group, working on each individual and working up a consensus. Members gave weekly accounts "of their temptations, triumphs, and faults," and at Love Feasts of cake and water recounted their salvation experiences, or "the goodness of God to their souls."[9]

Perhaps more important than anything else, Methodists sang together, pouring out emotion into hymns bringing the Methodist "confession of faith" to blacks, but at the same time "blackening" it, or making it more emotional and improvisational, for whites. Methodist James Meacham, preaching on the "Grensville Circuit," in Virginia in 1789, repeatedly sang with blacks and has left evidence of how deeply it affected him:

Tuesday. . . . [This] evening the dear black bretheren [sic] began to sing as they ware in their cottage. I went to join them, we went to prayer. . . .
Saturday. . . . Some time in the Night—I judge near the Middle watch—I awaked in raptures of Heaven by the sweet Echo of Singing in the Kitchen among the dear Black people (who my Soul loves.) I scarcely ever heard anything to equal it upon earth. I rose up and strove to join them.[10]

Jarratt was concerned about this black-style singing that he believed led to emotional "excesses," but Francis Asbury counseled that as long as proper attention was paid to Methodist rules, ecstatic emotion could well accompany proper practice. After a meeting at Accomac courthouse he advised, "attend to preaching, prayer, class meeting, and love feast; and then, if they will shout, why let them shout."[11] Asbury did not reject shouting and emotion: it had brought him and the church hundreds if not thousands of converts. And he did not reject the black who brought this emotion to the church. Wherever Asbury went, hundreds came to hear, and large numbers of blacks were always among them. "Here are Negroes who have astonished masters of families, understanding men, when they have heard them pray."[12] Clearly Asbury himself was astonished and very pleased.

As was usual in these emotional revivals, they seemed to reach an excited peak and then declined quickly after. Blacks and whites continued going to class meetings, but mass meetings were not held again until 1785 when a second wave of Methodist excitement began, now that of an independent church. Again, thousands attended protracted meetings. At one such meeting in Brunswick at the height of the excitement on July 28, 1787, Philip Cox, a participant, reported, "it is thought above a hundred whites found peace with God, besides as many negroes on that day." This extreme excitement, with both blacks and whites participating, was repeated in Sussex where blacks "lay struggling till they beat the earth with their hands, head and feet, while others kicked holes in the ground," and many whites were "so convulsed that they could neither speak not stir."[13]

Many slaves became Methodists. This was reflected in the advertisements for runaways, which now often noted that the slaves were Methodist exhorters. One Maryland owner commented that his "property," Sam,

was raised in a family of religious persons, commonly called Methodists, and has lived with some of them for years past, on terms of perfect equality. . . . He has been in the use [sic] of instructing and exhorting his fellow creatures of all colors in matters of religious duty.[14]

The Methodist excitement was followed by a new and larger wave of Baptist revivals. Thousands joined Baptist churches in the late 1780s. However, although blacks still played an important role, the white Baptists had by this time changed radically. The Baptist church, of the 1750s, 1760s, and 1770s, had been a church of the dispossessed. Black slaves and poor whites had suffered for their faith; blacks had been whipped and whites jailed and hounded out of Virginia. They had prided themselves on being a church of the lowly and persecuted. However, by the late 1780s many white Baptists had moved up in social class, and many of the "middling sort" now joined them, along with a few from the elite. This new Baptist church began to be self-conscious about its relationship with blacks and its attitudes toward slavery.[15]

Toward the end of the eighteenth century, and in the nineteenth, black Baptists were increasingly meeting separately, both as congregations and as subcongregations within the mixed churches. The whites in these mixed Baptist churches began to try to control black preachers and reduce the emotionality of services.[16]

In 1788, Water Lick Church counseled Brother Daniel not to call meetings in his own home. It seems likely that Daniel continued to preach, as his "conduct" was censured, and he apparently upset the church's peace in 1789. In January of 1793, this same Negro Daniel (along with Negro Jane) asked for a formal letter of dismissal (from Water Lick Church in Shenandoah County) stating that they wanted to join Buck Marsh Church. Buck Marsh was in the northern section of the adjoining county (Frederick), and it is likely that Peter Catlett, his owner, either moved Daniel to new land or sold him (perhaps with his wife).[17]

Daniel joined a church that had already reacted to black preaching:

The Church taking into Consideration the Conduct of a Number of the Black Members, who taking upon them to be teachers & preachers of funerals . . . so conclude as Such conduct is a general dissatis-

faction to the Church, resolved that such as May take that liberty shall be accountable to this Church for such conduct without first obtaining Liberty or license from the Church.[18]

The whites did not stop black preaching, but they did object to some of the preachers. Brother Ned, cited for drinking too much and falsely accusing a black sister, and Billy or William Lewis (servant to Col. Stubblefield), cited for disorderly conduct, were ordered not to preach. So was Jesu, the property of Mr. Henderson. Jesu was simply "forbid by the Church" with no grounds stated, but he "took on him to preach" notwithstanding the censure of the church. (The blacks who were "acceptable" preachers were not listed. Brother Daniel may have been among them.)[19]

This church, Buck Marsh, had a large and growing black population, and many more black men than white men were members. In 1788, there were 26 white and 40 black men, 100 white and 32 black women. Had they been together and *had* the blacks kept their vote (and had women been denied it), black men would have been in the great majority. Separation gave the whites a way of avoiding this issue directly (although they eventually did try to impose their authority), and it gave the blacks the freedom to act on their own and in their own fashion. Separated, Afro-American patterns could more freely be observed in this period when whites were becoming self-conscious about them.[20]

The issue of authority had to be faced in a more open fashion. Blacks, as charter members and "free" in the faith, had been voting in Baptist churches. This becomes clear when, at the close of the century, voting became an issue and whites became very nervous about this equality. In 1792, the Emmaus Baptist Church of Charles City specifically limited the vote to "free male members," clearly including free black men in this category. This became the most acceptable line of demarcation for Baptists, and as the number of free blacks in Virginia had grown conspicuously after the revolution (from 1,800 in 1782 to 12,766 in 1790), it was not a meaningless "right" they conferred.[21] Nevertheless, most black Baptists were slaves.

The churches moved to act in unison and to get advice from their association meetings. In 1797, the Roanoke Baptist Association considered the issue, and in 1801 and 1802, the Dover Association grappled with it. It was not a simple problem for them. (It should be remembered that this was after Gabriel's Conspiracy of 1800.) After a year's debate they came to the following position: "No person is entitled to exercize authority in the church, whose situation in social life, renders it his duty to be under obedience to the authority of another, such as minor sons, and servants." Servants, they felt, were "very useful in certain stages of discipline, [and] they may admonish, reprove, or rebuke" other servants.[22] This was *advice* to the churches, and each church could go its own way. Most churches in Virginia chose the Dover path, which it should be emphasized gave free blacks "authority," and recommended each "group" deal with "its own." In giving black congregations and subcongregations virtual independence, they gave blacks the right to vote on their own church lives.[23]

The issue of slavery was now resolved in a similar fashion. In 1785 and again in 1789, the Baptist General Committee had termed slavery "a violent deprivation of the rights of nature" and had suggested that the legislature could end this "horrid evil" in a "great Jubilee." The Methodists had also openly condemned the institution. Methodist James O'Kelly, an itinerant preacher in Virginia in 1778, had been one of the majority condemning slavery at the Baltimore Conference of 1780, crying "Remember, that 'of one blood God made all nations', Africa not excepted." The Conference decision was binding on Virginia.[24]

Sharing these views, many Virginia Methodists and Baptists as well as Quakers had, in the last quarter of the eighteenth century, manumitted their slaves. However, the Methodist Church abandoned its official antislavery stance within a year of its passage. In 1793, the Baptist General Committee debated the same issue again and this time decided "by a large majority (after considering it a while) that the subject be dismissed from this committee, as it belongs to the legislative body." All were to be free to act as they saw fit. David Barrow and others who shared his views eventually abandoned Virginia. However, most antislavery Baptists and Methodists, such as Benjamin Watkins, continued in "the vineyard." They were eventually labeled "eccentric," the nineteenth-century code word still used in Southern writings that almost always signifies a treatment of blacks that was different from most.[25]

Whites who had shared intensive and extensive experiences with blacks did not change as rapidly as these organizational decisions might suggest. The Ketockton Association of Baptist Churches, an old Association made up of mixed churches with many black members, would not accept the Baptist General Committee's guidelines. They had been debating the issue for over a decade, when in 1797, they finally felt constrained to publish their views finding "Hereditary slavery a transgression of the Divine Law." They advocated gradual manumission and came up with a rare plan:

1st   All Slaves 14 years old & under, to be free at 22 years of age.
2d   All above 14, and under 20, to be free at 25.
3d   All above 20 and under 25, to be free at 28.
4th   All above 25 to serve 5 years.
5th   All born after this date shall be entitled to the same rights and
*   privileges as children born of Negroes heretofore emancipated.*
6th   All who have been purchased with money, shall serve ten years
*   from the time of such purchase.*[26]

The plan was sent out to each church for comment, but that was the last time it was mentioned in the minutes. The people must have rejected it or simply tabled the plan, as more of the churches now accepted the "peculiar institution."

Blacks and whites still had to be in fellowship, but now the white hand was often offered only if the black bent his knee. A case at Smith's Creek in 1794 illustrates this change very well. Trouble had been reported between two members, white Sister Margaret Harrison and black Brother "Moor's Joe." Although all the details of the problem are not recorded, its resolution was as follows:

Sister Margaret Harrison being present herself, was enquired of concerning the Nonfellowship between her & Moor's Joe, & she came to so far as to forgive sd Brother Joe his fault against her, or that which she view'd as a fault in him; and agreed that he might keep his Place in the Church, as well as herself, and that she would not neglect her Duty in the Church on this Account; but this she undertook on Condition that said Joe shall not have the Previledge [sic] of her Wench Dine, as his wife.[27]

Peace was restored; both individuals, having been suspended, were reinstated, but Joe was forbidden to marry Dine on the decision of Dine's mistress. No discussion was held on that issue, and peace clearly came on the slaveowner's terms alone.

The last decades of the eighteenth century were distinguished by a strange mix in race relations in Virginia. On the one hand the races were moving apart, but on the other, the period saw a peak in certain types of interaction. Given the shared experiences of such large numbers in the 1770s and 1780s, many more whites had heard black preachers, and some small numbers were ready to accept them as the official preachers at their "white" churches.

Richard Dozier, Robert Carter's overseer in the Northern Neck, recorded in his diary his varying reactions to seven black sermons. His description suggests the extent of racial interaction, the normalcy of its occurence, and the way in which one individual changed his view of blacks' ability:

May 26, Sunday 1782. . . . I went in the evening to hear a Negro speak near Mr. Kelsick's (called Lewis). He spoke by way of exh'n [exhortation] to about 400 people. I think with the greatest sensibility I ever expected to hear from an Ethiopian he pointed out the state man was in by nature and laid before us the evidence of a sinful nature by the conduct of people, and entreated them to rest not in an unconverted state but come and accept of Christ by faith that they might be reconciled to God.

August 12, 1786. Negro Lewis Belonging to Mr. Brockenbrough in Essex. Spake Aug. 12, Sunday, to about 300 people at Mr. Jno. Coates, on Jude. He read the latter part of the ch. to the astonishment of the auditory. His gift exceeded many white preachers.

At night a negro who rides with Mr. Asberry [sic] preached on "Ye were sometime darkness, but now. . . ." Pointed out the dark state of the soul by nature; how they were brought to the light, and how they should walk as children, all in a clear and most wonderful manner. Mr. Ellice spake a few words. Abt. 50 people.

Monday, April 27th, 1789. Negro Jacob, a slave, came from the Eastern Shore with one Mr. Bacon, who preached at Farnham meeting house on Lu. 8:12. A most wonderful preacher. Oh, see God choosing the weak things of this world to confound the things that are mighty. The said Mr. Bacon exhorted.

Negro Lewis [preached] Farnham mtg. house. Sunday, June 27, [1790], Job 14:10 Abt. 400 people.

Lewis, belonging to Dr. Brockenbrough. [Preached at] Mrs. Allison's Nov. 2, [1794] Sunday Ps. 49:15.
A funeral of a child. See the power of God, —a poor Ethiopian. Abt. 150 people.

Negro Harry (A smith) belonging to Mr. C. Carter, preached a funeral at Dan'l Jackson's on Mark 10:15, Sept, 27, 1801. Abt. 100 blacks and 20 whites.[28]

In this period, at least two black men served as official preachers to Virginia Baptist "white" congregations. Jacob or Josiah Bishop, who had been a slave in Northhampton, was the official pastor of the Court Street Church in Portsmouth, serving from circa 1792 to 1802. Black William Lemon, pastor at Gloucester Church (also known as Pettsworth or Ware) in Gloucester County, between 1799 and 1801, led a revival at the church and represented its congregation at the "white" Dover Association meetings in 1797, 1798, and 1801.[29] "Uncle Jack," born in Africa circa 1758, and brought to Virginia seven years later, became a well-known preacher in Nottaway County. Converted by Presbyterian John Blair Smith, he chose to become a Baptist and was widely noted for his piety, erudition, and charisma. On the petition of whites he was formally licensed, preaching from 1790 to 1832. He converted many, including some whites, his master's son among them. Many others were impressed by the demands he made of both blacks and whites for "Christian submission."[30] (See Figure 41.)

Although whites and blacks did move further apart toward the close of the eighteenth century, the influence they had had on each other was deep and lasting. The Rev. John Early, a Methodist circuit preacher in the Portsmouth area in 1808, preached both to racially mixed groups as well as to separate congregations. On Sunday, August 7, 1808, he "appointed a love feast for . . . the black people at one hour after sun up and for the white people at nine o'clock." Interestingly, Early set an almost-African-style time for the blacks—"one hour after sunrise"—and clock time ("nine o'clock") for the whites. The meetings too were somewhat different. "I attended and commented to the black people and had a powerful time among many and felt truly pleased with them and Brother Boyd gave the love feast, that is, Bread and water, and many spoke feelingly of the goodness and power of God."[31] Later, when he met with the whites, he had a different and much colder experience. He found himself being critical, calling the people to task (or "rubbing" them) for their "naked breasts," their ornaments, and costly clothes.[32]

When Early preached to a mixed audience of whites and blacks, he noted very interesting things about himself: he was noisy and demonstrative. "While I was preaching I hollered very loud (as I commonly did) and stamped with my feet."[33] He felt constrained, however, to cite

212

FIGURE 41. Uncle Jack and a white congregation. Jack preached in Nottoway County, 1790-1832. This picture was drawn for William White's *The African Preacher*, 1849. Photo courtesy of the Rare Book Room, The Free Library of Philadelphia.

a Biblical justification for his actions: Ezekiel 6:11. "Thus saith the Lord God; Smite with thine hand, and stamp with thy foot, and say, Alas for all the evil abominations of the house of Israel!" Early was still willing to "holler," if somewhat self-conscious about it, and he was still willing to castigate slavery in his homespun way. When a plague of frogs tormented Virginia, "I told them I expected it was a judgement against slavery and their other wickednesses."[34]

Throughout Virginia, and throughout the South, blacks and whites continued to share some religious experiences, but the great period of intensive mass interaction had passed. It had, however, deep and lasting effect on both communities.[35]

16. Attitudes Toward Death and the Afterlife in Virginia

AFRICAN and English ideas of death and afterlife were merged in eighteenth-century Virginia. Ralph Roberts, a slave born circa 1794 on a plantation some 30 miles north of Richmond, was not a reborn Christian. When his wife died, he did not know who had been the cause and was greatly troubled. He felt considerable personal guilt, as he had taken her from her first husband, yet he vaguely felt that poor whites in the neighborhood, who had resented her free status and demanded her removal, were really "responsible." This lack of resolve, this confusion over the cause of her death (which he probably did not understand) as much as the death itself, upset Roberts deeply. "I became morose, quarrelsome, and vengeful. Like Cain, my hand was against every man and every man's hand against me." Later, having become a Christian, he felt he had "deserved to lose her" and was calmed by the justice of her death.[1]

Many blacks knew they were becoming Christians. They accepted that it was the Great God or Spirit that would greet them in heaven, and they accepted a single heaven for all people. But they welcomed African-style spirit guides on their conversion journeys (most often "a little man"), they continued to accept the duality of their souls, and they expected to shout and mourn in heaven. They believed forefathers were waiting there, and they assumed they would continue their kinship line in heaven, much as Africans had expected to in the afterlife.[2]

Blacks expected the afterlife to begin at death. Bodily resurrection at the second coming of Christ was sung about and talked about, but the immediate experience of heaven was expected. An old black man, thanking a white supporter for his aid to a black church, cried out, "May you live long, Sir, and when you die, may you not die eternally."[3]

The simple outline of Christianity given by Banna, one of the *Amistad* captives, suggests the emphasis that new Afro-Christians put on death, dying, and the afterlife. "The Great god . . . Sent his Son into the world to Save us from going down to held [sic]," he wrote. If they repent of their sins, "he will take them up to Heaven when they die   there they Shall [be] glad and happy and full of Joy."[4]

Afro-Americans melded African and Christian beliefs into one whole. Spirit power certainly was still respected, but amulets were now often made of three parts, seen as representing the Father, the Son, and the Holy Ghost. After all, the English came to Virginia believing in amulets and shared their beliefs with blacks, accepting many African "superstitions" as their own. Blacks had good reason to believe that use of spirit was Christian too.

But the Great God came into everyday life in a new way, and sin competed with breaking taboos as a causal agent.

Once, when Thomas Jefferson was ill, Hannah, one of Jefferson's black family all her life and caretaker at his retreat house at Poplar Forest, wrote him a simple but powerful message:

I heard that you did not expect to come up this fall   I was sorry to hear that you are so unwell you could not come   it grieve me many time   but I hope as you have been so blessed in this that you considered it was God that done it and no other one   we all ought to be thankful for what he has done for us   we ought to serve and obey his commandments that you may set to win the prize and after glory run

Master I do not [know that] my ignorant letter will be much encouragement to you as knows I am a poor ignorant creature. . . .

adieu, I am your humble servant
Hannah[5]

Here Hannah was preaching to Thomas Jefferson, and her message is clear:

1. God sent your illness.
2. This illness is a blessing that can lead to your conversion.
3. You can act to achieve conversion. (You have *not* been following the commandments!)
4. The "prize" you will get is life everlasting.

Her message seems to have come from Philippians 3:14: "I press toward the goal to win the prize which is God's call to the life above, in Christ Jesus." Hannah may have claimed ignorance and humility, but she seems to have been confident that she understood more about salvation than Thomas Jefferson did and was ready to instruct him. His sickness was the "omen" she understood. Whereas an African might have looked for the human causal agent (who had used spirit), Hannah was certain his illness was sent by God.

Many blacks got sick before conversion: sin-sick, they called it. The slave David George, born in Essex County, Virginia, circa 1742, wrote "I was sin. I felt my *own* plague; and I was so overcome that I could not wait upon my master. I told him *I was ill.*" A spiritual adjured

"Tak car' de sin-sick soul." Taking care was going to the Lord. The Lord took away David George's distress by "healing" him. Conversion was a healing event, and Christ was the Great Healer. His use of his spirit power could heal every individual. All illness thus shared in being sin-sickness: It *was* caused by sin too.[6]

Death itself was a healing and liberating event. "I bless de Lord I'm going to die." Death for most Afro-Christians was a positive event as the individual was given cause to believe "I'm boun' ter go ter heaven when I die." Heaven was to be every Christian's home. Most black Christians did not have any doubt about it. Everyone saved was going to be there. Hell was a danger for the unconverted. It was visited by almost every convert during conversion "travel," but the spirit guide led the convert up and away from this torment to heaven. Once there, God, or Christ, or spirit assured the convert of eternal salvation and sent the soul back to earth to spread the good word, but promised a home in heaven.[7]

Some converted Afro-Americans did begin to take the Christian idea of sin very much to heart and to worry about their own salvation, even after conversion. David George felt that "my sins had crucified Christ"; what if the converted person continued to sin? Andrew Burnaby was caught up short by the spiritual depth and very "white Protestant" comment on death made by a slave in the Northern Neck of Virginia in 1760:

An occurrence happened to me in the course of this day's travelling, which . . . made a considerable impression upon me at the time. . . . In passing either Acquia, Quantico, or Occoquan rivers, I do not recollect which, I was rowed by an old gray-headed negro who seemed quite exhausted and worn down by age and infirmity. I inquired into his situation, and received for answer, that he had been a slave from his youth, and had continued to work for his master till age had rendered him unfit for service; that his master had then kindly given him a small piece of ground, and the profits of the ferry, which were indeed very inconsiderable, for his maintenance; and that with these means of subsistence he awaited the hour when it might please God to call him to another life. I observed that he must naturally wish for that hour, as it would release him from his present sufferings. His answer was, no; for he was afraid to die. On my questioning him, why he was afraid to die: whether he had any thing upon his conscience that gave him uneasiness; or whether he had not been honest and faithful to his master? He answered, yes; I have always

216

done my duty to the best of my power: but yet I am afraid to die: and was not our Saviour himself afraid to die? The answer was so unexpected, and so far beyond what I supposed to be the intellectual capacity of the poor negro, that it sunk deep into my mind, and I was lost for a moment in silence.[8]

Most Afro-Christians apparently did not share this concern. If saved, they knew themselves to be saved eternally. They had been in heaven and had personally received God's promise of their return. Most Afro-Christians also remained convinced that spirit workers or conjurers had real power. Some were able to absorb this positively: Christ had been a spirit worker, so his followers could use his spiritual power. Some, however, saw all conjure work as the work of the Devil: "De Debbil is a liar and a conjurer, too, An' ef you don't mind he'll conjure you." Others divided magic work into good "white" magic and bad "black" magic, much as the English had in the seventeenth century.

Fetishes were still widely believed to cause death. Take "Hair from a horse's tail, a snake's tooth, and gunpowder. Wrap in a rag and bury under your enemey's doorstep." (This is recorded as a "Fetish to cause Death" but is probably missing some elements. Most such fetishes used blood, soil from cemeteries, and red fabric.) In the eighteenth century, and long after, omens and signs were observed. "If a dead tree falls when the wind is not blowing it is a sign of death." If you sweep after dark, "You'll sure sweep out some member uv de fam'ly." "If you carry a hoe or spade [in the house] you will dig a grave soon." "If a new window is cut in an old house, some member of the family will die."[9]

Spirits were widely believed to be present, and they too could cause death. It was accepted that "It is not good to answer the first time your name is called. It may be a spirit and if you answer it, you will die shortly. They never call more than once at a time, so by waiting you will miss probable death." Hags or witches could ride one in the night and bring illness that would eventually cause death. As Puckett learned, many saw hags as Christian witches. "Dey's done sold deir soul ter de debbil . . . an' ole Satan gi' dem pow'r ter change ter anything dey wants." In Virginia it was believed that "the hag turns the victim on his or her back. A bit (made by the witch) is then inserted in the mouth of the sleeper and he or she is turned on all-fours and ridden like a horse. Next morning the person is tired out, and finds dirt between the fingers and toes."[10]

But Jesus could overcome all these powers. He could take care of witches, bad medicine, and fetishes put under doorsteps.

> Ole Satan's camp aroun' my house,
> An's a stumblin' block in my way,
> But Jesus is my bosom friend,
> He moved it all away.[11]

Blacks, with a new sense of both time and place, sang:

> He have been wid us, Jesus,
> He still wid us, Jesus,
> He will be wid us, Jesus,
> Be wid us to the end.[12]

There was great assurance in this!

Although heaven was vouchsafed to the black Christian, Christian slaves remained anxious about funerals, much as their African parents had been. A funeral still had to be a fine affair. A second funeral service was still held, an important African practice at which leave-taking from the soul was properly celebrated. Christian slaves still believed that the souls of the departed could give messages on the way to the grave and at the funeral. An improper funeral might still lead the soul to haunt the living.[13]

Many whites changed their ideas about death and dying during this period when they were in intimate contact with blacks. White funerals became far more emotional affairs, echoing the ecstasy blacks often experienced at that time. John Leland, working with the Virginia Baptists between 1776 and 1791, has left us a record of the fact that he often converted people at funerals. He clearly entered into emotional and even ecstatic prayer, singing and using his body. One of his funeral songs that has been preserved echoes the black expectation of joining with Jesus, although it suggests far more hesitation in its refrain:

> O when shall I see Jesus
> And dwell with him above.[14]

Leland observed that "Funeral sermons in Virginia are seldom preached at the time of internment, but sometime afterwards."[15] Robert Hunter, visiting Virginia in December of 1785, attended such a delayed commemoration. His brief diary notation provides further evidence that this second rite was an established pattern and hints that the event was a highly emotional one:

218

It is the custom in this part of the country to have the funeral service performed two or three weeks after the person is buried—a very foolish one in my opinion, as it only serves to renew the grief of the relations.[16]

It is possible that the second funeral of the blacks had influenced whites. This possibility should be evaluated in light of the extraordinary fact that some whites adopted Afro-American practices at their burials and graveyards.

In an interesting analysis, D. G. Jeane has pointed out that many white graveyards in the Upland South, from Virginia to Texas, are markedly distinctive in terms of "a) site, b) size, c) vegetation, d) decoration, and e) cultus of piety." In Virginia, such cemeteries have been identified in Northampton, Isle of Wight, and Hanover counties as well as further west in Pittsylvania, Amhearst, Tazewell, Russell, and Lee counties. They are on hilltops; they tend to be small and family-oriented; cedars, crepe myrtle, gardenias, and roses are preferred, and except for this approved vegetation the ground is scraped clean; very idiosyncratic decoration is created; and families reunite once or twice a year to scrape and repair the graves, remember the dead, and celebrate with a festive meal at the cemetery.[17] (See Figure 42.)

The decoration and the cultus are of greatest importance. These cemeteries generally have mounded graves, homemade markers, and objects placed upon them. "Seashells, inverted mason jars or wine bottles . . . and other paraphernalia can be observed." Children's graves are distinguished from those of adults—they "frequently have marbles, toys, animal figurines, dolls, and shells."[18] Clearly items used by the dead were placed on the graves.

The direct parallel between black graves in the South and those on the West Coast of Africa is very strong. John Vlach cites similar practices in South Carolina as well as in the Congo, Gabon, Nigeria, Ghana, and the Ivory Coast.[19] Both Africans and Afro-Americans mounded and scraped the grave, used shells for decoration, placed articles used by the deceased on the grave, marked each grave uniquely, and covered their graves with gravesheds.[20] All these practices were followed by some whites in the Upland South. In fact, whites have been known to place food on graves, a central African and Afro-American pattern. Although researchers have looked for European roots for these practices, they have been hard put to find relevant folkways.[21]

Black influence seems undeniable. The interaction between whites and blacks is symbolically seen in the graveyards: Today the only re-

FIGURE 42. An Upland South grave. A twentieth-century example of an Upland-South-style grave found at Mt. Olivet Cemetery, in Washington, D.C., 1944. Mt. Olivet was then a white cemetery. Note the use of mounding and shells, both an African style of grave decoration. Photo courtesy of the Library of Congress.

corded sites with gravesheds are white cemeteries, whereas black cemeteries increasingly have clocks as grave "offerings." Perhaps white time has invaded the black world, even in death, whereas black recognition of spirit has clearly influenced white practices. Spirits were remembered yearly, honored, "placated" with their personal goods, and protected from wind and rain. They remain an important focus for their extended kin who celebrated with meals at the sites. White spirits and black spirits were being treated similarly.[22]

In the eighteenth century blacks were often with whites at deathbeds, as reported at Martha Jefferson's and George Washington's, and later at Thomas Jefferson's. Funerals for blacks were often attended by substantial numbers of whites, and funerals for whites were attended by blacks. They cried together, sang together, and experienced spirit together. Sometimes they were buried next to each other, in the same sacred place. The seventeenth-century graveyard at the Clifts plantation has five white graves to the north and ten black and one white in a row to the south.[23] Jefferson originally planned his graveyard at Monticello as a white *and black* resting place, although a segregated one.[24]

Eighteenth-century-Virginia graveyards have yet to be widely investigated. Many black cemeteries and many white cemeteries are no longer marked; perhaps among them were mixed black and white burial places. Hints from the ex-slave narratives suggest this might have been the case.[25]

Whether buried next to each other or not, blacks and whites went to funerals together. Frank Bell's slave grandfather was born circa 1728, and when he died at approximately 118 years of age, his "master," John Fallon, and a good percentage of the white and black family (150 slaves), came to the funeral. They were joined by many whites and blacks from the neighborhood who had known him. White slaveowner Fallon read the service at the graveside "an' all de folks was standin' there weepin' and wailin'." Blacks and whites were sending his spirit off to its new home, in a Christian yet African-style ritual.[26]

In the early eighteenth century this had not been the case. Then, white Anglicans felt "sorrow was to be shunned, and feelings were to be contained." Thomas Jones, William Byrd ii, Francis Taylor, and Robet Wormley Carter, for example, all found expression of grief disturbing and called for moderation and restraint.[27] These eighteenth-century Anglicans "seemed comfortable in this world," emphasizing life, with little overt concern given to the afterlife. However, over the course of the century white attitudes toward death, both in England and in Virginia, underwent significant development.[28]

A new focus on mortality was expressed by Isaac Watts, the English hymnist who published, between 1707 and 1719, an important body of songs dealing in part with death. Watts presented graphic images of the place where "greedy worms" will "gnaw my flesh," but he maintained that the true saint "yields his body to the dust" willingly, although he can be certain of no more than that his soul will "fly to unknown lands."[29]

Anglican missionaries in the colonies, revival preachers such as George Whitefield and Jonathan Edwards, and subsequently myriad Methodist and Baptist preachers, popularized Watts's hymns in America. The extraordinary diffusion and popularity of these hymns was an important cultural development. Peoples of a great range of churches (Anglicans, Congregationalists, Presbyterians, Baptists, and Methodists) sang these hymns, and they sang them to melodies that were already part of the popular culture. After the 1740s an American was likely to find that "the hymns of Watts became involved with . . . [his or her] vocal cords, . . . diaphragm, and lungs very early in life."[30] Blacks shared in this cultural development. Along with Bibles, Watts hymnals were among the first books given to blacks. Both blacks and whites quickly came to know his songs as though they were old folksongs, and they became an important part of a growing "common" heritage.

Watts sang of welcoming death, an attitude shared and expanded upon in the hymns of Charles Wesley and George Whitefield, but these hymns generally did not present a joyous picture of heaven, and their imagery cannot entirely account for the new Virginia view. Watts did write a popular hymn, "A Prospect of Heaven Makes Death Easy," in which heaven was depicted as "pure delight," "infinite day," and "everlasting spring."[31] However, in general, although Watts and Wesley expressed a strong desire in their hymns for death, heaven remained literally "an unknown land," whereas the image of the dead body was explicit. Charles Wesley's funeral hymn, sung at George Whitefield's burial, well suggests the tone of these works:

> Ah, lovely appearance of death,
>   No sight upon earth is so fair;
> Not all the gay pageants that breathe,
>   Can with a dead body compare.

> *With solemn delight I survey*
>   *The corpse when the spirit is fled;*
> *In love with the beautiful day,*
>   *And longing to lay in his stead.*[32]

Watts's and Wesley's verses are generally bleak and dour when compared with the "bright" (and detailed) images of heaven that can be
found in the slaves' visions recounted in Virginia and in the new folksongs sung in the South.

After the turn of the century, the new Southern Methodist hymnals
began to include songs about "making heaven my home." They were
already folk hymns among the people:

> *Farewell vain world I'm going home,*
> *My Jesus smiles and bids me come;*
> *Sweet angels shall convey me home,*
> *Away to New Jerusalem.*

> *I bless the Lord I'm born to die,*
> *From grief and woe my soul shall fly;*
> *Bright angles [sic] beckon me away*
> *To sing God's praise in endless day.*[33]

By the late eighteenth century heaven was being written of widely
by whites. The dying spoke to their kin of the afterlife as a perfect
world where "we shall ere long be reunited never again to be separated
from those we love." "We'll meet in heaven" became the acceptable
parting for loved ones, as deathbed scenes became ecstatic experiences, and white Virginians began to speak of preferring the life after
death to the present one.[34]

The correspondence of this new white attitude toward death and vision of the afterlife with that of Africans and Afro-Americans is very
close. Blacks were always highly concerned with life after death, and
life with forefathers. They had always "known" that kin would be
waiting and would provide a joyful homecoming. These concerns and
expectations now became "white" ones as well.

In the 1760s Virginia slaveowner Rev. James Maury wrote that his
mother had "made a most glorious end! Which God grant we may all
have the happiness to make whenever we shall be called upon!"
Maury expressed his hope to join her in the Heavenly Jerusalem
"where alone is fulness of joys and pleasures for evermore."[35]

This "Virginia style" of leave-taking was later found in Kentucky and Indiana, where there were many Virginia settlers, both white and black. In fact, this approach to death began to appear, along with Methodism and Baptism, all along the frontier, until by the second half of the nineteenth century, "Heaven our Home" was the theme of most popular consolation literature, and happiness at death was generally considered the proper "witness." This may be seen when at a deathbed Louisiana Hubbard reported "a blessed season of delightful peace and was almost constrained to shout."[36]

When the mother of John Rickets of Franklin County, Indiana, died, he wrote his brother in Kentucky:

I feel gratified to inform you that she left the world in the triumfs [sic] of faith, in her dying moments Jesse and myself Sung a Cupple of favorite hyms and She Slapt her hands and shouted give glory to god and retained her senses while she had breath and gave us all a great deel of satisfaction to See her happy. Such a great witness that she went happy out of the world.[37]

A Methodist hymn adjured:

I hope to praise him when I die
And shout *salvation as I fly.*[38]

White Methodists were certainly emotional and vocal, but the shout, involving ecstatic movement as well as vocalization, had come into the tradition from the black experience, via the revivals. It was *the* way to get "happy," ecstatic, or "high." It involved singing, rhythmic body motion, clapping, and vision travels.

The Virginia religious press, at the opening of the nineteenth century, was filled with joyous testimonies describing deathbed scenes, as young and old, male and female, white and black, went "happy" to their true home.[39] A Southern Baptist preacher who worked extensively with blacks reported his wife suffered painful trials before her death in 1790, but when "asked whether she was happy in her soul, she replied 'Yes, O yes!' These were the last words we could understand from her. A few hours after she breathed out her precious soul into the arms of the adored Redeemer, whom she sincerely loved."[40]

The happy death, and heaven a home, was a reward for a righteous life. Samuel Davies reminded *all* his parishioners that they would stand before "the tribunal of the Supreme Judge" where they would have to testify about their own lives, and they would also have to stand witness for the lives of all those they had known. Wives would be called on to testify about husbands, children about parents, slaves about masters, as well as masters about slaves, children, and wives. "We must all meet in the region of spirits. . . . They who lived or conversed together upon earth, and were spectators of each other's conduct, will then turn mutual witness against each other."[41]

Davies, Jarratt, Leland, and the other whites active in Virginia churches put far more emphasis on the possibility of converted Christians' falling back into sin than did blacks. These whites emphasized that even people *in* the churches could find themselves on the "left hand" of God or rejected at the heavenly tribunal. Their own behavior could put them there. Although blacks used the same imagery, those on the left were the unconverted, whereas those who had "it" were all on the right. Jesus had "washed" their sins away. "Colored people used to starve themselves and pray and seek sometimes a month or more" before they had a conversion experience. "[B]ut when they got it, they had it." "It" was a rite of passage, and once one had "come through," the experience could not be "lost" as a conviction could.[42]

17. Conclusions

IN JUNE OF 1793, Stith Mead, an itinerant white Methodist preacher in Virginia, wrote home to his family: "O ~~Daddy, Mamy,~~ [sic] Father, Mother, Brothers, Sisters, Black People my Soul is expanded towards you, who of you will try to meet me in Heaven." Eighteenth-century religious experiences left black and white Christians expecting to meet one another in heaven. There they would witness for one another, as they were "brothers and sisters in the Lord." There, most believed that black and white redeemed would "live together, and love one another throughout a long and happy eternity." A shared church life had prepared them for this. The church had absorbed the goals of the early visions of the new world: the church had become the Garden of Eden.[1]

The Black Creek Church was a church of blacks and whites together, begun in Southampton County in 1774. It had rejected slave-owner barbarity and had come to see slavery as "unrighteous." In 1786, the church members sat down to renew their covenant and to write a new testament. They recognized the church as something mystical, something far more than the sum of its members: *"The Church of Christ is a garden enclosed, a Spring sealed, a fountain shut up."*[2] For half a century this garden was a black and white one, and blacks came to accept a personal Christ, a very white-Christian understanding, while whites came to accept that "death was not a fearsome prospect but a step toward one's genuine fulfillment," a very African perception. Fithian noted that Robert Carter's children, "seem all to be free of any terror at the Presence of Death. *Harry* in special signified a Wish that his turn may be next." As a result of contact with blacks, spirit and spirits had become far more real to whites. Samuel Davies talked of heaven as the "region of spirits," and John Williams worried about which spirit was moving him.[3]

Many blacks were left with confusion as to death's cause. God gave life and took it, but many good Christians used tricks and magic power. Both blacks and whites had come to accept that God would call them to life everlasting, and they saw that as the place of real fulfillment. But life on this earth could not be wasted; it had to be lived to the fullest, preparing the spirit for its judgment. Martha Zeigler, born a slave in Virginia, said when she was 80:

I done got right with de Lord, and I am ready to go any time He calls me. I'se ready to stay here long as He wants me to, cause I done fell in good hands, but all the same I'se waiting to go. De Lord Knows I done the best I could with Whatever come to hand, and I'se trusting the rest to Him.[4]

In their understandings of life and death whites were being influenced by blacks, most often without their being aware of it; occasionally, though, they recognized and acknowledged it. Edward Baptist recalled that at the age of 10 he "was the subject of deep religious impressions, was conscientiously regular at prayer," having been taught by "a negro in the family who said he was seeking the Lord." Baptist was "looking out for voices, and visions."[5]

Ann Randolph Meade Page, wife of Mathew Page, Esquire, and mistress of Annfield in Frederick County, a plantation with some 200 slaves, was deeply influenced by black piety and exhortation and was well aware of it. In 1800, depressed after an illness, she had a crisis that found expression in her rejection of Sunday postchurch dinner parties, an important symbol of elite white life.

I . . . began to feel that my fellow-creatures in bondage upon the plantations ought to take the place in my mind and time, of this frequent dining about. . . . Not long after this, on a Sabbath after church, I was going, according to the general custom, to dine out; but the Spirit of God spoke better counsel, and enabled me [to] turn into a solitary November home, without a white person near. This was the first time I had returned home on Sunday from a religious motive. I shut myself up in my room, where my soul was engaged with the thoughts of judgment and eternity.[6]

Mrs. Page's servants were apparently well aware of her state and recognized it as "sin-sickness." They had the remedy and provided it:

While thus engaged in my chamber, an old blind negro woman was led in, who was a dear child of God. We began a conversation in which she used expressions respecting entire confidence in Christ, which made an indelible impression upon my mind. . . . I think I owe her, under God, much of my religious joy in after-years. Dear old creature, I often visited her in her cottage; and witnessed the evidences of her triumphant faith. She was a living example of Christ formed in the soul, the hope of glory.[7]

Page came to have a "never-failing" and "overcoming love" for the blacks in her family. She knew she would "meet them at the judgment-seat of my Lord and Master." Page's Lord and Master spoke through nature and was approached through ecstasy. Near death, which she awaited with joy, she reported, "I have sweet and heavenly visions as I lie upon this bed." Her son-in-law recorded that just before her death, at midnight,

a cloud arose, attended with heavy thunder and the most vivid flashes of lightning, creating in those around her bed the usual impressions of alarm. A tree near the house was torn in pieces by the stroke, which also broke the glass in the room opening into her chamber. With an animated countenance she said, pointing to the windows through which she saw the fields illuminated by the electric fluid: "How glorious, how delightful is this to me—see—this is the power of MY GOD.*"*[8]

Ann Page's understanding of death and the afterlife was radically different from that of William Byrd some 100 years earlier. He, and many of his generation, had never been sure about the nature of life after death. He hazarded that "Some sagacious men [may] make a shrewd guess at many things that will happen thereafter," but he clearly thought it no more than a guess. Byrd did not hold dead bodies in awe, nor did he expect souls or spirits to be troubled by the digging up of bones. In 1710, some five years after his father had died (but fourteen years after he had last seen him), Byrd had his bones dug up and "looked" at him. The sight led him to say simply: "[H]e was so wasted there was not anything to be distinguished."[9]

Later in the century whites were unlikely to have undertaken such an experiment. The belief that cemeteries were places where spirits often gambled had been reinforced, and bones were not to be treated lightly. The world to come was also known in a different way, with more than a hint of an African perception, but most often voiced in a very English manner.

In 1765, the Rev. Peter Fontaine, Jr., born in Virginia, brought up with blacks, and a slaveowner himself, "knew" much more about heaven than had Byrd. He was ready to advise his uncle, John Fontaine, living in England, a man some thirty years older than himself, that

we ought to stand always prepared for the painful divorce, and not set our affections on the good things of this world, which are only intended by our good God as comforts and refreshments in our pilgrimage upon the journey to that other world, which is our proper home. May God grant, my dear uncle, that all of us may so run this short

228

race, as that we may reap those joys which have no bitterness, and no bounds, in that everlasting world, to which you, that are seventy odd, and I that am forty odd, are equally hastening, and in which you only have a little the start; where I hope we shall not only be better acquainted with each other, know personally, and converse by word of mouth, and have no dangerous ocean of three thousand miles between us. But the very essence of all joy will be, that we shall know the Great Father of all our blessings and enjoyments, whom to know is eternal life.[10]

Afro-Americans could share this vision, although they were likely to describe it rather differently. In repetitive hymns they sang of mother, father, and all the family, waiting in heaven.

> *In that morning, true believers,*
> > *In that morning*
>
> *We will sit aside of Jesus.*
> > *In that morning,*
>
> *If you should go fore I go,*
> > *In that morning*
>
> *You will sit aside of Jesus*
> > *In that morning.*[11]

The basic elements of heaven as a joyful family home were shared by blacks and whites. Other issues are less clear.

In Africa, death was believed to have been caused by a human being through the agency of a malevolent spirit.[12] Virtually all evil and all good occurrences were attributed to spirits, controlled by both the living and the dead. Kagame maintains that this view of casuality is part of a closed system of thought, diametrically opposed by Cartesian logic, and that "it cannot evolve, and is abandoned entirely if a different conception of the world is acquired."[13] In America, most black Christians came to see Christ as an important causal agent in their lives. Perhaps he had replaced the family of African spirits, and although a stronger more positive spirit, he was still held responsible for the outcome of events.

IV

Coda

18. Coherent World Views

WHEREVER BLACKS lived in eighteenth-century America they affected the collective consciousness, and people in all classes—the elite, the "middling sort," the poor, and the slaves—shared values. Their world views were *not* identical; they were influenced by the histories of their parents, clans, classes, and races; but they were related to each other in an organic fashion. By the end of the eighteenth century, whites and blacks shared family, clan, and even folk histories that could not be separated one from the other. By then, both blacks and whites held a mix of quasi-English and quasi-African values. Sometimes these values played against one another and caused great difficulty for the individual; but in the folk religions that swept America in the last third of the century, the Baptists and Methodists, both black and white, achieved a coherent unification of these values. In some aspects the African and the English values reified each other; in other areas unconscious choices were made, and in many cases values from the past of the "other" group were adopted.[1]

The traditional English and African concepts of cyclical time attached to holy place reinforced each other and helped Southern folk, black and white, to weld new ties to their homes. The African appreciation of kin ties, spirit, and spirit power helped whites to forge closer ties to their living families and to conceptualize both spiritual life after death and the continuance of family ties in the afterworld. Wider kin ties became more important, and the African understanding of heaven as home became an American expectation. The white approach to a personal Christ gave every black Christian a new appreciation of individual rather than collective experience, as myriad blacks and whites knew themselves to be reborn.

The Calvinist approach to purpose—the finding of a calling in life and the dedication of life to that calling—was in its wider sense rejected. For the religious Baptist or Methodist, the only real calling was that of spreading the good word. For the nonreligious, slow time, love of place, and appreciation of soul, led to love of a special Southern-style good life. Work was minimal and pleasures of place such as hunting, fishing, sitting, and storytelling were particularly emphasized, as were those of the body—dancing, music-making, eating, and sex.

There was at least one other important Virginia tradition, that of a small intellectual elite. This tradition was influenced by black values as well, although not in obvious ways. Jefferson provides an interest-

FIGURE 43. Thomas Jefferson's chess set: Africans "in" the white world. This set may well have been carved by blacks and brought to the West by Portuguese traders. Strangely, it has a king with African features among the white pieces, whereas the "blacks" are painted red. Note the difference in physiognomy between the white king, the black elite, and the black pawns; the African staff of office held by black and white alike; and the European dress on the black queen. The white queen is no longer in the set. [A similar African (red) and European (white) set is in the Metropolitan Museum collection.] Photo courtesy of the Thomas Jefferson Memorial Foundation, Inc.

ing example. His concern with time was in part a reaction against blacks' perceptions and practices, but his love of place was reinforced by theirs. Jefferson's emphasis on rationality and life in this world was also in part developed in opposition to black views, but it was not only through opposition that blacks influenced him.

Jefferson came to show a deep personal concern with Jesus. Whereas his first editing of the Gospels in 1804 was apparently done in reaction to Joseph Priestley's *Socrates and Jesus Compared* (1803), his second redaction in 1819 was a personal work, perhaps kept secret, and done "strictly for his own moral and religious instruction." Dickinson W.

Adams, who has given it close analysis, believes Jefferson read it nightly, and that he had "hope for a life after death."[2]

Although Jefferson himself was unlikely to have thought that blacks had influenced him, it is very likely that the black perception of Jesus as one of the family, as one who still lived with the generations gone before and who affected both the dead and the living, had deep subliminal effect on him. Jefferson too was responding to Jesus as a man who could have been his friend. His gospel eliminated all the miracles and tried to picture Jesus as a *rational* as well as a supremely moral man, much as Jefferson saw himself. However, as Hannah had hoped, Jefferson may have come to accept, unwittingly, that "it was God that done it" (brought him low) ". . . and no other one."

In his "Death-bed Adieu" to Martha, Jefferson wrote of going "to my fathers" and to the "two seraphs [who] await me." He did indeed seem to harbor some hope of finding his family, and perhaps subconsciously recognizing the association with the African view, he echoed his early poem on slavery by noting "I welcome the shore / Which crowns all my hopes or which buries my cares."[3]

When Jefferson died, a white flag was hung on a bush to signal his death to those of the family living at Tufton plantation, below Monticello. It may well have been accidental, but in parts of Ghana, Upper Volta, the Ivory Coast, and the Congo, and among blacks in the West Indies and in New Orleans, white is the proper mourning color and connotes death. The English, and most Americans, use black for mourning—in clothes, in churches, and in symbolic flags on the houses of the deceased.[4]

Jefferson and the other members of the elite shared a concern with the ancient past and with Latin and Greek. The elite's interest in this past should be read as a legitimation of their civility. From the very outset, at the very start of colonization, they took great pains to treasure this knowledge. It was the hallmark of their supposed identity; they saw it as the key to their true selves. They were the heirs of a great civilization, and they were carrying it on. They wanted to be "educated gentlemen," and they saw Latin as the symbolic key to their character. The "accidental" fact that slavery became a Virginia institution reinforced their identification with Rome.[5]

College secret societies, such as the Cliosophic Society at Princeton, gave each member a secret name, most often in Latin. Ironically, some, such as Hannibal and Brutus, were the same as the demeaning slave names.[6] For use in a more public fashion, every male member of the elite inherited or chose a family herald with a Latin phrase as his special motto. Used as his private bookmark and seal, this motto expressed his key concern in quintessential form. It was his mark or signature, a symbol of his self.[7] William Byrd II used *Pallescere Nulla Culpa* or "No Guilt is Insignificant"; Landon Carter, *Purus Scleris*, or "Pure of Sin"; George Washington's motto was *Exitus Acta Probat*, "One's end is a test of his deeds."[8] All were concerned with guilt and responsibility. How strange that they should have turned to Latin for their moral tenets, almost hiding them from themselves as it were. (Washington, as others in the elite, did *not* know Latin.) Nor did the Bible serve them in this regard. They did not generally quote it in their letters or their diaries or commonplace books. (Byrd's Commonplace Book, for example, is a compendium of Latin wisdom sayings in English translation and of ribald stories, with only one extended reference to a modern Christian volume.[9])

The Latin motto Thomas Jefferson proposed for the United States seal meant "Rebellion to Tyrants is Obedience to God." The fact that he must have unconsciously associated this tyranny with slaveholding as well is evidenced by the picture suggested as the appropriate illustration for the seal. Jefferson originally proposed a picture of "the children of Israel in the wilderness, led by a cloud by day and a pillar by night, "but he accepted Franklin's suggestion that it should be of Moses causing the waters to cover Pharaoh and his chariots.[10] Both images clearly denote the saga of the Israelites being freed from slavery. In the Great Seal of the United States, the attachment to Latin and classical culture as well as to Biblical symbolism and the involvement with black slaves all came together. It has been suggested that the "allusions, similes, metaphors and concrete images which . . . [the rebelling colonists] utilized reveal how profoundly and disturbingly chattel slavery was embedded in their consciousness."[11] Revolutionary colonists certainly did not want to be "slaves to England," but in Virginia, most whites were also to conclude that they did not want to live without black slaves. Near the end of his life Jefferson was to say both that "the South agrees with the Negroes best" and that he feels "they are possessed of the best hearts of any people in the world."[12] He too wanted to continue to share in their joint world.

Had blacks been asked they would not have given the same answer. Blacks spoke of the pasts they shared with whites, but they had different visions of the future. Aunt Christian, master cook in the Burwell household in Mecklenburg County, remembered Kingsmill, near Williamsburg, which Lewis Burwell IV had left in 1775, taking his black and white family together to Botetourt Court. Aunt Christian reminded young Letitia Burwell of their joint family history, going back to the early 1700s, and of the "rights" it gave her:

[A]int I bin—long fo' dis yer little marster whar is was born—bakin' de bes' loaf bread, an' bes' beat biscuit and rice waffles, all de time in my ole marster time! An' I bin manage my own affa'rs, an I gwine manage my own affa'rs long is I got breff. Kase I 'members 'way back yonder in my mamy time fo' de folks come fum de King's Mill plantation nigh Williamsbu'g. All our black folks done belonks to de Burl fambly uver sence dey come fum Afiky. My gran-mammy 'member dem times when black folks lan' here stark naked, an' white folks hab to show 'em how to war close. But we all done come fum all dat now, an' I gwine manage my own affa'rs.[13]

When Lewis Burwell II died in 1710, he left "Farlow's Neck ..., Harrop Plantation and the Quarterland," all part of what was soon to be called Kinsgmill, to Lewis Burwell III, who built a mansion house there, probably in the 1720s.[14] Aunt Christian's family memories went back to that time, when the Africans and the English began a joint life together as slaves and masters (and servants, laborers, and apprentices).

Aunt Christian spoke of her own age in very African terms. She had been baking bread before Letitia Burwell's father had been born. She recognized that her sense of self and her independence were related to her knowledge or "hold" on the past; but she, as her very name tells us, was a Christian and was determined to use her understanding of where she had "come from" to forge a new future.

In America, African world views had come under attack. They had lost their ties to an independent social structure. Separate taboos and "superstitions" were often manipulated by magic workers who were no longer part of an ordered social fabric and often wielded extreme power. The Afro-Christian faith reabsorbed African values and white Christian values into a new coherent whole and established a new ordered social framework. A black person, such as Aunt Christian, who had come through and been reborn, was likely to have a coherent world view that united African understandings of spirit as "cause" of all, with Christian understandings of the future and the heavenly place that awaited. This new world view and the new church community helped slaves to find wholeness and purpose, even in slavery; it also affected some whites as they grew in spiritual experience.

John Woolman (1720–1772), born in New Jersey to parents who were members of the Society of Friends, chose to travel to Virginia when he was 26 (1746) and again at age 37 (1757). Quakers widely regarded journeys as providing the framework for spiritual change and chose their destinations with care, looking for God's guidance. Woolman, in deciding to go to Virginia, purposely placed himself in what was for him a very painful position in order to talk with both slaves and slaveowners and to know the reality they faced. He anticipated being influenced, and indeed in Virginia he found his heart "made tender," by the slaves" situations. Where owners "laid heavy burdens on their slaves, my exercise was often great, and I frequently had conversation with them in private concerning it. . . . [S]o many vices and corruptions [are] increased by . . . this way of life, that it appeared to me as a dark gloominess hanging over the land." Woolman confronted slaveowners, not in anger but in pain, sure that God would not countenance the continuation of slavery. He embarrassed them by paying them and asking them to pass the payment on to their slaves, as wages for serving him. Whites spoke of blacks' servitude as the punishment of Cain, and he reminded them that we all come from Noah. He knew that "The love of ease and gain are the motives . . . of keeping slaves."[15]

After his first visit to Virginia, Woolman spent considerable time thinking and writing about slavery. In 1754, after much soul searching, he published *Some Considerations on the Keeping of Negroes* . . . , a small book that reached a very wide audience. All the yearly meetings of the Quakers in America received copies, as did the English Friends. His argument was simply: "Did not He that made us make them?"[16]

Woolman was one of a small group of reformers who became very active in speaking with Friends on this issue, and the meetings began to change their policy, slowly, through a talked-up consensus. In 1758, as part of what was becoming a major reform movement in Quaker polity, the Philadelphia Yearly Meeting condemned slave trading, and by 1776, it had moved to reject any Quaker ownership of slaves. Woolman certainly should have had good reason to have been at peace with his own role in this development, although it came to its last stage some four years after his death.[17] Nevertheless, Woolman experienced a major crisis in January of 1770, and it revolved around blacks, their place in the world, and Woolman's identity.

In his journal for 1772, Woolman recorded the following emotional history:

In a time of sickness, a little more than two years and a half ago, I was brought so near the gates of death that I forgot my name. Being then desirous to know who I was, I saw a mass of matter of a dull gloomy color between the south and the east, and was informed that this mass was human beings in as great misery as they could be, and live, and that I was mixed with them, and that henceforth I might not consider myself as a distinct or separate being. In this state I remained several hours. I then heard a soft melodious voice, more pure and harmonious than any I had heard with my ears before; I believed it was the voice of an angel who spake to the other angels; the words were, "John Woolman is dead." I soon remembered that I was once John Woolman, and being assured that I was alive in the body, I greatly wondered what that heavenly voice could mean. I believed beyond doubting that it was the voice of an holy angel, but as yet it was a mystery to me.

I was then carried in spirit to the mines where poor oppressed people were digging rich treasures for those called Christians, and heard them blaspheme the name of Christ, at which I was grieved, for his name to me was precious. I was then informed that these heathens were told that those who oppressed them were the followers of Christ, and they said among themselves, "If Christ directed them to use us in this sort, then Christ is a cruel tyrant."[18]

Woolman immediately sought the meaning of his vision, and he recognized that the "dark mass of human misery" was the slavery he had seen in Virginia and elsewhere. "After this sickness I spake not in public meetings for worship for nearly one year, but my mind was very often in company with the oppressed slaves as I sat in meetings . . . [where] the Divine gift operated [in me] by abundance of weeping, in feeling the oppression of this people."[19] Woolman came to believe that this vision meant that he should take on further responsibility for slaveholding. Christians were oppressing blacks: *They* were blaspheming Christ's name. Woolman would not consciously use such harsh language, but his unconscious provided it for him.

What Woolman may never have realized was how like a black vision experience his own "coming through" had been. He too had been called by name; he had died; and he had been taken to see hell. He had also come to a final awareness of heavenly acceptance, although this apparently came in a separate vision in which God gave Woolman a harsh message and the task to return to life and "open this vision" by indicating the supporters of slavery "shall be broken to pieces."[20]

This patterned vision travel had once been a white one; medieval folk legends and literature preserve it.[21] But although it came down into the Puritan tradition as a model, as in Bunyan's *Pilgrim's Progress* (1678), the spiritual autobiographies of Quakers, Anglicans, and Puritans, even of Bunyan himself, indicate that in the early modern period rebirths were generally experienced in time present, suddenly, and not in extended travels to hell and heaven.[22] Whitefield, for example, had an experience seven weeks after Easter 1735, when he felt "the spirit of God take possession of my soul, and, as I hope, seal me unto the day of redemption."[23] Wesley's "Aldergate Experience" of May 24, 1738, when "I felt my heart strangely warmed," and "an assurance was given me," became an important model of sudden rebirth for the concerned in the eighteenth century.[24]

The roots of the black vision pattern, the "travels" in time, are not at all clear. Elements are African, but it would appear that blacks had adopted and adapted the once traditional Christian vision travel.[25] In Woolman's case they deeply influenced a white who found his way "through" by its means. After revival contact with blacks, whites were far more likely to report more detailed spirit journeys. When Methodist Richard Whatcoat heard the testimony of Nancey Jeferis in Virginia in 1789, he reported she had "Lost her Speech four Days & Nights But God was with her She Saw A Glorious place and heared heavenly Music; and also Heard the Screeks & Crys of Damned Souls."[26]

In general, white Southern Baptists and Methodists, unlike the English, came to be far more interested in the conversion experience than in the redemption of time afterwards, emphasized by Wesley. By the nineteenth century, however, many whites, unaware of the historic roots of vision travels, rejected such "dreams, visions, trances [and] voices" as non-Christian.[27]

In the nineteenth century, the social and emotional distance between whites and blacks grew, both in daily life and in the churches. For some blacks, achieving freedom in Christ became in part a blow against white oppression.[28] However, in the eighteenth century many blacks and whites had found a joint path to spiritual freedom and coherent world views and had often helped each other along this way.

Most blacks began to think of themselves as Christians, although their religion (and their world view) retained African values and perceptions. Both time and place were still seen much in traditional terms, with unique events and sacred places of special import. However, the High God had been generally accepted as the cause of death, with sin an important causal factor; but sin was more likely to be seen as a violation of a taboo than as a moral failing. "Magic" was still recognized as potent and possibly God-given, although it was more likely to be from the Devil. The "little me," an inner soul, was recognized as existing before the body and as separable and capable of journeying to hell and heaven. Individuals were still to aim for wholeness, and kin determined social life both on the earth and after death. Placating their spirits was very important, and funerals remained the most significant transitional rites.

Whites had come to share many African perceptions without being aware of it. African attitudes to time and place had reinforced old Christian views, and an African esthetic had altered both building styles and techniques. Belief in magic had been reinvigorated, and it was accepted that human beings could sometimes cause death through its power. Spirits were perceived in a new way. Life after death was seen as a "homecoming," and kin were expected to welcome the spirits. Funerals became far more important, and graveyards were recognized as places where spirits should be honored. In sharing day-to-day life with blacks, some whites had "slided over" into their ways of working, some were influenced by their perceptions of time and space, and eventually some were unconsciously made ready to share black traditions of seeking spirit in ecstasy.[29]

Thomas Rankin was overwhelmed by "the presence of the Lord in their midst" when he was at a Methodist meeting in Virginia in July of 1775. Blacks and whites were crying, moaning, and shouting, and Rankin was brought to a vision of redemption: "Verily, the God of Glory has wrought a very great work among this people. . . . Virginia, I believe, will be as the Garden of the Lord, as Eden before him."[30] However, if Virginia "was like the Garden of the Lord, it was [also] like the land of Egypt" (Genesis 13:10), both with its slaves and slave-owners. Blacks knew this when they sang of Israel in bondage and of Moses. Whites had told blacks these sacred stories, but blacks had made them their own.

Blacks and whites were together in church, house, field, and garden. They had variant visions of the future, but they shared an important part of time present as well as time past. Surveying Southern culture in the twentieth century, Henry Glassie has suggested that we ought to ask ourselves "why the children of white farmers in the Lowland South are often given carefully homemade Negro dolls with which to play."[31] (See Figure 44.) I think the beginning of the answer lies in the eighteenth century, when blacks and whites played together both as children and later before God.

FIGURE 44. A white's homemade black doll. "When this cloth doll was new, in about 1937, it had a railroad red bandana around its neck. A couple of generations of white children have left the doll, named after an elderly, well-liked, local Negro, in good condition; North Garden, Albemarle County, Virginia (September, 1965)." Reprinted with permission of Henry Glassie, from *Pattern in the Material Folk Culture of the Eastern United States* (Philadelphia, 1968).

Notes

INTRODUCTION

1. Wesley M. Gewehr, *The Great Awakening in Virginia, 1740–1790* (Chapel Hill, 1930), 72, 96, 169, 170, 235–239, 241–253, 261.
2. Mechal Sobel, *Trabelin' On: The Slave Journey to an Afro-Baptist Faith* (Westport, Conn., 1979). For a revisionist view of the Awakening, as well as a detailed bibliography, see Jon Butler, "Enthusiasm Described and Decried: The Great Awakening as Interpretive Fiction," *Journal of American History* 69 (1982), 305–325.
3. Colonial population estimates vary widely. See the excellent discussion and analysis in Allan Kulikoff, "A 'Prolifick' People: Black Population Growth in the Chesapeake Colonies, 1700–1790," *Southern Studies* 16 (1977), 391–428; Kulikoff, "The Origins of Afro-American Society in Tidewater Maryland and Virginia, 1700 to 1790," *William and Mary Quarterly* 35 (1978), 226–259 (all references to *William and Mary Quarterly* are to the third series, unless otherwise noted); Kulikoff, *Tobacco and Slaves: The Development of Southern Cultures in the Chesapeake, 1680–1800* (Chapel Hill, 1986); E. B. Greene and V. D. Harrington, *American Population Before the Federal Census of 1790* (New York, 1932); U.S. Bureau of the Census, *Historical Statistics of the United States. Colonial Times to 1970*, 2 vols. (Washington, D.C., 1975), Table 21–19, a:1168; Robert V. Wells, *The Population of the British Colonies in America Before 1776: A Survey of Census Data* (Princeton, 1975); Wesley Frank Craven, *White, Red and Black: The Seventeenth-Century Virginian* (Charlottesville, 1971); Edmund S. Morgan, *American Slavery, American Freedom: The Ordeal of Colonial Virginia* (New York, 1975). The following table is a rough estimate of black and white population based on the above sources:

Year	Black	White	Year	Black	White
1650	400	18,000	1760	140,500	200,000
1680	3,000	40,000	1770	187,500	260,000
1700	15,000	45,000	*		
1710	19,000	55,000	1780	223,500	317,000
1730	36,500	84,000	1790	305,000†	432,000
1750	107,000	130,000			

* In 1778, the foreign slave trade to Virginia was legally closed.

† In 1790, of the 305,000 blacks, 292,500 were slaves, 12,500 were free.

The black population was unevenly distributed: All through the eighteenth century, some areas had a relatively high black population, whereas others, essentially those on the "moving" western frontier, were primarily white. See the map in the Introduction. William Byrd ɪɪ's comments are from his letter to John Perceval, Earl of Egmont, July 12, 1736, in *The Correspondence of the Three William Byrds of Westover, Virginia, 1684–1776*, ed. Marian Tinling, 2 vols. (Charlottesville, 1977), 2:487. In the latest study of interregional migration, 1800–1860, McClelland and Zeckhauser conclude that "To the common view of an East–West flow [of population] must now be added the uncommon view of a *major South–North flow throughout the entire 60 year period*." White Virginians emigrated to southern, western, and northwestern communities. Peter D. McClelland and Richard J. Zeckhauser, *Demographic Dimen-*

sions of the New Republic: American Interregional Migration, Vital Statistics, and Manumissions, 1800–1860 (Cambridge, England, 1982), 7. On black
population movement out of Virginia, see Allan Kulikoff, "Uprooted Peoples:
Black Migrants in the Age of the American Revolution, 1790–1820," in *Slavery and Freedom in the Age of the American Revolution*, ed. Ira Berlin and
Ronald Hoffman (Charlottesville, 1983), 143–173.

4. Philip D. Morgan, "Slave Life in the Virginia Piedmont, 1720–1790: A Demo-
   graphic Report," Conference on "The Colonial Experience: The Eighteenth
   Century Chesapeake," Baltimore, September 1984, mimeographed; Richard S.
   Dunn, "Black Society in the Chesapeake, 1776–1810," in *Slavery and Freedom
   in the Age of the American Revolution*, ed. Ira Berlin and Ronald Hoffman
   (Charlottesville, 1983), 49–82. I am indebted to Allan Kulikoff for information
   on the growth of the slave population in the 1770s and 1780s. Communication,
   November 1985.

5. Not all the colonies had the same experience with racial interaction. In South
   Carolina, for example, blacks quickly became a far higher percentage of the
   population and often worked "alone" on their tasks. The case in Virginia, however, had much wider ramifications. First, its white population was much
   larger, and second, it became the home "base" from which a large white and
   black population moved to the South, West, and Northwest, taking Virginia's
   culture along with it. On South Carolina see Philip D. Morgan, "Work and Culture: The Task System and the World of Low-country Blacks, 1700 to 1800,"
   William and Mary Quarterly 39 (1982), 563–599.

6. Elizabeth Donnan, *Documents Illustrative of the History of the Slave Trade to
   America*, 4 vols. (New York, [1930–1935] 1969); Philip D. Curtin, *The Atlantic
   Slave Trade: A Census* (Madison, Wis., 1969), 125, 157–158, 161, 188, 245;
   Herbert S. Klein, "Slaves and Shipping in Eighteenth Century Virginia," *Journal of Interdisciplinary History* 3 (1975), 383–412, reprinted in Klein, *The Middle Passage: Comparative Studies in the Atlantic Slave Trade* (Princeton,
   1978), 121–140; Walter Minchinton, Celia King, and Peter Waite, eds., *Virginia
   Slave Trade Statistics, 1698–1775* (Richmond, 1984). Susan A. Westbury,
   "Colonial Virginia and the Atlantic Slave Trade" (Ph.D. dissertation, University of Illinois, 1981), has found records of some 7,020 slaves imported into Virginia that Donnan was unaware of. Westbury concludes that the Virginia slave
   trade with Africa was as large as—and possibly larger than—South Carolina's.
   Jim Potter suggests that in "the colonial period some hundred thousand slaves
   were imported into Virginia." Potter, "Demographic Development and Family
   Structure," in *Colonial British America: Essays in the New History of the
   Early Modern Era*, ed. Jack P. Greene and J. R. Pole (Baltimore, 1984), 139. On
   African origins see Patrick Manning, "The Slave Trade in the Bight of Benin,
   1640–1890," in *The Uncommon Market: Essays in the Economic History of
   the Atlantic Slave Trade*, ed. Henry A. Gemery and Jan S. Hogendorn (New
   York, 1979), 107–142; Melville Herskovits found that of the Virginia slaves
   whose African origins could be identified, more were from the Niger Delta
   than any other region, almost as many came from the Gold Coast, and sizable
   groups had arrived from Senegambia and Angola. Herskovits, *The Myth of the
   Negro Past* (Boston, [1941] 1958), 46–48. James A. Rawley has interpreted currently available data as indicating that 38 percent of all African slaves brought
   into Virginia, from 1710 to 1760, were from the Bight of Biafra. Rawley, *The
   Transatlantic Slave Trade: A History* (New York, 1981), 335. See also Marion

Dusser De Barenne Kilson, "West African Society and the Atlantic Slave Trade, 1441–1865," in *Key Issues in the Afro-American Experience,* ed. Nathan I. Huggins et al. (New York, 1971), 48. Analysts are agreed that the African population in Virginia differed significantly from the South Carolina one, where the Bight of Biafra accounted for only two percent of the migrants whereas two-fifths were Angolans. On Virginia planter preferences for Gold Coast and Gambia slaves see Darold D. Wax, "Preferences for Slaves in Colonial America," *Journal of Negro History* 58 (1973), 391, 395, 396. The Igbo, a Kwa-speaking people of eastern Nigeria, are often referred to as the Ibo. For currently preferred ethnic group terminology, see Roland Oliver and Michael Crowder, eds., *The Cambridge Encyclopedia of Africa* (Cambridge, England, 1981), 78–88.

7. For an analysis of the problems involved in assessing African history see Douglas L. Wheeler, "Toward a History of Angola: Problems and Sources," in *Western African History,* ed. D. F. McCall et al. (New York, 1969), 45–68; Jan Vansina, *Oral Tradition: A Study in Historical Methodology* (Chicago, 1965).

8. Simon Ottenberg, "Ibo Receptivity to Change," in *Continuity and Change in African Cultures,* ed. William R. Bascom and Melville J. Herskovits (Chicago, [1959] 1962), 130–143.

9. For an introduction to the range of African beliefs, see Daryll Forde, *African Worlds: Studies in the Cosmological Ideas and Social Values of African Peoples* (London, [1954] 1970); John S. Mbiti, *Introduction to African Religion* (London, 1975); Geoffrey Parrinder, *West African Religion: A Study of the Beliefs and Practices of Akan, Ewe, Yoruba, Ibo and Kindred Peoples* (London, [1949] 1969); Benjamin C. Ray, *African Religions: Symbol, Ritual, and Community* (Englewood Cliffs, N.J., 1976).

10. Amelia County had the largest population of new arrivals after 1750. P. Morgan, "Slave Life," 5 and Table 4, maintains that 60 percent of Amelia County's adult slaves were African in 1755 and 20 percent in 1782. See also R. Dunn, "Black Society," 58–69; Amelia County Records, Virginia State Library (microfilm). For a bibliography of extant Virginia records, see David H. Flaherty, "A Select Guide to the Manuscript Court Records of Colonial Virginia," *American Journal of Legal History* 19 (1975), 112–137.

11. Carl Bridenbaugh, *Vexed and Troubled Englishmen, 1590–1642* (New York, 1968); James Sears McGee, *The Godly Man in Stuart England: Anglicans, Puritans, and the Two Tables, 1620–1670* (New Haven, 1976), 14, 237, 245; J. J. Scarisbrick, *The Reformation and the English People* (Oxford, 1984), 136–188; G. R. Elton, "Contentment and Discontent on the Eve of Colonization," in *Early Maryland in a Wider World,* ed. David. B. Quinn (Detroit, 1982), 105–118; David B. Quinn, "Why They Came," in *Early Maryland in a Wider World,* ed. David B. Quinn (Detroit, 1982), 119–148; Perry Miller, *Errand Into the Wilderness* (New York, 1956), 108, 139, 183; Babette M. Levy, "Early Puritans in the Southern and Island Colonies," in *American Antiquarian Society Proceedings* 70 (1960), pt. 1, 86, 119, 308.

12. Darrett B. Rutman, "The Evolution of Religious Life in Early Virginia," *Lex et Scientia* 14 (1978), 190–214. For a variant view see Herbert Leventhal, *In the Shadow of the Enlightenment: Occultism and Renaissance Science in Eighteenth-Century America* (New York, 1976).

13. Richard R. Beeman, *The Evolution of the Southern Backcountry: A Case Study of Lunenburg County Virginia, 1746–1832* (Philadelphia, 1984), 22, 23,

56, 94; Carole Shammas, "English-Born and Creole Elites in Turn-of-the-Century Virginia," in *The Chesapeake in the Seventeenth Century: Essays on Anglo-American Society*, ed. Thad W. Tate and David L. Ammerman (New York, 1979), 274–296; Darrett B. Rutman and Anita H. Rutman, *A Place in Time: Middlesex County, Virginia, 1650–1750* (New York, 1984), 76, referred to below as Rutman, *A Place in Time I*, and Rutman and Rutman, *A Place in Time: Explicatus* (New York, 1984), referred to below as Rutman, *A Place in Time II*. The Rutmans find that in Middlesex County 55 percent of the white population was Virginian-born in 1700, 77 percent in 1724, and over 90 percent by 1750. For the seventeenth-century background, see E. Morgan, *American Slavery, American Freedom*; W. Craven, *White, Red and Black*, 25 and 30; Lois Green Carr and Russell R. Menard, "Immigration and Opportunity: The Freedman in Early Colonial Maryland," in *The Chesapeake in the Seventeenth Century*, ed. Tate and Ammerman, 239. See also Mildred Campbell, "Social Origins of some Early Americans," in *Seventeenth-Century America: Essays in Colonial History*, ed. James Morton Smith (New York, [1959] 1972), 76; David Galenson, "British Servants and the Colonial Indenture System in the Eighteenth Century," *Journal of Southern History* 44 (1978), 41–66; Galenson, *White Servitude in Colonial America: An Economic Analysis* (Cambridge, England, 1981); James Horn, "Servant Emigration to the Chesapeake in the Seventeenth Century," in *The Chesapeake in the Seventeenth Century*, ed. Tate and Ammerman, 3–50; Russell R. Menard, "From Servants to Slaves: The Transformation of the Chesapeake Labor System," *Southern Studies* 16 (1977), 355–390; Richard S. Dunn, "Servants and Slaves: The Recruitment and Employment of Labor," in *Colonial British America*, ed. Greene and Pole, 157–194.

14. Rutman, *A Place in Time I*, 73, 75.

15. Beeman, *Evolution of the Southern Backcountry*, 14–15, 22–24, 56, 78–80, 99, 171–172. See Forrest McDonald and Ellen Shapiro McDonald, "The Ethnic Origins of the American People, 1790," *William and Mary Quarterly* 37 (1980), 179–199 for data and bibliography.

16. On methodological problems in relation to slave data, see C. Vann Woodward, "History from Slave Sources," *American Historical Review* 79 (1974), 470–481; John W. Blassingame, "Using the Testimony of Ex-Slaves: Approaches and Problems," *Journal of Southern History* 41 (1975), 473–492; Norman Yetman, "Ex-Slave Interviews and the Historiography of Slavery," *American Quarterly* 36 (1984), 181–210. David Hall suggestively discusses some key problems in the study of popular culture in his "Introduction" to *Understanding Popular Culture: Europe from the Middle Ages to the Nineteenth Century*, ed. Steven L. Kaplan (Berlin, 1984), 5–18. Poor whites in eighteenth-century Virginia have not been studied in any depth. See the bibliographic essay in J. Wayne Flynt and Dorothy S. Flynt, *Southern Poor Whites: A Selected Bibliography of Published Sources* (New York, 1981).

17. Thomas Luckman, *The Invisible Religion: The Problem of Religion in Modern Society* (New York, 1967), 52–54, 61; see also Luckman and Peter L. Berger, *The Social Construction of Reality: A Treatise in the Sociology of Knowledge* (London, 1966). A broad survey of work on world views can be found in W. T. Jones, "World Views: Their Nature and Function," *Current Anthropology* 13 (1972), 79–109.

18. Luckman, *The Invisible Religion*, 51–68; Peter Berger, *The Sacred Canopy* (Garden City, N.Y., 1969).

19. J. L. Dillard, *Black English: Its History and Usage in the United States* (New York, 1972).

20. Maurice Mandelbaum, *The Anatomy of Historical Knowledge* (Baltimore, 1977), 138–139. See also Peter Gay, *Art and Act: On Causes in History—Manet, Gropius, Mondrian* (New York, 1976), x, 7.

21. See, for a striking recent example, Daniel Blake Smith, *Inside the Great House: Planter Family Life in Eighteenth-Century Chesapeake Society* (Ithaca, 1980), 19, who found that "Slavery . . . remains almost impervious to study—at least in the seventeenth and eighteenth centuries—simply because of the paucity of surviving sources. . . . The silence of the documents on the slave experience in planter households is overwhelming."

22. Mandelbaum does consider the issues raised here but "dismisses" them. Mandlebaum, *The Anatomy of Historical Knowledge*, 192. An excellent introduction to important aspects of early American cultural history can be found in James Deetz, *In Small Things Forgotten: The Archeology of Early American Life* (Garden City, N.Y., 1977). On overdeterminism in history see Peter Gay, *Freud for Historians* (New York, 1985), 50, n. 8; 186–187.

23. Melville J. Herskovits and William R. Bascom, "The Problem of Stability and Change in African Cultures," in *Continuity and Change*, ed. Bascom and Herskovits, 8.

24. A comprehensive overview of the vast "new history" of the colonial era can be found in the bibliographic essays in Greene and Pole, eds., *Colonial British America*.

25. Rhys Isaac, for example, in his fine study of eighteenth-century Virginia, accepts this view of a "divergent" black culture and does not consider black–white interaction in depth. Isaac, *The Transformation of Virginia, 1740–1790: Community, Religion, and Authority* (Chapel Hill, 1982), 407, n. 16. However, in a "divergent" appendix Landon Carter and his slaves are seen as dramatic actors on the same stage. Isaac, 323–356; reprinted from "Ethnographic Method in History: An Action Approach," *Historical Methodology* 12 (1980), 43–61. See Michael Craton, ed., "Roots and Branches; Current Directions in Slave Studies," *Historical Reflections* 6, no. 2 (Summer 1979), entire issue; Peter H. Wood, " 'I Did the Best I Could For My Day': The Study of Early Black History During the Second Reconstruction, 1960 to 1976," *William and Mary Quarterly* 35 (1978), 185–225.

26. Melville J. Herskovits made a strong argument for this position long ago, but strangely few investigations have followed up his leads. See "What has Africa Given America?" in his *The New World Negro: Selected Papers in Afroamerican Studies* (Bloomington, 1966), 168–174; and Herskovits, *Myth of the Negro Past*. C. Vann Woodward briefly but significantly considered the relatedness of black and white cultures in "Clio with Soul," *Journal of American History* 56 (1969), 5–20. Peter H. Wood's significant evaluation of Africans' contributions to rice culture in *Black Majority: Negroes in Colonial South Carolina from 1670 through the Stono Rebellion* (New York, 1974) has been further substantiated by Daniel C. Littlefield in *Rice and Slaves: Ethnicity and the Slave Trade in Colonial South Carolina* (Baton Rouge, 1981), but neither Wood nor Littlefield explored cultural interaction in depth. Perhaps the most important

consideration of slave–master cultural interrelationships is to be found in Eugene Genovese's study of antebellum life, *Roll, Jordan Roll: The World the Slaves Made* (New York, 1974). Among the many innovative analyses of slave society, Raimondo Luraghi, *The Rise and Fall of the Plantation South* (New York, 1978) and Willie Lee Rose, *Slavery and Freedom* (New York, 1982) should be singled out. Sidney Mintz and Richard Price have written a wide-ranging analysis of methodological approaches to black–white interaction in *An Anthropological Approach to the Afro-American Past: A Caribbean Perspective* (Philadelphia, 1976). Gary Nash has broadly considered the interactions of Europeans, Africans, and native Americans in his fine essay, *Red, White and Black: The Peoples of Early America* (Englewood Cliffs, N.J., 1974). This triracial mix, most important in the South, has not been analyzed in depth by anyone else. Allan Kulikoff, in *Tobacco and Slaves*, 381–420, discusses white–black relationships on small farms and between white overseers and slaves, covering a wide range of relevant economic and social issues and providing an excellent analysis of Chesapeake society. He strongly argues that there were two "Southern cultures in the Chesapeake, 1680–1800."

CHAPTER 1

1. Luckman, *The Invisible Religion*, 53.
2. Ibid., 51–68.
3. This summary description of world views is taken from Sobel, *Trabelin' On*, 3–5.
4. Christopher Hill, *The World Turned Upside Down: Radical Ideas During the English Revolution* (London, 1972), 12. For a discussion of and bibliography on modernization, see Michael Zuckerman, "Dreams That Men Dare to Dream: The Role of Ideas in Western Modernization," *Social Science History* 2 (1978), 332–345; Dean C. Tipps, "Modernization Theory and the Comparative Study of Societies: A Critical Perspective," *Comparative Studies in Society and History* 15 (1973), 199–226; Joyce Appleby, "Value and Society," in *Colonial British America*, ed. Greene and Pole, 290–316, surveys contemporary historians who regard values as "the principal cohesive force in society."
5. Christopher Hill, *Reformation to Industrial Revolution: The Making of Modern English Society. Vol. 1: 1530–1780* (New York, 1968), 228; Keith Thomas, *Religion and the Decline of Magic: Studies in Popular Beliefs in Sixteenth and Seventeenth Century England* (London, 1971), 160; Patrick Collinson, *The Religion of Protestants: The Church in English Society, 1559–1625* (Oxford, 1982), 198.
6. Bernard Gilpin, 1552, cited by Thomas, *Religion and the Decline of Magic*, 278. See Scarisbrick, *The Reformation and the English People*, 46, 106, 136–161; Imogen Luxton, "The Reformation and Popular Culture," in *Church and Society in England: Henry VIII to James I*, ed. Felicity Heal and Rosemary O'Day (London, 1977), 57–77; Christopher Hill, "Science and Magic in Seventeenth-Century England," in *Culture, Ideology and Politics: Essays for Eric Hobsbawn*, ed. Raphael Samuel and Gareth S. Jones (London, 1982), 176–193.
7. Clare Gittings, *Death, Burial and the Individual in Early Modern England* (London, 1984), 40.

8. G. J. Cuming, *A History of Anglican Liturgy*, 2d ed. (London, [1969] 1982), 10–11, 64–66, 111–112.

9. Gittings, *Death, Burial and the Individual*, 151.

10. See William Byrd II's 1725 essay on the extent of English belief in arational means in "The Female Creed," in *Another Secret Diary of William Byrd of Westover, 1739–1741; with Letters and Literary Exercises, 1696–1726*, ed. Maude A. Woodfin and Marion Tinling (Richmond, 1942), 445–476. (This volume is referred to below as Byrd, *Diary 1739–1741*.)

11. A. J. Gurevich, "Time as a Problem of Cultural History," in *Cultures and Time*, ed. L. Gardet et al. (Paris, 1976), 229–245.

12. On causality and social change in this period, see Christopher Hill, *Change and Continuity in Seventeenth-Century England* (London, 1974).

13. On English world views, see Bridenbaugh, *Vexed and Troubled Englishmen*; Wallace Notestein, *The English People on the Eve of Colonization, 1603–1630* (New York, 1962); Christopher Hill, *Society and Puritanism in Pre-Revolutionary England* (New York, 1964); Keith Wrightson and David Levine, *Poverty and Piety in an English Village; Terling, 1525–1700* (New York, 1979); Wrightson, *English Society: 1580–1680* (New Brunswick, N.J., 1982); Paul Delany, *British Autobiography in the Seventeenth Century* (London, 1969).

14. On Anglican and Puritan calendars and sense of time, see Horton Davies, *Worship and Theology in England; From Andrewes to Baxter and Fox, 1603–1690* (Princeton, 1975), 215–252. On the Anglicans in this period, see Collinson, *The Religion of Protestants*.

15. Herskovits, *Myth of the Negro Past*; Mintz and Price, *An Anthropological Approach*; Roger D. Abrahams, "The Shaping of Folklore Traditions in the British West Indies," *Journal of Inter-American Studies* 9 (1967), 456–480; Alan P. Merriam, "African Music," in *Continuity and Change*, ed. Bascom and Herskovits, 49–86; Sobel, *Trabelin' On*, 3–21.

16. Newell S. Booth, Jr., "Time and Change in African Traditional Thought," *Journal of Religion in Africa* 7 (1975), 81–91.

17. James W. Fernandez, *Bwiti: An Ethnology of the Religious Imagination in Africa* (Princeton, 1982), 49–98.

18. Mbiti, *Introduction to African Religion*, 34–35; Ray, *African Religions*, 17, 20, 41–42, 155, 167.

19. Dominique Zahan, *The Religion, Spirituality and Thought of Traditional Africa* (Chicago, [1970] 1979), 20–23.

20. Alexis Kagame, "The Empirical Apperception of Time and the Conception of History in Bantu Thought," in *Cultures and Time*, ed. Gardet et al., 89–116; Robin Horton and Ruth Finnegan, *Modes of Thought: Essays on Thinking in Western and Non-Western Societies* (London, 1973).

21. Geoffrey Parrinder, *African Traditional Religion* (London, 1954), 134–141. See bibliography in Patrick E. Ofori, *Black African Traditional Religions and Philosophy: A Select Bibliographic Survey of the Sources from the Earliest Times to 1974* (Nendeln, Lichtenstein, 1977).

CHAPTER 2

1. Rollo May, "Contributions of Existential Psychotherapy," and Henri F. Ellenberger, "A Clinical Introduction to Psychiatric Phenomenology and Existen-

tial Analysis," in *Existence: A New Dimension in Psychiatry and Psychology*, ed. May et al. (New York, 1958), 37–91, 92–126. See Derek de Solla Price, "Clockwork Before the Clock and Timekeepers Before Timekeeping," in *The Study of Time II*, ed. J. T. Fraser and N. Lawrence (Berlin, 1975), 367–380; Gurevich, "Time as a Problem of Cultural History." Edward T. Hall has written several very suggestive studies dealing with perception of time and space. See especially *The Silent Language* (Garden City, N.Y., 1959), 23–42, and *The Dance of Life: The Other Dimension of Time* (Garden City, N.Y., 1983); Yi-Fu Tuan, "Space Time, Place: A Humanistic Frame," in *Making Sense of Time*, vol. 1, ed. T. Carlstein et al. (London, 1978), 1:7–16. Thomas J. Cottle and Stephen L. Klineberg, *The Present of Things Future: Explorations of Time in Human Experience* (New York, 1974); David S. Landes, *Revolution in Time: Clocks and the Making of the Modern World* (Cambridge, Mass., 1983), 17–84; Georges Gurvitch, *The Spectrum of Social Time* (Dordrecht, 1964); Jacques LeGoff, *Time, Work, and Culture in the Middle Ages* (Chicago, 1980); Carlo Cipolla, *Clocks and Culture, 1300–1700* (New York, 1967).

2. Nina Gockerell, "Telling Time Without a Clock," in *The Clockwork Universe: German Clocks and Automata 1550–1650*, ed. Klaus Maurice and Otto Mayr (New York, 1980), 131, n. 2. Our term noon is from nones, although it originally designated approximately 3 P.M. The Anglican Church fused matins, lauds, and prime into one morning prayer time; dropped the "little hours" of terce, sext, and none; and fused vespers and compline in the evening. See Cuming, *History of Anglican Liturgy*, 7–9, 48.

3. E. P. Thompson, "Time, Work-Discipline and Industrial Capitalism," *Past and Present* 38 (1967), 58.

4. David D. Hall, "The Mental World of Samuel Sewall," in *Saints and Revolutionaries: Essays on Early American History*, ed. Hall et al. (New York, 1984), 75–98; D. Hall, "The World of Print and Collective Mentality in Seventeenth-Century New England," in *New Directions in American Intellectual History*, ed. John Higham and Paul K. Conkin (Baltimore, 1979), 166–180; G. T. Salusbury-Jones, *Street Life in Medieval England*, 2d ed. (Hassocks, Sussex, [1948] 1975), 167–197.

5. Ivy Pinchbeck and Margaret Hewitt, *Children in English Society*, 2 vols. (London, 1969–1973), 1:7.

6. Hill, *Reformation to Industrial Revolution*, 88. Keith Thomas, "Age and Authority in Early Modern England," *Proceedings of the British Academy* 62 (1976), 205–248. I am indebted to Keith Thomas for sharing data on English perceptions of age that confirm this view. Arthur E. Imhof, in a communication of February 1985, suggests that most Germans of this period could also have known their baptism dates, registered from circa the second half of the sixteenth century, but they had no need or desire to know them.

7. John R. Gillis, *Youth and History: Tradition and Change in European Age Relations, 1770–Present* (New York, 1981), 4.

8. Gillis, *Youth and History*, 5; Edward T. Hall, *The Hidden Dimension* (Garden City, N.Y., 1966), 173–174; Hall, *Beyond Culture* (Garden City, N.Y., 1976), 14–15.

9. Denys Thompson, ed., *Change and Tradition in Rural England: An Anthology of Writings on Country Life* (Cambridge, England, 1980), 125–126.

10. Thomas, *Religion and the Decline of Magic*, 615–621.

11. The pendulum was perfected circa 1658; pocket watches proliferated after 1674; and in the 1680s England became the center of watch and clock manufacture. Cipolla, *Clocks and Culture*, 65–69.

12. Thomas Ken, *The Prose Works of the Right Reverend Thomas Ken, D.D.*, ed. W. Benham (London, 188?), 224.

13. Ken, in *The English Sermon: An Anthology, Vol. 2: 1650–1750*, ed. Charles Herbert Sisson (Manchester, England, 1976), 181.

14. Henry, *Diaries and Letters of Philip Henry, M.A.*, ed. M. H. Lee, cited by Gerald R. Cragg, *Puritanism in the Period of the Great Persecution, 1660–1688* (Cambridge, England, 1957), 134. Hill, *Society and Puritanism*, 127.

15. Charles E. Hambrick-Stowe, *The Practice of Piety: Puritan Devotional Disciplines in Seventeenth Century New England* (Chapel Hill, 1982), 174, 190, 191.

16. Charles H. George and Katherine George, *The Protestant Mind of the English Reformation, 1570–1640* (Princeton, 1961), 143.

17. John Wesley, *The Journal of the Rev. John Wesley*, ed. N. Curnock, 8 vols. (London, 1909–1916), 1:82–83; also in John Wesley, *The Works of John Wesley*, 3d ed., 14 vols. (Grand Rapids, 1984), 1:103. In Georgia in August of 1737, at the outset of his preaching career, Wesley was accused of instituting hours of prayer for wives and servants "very inconsistent with the labour and employments of the Colony." "List of Grievances" in R. M. Cameron, ed., *The Rise of Methodism: A Source Book* (New York, 1954), 126.

18. "Doctrinal Minutes" of the Conference of June 1774, in *The Rise of Methodism*, ed. Cameron, 356–357.

19. See Alan Smith, *The Established Church and Popular Religion, 1750–1850* (London, 1970), 33–41; Robert F. Wearmouth, *Methodism and the Common People of the Eighteenth Century* (London, 1945), 217–362.

20. E. P. Thompson, "Time, Work-Discipline and Industrial Capitalism," 73.

21. J. Arbuthnot, 1773, cited by J. L. Hammond and Barbara Hammond, *The Village Laborer, 1760–1832: A Study in the Government of England Before the Reform Bill* (New York, [1920] 1970), 13.

22. G. Markham, 1636, cited by E. P. Thompson, "Time, Work-Discipline and Industrial Capitalism," 77.

23. Joseph Arch, "The Autobiography of Joseph Arch," in *Change and Tradition in Rural England*, ed. D. Thompson, 110; E. P. Thompson, "Time, Work-Discipline and Industrial Capitalism," 54.

24. Ann Kussmaul, *Servants in Husbandry in Early Modern England* (Cambridge, England, 1981), 45–46.

25. Landon Carter, *The Diary of Colonel Landon Carter of Sabine Hall, 1752–1778*, ed. Jack P. Greene, 2 vols. (Charlottesville, 1965).

26. On labor traditions, see R. W. Malcolmson, *Life and Labour in England 1700–1780* (New York, 1981); Wrightson, *English Society: 1580–1680*; Eric Kerridge, *The Farmers of Old England* (London, 1973); D. Thompson, ed., *Change and Tradition in Rural England*; Peter Laslett, *The World We Have Lost: England Before the Industrial Age*, 2d ed. (London, 1971); G. E. Fussell, *The English Rural Labourer* (London, 1949); Dorothy Marshall, *The English Domestic Servant in History* (London, 1949); J. Jean Hecht, *The Domestic Servant Class in Eighteenth-Century England* (London, 1956); Kussmaul, *Servants in Husbandry*; E. P. Thompson, "Time, Work-Discipline and Industrial Capitalism";

Keith Thomas, "Work and Leisure in Pre-Industrial Society," *Past and Present* 29 (1964), 50–62.

27. Anonymous, "The Trade of England Revived" (1681), 8; D. Defoe, *The Behavior of Servants* (1724), 84; J. Locke, *Report to The Board of Trade* (1697), 102; R. Dunning, *A Plain and Easie Method* (1886), 1; J. Massie, *Considerations Relating to the Poor* (1757), 58; all cited by Dorothy Marshall, *The English Poor in the Eighteenth Century* (London, 1926), 30–31.

28. Rennie, Brown, and Sheriff, *General View of the Agriculture of West Riding* (1794), 25, cited by E. P. Thompson, *The Making of the English Working Class* (London, 1963), 237.

29. E. Morgan, *American Slavery, American Freedom*, 64.

30. D. C. Coleman, "Labour in the English Economy of the Seventeenth Century," in *Seventeenth Century England: Society in an Age of Revolution*, ed. Paul S. Seaver (New York, 1976), 125–128.

31. E. P. Thompson, *The Making of the English Working Class*.

32. Paul Bohanan, "Concepts of Time among the Tiv of Nigeria," *Southwestern Journal of Anthropology* 9 (1953), 253; J. B. Danquah, *The Akan Doctrine of God: A Fragment of Gold Coast Ethics and Religion* (London, 1968).

33. E. E. Evans-Pritchard, "Nuer Time Reckoning," *Africa* 12 (1939), 189–216; abridged in Evans-Pritchard, *The Nuer: A Description of the Modes of Livelihood and Political Institutions of a Nilotic People* (Oxford, 1968), 104–108. East Europeans often used similar descriptions of time, as the time when "the people come from the field" or the time when "the herd returns." Gockerell, "Telling Time Without a Clock," 131–143.

34. E. P. Thompson, "Time, Work-Discipline and Industrial Capitalism," 58, notes that use is made of some set periods of time, as "the time it takes to cook rice in."

35. Evans-Pritchard, "Nuer Time Reckoning," 208.

36. Gwilym I. Jones, "Ibo Age Organization with Special Reference to the Cross River and North-Eastern Ibo," *Journal of the Royal Anthropological Institute of Great Britain and Ireland* 92 (1962), 191–221; Evans-Pritchard, "Nuer Time Reckoning," 211; Bohanan, "Concepts of Time Among the Tiv," 258.

37. Bohanan, "Concepts of Time Among the Tiv," 275, 261.

38. T. O. Beidelman, "Kaguro Time Reckoning: An Aspect of the Cosmology of an East African People," *Southwestern Journal of Anthropology* 19 (1963), 18. Booth, "Time and Change," 8; Kagame, "The Empirical Apperception of Time," 89–116.

39. H. B. Green, "Temporal Attitudes in Four Negro Subcultures," in *The Study of Time*, ed. J. T. Fraser et al. (Berlin, 1972), 402–417.

40. Olaudah Equiano, "The Life of Olaudah Equiano, or Gustavus Vassa, the African" (1784), in *Great Slave Narratives*, ed. Arna Bontemps (Boston, 1969), 14.

41. Equiano, "The Life of Olaudah Equiano," 10, 13. On Equiano's background, see Philip D. Curtin, "Olaudah Equiano of the Niger Ibo," in *Africa Remembered: Narratives by West Africans from the Era of the Slave Trade*, ed. Curtin (Madison, Wis., 1967), 60–98; G. T. Basden, *Niger Ibos* (London, 1938); Daryll Forde and G. I. Jones, *The Ibo and Ibibio-Speaking Peoples of Southeastern Nigeria* (London, 1962).

42. Victor C. Uchendu, "Social Determinants of Agricultural Change," in *Agricultural Change in Tropical Africa*, ed. Kenneth R. M. Anthony et al. (Ithaca,

1979), 205; Uchendu, *The Igbo of Southeast Nigeria* (New York, 1965), 22–38. On Tiv work patterns see Akiga, *Akiga's Story: The Tiv Tribe as Seen by One of Its Members*, trans. Rupert East, 2d ed. (London, 1965), 342.

43. Douglas Grant, *The Fortunate Slave: An Illustration of African Slavery in the Early Eighteenth Century* (London, 1968), 13. On materialistic values in West Africa see Robert A. LeVine, *Dreams and Deeds: Achievement Motivation in Nigeria* (Chicago, 1966), 3–7; Uchendu, "Social Determinants of Agricultural Change," 204–205.

44. Suzanne Miers and Igor Kopytoff, eds., *Slavery in Africa: Historical and Anthropological Perspectives* (Madison, Wis., 1977); Martin Klein and Paul E. Lovejoy, "Domestic Slavery in West Africa," in *The Uncommon Market*, ed. Gemery and Hogendorn, 181–212; Lovejoy, *Transformations in Slavery: A History of Slavery in Africa* (Cambridge, England, 1983); Claire Robertson and Martin A. Klein, eds., *Women and Slavery in Africa* (Madison, Wis., 1983).

45. Alan Lomax, "The Homogeneity of African-Afro-American Musical Style," in *Afro-American Anthropology: Contemporary Perspectives*, ed. Norman E. Whitten, Jr., and John F. Szwed (New York, 1970), 192.

CHAPTER 3

1. Equiano, "The Life of Olaudah Equiano," 35.

2. *Virginia Gazette* (Rind) Sept. 22, 1768, July 19, 1754, cited by Gerald W. Mullin, *Flight and Rebellion: Slave Resistance in Eighteenth-Century Virginia* (New York, 1972), 45.

3. Nat Turner, *The Confessions of Nat Turner*, transcribed by Thomas R. Gray (Baltimore, 1831), reprinted in *The Southampton Slave Revolt of 1831: A Compilation of Source Material*, ed. Henry I. Tragle (Amherst, 1971), 310–315.

4. John W. Blassingame, ed., *Slave Testimony: Two Centuries of Letters, Speeches, Interviews, and Autobiographies* (Baton Rouge, 1977), 33, 44.

5. Blassingame, ed., *Slave Testimony*, 38, emphasis added.

6. Françoise Jean Marquis de Chastellux, *Travels in North America in the Years 1780, 1781, 1782*, trans. and ed. Howard C. Rice, 2 vols. (Chapel Hill, 1963), 2:435–440.

7. Benjamin Franklin, *The Writings of Benjamin Franklin*, ed. Albert Smyth, 10 vols. (New York, 1970), 8:606.

8. Ebenezer Hazard, "The Journal of Ebenezer Hazard in Virginia, 1777," ed. Fred Shelly, *Virginia Magazine of History and Biography* 62 (1954), 414: June 10, 1777.

9. L. Carter, *Diary*, Nov. 23, 1756; Jan. 21, 1757; Feb. 28, 1757; Aug. 31, 1778.

10. L. Carter, *Diary*, June 14, 1771; July 30, 1771; June 5, 1773.

11. John F. D. Smyth, *A Tour in the United States of America*, 2 vols. (London, 1784), 1:119, 121.

12. A. J. Morrison, ed., *Travels in Virginia in Revolutionary Times* (Lynchburg, 1922), 420. The town of Wilmington, N.C., passed a 10 o'clock curfew for slaves, noting that slaves took "uncurbed liberty at night [for] night is their day." See *The Wilmington Town Book, 1743–1778*, ed. D. Lennon and I. Kellam (Raleigh, 1973), cited by Jeffrey J. Crow, *The Black Experience in Revolutionary North Carolina* (Raleigh, 1977), 27–28.

13. Nicholson, cited by J. L. Dillard, *Perspectives on Black English* (The Hague, 1975), 29.

14. Grant, *The Fortunate Slave*, 14.

15. Fernandez, *Bwiti*, 273, 276, 438–439.

16. Smyth, *A Tour*, 1:46.

17. John Davis, *Travels of Four Years and a Half in the United States of America During 1798, 1799, 1800, 1801 and 1802* (New York, [1803] 1909), 413. An edited version appears in a later edition titled *Personal Adventures and Travels of Four Years and a Half in the United States of America* (London, 1817), 88ff.

18. Frederick Douglass, *Narrative of the Life of Frederick Douglass, An American Slave*, ed. Benjamin Quarles (Cambridge, Mass., 1973), 23.

19. See, for example, Paul Carrington, Account Book, 1755–1775; Richard Corbin, A List of Negroes & Stocks at Moss Neck this 18th Day of May 1778; Isaac Hite, Commonplace Book, 1776–1859; Croom-Hatcher-Dement Family Bible Records, 1742–1893; all at Virginia Historical Society. Records of fathers may be found in Jerome Family Papers, Slave Book, 1761–1865, microfilm, Colonial Williamsburg Foundation; Robert "King" Carter, "Will, probated General Court of Virginia, Oct. 16, 1732," reprinted in *Virginia Magazine of History and Biography* 5 (April 1898), 408–428 and 6 (July 1898), 1–22; and Bolling Family Papers, Register of Slaves, 1752–1890, Virginia Historical Society. See also Chapter 11.

20. Norman R. Yetman, *Life Under the "Peculiar Institution": Selections from the Slave Narrative Collection* (New York, 1970), 71.

21. Blassingame, ed., *Slave Testimony*, 481; Thomas Jefferson, *Thomas Jefferson's Farm Book*, ed. Edwin M. Betts (Charlottesville, 1976), 139.

22. G. Jones, "Ibo Age Organization"; Evans-Pritchard, "Nuer Time Reckoning"; Bohanan, "Concepts of Time Among the Tiv." Some slaves were coming to regard birthdates as important. Fithian recounts his making a list of "children, & their respective ages" for Dadda Gumby, who was a 94-year-old slave on Robert Carter's plantation. Philip Vickers Fithian, *Journal and Letters of Philip Vickers Fithian, 1773–1774: A Plantation Tutor of the Old Dominion*, ed. Hunter D. Farish (Williamsburg, 1943): July 13, 1774.

23. J. Davis, *Travels*, 413.

24. Blassingame, ed., *Slave Testimony*, 178.

25. George P. Rawick, ed., *The American Slave: A Composite Autobiography*, Series 1 and 2, 19 vols. (Westport, Conn., [1941] 1972), 18:59, 81, 104.

26. Rawick, *The American Slave*, 18:161, 113, 80.

27. Marie Jeanne Adams, "The Harriet Powers Pictorial Quilts," and Maude S. Wahlman and John Scully, "Aesthetic Principles in Afro-American Quilts," in *Afro-American Folk Art and Crafts*, ed. William R. Ferris (Boston, 1983), 67–68, 79–98; Gladys-Marie Fry, "Harriet Powers: Portrait of a Black Quilter," in *Missing Pieces: Georgia Folk Art 1770–1976*, ed. Anna Wadsworth (Atlanta, 1976), 16–23; John M. Vlach, *The Afro-American Tradition in Decorative Arts* (Cleveland, 1979), 43–67.

28. *Virginia Gazette* (P.), May 29, 1778. Between 1766 and 1780 there were at least two and sometimes three different *Virginia Gazettes* being published simultaneously. In order to distinguish between these competing papers, the editor or editors initials are given. (C. for Clarkson and Davis; D. for Dixon and Hunter, or Dixon and Nicolson; P. for Purdie; P.D. for Purdie and Dixon; Pi. for

Pinkey; and R. for Rind.) For full publication details see Lester J. Cappon and Stella F. Duff, *Virginia Gazette Index, 1736–1780*, 2 vols. (Williamsburg, 1950), l:vi–vii.

29. For a black's prediction that the End of Days would come on March 1, 1795, see [Martha Blodget, The Diary of Martha Blodget, in] "Cawson's Virginia in 1795–1796," ed. Marion Tinling, *William and Mary Quarterly* 3 (1946), 285. Black-Christian attitudes toward time are discussed in Sobel, *Trabelin' On*, 125–126, 245–246, and in Chapter 16.

30. J. Davis, *Travels*, 413.

31. Gillis, *Youth and History*, 5–9; Rawick, *The American Slave*, 18:110.

32. J. Davis, *Travels*, 417.

33. Ibid., 422.

34. Ibid., 424.

35. Peter Randolph wrote William Byrd iii, I "am rather inclinable to sell the young Negroes, for it will by no means answer to sell the workers. The only objection to this scheme is, that it will be cruel to part them from their parents." *The Correspondence of the Three William Byrds*, ed. Tinling, 2:628, Sept. 20, 1757; Richard S. Dunn, "A Tale of Two Plantations: Slave Life at Mesopotamia in Jamaica and Mount Airy in Virginia, 1799 to 1828," *William and Mary Quarterly* 34 (1977), 32–65; Dunn, "Black Society in the Chesapeake, 1776–1810," 179; Robert W. Fogel and Stanley L. Engerman, *Time on the Cross: The Economics of American Negro Slavery*, 2 vols. (Boston, 1974), 1.49–51.

36. The literature on slave adjustment is extensive, sparked in great part by Stanley Elkins's "Sambo thesis," but it is based almost entirely on nineteenth-century evidence. See Elkins, *Slavery: A Problem in American Institutional and Intellectual Life* (Chicago, 1959); Ann J. Lane, ed., *The Debate Over Slavery: Stanley Elkins and His Critics* (Urbana, 1971); Leslie H. Owens, *"This Species of Property": Slave Life and Culture in the Old South* (New York, 1976).

37. J. Davis, *Travels*, 405.

38. L. Carter, *Diary*, May 14, 1766; May 23, 1766.

39. Ibid., June 12, 1771.

40. Ibid., May 23, 1766; June 12, 1774; June 25, 1774. On respect for older slave workers, see William Lee to Francis Gildart: William Lee, Letterbooks, Sept. 26, 1787 – Aug. 17, 1788, October 9, 1787, Virginia Historical Society; Russell L. Blake, "Ties of Intimacy: Social Values and Personal Relationships of Ante-Bellum Slaveholders" (Ph.D. dissertation, University of Michigan, 1978), 127.

41. See Lewis E. Mason, Lists of Negroes, c. 1851–1854, Virginia Historical Society, which show that some slaves aged faster than others. Allan Kulikoff notes that whites also "aged" unnaturally. "Many whites did not know their birthdates, and as whites aged, they tended to guess their ages." Kulikoff, personal communication, March 1985, referring to the Maryland census records. Thomas notes the same process in England in "Age and Authority in Early Modern England," 235. David Hackett Fischer, *Growing Old in America* (New York, 1977), 82, 84, found that seventeenth- and eighteenth-century Americans often "rounded" their ages and "tended to represent themselves as older," as greater age was respected down through the Revolutionary period.

42. Orra Langhorne (1841–1904), in Blassingame, ed., *Slave Testimony*, 487. William Faulkner noted that he learned to be "respectful to age" from Caroline

Barr, his nursemaid, born a slave in 1840. *William Faulkner: A Life on Paper*, ed. Ann Abadie (Jackson, Miss., 1980), 86.

43. James Blair to Charles Dabney, April 1, 1769, reprinted in Michael Mullin, ed., *American Negro Slavery: A Documentary History* (Columbia, S.C., 1976), 71.

44. Thomas, "Age and Authority in Early Modern England," 207, 247.

CHAPTER 4

1. Elizabeth Sprigs to John Sprigs, Sept. 22, 1756, in *Root of Bitterness: Documents of the Social History of American Women*, ed. Nancy F. Cott (New York, 1972), 89. William Eddis was also convinced that white servants were treated more harshly than slaves, who were property for "life." Eddis, *Letters from America, Historical and Descriptive: Comprising Occurrences from 1769 to 1777 Inclusive* (London, 1792), 69–70. See the early studies by James C. Ballagh, *A History of Slavery in Virginia* (Baltimore, [1902] 1968); and Ballagh, *White Servitude in the Colony of Virginia: A Study of the System of Indentured Labor in the American Colonies* (Baltimore, 1895).

2. Gloria L. Main, *Tobacco Colony: Life in Early Maryland, 1650–1720* (Princeton, 1982), 106, 132, 186; E. Morgan, *American Slavery, American Freedom*, 319. Both Main and Morgan suggest that the lower class racial sharing of the seventeenth century gave way to separation in the eighteenth. See T. H. Breen, "A Changing Labor Force and Race Relations in Virginia, 1660–1710," *Journal of Social History* 7 (1973), 3–25; Breen and Stephen Innes, *"Myne Owne Ground": Race and Freedom on Virginia's Eastern Shore, 1640–1676* (New York, 1980).

3. Testimony of Robert Clark, white indentured servant, Lancaster County Order Book, Sept. 11, 1667, cited by Abbot Emerson Smith, *Colonists in Bondage: White Servitude and Convict Labor in America, 1607–1776* (Chapel Hill, 1947), 257; T. H. Breen, James H. Lewis, and Keith Schlesinger, "Motive for Murder: Servant's Life in Virginia, 1678," *William and Mary Quarterly* 40 (1982), 106–120.

4. Robert Beverly, *The History and Present State of Virginia* (London, 1705), 251; Hugh Jones, *The Present State of Virginia*, ed. Richard L. Morton (Chapel Hill, [1724] 1956), 36. Beverly suggests that the clothing and food of blacks differed somewhat from that of whites, but that their work was the same. Byrd's Diary suggests a white artisan was offended to be served slave-style corn bread. Byrd. *Diary 1709–1712*, March 2, 1711. Cf. Richard S. Dunn, "Masters, Servants and Slaves in the Colonial Chesapeake and the Caribbean," in *Early Maryland in a Wider World*, ed. Quinn, 242–266. Kulikoff deals at length with declining white indentured servitude, the growing trend to train slaves, and black and white work contact. See *Tobacco and Slaves*, 381–420. Joan Rezner Gundersen, "The Double Bonds of Race and Sex: Black and White Women in a Colonial Virginia Parish," *Journal of Southern History* 52 (1986), 351–372. On the work of black women in slavery, primarily in the nineteenth century, see Bell Hooks, *Ain't I A Woman: Black Women and Feminism* (Boston, 1981), 15–50; and Jacqueline Jones, *Labor of Love, Labor of Sorrow: Black Women, Work, and the Family from Slavery to the Present* (New York, 1985), 11–43; Lorena S. Walsh, "Changing Work Roles for Slave Labor in Chesapeake Agriculture,

1620–1820," Conference on "The Colonial Experience: The Eighteenth Century Chesapeake," Baltimore, September 1984, mimeographed."

5. E. Morgan, *American Slavery, American Freedom*, 328.

6. Reported appeal of rebel Wheeler to servant John Finley, who claimed he did not join the rebellion. Sept. 13, 1677, Charles City County Records, Orders, 1677–1679, 190, cited by William L. Shea, *The Virginia Militia in the Seventeenth Century* (Baton Rouge, 1983), 114.

7. Shea supports this view in *The Virginia Militia*, 114. Bacon claimed "to plead the cause of the oppressed." Cf. "Bacon's Manifesto," Fall 1676, in Warren M. Billings, ed., *The Old Dominion in the Seventeenth Century: A Documentary History of Virginia, 1606–1689* (Chapel Hill, 1975), 278.

8. Thomas Grantham, "Account of my Transactions" [1677] Sir Henry Coventry Papers, 78:301–302, Longleat House, England, cited by Shea, *The Virginia Militia*, 117; participation estimated by Stephen Saunders Webb, *1676, The End of American Independence* (Cambridge, Mass., 1985), 6, 123, 125.

9. Thad W. Tate, *The Negro in Eighteenth-Century Williamsburg* (Williamsburg, 1965), 91; Adele Hast, "The Legal Status of the Negro in Virginia, 1705–1765," *Journal of Negro History* 54 (1969), 217–239; A. Leon Higginbotham, Jr., *In the Matter of Color; Race and the American Legal Process: The Colonial Period* (New York, 1978), 19–60; Helen T. Catterall, ed., *Judicial Cases Concerning American Slavery and the Negro*. Vol. 1: *Cases from the Courts of England Virginia, West Virginia and Kentucky* (New York, 1968).

10. William W. Hening, ed., *The Statues at Large, Being a Collection of all the Laws of Virginia, from the First Session of the Legislature in the Year 1619*, 13 vols. (Richmond, 1809–1823), 2:481–482, 3:447–462, 4:126–134, 6:104–112.

11. For other counties see Robert E. Brown and B. Katherine Brown, *Virginia 1705–1786: Democracy or Aristocracy?* (East Lansing, 1964), 75; Jackson Turner Main, *The Social Structure of Revolutionary America* (Princeton, 1965), 45–46; Beeman, *The Evolution of the Southern Backcountry*, 65–67, 110, 208; Rutman, *A Place in Time*, 1:184, n. 42, 271; 2:121–124; P. Morgan, "Slave Life in the Virginia Piedmont," Appendix 1; Kulikoff, *Tobacco and Slaves*, 134, 136–137, 140, 152, 154, 208–209, 430; R. Dunn, "Black Society in the Chesapeake," 49–82; Peter Joseph Albert, "The Protean Institution: The Geography, Economy and Ideology of Slavery in Post-Revolutionary Virginia" (Ph.D. dissertation, University of Maryland, 1976).

12. Sarah S. Hughes, "Slaves for Hire: The Allocation of Black Labor in Elizabeth City County, Virginia, 1782–1810," *William and Mary Quarterly* 35 (1978), 260–286; Kulikoff, *Tobacco and Slaves*, 139–140, 342–343, 405–407, 431.

13. Washington's agreement with William Powell, overseer at his "mother's Quarter on the Rappahannock," *The Diaries of George Washington*, ed. Donald Jackson et al., 6 vols. (Charlottesville, 1976–1979), 3:59, Sept. 12, 1771.

14. Washington to William Pearce, his farm manager, Jan. 25, 1795, *The Writings of George Washington, From the Original Manuscript Sources, 1745–1799*, ed. John C. Fitzpatrick, 39 vols. (Washington, D.C., 1931–1944), 34:103. Bloxham had come from England to manage Washington's estate in April of 1786. Whiting was manager from May 1790 until his death in 1793. Cf. Washington, *The Diaries*, 4:315, 337; *The Writings*, 31:36; 33:26, 192.

15. Edward Kimber, "Eighteenth-Century Maryland as Portrayed in the 'Itinerant Observations of Edward Kimber,'" *Maryland Historical Magazine* 51 (1956),

327–328, cited by Kulikoff, "The Origins of Afro-American Society," 236; and in [Kimber,] "Observations in Several Voyages and Travels in America in the year 1736; from the *London Magazine*, July 1746," *William and Mary Quarterly*, 1st series, 15 (1907), 149.

16. Washington, *The Writings*, 33:141, Oct. 27, 1793; 188, Dec. 18, 1793.
17. Inventory of the Estate of William Byrd ... In the County of Henrico at the Falls of the James River, June 1746, Huntington Library. Robert Rose, *The Diary of Robert Rose: A View of Virginia by a Scottish Colonial Parson, 1746–1751*, ed. Ralph E. Fall (Verona, Va., 1977), 340–341. Rose also had a quarter where one white was together with five blacks, and a quarter with 39 blacks with no white person resident.
18. Smyth, *A Tour*, 1:74–76. For a discussion of housing see Chapter 9, below.
19. James Revel, "The Poor Unhappy Transported Felon's Sorrowful Account of his Fourteen Years Transportation at Virginia in America" [c. 1680], ed. John M. Jennings, *Virginia Magazine of History and Biography* 56 (1948), 180–186, reprinted in *The Old Dominion in the Seventeenth Century*, ed. Billings, 140.
20. Washington, *The Diaries*, 2:164–165, July 29, 1769.
21. Galenson, *White Servitude in Colonial America*, 131–133, 138–139, 166, 174; Menard, "From Servants to Slaves," 360–369; An Inventory of all the Personal Estate of the Hon. Robert Carter, County of Lancaster, Esq., Deceased, Carter Family Papers, Virginia Historical Society.
22. Jefferson, *Farm Book*, 148–184.
23. John Harrower, *The Journal of John Harrower: An Indentured Servant in the Colony of Virginia, 1773–1776*, ed. Edward M. Riley (Williamsburg, 1963), 48, 76. Harrower described Caroline as "a great high Gir[l]e ... as Black as the D__s A__se."
24. Marcus W. Jernegan, *Laboring and Dependent Classes in Colonial America, 1607–1783* (New York, 1931), 3–23; John R. Commons et al., eds. *A Documentary History of American Industrial Society*, 10 vols. (New York, [1910–1911] 1958), 2:314–328; Raymond Pinchbeck, *The Virginia Negro Artisan and Tradesman* (Richmond, 1926), 42; Jefferson, *Farm Book*, 484–486.
25. William Byrd, "A Progress to the Mines," in *History of the Dividing Line and Other Notes from the Papers of William Byrd of Westover in Virginia, Esquire*, ed. Thomas Wynne, 2 vols. (Richmond, 1866), 2:41–82.
26. L. Carter, *Diary*, 253, 259, 706.
27. Washington, *The Writings*, 33:221–224.
28. Mullin, *Flight and Rebellion*, 94–96, has analyzed all Virginia runaway advertisements and finds a very high incidence of skilled workers, especially woodworkers. See Lathan A. Windley, ed., *Runaway Slave Advertisements: A Documentary History from the 1730s to 1790. Vol. 1: Virginia and North Carolina* (Westport, Conn., 1983); Windley, "A Profile of Runaway Slaves in Virginia and South Carolina from 1730 through 1787" (Ph.D. dissertation, University of Iowa, 1974); Tate, *The Negro in Eighteenth-Century Williamsburg*, 41, believes most slaves in Williamsburg were household servants. "Number and Occupations of Certain Slave Owners in Richmond in 1782" from United States Bureau of the Census, *Heads of Families, First Census of the United States Taken in the Year 1790* (Washington, D.C., 1908), "State Enumeration of Virginia, 1782–1785," 57, 94–96, compiled by Pinchbeck, *The Virginia Negro Artisan and Tradesman*, 40.

29. Lee, Feb. 23, 1773, Lee Family Papers, Virginia Historical Society.
30. Pinchbeck, *The Virginia Negro Artisan and Tradesman*, 29–30.
31. Isaac Jefferson, "Memoirs of a Monticello Slave as Dictated to Charles Campbell by Isaac Jefferson at Monticello," in *Jefferson at Monticello*, ed. James A. Bear, Jr. (Charlottesville, 1967), 14–15. Bear notes, correcting Isaac Jefferson, that the white man involved was probably James Bringhurst, an "ironmonger," and the time, 1790–1794. Ibid., 126, n. 52.
32. Washington's will is reprinted in his *Writings*, 37:275–303. Robert Carter's manumission records in Memorandum Book, Vols. 11–12: 1777–1791, microfilm, Colonial Williamsburg Foundation. See also Deed of Gift, Westmoreland County, August 1791, Order Book, 1791, Virginia State Library; Robert Carter Letter Books, 1791–1793, microfilm, Colonial Williamsburg Foundation. Flournoy's will is reprinted in the *Virginia Magazine of History and Biography* 2 (1894), 210, cited by Pinchbeck, *The Virginia Negro Artisan and Tradesman*, 30. See also Whittington B. Johnson, "Black Patterns of Employment, 1750–1820," in *From Freedom to Freedom: African Roots in American Soil*, ed. Mildred Bain and Ervin Lewis (New York, 1977), 264–267; James E. Newton, "Slave Artisans and Craftsmen: The Roots of Afro-American Art," *Black Scholar* 9 (1977), 35–44; Leonard Stavisky, "The Origins of Negro Craftsmanship in Colonial America," *Journal of Negro History* 32 (1947), 417–429; Newton and Ronald L. Lewis, eds., *The Other Slaves: Mechanics, Artisans and Craftsmen* (Boston, 1978). Kulikoff, *Tobacco and Slaves*, 396–408, discusses black apprenticeship at great length and provides much new evidence.
33. Jefferson, *Notes on the State of Virginia* (New York, [1787] 1964), 134.
34. Jefferson's will, *Writings*, 18:465–470; Jefferson, *Farm Book*, 27–28. L. Carter, *Diary*, 158–159, 351, 526.
35. Washington, *The Writings*, 33:134, 203–204, 394–395; 34:24; 37:11. Cf. *Maryland Gazette*, Oct. 15, 1770, cited by Kulikoff, "The Origins of Afro-American Society," 250. Act to control the sale of goods stolen by slaves passed by the General Assembly, Oct. 3, 1705. Henry Grimes, born in Virginia in 1784, wrote of his white overseer's family: "They were very poor, and secretly bought things from the negroes which they had stolen from my master." *Life of William Grimes, The Runaway Slave Brought Down to the Present Time* (New Haven, 1855), 22. Henry Bibb (b. 1815) attests to such illegal black and white activity in the nineteenth century in *Narrative of the Life and Adventures of Henry Bibb, an American Slave* (New York, 1849), 69. See J. Wayne Flynt, *Dixie's Forgotten People: The South's Poor Whites* (Bloomington, 1979).
36. Proclamation of Gov. F. Nicholson, July 10, 1700, Essex County, Orders, 1699–1702, microfilm, Virginia State Library. Cf. for example, whites charged with "dealing" with slaves in Henrico County, May 1, 1708, March 1, 1708/1709, Order Books, 1707–1709, 37–38, 122–123; William Byrd to Benjamin Lynde, Feb. 20, 1736, in *Correspondence*, 2:474; L. Carter, *Diary*, 648, 649; Robert Carter to Christopher Collins, Oct. 7, 1791, Letter Books, 1791–1793, microfilms, Colonial Williamsburg Foundation.
37. Deposition of Roger Court Crotosse, 1684, Accomac County, Deeds, Wills and Inventories, 1676–1690, 389–390, reprinted in Billings, *The Old Dominion*, 144–146.
38. Adele Hast, *Loyalism in Revolutionary Virginia: The Norfolk Area and the Eastern Shore* (Ann Arbor, 1982), 185.

39. Revel, "The Poor Unhappy Transported Felon's Sorrowful Account," 192; Robert Carter, April 4, 1727, Diary, 1722–1727, microfilm, University of Haifa. For nineteenth-century evidence of blacks and whites working together see Philip S. Foner and Ronald L. Lewis, eds., *The Black Worker: A Documentary History from Colonial Times to the Present.* Vol. 1: *The Black Worker to 1869* (Philadelphia, 1978), 103–113; Claudia Goldin, *Urban Slavery in the American South, 1820–1860: A Quantitative History* (Chicago, 1976), 28–33.

40. Pinchbeck, *The Virginia Negro Artisan and Tradesman,* 32.

41. Robert Carter, Bills of Lading to Casar (Slave) and William Lawrence (Negro), 1774, Carter Family Papers, Virginia Historical Society.

42. For excellent analyses of interaction in the seventeenth-century Chesapeake see G. Main, *Tobacco Colony,* and E. Morgan, *American Slavery, American Freedom.* Mullin's fine study of eighteenth-century Virginia, *Flight and Rebellion,* does not focus on blacks' influence on whites. For the nineteenth century, see Eugene D. Genovese, " 'Rather be a Nigger than a Poor White Man': Slave Perceptions of Southern Yeoman and Poor Whites," in *Toward a New View of America, Essays in Honor of Arthur C. Cole,* ed. Hans L. Trefousse (New York, 1977), 79–96; and Avery Craven, "Poor Whites and Negroes in the Ante-bellum South," *Journal of Negro History* 15 (1930), 14–25. For explorations of black–white interaction in specific areas see Larry G. Bowman, "Virginia's Use of Blacks in the French and Indian War," *Western Pennsylvania Historical Magazine* 53 (1970), 57–63; James H. Johnston, "The Participation of White Men in Virginia Negro Insurrections," *Journal of Negro History* 16 (1931), 158–167; Marianne B. Sheldon, "Black–White Relations in Richmond, Virginia, 1782–1820," *Journal of Southern History* 45 (1979), 27–44.

43. D. Thompson, *Change and Tradition in Rural England,* 8, 135, 197; Peter Laslett, *The World We Have Lost,* 73, citing Best's Farming Book (1641), 93.

44. Yetman, *Life Under the "Peculiar Institution,"* 267.

45. Flora Thompson, *Lark Rise to Candleford* (1945) reprinted in D. Thompson, *Change and Tradition in Rural England,* 197–198.

46. Akiga, *Akiga's Story,* 87.

47. Philip O. Nsugbe, *Ohaffia: A Matrilineal Ibo People* (Oxford, 1974), 23.

48. Henry Williams, quoted in Georgia Writers Project, *Drums and Shadows: Survival Studies Among the Georgia Coastal Negroes* (Athens, Ga., 1940), 179. See also 137, 157, 160, 163, 178.

49. Nineteenth-century camp meetings were most often held in August. See Bernard A. Weisberger, *They Gathered at the River: The Story of the Great Revivalists and their Impact Upon Religion in America* (Boston, 1958), 24, 25, 31.

CHAPTER 5

1. T. H. Breen, "Of Time and Nature: A Study of Persistent Values in Colonial Virginia," in his *Puritans and Adventurers: Change and Persistence in Early America* (New York, 1980), 164–196.

2. Thomas J. Wertenbaker, "The Mind of the Tobacco Aristocrat," in his *The Golden Age of Colonial Culture,* 2d rev. ed. (Ithaca, [1942] 1949), 105–126; Thomas Jefferson, *The Papers of Thomas Jefferson,* ed. Julian P. Boyd, 21 vols. (Princeton, 1950–1982), 18:146. On the meaning of classical symbols in colonial Virginia see Part Four, Coda.

3. See Robert B. Semple, *A History of the Rise and Progress of the Baptists in Virginia* (Richmond, 1810); John S. Moore, "Writers of Early Virginia Baptist History: John Williams," *Virginia Baptist Register* 14 (1975), 633–647.

4. Washington, *The Diaries*, 2:30; Rose, *The Diary*, January 21, 1746.

5. William Byrd, *The Secret Diary of William Byrd of Westover, 1709–1712*, ed. Louis B. Wright and Marion Tinling (Richmond, 1941), 1. (This volume is referred to below as Byrd, *Diary, 1709–1712*.) For variant interpretations of Byrd and slavery see Mullin, *Flight and Rebellion*, 3–33; Michael Zuckerman, "William Byrd's Family," *Perspectives in American History* 12 (1979), 255–311; Pierre Marambaud, *William Byrd of Westover, 1674–1744* (Charlottesville, 1971); Michael S. Greenberg, "Gentlemen Slaveholders: The Social Outlook of the Virginia Planter Class" (Ph.D. dissertation, Rutgers University, 1972); Joseph R. Conlin, "Another Side to William Byrd of Westover: An Explanation of the Food in His Secret Diaries," *Virginia Cavalcade* 26 (1977), 125–132.

6. Byrd, *Diary, 1709–1712*, 1709: Feb. 8, 16; April 17; May 23; June 10; July 30; Aug. 8, 27; Sept. 3, 16, 19; Nov. 30; Dec. 1, 16. 1710: Jan. 6; Mar. 3; July 15; Aug. 31; Oct. 8, 9. 1711: Feb. 2, 27; Dec. 31. 1712: Mar. 2; May 22; *Diary, 1739–1741*: Jan. 7, 1740.

7. Byrd, *Diary, 1709–1712*, 148.

8. Byrd, *Diary, 1739–1741*, 173, infra.

9. Peter Fontaine to Moses Fontaine, Nov. 4, 1749, in James Fontaine, *Memoirs of a Huguenot Family*, ed. Ann Maury (Baltimore, 1973), 333.

10. L. Carter, *Diary*, refers by name to 25 house servants, 41 field hands, and 83 skilled workers. To compare with his total slave family, see An Inventory of the Estate of Landon Carter, Esqr. Dec'd, Taken Feb. 1799, Landon Carter Papers, University of Virginia.

11. Washington, *The Diaries*, 1:xxxvi.

12. Silvio A. Bedini, "Thomas Jefferson, Clock Designer," *Proceedings of the American Philosophical Society* 108 (1964), 164. The Great Clock was installed early in 1793. On the bells at Robert Carter's plantation, which rang from 8 A.M. to 3 P.M., see Fithian, *Journal*, 157.

13. Ibid., 164, 167, 170, 171. Isaac Jefferson, "Memoirs of a Monticello Slave," 12–13.

14. Thomas Jefferson to Thaddeus Kosciusko, Feb. 26, 1810, in *The Domestic Life of Thomas Jefferson*, Sarah N. Randolph (Charlottesville, [1871] 1978), 331; see also Jefferson to Dr. Vine Utley, March 21, 1819, *Papers of Thomas Jefferson*, 15:187–488. For variant views of Jefferson's day plan, see James A. Bear, Jr., ed., *Jefferson at Monticello* (Charlottesville, 1967), 125, n. 37.

15. Jefferson, *The Family Letters of Thomas Jefferson*, ed. Edwin M. Betts and James A. Bear, Jr. (Colombia, Mo., 1966), 395, Dec. 20, 1809.

16. *Papers of Thomas Jefferson*, 4:446–448, Nov. 28, 1783.

17. Jefferson, *Family Letters*, 39, May 3, 1787.

18. Ibid., 41–42, May 21, 1787.

19. *Papers of Thomas Jefferson*, 11:250, 349, March 28 and May 5, 1787.

20. Bedini, "Thomas Jefferson, Clock Designer," 163.

21. Martha Jefferson, in Jefferson, *Family Letters*, 388, Mar. 2, 1809; 68, Jan. 16, 1791.

22. Martha Washington, 1797, in *Martha Washington*, Anne Hollingsworth Wharton (New York, 1897), 265.
23. L. Carter, *Diary*, 1138–1139, Aug. 2, 1778.
24. Washington, *The Writings*, 36:117–118, 135–137; 37:100, 368–370.
25. William Byrd, *William Byrd's Histories of the Dividing Line Betwixt Virginia and North Carolina*, ed. William K. Boyd (Raleigh, 1929), 304–305.
26. James Fontaine, *Memoirs*, 331, Nov. 4, 1749; See Peter Fontaine, Sermon Preached at Westover, May 10, 1727, transcript, Colonial Williamsburg Foundation; Andrew Burnaby, *Travels Through the Middle Settlements in North-America in the Years 1759 and 1760 . . .* , 3d ed. (New York, [1798] 1904), 53–54. Nicolas Cresswell, *The Journal of Nicholas Cresswell, 1774–1777* (New York, 1924), 268.
27. Gen. Charles Lee to William Byrd III; April 1, 1776, in *The Correspondence*, 2:818.
28. Thomas Anburey, *Travels Through the Interior Parts of America*, 2 vols. (Boston, [1789] 1923), 2:190–191. See similar description in Smyth, *A Tour*, 1:35, 41–43; and the very same description in Jedidiah Morse, *American Geography* (London, 1792) 388. Chastellux, *Travels in North America*, 2:435–441.
29. Burnaby, *Travels Through the Middle Settlements*, 53–60; Henry Hartwell, James Blair, and Edward Chilton, *The Present State of Virginia and the College*, ed. H. D. Farish (Williamsburg, [1697] 1940), 9.
30. Byrd to John Perceval, Earl of Egmont, July 12, 1736, *Correspondence*, 2:487–488.
31. David Bertelson, *The Lazy South* (New York, 1967); C. Vann Woodward, "The Southern Ethic in a Puritan World," *William and Mary Quarterly* 25 (1968), 343–370; Rhys Isaac, "Idleness Ethic and the Liberty of Anglo-Americans," *Reviews in American History* 4 (1976), 47–52; H. C. Brearley, "Are Southerners Really Lazy?" *American Scholar* 18 (1948–1949), 68–75; Elkanah Watson, *Men and Times of the Revolution; or, Memoirs of Elkanah Watson, Including His Journals of Travels in Europe and America . . . , 1777–1842*, 2d ed. (New York, [1857] 1861), 72.

CHAPTER 6

1. Genovese, *Roll, Jordan, Roll*, 285–324. See James A. Henretta, "Families and Farms: *Mentalité* in Pre-Industrial America," *William and Mary Quarterly* 35 (1978), 3–32.
2. Byrd, *Diary, 1717–1721*, 492, Dec. 28, 1720. Holy Innocents' Day commemorates the supposed slaughter of the children of Bethlehem on Herod's order. See Marion B. Stowell, *Early American Almanacs: The Colonial Weekday Bible* (New York, 1977).
3. On Igbo "pawns" see Victor C. Uchendu, "Slaves and Society in Igboland, Nigeria," in *Slavery in Africa*, ed. Miers and Kopytoff, 130.
4. Fithian, *Journal*, July 3, 1774. See Herskovits, "What Has Africa Given America?" 168–174, for a discussion of African influence on polite behavior in the South.
5. Equiano, "The Life of Olaudah Equiano," 10.
6. Studies in Maryland indicate that in Annapolis some 12 percent of the inventoried free population had watches by the time of the Revolution. A break-

down of St. Mary's population into three classes indicates that whereas 80 percent of the wealthiest did come to have timepieces, only some five estates out of the 550 of the poorest third did. See Mark P. Leone, "Material Culture of the Georgian World," Conference on "The Colonial Experience: The Eighteenth Century Chesapeake," Baltimore, September 1984, mimeographed; Lois Green Carr and Lorena S. Walsh, "Inventories and Analysis of Wealth and Consumption Patterns in St. Mary's County, Maryland, 1658–1777," *Historical Methods* 13 (1980), 81–104. For comparative data on Virginia, see the published inventories in Alice Hanson Jones, *American Colonial Wealth: Documents and Methods*, 3 vols. (New York, 1978), 2:1295–1403, with data from seven counties in Virginia in 1774, which indicate that ownership of watches and clocks may well have been even more limited in Virginia.

7. Byrd, *Diary, 1709–1712*, April 7, 1709; Dec. 13, 1709; June 18, 1710; Dec. 31, 1710.
8. Byrd, "Inamorato L'Oiseaux" or "Enamored Bird," in *Diary, 1739–1741*, 276–282.
9. Ken, *The Prose Works of Thomas Ken*, 257.
10. Bedini, "Thomas Jefferson, Clock Designer," 180.
11. Robert Farris Thompson, "An Aesthetic of the Cool: West African Dance," *American Forum* 2 (1966), 85–102.
12. Darrett B. Rutman, Charles Wetherell, and Anita H. Rutman, "Rhythms of Life: Black and White Seasonality in the Early Chesapeake," *Journal of Interdisciplinary History* 11 (1980–1981), 29–53. (Different patterns in regard to deaths and marriages were also noted.) A similar pattern for births among blacks and whites in King William Parish has been found by Gundersen, "The Double Bonds of Race and Sex," 363–365. G. R. Quaife, *Wanton Wenches and Wayward Wives: Peasants and Illicit Sex in Early Seventeenth Century England* (London, 1979), 78, 81, found a March peak in births in seventeenth-century Somerset. Rutman et al. have other fragmentary evidence of both the old English and the African patterns.
13. There is a very interesting description of a slave Christmas gathering, in South Carolina, sometime between 1783 and 1805, at which African languages were heard and African sports were witnessed, in A.S.S., "Sketches of the South Santee," *American Monthly Magazine* 8 (Oct., Nov., 1836), reprinted in *Travels in the Old South: Selected from Periodicals of the Times*, ed. Eugene L. Schwabb (Lexington, 1973), 11; Kenneth M. Stampp, *The Peculiar Institution: Slavery in the Ante-Bellum South* (New York, 1956), 166, 290. Easter cockfights are noted in Fithian, *Journal*, April 4, 1774.
14. Byrd, *Diary, 1709–1712*, Dec. 25, 1709; Fithian, *Journal*, Dec. 24, 1793, 39; April 4, 1774, 91.
15. Rutman, Wetherell, and Rutman, "Rhythms of Life," 38, found white marriages highest in April, followed by February, January, and December but Kulikoff has found a significant rise in December and January in white weddings in the second half of the eighteenth century. Kulikoff, *Tobacco and Slaves*, 256.
16. See Part Three. For a comparison with New England developments, see James P. Walsh, "Holy Time and Sacred Space in Puritan New England," *American Quarterly* 32 (1980), 79–95.

17. Newbell Niles Puckett, *Folk Beliefs of the Southern Negro* (New York, [1926] 1968), 570.

CHAPTER 7

1. On the concept of space and attitudes toward it, see E. Hall, *The Hidden Dimension*, 39–48; E. Hall, *The Silent Language*, 187–210; Yi-Fu Tuan, *Topophilia: A Study of Environmental Perception, Attitudes and Values* (Englewood Cliffs, N.J., 1974); Tuan, "Rootedness Verses Sense of Place," *Landscape* 24, no. 1 (1980), 3–8; Tuan, "Space, Time, Place: A Humanistic Frame," and Susan-Ann Lee, "The Value of the Local Area," in *Valued Environments*, ed. J. R. Gold and J. Burgess (London, 1982), 161–171; Erick Isaac, "Religion, Landscape and Space," *Landscape* 9, no. 2 (1959–1960), 14–18.
2. Zahan, *The Religion, Spirituality and Thought of Traditional Africa*, 77; Susan Denyer, *African Traditional Architecture: An Historical and Geographical Perspective* (London, 1978), 19; Curtin, *Africa Remembered*, 23–24, 195–197.
3. A. E. Afigbo, "Prolegomena to the Study of the Culture History of the Igbo-speaking Peoples of Nigeria," in *West African Cultural Dynamics: Archeological and Historical Perspectives*, ed. B. K. Swartz, Jr., and R. E. Dumett (The Hague, 1980), 316–317; Labelle Prussin, "An Introduction to Indigenous African Architecture," *Journal of the Society of Architectural Historians* 33 (1974), 183–205; Uchendu, *The Igbo of Southeast Nigeria*, 96, Richard N. Henderson, *The King in Every Man: Evolutionary Trends in Onitsha Ibo Society and Culture* (New Haven, 1972), 115, 176, 177, 183.
4. Mary Douglas, "The Lele of Kasasi," in *African Worlds: Studies in the Cosmological Ideas and Social Values of African Peoples*, ed. Daryll Forde (London, [1954] 1970), 1–26.
5. Marcel Griaule and Germaine Dieterlen, "The Dogon of the French Sudan," in *African Worlds*, ed. Forde, 83–110.
6. E. Isaac, "Religion, Landscape and Space," 16; Denyer, *African Traditional Architecture*, 19, 25.
7. Zahan, *The Religion, Spirituality and Thought of Traditional Africa*, 66–75.
8. Meyer Fortes, *The Web of Kinship Among the Tallensi* (London, [1949] 1957), 49–63.
9. Equiano, "The Life of Olaudah Equiano," 8–9; Julius F. Glück, "African Architecture," in *Peoples and Cultures of Africa—An Anthropological Reader*, ed. E. P. Skinner (Garden City, N.Y., 1973), 230–244. Oliver points out that the style of house Equiano described is no longer built in Benin, where Yoruba architectural influence is now dominant, but it can still be found in an adjacent area. Paul Oliver, ed., *Shelter in Africa* (London, 1971), 7–24.
10. Denyer, *African Traditional Architecture*, 133–158; Denyer has found rectangular, free-standing, saddle-back roofed houses among "Ibo, some rural Hausa (Nigeria); Asante (Ghana); southern Togo; southern Benin; southern Ivory Coast." See also Glück, "African Architecture," 234; John Skolle, "Adobe in Africa: Varieties of Anonymous Architecture," *Landscape* 12, no. 2 (1962), 15–17; Mod Mekkawi, *Bibliography on Traditional Architecture in Africa* (Washington, D.C., 1978); Labelle Prussin and David Lee, "Architecture in Africa: An Annotated Bibliography," *Africana Library Journal* 4 (1973), 2–32.

11. Meyer Fortes, *Oedipus and Job in West African Religion* (Cambridge, England, 1959); William R. Bascom, *Ifa Divination* (Bloomington, 1969); E. E. Evans-Pritchard, *Witchcraft, Oracles and Magic Among the Azande* (Oxford, 1937); Lovejoy, *Transformations in Slavery*, 82–83.

12. John Aubrey, *Remaines of Gentilisme and Judaisme* (Nendeln, Lichtenstein, [1881] 1967), 33.

13. Ibid., 33, 40, 223, 243, 245.

14. Thomas, *Religion and the Decline of Magic*; Keith Thomas, *Man and the Natural World: Changing Attitudes in England, 1500–1800* (London 1983); William H. Seiler, "Land Processioning in Colonial Virginia," *William and Mary Quarterly* 6 (1949), 416–436. Ronald Neale, *Bath, 1680–1950; A Social History; or A Valley of Pleasure, Yet a Sink of Iniquity* (London, 1981).

15. D. Thompson, *Change and Tradition in Rural England*, 33.

16. Arnold Rattenbury, "Methodism and the Tatterdemalions," in *Popular Culture and Class Conflict, 1590–1914: Explorations in the History of Labour and Leisure*, ed. E. Yeo and S. Yeo (Sussex, 1981), 38; cf. Gold and Burgess, eds., *Valued Environments*; Kerridge, *The Farmers*, 164–166; Wrightson, *English Society: 1580–1680*, 35, 140; Malcolmson, *Life and Labour in England, 1700–1780*.

17. George Stuart, "The Wheelwrights' Way of Life," in *Change and Tradition*, ed. D. Thompson, 217.

18. Henry Glassie, *Folk Housing in Middle Virginia: A Structural Analysis of Historic Artifacts* (Knoxville, Tenn., 1975), 118; Kerridge, *The Farmers*, 164–165; Fussell, *The English Rural Labourer*, 50, 66–67; Wrightson, *English Society: 1580–1680*, 35, 140; J. T. Smith, "The Evolution of the English Peasant House to the Late Seventeenth Century: The Evidence of Buildings," *Journal of the British Archaeological Association* 33 (1970), 122–147; Eric Mercer, *English Vernacular Houses: A Study of Traditional Farmhouses and Cottages* (London, 1975).

19. John R. Stilgoe, *Common Landscape of America, 1580 to 1845* (New Haven, 1982), 16.

20. Michael MacDonald, *Mystical Bedlam: Madness, Anxiety and Healing in Seventeenth-Century England* (Cambridge, England, 1981); Hill, "Science and Magic in Seventeenth-Century England"; Bernard Capp, *English Almanacs, 1500–1800: Astrology and the Popular Press* (Ithaca, 1979); Leventhal, *In the Shadow of the Enlightenment*.

21. D. Hall, "The Mental World of Samuel Sewall," 76.

22. William Byrd, "The Female Creed," c. 1725, in *Diary, 1739–1741*, 445–475.

23. William Byrd, *The London Diary (1717–1721), and Other Writings of William Byrd of Virginia*, ed. Louis B. Wright and Marion Tinling (New York, 1958), 78, 102, 115. (This volume is referred to below as Byrd, *Diary, 1717–1721*.)

24. Wrightson, *English Society: 1580–1680*, 220–221.

25. Trance and possession were accepted by religious people in both societies, but to a very different degree. Erika Bourguignon estimates that 81 percent of contemporary sub-Saharan societies have some type of possession belief. Cf. "Ritual Dissociation and Possession Belief in Caribbean Negro Religion," in *Afro-American Anthropology*, ed. Whitten and Szwed, 91. John Beattie and John Middleton, eds., *Spirit Mediumship and Society in Africa* (London, 1969). See below, Chapter 8. Trance and vision experiences were always known to Chris-

tians, but the revivals gave rise to public and extensive excitements. Their exact extent is in question; it may well be that in their later development, churches of Baptist and Methodist denominations did not choose to dwell on this period of early excitement, and the revivals in Wales, Cornwall, and the Isle of Man have not been adequately studied. For Wesley, on visions, see *John Wesley: The Man and his Thought*, ed. Ole E. Borgen (Leiden, 1966), 40; Umphrey Lee, *The Historical Background of Early Methodist Enthusiasm* (New York, 1967), 138.

CHAPTER 8

1. Leventhal, *In the Shadow of the Enlightenment*, 100; Jon Butler, "Magic, Astrology and the Early American Religious Heritage, 1600–1760," *American Historical Review* 84 (1979), 317–346; Butler, "The Dark Ages of American Occultism, 1760–1848," in *The Occult in America: New Historical Perspectives*, ed. Howard Kerr and Charles L. Crow (Urbana, 1983), 58–78; Rutman, "The Evolution of Religious Life in Early Virginia."
2. Byrd, *Correspondence*, 2:463; cf. Fletcher S. Bassett, "Wind-Makers and Storm Raisers," in *Legends and Superstitions of the Sea and of Sailors*, ed. Bassett (London, 1885), 101–147. See William Shakespeare, *Macbeth*, Act 1, Scene 3, where the witch threatens "I'll give thee a wind."
3. Harrower, *The Journal of John Harrower*, 33.
4. On the occult in New England, see John Demos, *Entertaining Satan: Witchcraft and the Culture of Early New England* (New York, 1982); Richard Dorson, ed., *America Begins: Early American Writings* (Greenwich, Conn., 1950), 348–349, 353–356, 362–366; Richard Weisman, *Witchcraft, Magic and Religion in 17th-Century Massachusetts* (Amherst, 1984), Appendix A, 192–203, documents 34 Massachusetts witchcraft cases prior to the Salem trials but notes that there were many more cases. Appendix B, 204–207, lists 18 defamation suits brought by people who had been called witches. At the Salem trials some 141 were accused. Background evidence and excerpts from the transcript of the Sherwood trial are reprinted in Edward Ingle, "A Virginia Witch," *Magazine of American History* 10 (1883), 425–427; "Record of the Trial of Grace Sherwood, in 1705, Princess Anne County, for Witchcraft," in *Collections of the Virginia Historical & Philosophical Society* 1 (1833), 69–78; Record of a Council Meeting, March 8, re: Witchcraft, (Atny. Genl.), April 15, 1706, in Colonial Papers, 1907, #36, 1706 Folder 17, Virginia State Library; and in Edward W. James, "Grace Sherwood, the Virginia Witch," *William and Mary Quarterly*, 1st series, 3 (1894–1895), 96–101, 190–192, 242–244; 4 (1895–1896), 18–22. Little is known of Grace Sherwood's background, but James claims her father was "a substantial mechanic and small land owner" and reprints his will leaving son-in-law James Sherwood 50 acres of land. Most interestingly he notes, "one writer thought she was a member of the despised free negro class." Ibid., 96.
5. Princess Anne Co., Feb. 4, 1697/1698, March 3, 1697/1698, Sept. 10, 1698, reprinted in James, "Grace Sherwood, the Virginia Witch," 99–101.
6. Inventory, Princess Anne Co., Sept. 3, 1701, reprinted in James, "Grace Sherwood, the Virginia Witch," 190.

7. Princess Anne Co., Oct. 7, 1705, reprinted in James, "Grace Sherwood, the Virginia Witch," 191.

8. Princess Anne Co., Jan. 3, 1705/1706, Feb. 7, 1705/1706, reprinted in James, "Grace Sherwood, the Virginia Witch," 191.

9. Michael Dalton, *The Countrey Justice* (London, 1618), 243.

10. Virginia Council Book, April 16, 1706, reprinted James, "Grace Sherwood, the Virginia Witch," 244–245.

11. Princess Anne Co., May 2, 1706, in *Collections of the Virginia Historical & Philosophical Society* 1 (1833), 75.

12. King James I, *Daemonology* (1597), in Ronald Holmes, *Witchcraft in British History* (London, 1974), 11.

13. Princess Anne Co., July 5, 1706, July 10, 1706, in *Collections of the Virginia Historical & Philosophical Society* 1 (1833), 77.

14. Princess Anne Co., July 10, 1706, in *Collections of the Virginia Historical & Philosophical Society* 1 (1833), 78.

15. Ingle, "A Virginia Witch," 427; Grace Sherwood's will in Princess Anne Co., Oct. 1, 1740, reprinted in James, "Grace Sherwood, the Virginia Witch," 19. Sherwood left son John Sherwood all her property except for 5 shillings each for sons James and Richard.

16. Floyd Painter, "An Early Eighteenth Century Witch Bottle: A Legacy of the Wicked Witch of Pongo," *The Chesopiean: A Journal of North American Archeology* 18 (1980), 62–71.

17. Painter, "An Early Eighteenth Century Witch Bottle," 62–63.

18. Robert Burton, *Anatomy of Melancholy* (Oxford, 1621), 289, in Alan Macfarlane, *Witchcraft in Tudor and Stuart England: A Regional and Comparative Study* (London, 1970), 115.

19. Rutman, "The Evolution of Religious Life in Early Virginia," 193–194. Mary Lee, who was on the ship *Charity* in 1659, "confessed." In 1659, when a Capt. Bennette executed Katherine Grade at sea, having found her a witch, he came under investigation in Virginia. See Fred Drake, "Witchcraft in the American Colonies, 1647–62," *American Quarterly* 20 (1968), 706.

20. See variant view in Richard Beale Davis, "The Devil in Virginia in the Seventeenth Century," in his *Literature and Society in Early Virginia, 1608–1840* (Baton Rouge, 1973), 14–41. Davis believes that Southerners were not particularly concerned with the devil or witchcraft. See Philip Alexander Bruce, *Institutional History of Virginia in the Seventeenth Century*, 2 vols. (Gloucester, Mass., [1910] 1964), 1:278–289; Jeremy Minter, *Scripture Proofs of Sorcery and Warning Against Sorcerers* (Richmond, 1814).

21. Rutman, "The Evolution of Religious Life in Early Virginia," 190–214. Harding, found guilty of witchcraft in Northumberland County in 1656, was given 10 stripes and banished.

22. Ibid., 194–195.

23. Butler, "Magic, Astrology and the Early American Religious Heritage, 1600–1760," 326–328, cites the library lists of Ralph Wormley (d. 1701), Richard Lee (d. 1715), Edmund Berkley (d. 1718), and Thomas Teackle (d. 1696 or 1697) as containing extensive occult literature.

24. *Virginia Gazette* (P.D.) June 29, 1769. A "virtue" was an object having "occult efficacy or power." *Oxford English Dictionary* (Oxford, 1961), 12:239.

25. The Autobiography of John Craig, Historical Foundation of the Presbyterian

and Reformed Churches, Montreat, N.C., cited by Butler, "Magic, Astrology, and the Early American Religious Heritage," 338, 342.

26. George Webb, *The Office and Authority of a Justice of the Peace* (Williamsburg, 1736), 61, 62.

27. MacDonald, *Mystical Bedlam*, 198–231; Thomas, *Religion and the Decline of Magic*, 126. Ephesians 4:11, 5:21. I Corinthians 12:10; 14.

28. Byrd, *Diary, 1709–1712*, Dec. 29 and 31, 1710, 278–279. For Byrd's dreams see *Diary, 1709–1712*, 1709: April 8, 18; July 15. 1710: Jan. 5; March 31; April 10; June 18, 21; July 21; Aug. 21, 29; Dec. 31. 1712: Jan. 16, 19. *Diary, 1717–1721*, 1720: Aug. 27; Dec. 2. 1721: Jan. 2. *Diary, 1739–1741*, 1740: Feb. 12; March 18; Dec. 20. 1741: April 24.

29. See Byrd's Creed, in *Diary, 1709–1712*, xxviii; Norman Viering, "The First American Enlightenment: Tillotson, Leverett and Philosophical Anglicanism," *New England Quarterly* 54 (1981), 307–344; Marambaud, *William Byrd of Westover*; Zuckerman, "William Byrd's Family"; Lewis P. Simpson, "William Byrd and the South," *Early American Literature* 7 (1972), 187–195; David Smith, "William Byrd Surveys America," *Early American Literature* 11 (1976), 296–310; Marshall Fishwick, "The Pepys of the Old Dominion," *American Heritage* 11 (1959), 5–7, 117–119; Louis B. Wright, "William Byrd of Westover: An American Pepys," *South Atlantic Quarterly* 39 (1940), 259–274.

30. Byrd, Commonplace Book, c. 1722–1732, 105, Virginia Historical Society, records a tale of a witch riding people.

31. Ralph Lane, Sept., 1585, in a letter to Richard Hakluyt, which Hakluyt published in *Principal Navigations*, 8 vols. (London, [1589] 1927–1928), 4:140, and is reprinted in *Sixteenth Century North America: The Land and the People as Seen by the Europeans*, Carl O. Sauer (Berkeley, 1971), 254–256.

32. Michael Drayton, *The Works of Michael Drayton,* ed. J. W. Hebel, 5 vols. (Oxford, 1961), 2:362. Cf. the Edenic vision preached to the men going out to Virginia by William Symonds in *Virginia: A Sermon Preached at White-Chapel, London 1609* (Amsterdam, [1609] 1968), 24; Bertelson, *The Lazy South*, 14. For contemporary attitudes toward the Biblical Eden, see Arnold Williams, *The Common Expositor: An Account of the Commentaries on Genesis, 1527–1633* (Chapel Hill, 1948).

33. Daniel Blake Smith, "Mortality and Family in the Colonial Chesapeake," *Journal of Interdisciplinary History* 8 (1978), 403–427. Lewis P. Simpson, *The Dispossessed Garden: Pastoral and History in Southern Literature* (Athens, Ga., 1975), 16; Louis B. Wright, *The Colonial Search for a Southern Eden* (University, Ala., 1953); Leo Marx, *The Machine in the Garden: Technology and the Pastoral Ideal in America* (London, 1964), 75–79, 101–112.

34. Beverly, *The History and Present State of Virginia*, 298–299.

35. Byrd, *Correspondence*, 1:179, n. 1, 827; William Byrd I to Warham Horsmanden, March 1684/1685, 1:32.

36. Westover was a 1,200-acre plantation purchased by W. Byrd I in 1688. Byrd, *Correspondence*, 1:106, n. 3, and 121, 132, 135; Clare Cooper, "The House as Symbol of the Self," in *Designing for Human Behavior: Architecture and the Behavioral Sciences*, ed. J. Lang et al. (Stroudsburg, Penn., 1974), 130–146.

37. W. Craven, *White, Red and Black*, 107, n. 45, cites Abstract of Patent Book 8, 413, "for a patent to William Byrd in 1696 which included 100 Negroes in the total of 113 headrights." Byrd may well have resold many of these slaves. The

small stone house is pictured in the Byrd Title Book, Byrd Family Papers, Virginia Historical Society.

38. See Jean Devisse, *The Image of the Black in Western Art*, 2 vols. (New York, 1979); see A Mappe of Paradise belonging to Richard Lee, and the Will of Richard Lee, March 3, 1714, in Lee Family Papers, 1742–1795, microfilm, University of Haifa.

39. Byrd, *Diary, 1709–1712*, Aug. 27, 1710. Byrd owned a copy of the translation and commentary on "Solomon's Song" made by the Puritan Hebraicist Henry Ainsworth in 1623. Ainsworth noted that the bride's color was black and that she was "beautiful, amiable and to be desired," apparently accepting that the book told of the marriage of Solomon to Pharaoh's daughter. Henry Ainsworth, *Solomon's Song of Songs in English Metre with Annotations and References to Other Scriptures* (London, 1623). "A Catalogue of the Books in the Library at Westover Belonging to William Byrd, Esqr.," is in *The Writings of Colonel William Byrd of Westover in Virginia, Esquire*, ed. John S. Bassett (New York, 1901), 413–443. See George L. Scheper, "Reformation Attitudes Toward Allegory and the Song of Songs," *PMLA* 89 (1974), 551–562.

40. Byrd, *Diary, 1709–1712*, Sept. 23, 1711.

41. Byrd to Charles Boyle, July 5, 1726, *Correspondence*, 1:355.

42. Byrd, *Histories of the Dividing Line Betwixt Virginia and North Carolina*. The Governor of North Carolina was then Charles Eden, and the name Eden was a play on his name as well. Heluetische Societat, or Wilhelm Vogel [William Byrd], *Neu-gefundenes Eden* (Bern, Switzerland, 1737). On its authorship, see Tinling, in *Correspondence*, 2:507, n. 2; and Percy G. Adams, "The Real Author of William Byrd's Natural History of Virginia," *American Literature* 28 (1956–1957), 211–220.

43. Byrd to John Perceval, July 12, 1736, *Correspondence*, 2:487–488.

44. Byrd, *Correspondence*, 2:613; Sam Byrd's trial record, Executive Papers of Gov. James Monroe, Sept.–Dec. 1800, Virginia State Library. See also Virginia, Auditor of Public Records, Condemned, Executed and Transported Slaves, 1783–1865, Virginia State Library.

45. Jefferson, *Thomas Jefferson's Garden Book, 1766–1824*, ed. Edwin M. Betts (Philadelphia, 1981), 50, March 31, 1774; Joan Lee Faust, "The Gardens at Monticello," *America* 1 (1973), 6–8; Carol McCabe, "Mr. Jefferson's Garden," *Early American Life* 14, no. 3 (1983), 44–49; William Howard Adams, *Jefferson's Monticello* (New York, 1983), 145–190. See John Prest, *The Garden of Eden: The Botanic Garden and the Re-Creation of Paradise* (New Haven, 1981).

46. William M. Kelso, *Kingsmill Plantations, 1619–1800: Archaeology of Country Life in Colonial Virginia* (Orlando, 1984), 167–176.

47. John Smith, *A Map of Virginia* (Oxford, 1612); map reprinted in *America in Maps: Dating from 1500 to 1856*, ed. Egon Klemp (New York, 1976), no. 33. Illustration from an engraving by William Hole, 1612, based on a DeBray engraving that in turn was based on a John White drawing done in North America. Cf. William P. Cumming, "Early Maps of the Chesapeake Bay Area: Their Relation to Settlement and Society," in *Early Maryland in a Wider World*, ed. Quinn, 267–310; E. M. Sanchez-Saavedra, *A Description of the Country: Virginia's Cartographers and Their Maps, 1607–1881* (Richmond, 1975); Mary R. Miller, *Place Names of the Northern Neck of Virginia: From John Smith's*

1606 Map to the Present (Richmond, 1983); Christian F. Feest, "The Virginia Indian in Pictures, 1612–1624," *The Smithsonian Journal of History* 2, no. 1 (Spring 1967), 1–30.

48. Map reprinted in Klemp, *America in Maps*, no. 37; Coolie Verner, "The Fry and Jefferson Map," *Imago Mundi* 21 (1967), 70–94.

49. George D. McJimsey, "Topographic Terms in Virginia," *American Speech* 15 (1940), 3–39, 149–180, 262–301, 381–420. McJimsey found only two topographic terms that were from black speech: mulatto land and niggerhead. Kelsie B. Harder, *Illustrated Dictionary of Place Names, United States and Canada* (New York, 1976), 16, 187, states that Angola was used as a name for "euphonious" reasons. Africa and blacks are *not* mentioned. J. L. Dillard, *Black Names* (The Hague, 1976), 12; *Thomas Jefferson's Farm Book*, ed. Betts, 9; Deetz, *In Small Things Forgotten*, 139, 141, 142; Rawick, *The American Slave*, 18:55; Kelso, *Kingsmill Plantations*, 208; Rutman, *A Place in Time I*, 165. The name Gumba Springs, Va., apparently has African roots, and a natural flight of rock stairs at Wyer's Cave, Virginia (17 miles from Stanton) was named Jacob's ladder by blacks. Miles Mark Fisher, *Negro Slave Songs in the United States* (Ithaca, 1953), 117. Negro Arm in Powhatan Co., and Negro Foot in Hanover Co., can be found in Ray O. Hummel, Jr., *A List of Places Included in Nineteenth Century Virginia Directories* (Richmond, 1960), 92, 93.

50. Michael L. Nicholls, "Origins of the Virginia Southside, 1703–1750: A Social and Economic Study" (Ph.D. dissertation, College of William and Mary, 1972), 139. I am grateful to Allan Kulikoff for bringing this to my attention. See also Beeman, *The Evolution of the Southern Backcountry*, 29–30; Rutman, *A Place in Time I*, 48–49, 73, 148, 236–240; Kevin P. Kelly, " 'In Dispers'd Plantations': Settlement Patterns in Seventeenth-Century Surry County, Virginia," in *The Chesapeake in the Seventeenth Century*, ed. Tate and Ammerman, 183–205; Carville V. Earle, *The Evolution of a Tidewater Settlement System: All Hallow's Parish, Maryland, 1650–1783* (Chicago, 1975).

51. The processioning statute, passed in 1662 and renewed in 1705, had each vestry divide the parish into precincts, each to be surveyed every four years by two "Processioners" as well as by the owners, who "shall goe in procession and see the marked trees of every man's land." Hening, *Statutes*, 2:102; Seiler, "Land Processioning," 419; Rutman, *A Place in Time II*, 145–147, 162 n. 15. The average age of a processioner in Middlesex was 37.6 years, and processioning was the seventh task "up" a hierarchy of tasks, as analyzed by the Rutmans. Land disputes fill virtually all the local court records. See, for example, York County, Orders, Wills, Inventories, 1720–1759; Judgments and Orders, 1759–1765, microfilm, Virginia State Library.

52. Thad M. Tate, "The Discovery and Development of the Southern Colonial Landscape: Six Commentators," *Proceedings of the American Antiquarian Society* 93 (1983), 289–311, discusses six individuals who saw space in terms of its "potential for exploitation."

53. Harrower, *The Journal of John Harrower*, 17, 44, 76, 171, notes 1–3.

54. Harrower, *The Journal of John Harrower*, 56.

55. Lorena S. Walsh and Russell R. Menard, "Death in the Chesapeake: Two Life Tables for Men in Early Colonial Maryland," *Maryland Historical Magazine* 69 (1974), 211–227; Rutman, *A Place in Time II*, 37–60.

56. Hakluyt, *Principal Navigations*, 4:140, in *Sixteenth Century North America*, Sauer, 245–246.

57. Adams, "The Real Author of William Byrd's Natural History of Virginia," 211–220. A copy of *Neu-gefundenes Eden* (Bern, Switzerland, 1737) is in Brown University Library.

58. See below, Parts Three and Four.

59. Rawick, *The American Slave*, 18:227; Leon F. Litwack, *Been in the Storm So Long: The Aftermath of Slavery* (New York, 1980), 326.

60. *Virginia Gazette* (P.D.) Sept. 12, 1771, in Mullin, *American Negro Slavery*, 82. Africans who were brought to Surinam thought they were still in Africa but at such a distance from home that they could not make contact with their own peoples. S. Allen Counter and David L. Evans, *I Sought My Brother: An Afro-American Reunion* (Boston, 1981).

61. Lt. Gov. Sir William Gooch to Board of Trade, Williamsburg, June 29, 1729, Colonial Office Papers 5/1322, 19ff. Virginia Colonial Records Project, microfilm, Colonial Williamsburg Foundation.

62. Curtin, *Africa Remembered*; Fisher, *Negro Slave Songs*, 49, 111–118. Fisher believed that "home" or "the promised land" in slave songs meant Africa.

63. Jefferson, *The Complete Jefferson*, ed. Saul K. Padover (Freeport, N.Y., [1943] 1968), 822–823. Poem reprinted by permission of the Massachusetts Historical Society.

64. Reuben Madison, interviewed 1827; George Pleasant, Sept. 6, 1833; in Blassingame, ed., *Slave Testimony*, 185, 19.

65. Puckett, *Folk Beliefs of the Southern Negro*, 115–166, 324. William Grimes, born a slave in Virginia in 1784, wrote that Aunt Frankee, a slave whose room he shared, was a witch who rode him in the night. Grimes, *Life of William Grimes*, 29.

66. Ellen Glasgow, *The Woman Within* (New York, 1954), 26. Glasgow, instructed by her black nursemaid, baptized trees in Virginia in the nineteenth century.

67. Robert Farris Thompson and Joseph Cornet, *The Four Moments of the Sun: Kongo Art in Two Worlds* (Washington, D.C., 1982), 150, 178–179; Thompson, *Flash of the Spirit: African and Afro-American Art and Philosophy* (New York, 1983), 143–145.

68. Stilgoe, *Common Landscape*, 138ff. For a different view of black influence, see Norman E. Whitten, Jr., "Contemporary Patterns of Malign Occultism Among Negroes in North Carolina," *Journal of American Folklore* 65 (1962), 311–325.

69. Although Leventhal, *In the Shadow of the Enlightenment*, 163, does not take at face value the white colonial claim that their knowledge of snakes' ability to "fascinate" came from Indians, he never raises the possibility of African influences. See Benjamin Bartram, "A Memoir Concerning the Fascinating Faculty Which Has Been Ascribed to the Rattle-Snake and Other American Serpents," in *Transactions of the American Philosophical Society* 4 (1799), 74–113; John Lederer, *The Discoveries of John Lederer* (Charlottesville, 1958), 15–16. Byrd, *The Correspondence*, 169, 260, 343, 414, 519. Byrd, a Fellow of the Royal Society as of April 29, 1696, presented a Virginia rattlesnake to the Society, July 20, 1697, and wrote them of its ability to "charm"; Raymond P. Stearns, *Science in the British Colonies of America* (Urbana, 1970), 281. See also Thomas Walduck, "Account of the Rattlesnake, Read Before the Royal So-

ciety, Jan. 7th, 1713/14" in "Colonial Rattlesnake Lore, 1714," ed. James R. Masterson, *Zoologica* 23 (1938), 213–216.

70. On African practices see Wilfred D. Hambly, *Serpent Worship in Africa* in Publications of Field Museum of Natural History, Anthropological Series, 21 (New York, [1931] 1968), 76. On Voodoo and Afro-American snake cults, see Sobel, *Trabelin' On*, 45–57; Herskovits, *Myth of the Negro Past*, 246; A. Metraux, *Voodoo in Haiti* (New York, 1959).

71. The contemporary Southern white snake cults may well be based on black beliefs, although this possibility has not been explored. Cf. Nathaniel Gerrard, "Serpent-Handling Religions of West Virginia," *Tennessee Folklore Society Bulletin* 36 (1970), 22–28.

72. Leventhal discusses white belief in three types of souls and in spirits in *In the Shadow of the Enlightenment*, 154–155, 184–185, 205–218. On African concepts of souls see Zahan, *The Religion, Spirituality and Thought of Traditional Africa*, 87, 90; Parrinder, *West African Religion*, 21, 97, 113; Sobel, *Trabelin' On*, 14, 46–48, 69, 108.

73. Thomas, *Religion and the Decline of Magic*, 29, 508; A summary of the extensive European beliefs in the curing properties of stones can be found in Sophie Lasne and André P. Gaultier, *A Dictionary of Superstitions* (Englewood Cliffs, N.J., 1984), 35–53. For early English stone medicine, see J.H.G. Grattan and Charles Singer, *Anglo-Saxon Magic and Medicine* (London, [1952] 1977), 66.

74. Nigel Barley, *Adventures in a Mud Hut: An Innocent Anthropologist Abroad* (New York, [1983] 1984), 102, records contemporary Dawoyo practices.

75. Robert A. Hodges, "Some Madstones of Virginia," *Pioneer America* 4 (1972), 1–8. White folk medicine in Virginia has not been systematically investigated. Herbal recipes for medicines are scattered through Virginia almanacs and commonplace books. (See, for example, a cure for venereal disease in Byrd's Commonplace Book, 13–14.) Only one Southern occult witchcraft book has been found—that of Joshua Gordon of South Carolina, c. 1784, now in the South Carolina Library, University of South Carolina. Cf. Butler, "Magic, Astrology, and the Early American Religious Heritage," 335–337. A selection of Southern folk cures can be found in Richard Dorson, *American Folklore* (Chicago, [1959] 1964), 17–18. See Peter H. Wood, "People's Medicine in the Early South," *Southern Exposure* 6 (1978), 50–53; Wyndham B. Blanton, *Medicine in Virginia in the Eighteenth Century* (Richmond, 1931); Blanton, "Washington's Medical Knowledge and Its Sources," *Annals of Medical History* 5 (1933), 52–61; Jean W. Robinson, "Black Healers During the Colonial Period and Early Nineteenth Century America" (Ph.D. dissertation, Southern Illinois University, 1979); Todd L. Savitt, *Medicine and Slavery: The Diseases and Health Care of Blacks in Antebellum Virginia* (Urbana, 1978); Ralph Kuna, "Hoodoo: The Indigenous Medicine and Psychiatry of the Black American," *Mankind Quarterly* 18 (1977), 137–151.

76. On the modern mix of black and white esoteric knowledge, no doubt the result of "mixing" since the seventeenth century, see Puckett, *Folk Belief of the Southern Negro* and Harry Hyatt, *Hoodoo, Conjuration, Witchcraft, Rootwork: Beliefs Accepted by Many Negroes and White Persons, These Being Orally Recorded Among Blacks and Whites*, 5 vols. (Hannibal, Mo., 1970). On earlier English use of amulets or sigils see MacDonald, *Mystical Bedlam*, 24, 30, 176, 213–216, 222, 294, n. 198.

77. James Gordon, "Journal of Col. James Gordon of Lancaster County, Virginia," *William and Mary Quarterly*, 1st series, 11 (1902–1903), 98–112, 195–205, 217–236; 12 (1903–1904), 1–12; on a white consulting a black doctor see March 23, 1760. Winthrop D. Jordan, *White Over Black: American Attitudes Toward The Negro, 1550–1812* (Chapel Hill, 1968), 343, reports 20 slaves were executed for poisoning in Virginia, 1772–1810. Many others were recognized as providing poisonous "medicines" but were acquitted of murder. See Sussex County, Court of Oyer and Terminer, March 10, 1755, Dec. 11, 1770, June 20, 1771. June 20, 1782, Dec. 2, 1786, Aug. 2, 1798, microfilm (on reel with Order Books, 1754–1764), Virginia State Library. See advertisements for slave "doctors," *Virginia Gazette*, Nov. 21, 1745; Nov. 4, 1763.

78. Savitt, *Medicine and Slavery*; on the hiring of white midwives for slaves, see, for examples, the 1792 tax records of Robert Carter (1728–1804), Carter Family Papers, Virginia Historical Society; and the Minutes of the Meherrin Baptist Church, Sept. 1, 1775, Virginia Baptist Historical Society. See L. Carter, *Diary*, infra., for extensive examples of his medical treatment of slaves; and Julia Cherry Spruill, *Women's Life and Work in the Southern Colonies* (New York, [1938] 1972), 75, 308, 311–312, for white women caring for ill slaves, including white nurses advertising to find work with slaves.

79. John Custis to Peter Collinson, 1742, in Custis Letter Book, typescript, 243, Custis Family Papers, Virginia Historical Society.

80. Lt. Gov. Gooch, to the Council of Trade and Plantations, June 29, 1729, and to the Bishop of London, Records of Lt. Gov. Gooch, 1727–1749, 3 vols., typescript, Virginia Historical Society; reprinted in *Virginia Magazine of History and Biography* 32 (1924), 227–231. H. R. McIllwaine, W. L. Hall, and B. J. Hillman, eds., *Executive Journals of the Council of Colonial Virginia, 1680–1775*, 6 vols. (Richmond, 1925–1966), 4:199, April 23, 1729.

81. See, for example, the reference to a "conjurer," Ben, whose testimony condemned another slave. In this case whites wrote to the Governor asking that he discount the word of such a man. State of Virginia, Calendar of State Papers, 1790–1792, 332–339, Virginia State Library.

82. Cf. Irving I. Zaretsky and Cynthia Shambaugh, *Spirit Possession and Spirit Mediumship in Africa and Afro-America: An Annotated Bibliography* (New York, 1978); Sheila S. Walker, *Ceremonial Spirit Possession in Africa and Afro-America: Forms, Meanings and Functional Significance for Individuals and Social Groups* (Leiden, 1972); Henry H. Mitchell, *Black Belief: Folk Beliefs in America and West Africa* (New York, 1975).

CHAPTER 9

1. Richard C. Bushman, "American High-Style and Vernacular Cultures," in *Colonial British America*, ed. Greene and Pole, 345–383. See Chapter 10. For examples of Great Houses, see Thomas Tileston Waterman, *The Mansions of Virginia, 1706–1776* (Chapel Hill, 1946); Waterman and John A. Barrows, *Domestic Colonial Architecture of Tidewater Virginia* (New York, [1932] 1969).

2. Carter Hudgins, "Exactly as the Gentry do in England: Culture, Aspirations, and Material Things in the Eighteenth Century Chesapeake," Conference on "The Colonial Experience: The Eighteenth Century Chesapeake," Baltimore,

September 1984, mimeographed, 5. G. Main, *Tobacco Colony*, 140–166, recognized this was the case in seventeenth-century Maryland.

3. Dell Upton, "Vernacular Domestic Architecture in Eighteenth-Century Virginia," *Winterthur Portfolio* 17 (1982), 96.

4. Carter L. Hudgins, "The King's Realm: An Archeological and Historical Study of Plantation Life at Robert Carter's Corotoman" (M.A. thesis, Wake Forest University, 1981), 23–24, as cited by Kelso, *Kingsmill Plantations*, 14, 110.

5. John Fontaine, *The Journal of John Fontaine, An Irish Huguenot Son in Spain and Virginia, 1710–1719*, ed. Edward P. Alexander (Williamsburg, 1972), 86.

6. W. Adams, *Jefferson's Monticello*, 39, 197. See Buford Pickens, "Mr. Jefferson as Revolutionary Architect," *Journal of the Society of Architectural Historians* 34 (1975), 257–279. This first Monticello building, which was later called the South Pavillion, was a single, all-purpose room, under which was a slave-run kitchen. Thomas Lord Fairfax at Greenway Court in the 1750s chose to live in a small cabin, giving the larger house to his overseer and guests. Roger R. Dawson, "Greenway Court and White Post: Virginia Home of Thomas, Lord Fairfax," *Pioneer America* 1 (1969), 33–39.

7. Hudgins, "Exactly as the Gentry do in England," 19, citing Lancaster County records.

8. William Byrd, "Journey to the Land of Eden," in *The Prose Works of William Byrd of Westover: Narratives of a Colonial Gentleman*, ed. Louis B. Wright (Cambridge, Mass., 1966), 385; on another journey Byrd lay on "a dirty and Wet Floor." *Histories of the Dividing Line*, ed. Boyd, 57. "Square" was used to mean an erect, straight, or right-angled building or one "having a solid, sturdy form." Cf. Jess Stein, ed., *The Random House Dictionary of the English Language* (New York, 1967), 1380.

9. Washington, *The Writings*, 1:17.

10. Fussell, *The English Rural Labourer*, 70.

11. Equiano, "The Life of Olaudah Equiano," 9.

12. Stratton inventory, Henrico County Records, 1697–1704, 138, as given in Philip Alexander Bruce, *Economic History of Virginia in the Seventeenth Century*, 2 vols. (Gloucester, Mass., 1935), 2:106.

13. Rutman, *A Place in Time I*, 168.

14. Carr and Walsh, "Inventories and Analysis of Wealth and Consumption Patterns in St. Mary's County, Maryland, 1658–1777," 83–87. St. Mary's was a Chesapeake area dependent on tobacco and was one-half black in 1750, in these aspects similar to many Virginia counties. See Russell R. Menard, Lois Green Carr, and Lorena S. Walsh, "A Small Planter's Profits: The Cole Estate and the Growth of the Early Chesapeake Economy," *William and Mary Quarterly* 40 (1983), 171–196. A very interesting nineteenth-century Virginia slave's will (June 18, 1856) is extant, that of Dangerfield Hunter, 1781?-Nov. 20, 1856, slave of Louis Abraham Pauly; typed copy, Virginia Historical Society. Hunter, or "Uncle Field," gave his nephew, friends, and perhaps other relatives, his bedstead, bedding, 3 split-bottom chairs, a corner "cubbord," a walnut table, a "big Pot, pot Rack and Pot Hooks," a basket, 2 crocks, 1 coffee pot, 1 quart pot, 1 large tin, 1 glass tumbler, 1 square basket, 2 boxes, 3 knives, 3 forks, 1 coffee mill, 2 plates, 1 tin, an iron fire shovel, and old frying pan, assorted clothing, and a walking stick.

15. *Virginia Gazette* (H.), April 10, 1752, Oct. 17, 1755, reprinted in *Runaway*

Slave Advertisements, ed. Windley, 27, 33; Devereux Jarratt, "The Autobiography of the Reverend Devereux Jarratt, 1732–1763," ed. Douglas Adair, *William and Mary Quarterly* 9 (1952), 367. (Osnaburg, spelled in various ways in the period, was a coarse linen or cotton fabric, widely used for slave clothing and that of the poor and "middling sort.") On Jarratt, see E. Clowes Chorley, "The Rev. Devereux Jarratt, 1732–1801," *Historical Magazine of the Protestant Episcopal Church* 5 (1936), 47–64; David Holmes, "Devereux Jarratt: A Letter and a Reevaluation," *Historical Magazine of the Protestant Episcopal Church* 47 (1978), 37–49.

16. J. T. Main, *The Social Structure of Revolutionary America,* 54; Main, "The Distribution of Property in Post-Revolutionary Virginia," *Mississippi Valley Historical Review* 41 (1954–1955), 241–258; Sarah S. Hughes, "Slaves for Hire," 285. See also Aubrey C. Land, "Economic Base and Social Structure: The Northern Chesapeake in the Eighteenth Century." *Journal of Economic History* 25 (1965), 639–654.

17. This view is shared in recent works by George W. McDaniel, *Hearth and Home: Preserving a People's Culture* (Philadelphia, 1982), 53; Dell Upton, "The Power of Things: Recent Studies in American Vernacular Architecture," *American Quarterly* 35 (1983), 268; Upton, "The Origins of Chesapeake Architecture," in *Three Centuries of Maryland Architecture: A Selection of Presentations Made at the Eleventh Annual Conference of the Maryland Historic Trust,* mimeographed (Annapolis, 1982), 45; and in older studies by Genovese, *Roll Jordan Roll,* 533, and A. Craven, "Poor Whites and Negroes," 20.

   Interesting comparisons of slave and free living standards and life styles in Virginia can be found in Kelso, *Kingsmill Plantations,* infra. For other relevant studies, based on different areas, see John S. Otto, "A New Look at Slave Life," *Natural History* 88 (1979), 8–30; Otto and Augustus M. Burns, III, "Black Folks and Poor Buckras: Archeological Evidence of Slave and Overseer Living Conditions on an Antebellum Plantation," *Journal of Black Studies* 14 (1983), 185–200; Otto, "Artifacts and Status Differences—A Comparison of Ceramics from Planter, Overseer, and Slave Sites on an Antebellum Plantation," in *Research Strategies in Historical Archeology,* ed. Stanley South (New York, 1977), 91–118; Otto, *Cannon's Point Plantation, 1794–1860: Living Conditions and Status Patterns in the Old South* (Orlando, 1984); Theresa A. Singleton, ed., *The Archaeology of Slavery and Plantation Life* (Orlando, 1985).

18. Chastellux, *Travels in North America,* 2:438.

19. Benjamin H. Latrobe, *The Virginia Journals of Benjamin Henry Latrobe, 1795–1798,* ed. Edward C. Carter, II, and Angeline Polites, 2 vols. (New Haven, 1977), 1:101, cited by Upton, "The Origins of Chesapeake Architecture," 45.

20. Durand de Dauphiné, *A Huguenot Exile in Virginia, or Voyages of a Frenchman Exiled for his Religion, with a Description of Virginia and Maryland,* trans. and ed. Gilbert Chinard (New York, [1687] 1934), 119–120, reprinted in Billings, *The Old Dominion in the Seventeenth Century,* 306. A similar village-like pattern was the norm in Barbados in the seventeenth century. Cf. Gary A. Puckrein, *Little England: Plantation Society and Anglo-Barbadian Politics, 1627–1700* (New York, 1984), 74–75.

21. I want especially to thank Professor Michael L. Nicholls of Utah State University, who has been extremely generous in sharing his manuscript, "Building the Virginia Southside: A Note on Architecture and Society in the Eighteenth

Century." He cites James Bates's inventory, "A List of White Persons and Houses taken in the County of Halifax, 1785," in Lists, Inhabitants and Buildings, 1782–1785, Box 2, Virginia State Library, Richmond.

22. Nicholls, "Building the Virginia Southside," 11.

23. Kelso, *Kingsmill Plantations*, 82, 96, 110, 113. See *Virginia Gazette* (D.N.), Feb. 24, 1781.

24. Historic American Building Survey, HABS VA 208, 2, photographs and loose papers, Library of Congress, citing *Virginia Gazette* and *Weekly Advertiser* (N.P.), Nov. 16, 1782. "All necessary outhouses" were commonly referred to in advertisements. Cf. Mathew Moody, Jr.'s description of his property, *Virginia Gazette* (P.D.), April 18, 1766.

25. See Fraser D. Neiman, *The "Manner House" Before Stratford: Discovering the Clifts Plantation* (Stratford, Va., 1980); Neiman, "Domestic Architecture at the Clifts Plantation: The Social Context of Early Virginia Building," *Northern Neck of Virginia Historical Magazine* 28 (1978), 3096–3128; Judith S. Hynson, Custodian of Records, Stratford Hall Plantation, Stratford, Virginia, correspondence, January 1984.

26. Washington, *The Writings*, 33: Dec. 22, 1793, 196; May 21, 1794, 376; Sept. 7, 1794, 495, 34: Nov. 2, 1794, 15; June 7, 1795, 212; June 21, 1795, 217. The move was not completed until 1795. Washington went to the expense of digging a well in order to relocate this housing. The map shows the new locations; no map of the old sites has been found, but the cabins were probably spread out asymmetrically, as at Muddy Hole farm. Dell Upton has found that "The surviving eighteenth and nineteenth century groups of quarters . . . are all set in straight lines, or in opposed straight lines." However, only the later and better slave housing survived. Upton, "Slave Housing in 18th-Century Virginia: A Report to the Department of Social and Cultural History, National Museum of American History, Smithsonian Institution" (Washington, D.C., 1982), typescript, 35. This is an excellent survey and analysis of available data on plantation housing.

27. Charles C. Wall, "Housing and Family Life of the Mount Vernon Negro," Mt. Vernon, [1954] 1962, typescript; "Slave Burial Ground and Slavery at Mount Vernon," The Mount Vernon Ladies Association of the Union, n.d.; Edward Chappell, "Slave Housing," *Fresh Advices* (Nov. 1982), 1–4; See Robert Schuyler, ed., *Archaeological Perspectives on Ethnicity in America* (New York, 1980); Steven L. Jones, "The African-American Tradition in Vernacular Architecture," in *The Archaeology of Slavery and Plantation Life*, ed. Theresa A. Singleton (Orlando, 1985), 195–214.

28. Washington, *The Writings*, 33: Sept. 7, 1794, 495, 34: Nov. 2, 1794, 15; Feb. 1, 1796, 434.

29. Wall, "Housing and Family Life of the Mount Vernon Negro," 33; Upton, "Slave Housing," 28.

30. Cheryl Hayes, "Cultural Space and Family Living Patterns in Domestic Architecture, Queen Anne's County, Maryland, 1750–1776" (M.A. thesis, Georgetown University, 1974), as cited by McDaniel, *Hearth and Home*, 43.

31. Thomas Nairne, *A Letter from South Carolina* (London, 1710), 49–50, cited by Carson et al., "Impermanent Architecture," 140.

32. Smyth, *A Tour*, 1:74–76.

33. J. Davis, *Travels*, 423. Slave gardens in Virginia are noted by Revel, "The Poor

Unhappy Transplanted Felon's Sorrowful Account," 182; Anburey, *Travels*, 1:192; Fithian, *Journal*, 96; [Kimber] "Observations in Several Voyages and Travels in America in the Year 1736," 148; Isaac Weld, *Travels Through the State of North America, and the Provinces of Upper and Lower Canada, During the Years 1795, 1796, and 1797* (London, 1799), 85.

34. J. Davis, *Travels*, 423. Both blacks and whites chose to build under or near trees, which probably defined proper or holy space for both. See Richard C. Poulsen, *The Pure Experience of Order: Essays on the Symbolic in the Folk Material Culture of Western America* (Albuquerque, 1982), 120, 137.

35. Jefferson, *Farm Book* Nov. 10, 1818, 41. See analysis of Jefferson's black family groupings and separations in Mary Beth Norton, Herbert Gutman, and Ira Berlin, "The Afro-American Family in the Age of the Revolution," in *Slavery and Freedom*, ed. Berlin and Hoffman, 175–192.

36. Jefferson, *Garden Book*, Dec. 1811, 466–467.

37. Jefferson, *Farm Book*, 76.

38. The remains of an earthfast 12' × 12' building in use c. 1740 were found by Kelso, at *Kingsmill Plantations*, 106; Upton has collected evidence of several 12' × 12' buildings, and others 12' × 14', 15', and 16'. Upton "Slave Housing," 31, 36, 68, citing Robert Carter's Account Book, 1785–1792, 47, 56, Virginia Historical Society, for evidence of a 12' × 12' quarter built for Carter's tenant, Thos. Blundel, 1787; and Surry County Orders, Deeds, Wills, 1654–1672, Virginia State Library, for evidence of a 12' × 12' quarter on the farm of Geo. Burchard, 1651. Upton documents 22 eighteenth-century quarters, comparing big house and slave quarter size and building material. Upton, *Slave Housing*, 68–70. John Harrower was living in a refurbished wooden cabin that was 12' × 20'. Harrower, *The Journal of John Harrower*, 56, 68.

39. L. Carter, *Diary*, Oct. 9, 1770, 509; Nov. 15, 1770, 523. Doleman may not have moved into this house. There was another old white person's cabin, that of Baker DeGratenreed, that Carter had bought, planning to use it for "two or three hands." It apparently became Doleman's. See *Diary*, Nov. 10, 1770, 522.

40. Kelso, *Kingsmill Plantations*, 31, 71, 85, 106, 117, 119–123, 127, 172, 202. The cellars ranged in size from approximately 3' × 2' to 5' × 8' and were from 2' to 3'6" deep. Kelso notes that they were also found at Monticello and cites his "Report of Archeological Excavations at Monticello, Albemarle County, Virginia, 1979–1983" (Charlottesville, 1984), 49–150. Carter referred to such storage places in his *Diary*, 495.

41. Washington, *The Writings*, 33:178.

42. In the mid-nineteenth century Olmstead (who traveled in Virginia in 1853 and 1854) reported that large numbers of whites were living in tiny cabins. Frederick Law Olmstead, *The Cotton Kingdom*, 2 vols. (New York, [1861] 1966), 1:31; *A Journey in the Back Country* (New York, 1860), 198, 205, 231–232; *A Journey in the Seaboard States* (New York, 1856), 384–386.

43. C. Carson et al., "Impermanent Architecture in the Southern American Colonies," *Winterthur Portfolio* 16 (1981), 135–196. Among the many special studies of great value, see Nicholas Luccketti, "17th-Century Planters in 'New Pocosin': Excavations at Bennett Farm and River Creek," *Notes on Virginia* 23 (1983), 26–29; Charles E. Hatch, Jr., *Popes Creek Plantation; Birthplace of George Washington* (Wakefield, Va., 1979); William T. Buchanan, Jr., and Edward F. Heite, "The Hallowes Site: A Seventeenth-Century Yeoman's Cottage

in Virginia," *Historical Archeology* 5 (1971), 38–48; Paul E. Buchanan, "The Eighteenth-Century Frame Houses of Tidewater Virginia," in *Building Early America: Contributions Toward the History of a Great Industry*, ed. Charles E. Peterson (Radnor, Penn., 1976), 54–73; Dawson, "Greenway Court and White Post"; Neiman, *The "Manner House" Before Stratford*; Neiman, "Domestic Architecture at the Clifts Plantation"; and the very perceptive work of Dell Upton, "Toward a Performance Theory of Vernacular Architecture: Early Tidewater Virginia as a Case Study," *Folklore Forum* 12 (1979), 173–196; Upton, "Traditional Timber Framing: An Interpretive Essay," in *The Material Culture of the Wooden Age*, ed. Brooke Hindle (Tarrytown, N.Y., 1981), 35–93; Upton, "Vernacular Domestic Architecture in Eighteenth-Century Virginia," and Upton, "Ordinary Buildings: A Bibliographical Essay on American Vernacular Architecture," *American Studies International* 19, no. 2 (Winter 1981), 57–75. A general overview of house types can be found in Peirce Lewis, "Common Houses, Cultural Spoor," *Landscape* 19, no. 2 (1975), 1–22; Lewis, "Learning from Looking: Geographic and Other Writing about the American Cultural Landscape," *American Quarterly* 35 (1983), 242–261, which has an excellent bibliography and a review of recent work in the field.

44. C. Carson et al., "Impermanent Architecture," 147, n. 30.
45. Ibid., 159.
46. Glassie, *Folk Housing*, 43. On "square," see above, note 8.
47. Glassie, *Folk Housing*, 163; Glassie, "The Types of Southern Mountain Cabin," in *The Study of American Folklore: An Introduction*, by Jan Harold Brunvand (New York, 1968), 338–370; Glassie, "Eighteenth-Century Cultural Process in Delaware Valley Folk Building," *Winterthur Portfolio* 7 (1972), 29–57; Deetz, *In Small Things Forgotten*, 138–154. Truro Parish ordered a new Vestry House, 16' × 16' in 1750; Minutes of the Vestry, 1732–1785, 58, cited by C. Carson et al., "Impermanent Architecture," 153, n. 46. Whites did build 12' × 12' units for their own use: The earthfast jail in Stafford County, Va., and the arms arsenal at Greenway Court were both this size. See Upton, "Traditional Timber Framing," 55; Dawson, "Greenway Court," 38. Not many eighteenth-century earthfast structures are still extant. Most of them decayed and were destroyed, and some were altered and are unrecognizable. For example, the Woodward House, 3017 Williamsburg Avenue, Richmond, Virginia, was originally a one-room wooden structure with loft built in 1716. It is still standing, but the roof was raised, and it is now two stories with a two-bay addition. Virginia Historic Landmarks Commission, photographs and loose papers, Richmond File, No. 133–141. See evidence on Cedar Park and Sotterly, two earthfast buildings in Maryland, extant but in very poor condition, in C. Carson et al., "Impermanent Architecture," 187–189.
48. Jefferson, *Notes on the State of Virginia*, query 15, 145.
49. Glassie, *Folk Housing*, 25, 51; Martin Wright, "Antecedents of the Double-Pen House Type," *Annals of the Association of American Geographers* 48 (1958), 109–117, suggests Scandinavian influence. Eugene M. Wilson, "Some Similarities Between American and European Folk Houses," *Pioneer America* 3 (1971), 8–14, sees the dogtrot as related to the central passage of folk houses in England, Wales, Slovakia, and Lithuania. John Opie, "A Sense of Place: The World We Have Lost," in *An Appalachian Symposium: Essays Written in Honor of Cratis D. Williams*, ed. J. W. Williamson (Boone, N.C., 1977), 113–

118, claims Scotch-Irish origins. Terry G. Jordan has made a comprehensive survey of European sources in *American Log Buildings: An Old World Heritage* (Chapel Hill, 1985). See also Richard H. Hulan, "Middle Tennessee and the Dogtrot House," *Pioneer America* 7 (1975), 37–46; Eugene M. Wilson, "The Single Pen Log House in the South," *Pioneer America* 2 (1970), 21–28; Fred Kniffen, "Folk Housing: Key to Diffusion," *Annals of the Association of American Geographers* 55 (1965), 549–577. Kniffen's work has been seminal and remains fresh and important today. Kniffen's 1936 "Louisiana House Types," reprinted in *Readings in Cultural Geography*, ed. P. Wagner (Chicago, 1962), 157–169, provides a taxonomy for vernacular houses; Kniffen and Glassie, "Building in Wood in the Eastern United States: A Time-Place Perspective," *Geographical Review* 56 (1966), 40–66.

50. Upton, "Traditional Timber Framing," 51, 60.

51. Equiano, "The Life of Olaudah Equiano," 9.

52. Denyer, *African Traditional Architecture*, 95.

53. Tie beams or collar beams were traditionally used to brace a roof truss some distance above its foot, forming an A. See these beams in the conjectural drawing of an early-seventeenth-century Virginia frame in Billings, *The Old Dominion*, 292, and Carson and Chinh Houng's reconstruction of a house described in a 1684 pamphlet for English migrants to the colonies, *Information and Direction to Such Persons as are Inclined to America, More Especially Those Related to the Province of Pennsylvania* (n.p., n.d.), 2, in "Impermanent Architecture in the Southern American Colonies," C. Carson et al., 143. Eighteenth-century Virginia roofs apparently ranged from the radically simplified, through the traditional English queen post roof (as on many Williamsburg houses), to the complex " 'modern' king post roof trusses" found at Stratford Hall (1725–1730). See D. T. Yeomans, "A Preliminary Study of 'English' Roofs in Colonial America," *APT Bulletin* 13 (1981), 9–18; Marcus Whiffen, *The Public Buildings of Williamsburg: Colonial Capital of Virginia* (Williamsburg, 1958), 70–75, 227, 231.

54. Denyer, *African Traditional Architecture*, illustration numbers 71, 80, 102, 106–111, 113, 117, 142, 149, and pages 138, 139, 141.

55. Beverly, *The History and Present State of Virginia*, 290. Separate kitchen buildings were known in medieval England and were built as a fire precaution. See Derek Portman, "Vernacular Building in the Oxford Region in the Sixteenth and Seventeenth Centuries," in *Rural Change and Urban Growth, 1500–1800*, ed. C. W. Chalkin and M. A. Havindin (London, 1974), 159–160.

56. John Michael Vlach, "The Shotgun House: An African Architectural Legacy," *Pioneer America* 8 (1976), 47–70; Vlach, "Shotgun Houses," *Natural History* 87 (1977), 50–57; Vlach "Architecture," in his *Afro-American Tradition in Decorative Arts*, 122–138; Sylvia Grider, "The Shotgun House," *Pioneer America* 7 (1975), 47–55.

57. Denyer, *African Traditional Architecture*, illustration number 79; Vittoria Alliata, *Le Case del Paradiso* (Milan, 1983), 45.

58. Denyer, *African Traditional Architecture*, 100–103.

59. Robert Carter to John Ballendine, Letterbook, 3, pt. 1, 138–139, Virginia Historical Society, cited by Mullin, *Flight and Rebellion*, 86. See Vlach, *The Afro-American Tradition in Decorative Arts*, 122–138; Peter H. Wood, "Whetting, Setting and Laying Timbers: Black Builders in the Early South," *Southern Ex-*

posure 8 (1980), 3–8; Robert E. Perdue, *Black Laborers and Black Professionals in Early America, 1750–1830* (New York, 1975); Catherine W. Bishir, "Black Builders in Antebellum North Carolina," *North Carolina Historical Review* 61 (1984), 423–461. Black skills and African roots have been recognized in regard to the banjo and the dugout canoe. See Phil Peek, "Afro-American Material Culture and the Afro-American Craftsman," *Southern Folklore Quarterly* 42 (1978), 109–134; Judith W. Chase, "American Heritage from Ante-Bellum Black Craftsmen," *Southern Folklore Quarterly* 42 (1978), 135–158. See also the seminal study by Robert Farris Thompson, "African Influence on the Art of the United States," in *Black Studies in the University: A Symposium*, ed. Armstead L. Robinson et al. (New Haven, 1969).

60. Pisé building at Bremo Bluff, Fluvanna County, and Four-Mile Tree Plantation, Surry County, are catalogued in the Historic American Building Survey, *Virginia Catalogue: A List of Measured Drawings, Photographs, and Written Documentation in the Survey* (Charlottesville, 1976), 67, 250. Eighteenth-century rammed-earth houses have been located in Washington, D.C., and in Prince George's County, Maryland. Cf. McDaniel, *Hearth and Home*, 271, n. 17. J. Davis mentioned them in the 1803 dedication of his book, *Travels*.

61. George Washington built an "arbor" for Patsy Custis at the "little bush village" of Berkeley Warm Springs. Fithian, *Journal*, 126. See a photograph of a gazebo at the Springs in George Cook Smith et al., eds., *Shadows in Silver: A Record of Virginia, 1850–1900 in Contemporary Photographs Taken by George and Huestic Cook* (New York, 1954), 154. C. Carl Anthony, "The Big House and the Slave Quarters," *Landscape* 20, no. 3 (1976), 8–19; 21, no. 1 (1976), 9–15. The round slave house at Keswick in Powhatan County, built in the nineteenth century, seems to be African in concept, although it is brick, 17 7/8' in diameter, and has a central fireplace. See picture in Historical American Building Survey, *Virginia Catalogue*, 206. Other pyramidal roofs and pisé buildings can be found in Smith, *Shadows in Silver*, 77, 103, 104. For a broad selection of eighteenth-century Virginia houses, emphasizing the more substantial, and more English in appearance, but including some smaller homes, see Virginia Historic Landmarks Commission, *The Virginia Landmarks Register* (Richmond, 1976).

CHAPTER 10

1. Kniffen, "Folk Housing," 555, 557; James R. O'Malley and John B. Rehder, "The Two-Story Log House in the Upland South," *Journal of Popular Culture* 11 (1977–1978), 904–915.
2. Genovese, *Roll Jordan Roll*, 775, n. 62. F. Douglass, *Narrative of the Life of Frederick Douglass*, 35–36.
3. Bushman, "American High-Style and Vernacular Cultures," 349. On the most symbolically important buildings in Virginia, see Whiffen, *The Public Buildings of Williamsburg*.
4. R. D. Laing, *The Politics of the Family, and Other Essays* (London, 1971); Martin Howarth-Williams, *R. D. Laing: His Work and Its Relevance for Sociology* (London, 1977).
5. Jack Greene, in L. Carter, *Diary*, 6. Greene's excellent introduction to the Carter *Diary* has been reprinted as *Landon Carter: An Inquiry Into the Per-*

sonal Values and Social Imperatives of the Eighteenth-Century Virginia Gentry (Charlottesville, 1967); William Rasmussen, "Sabine Hall, A Classical Villa in Virginia," *Journal of the Society of Architectural Historians* 39 (1980), 286–296; John Mead Howells, *Lost Examples of Colonial Architecture: Buildings That Have Disappeared or Been So Altered as to be Denatured* (New York, [1931] 1963), plate 137.

6. L. Carter, *Diary*, July 2, 1772, 704.

7. Ibid., Oct. 9, 1774, 870. See Robert Wormley Carter, Diary, in *Virginia Almanac for 1776*, Colonial Williamsburg Foundation; Louis Morton, "Robert Wormley Carter of Sabine Hall: Notes on the Life of a Virginia Planter," *Journal of Southern History* 12 (1946), 345–365; Daniel Blake Smith, "Autonomy and Affection: Parents and Children in Eighteenth-Century Chesapeake Families," *Psychohistory Review* 6 (1977–1978), 32–51.

8. L. Carter, *Diary*, April 17, 1773, 750–751.

9. Lucien Levy-Bruhl, *Primitives and the Supernatural* (New York, [1935] 1973), 241, 243.

10. L. Carter, *Diary*, July 25, 1776, 1064.

11. The number that joined Dunmore is in dispute. See Mullin, *American Negro Slavery*, 118–119; Hast, *Loyalism in Revolutionary Virginia*, 184; Benjamin Quarles, "Lord Dunmore as Liberator," *William and Mary Quarterly* 15 (1958), 494–507.

12. Frederick D. Nichols and James A. Bear, Jr., *Monticello* (Monticello, 1982); Fiske Kimball, *Thomas Jefferson, Architect* (New York, [1916] 1968); Frederick D. Nichols, *Thomas Jefferson's Architectural Drawings*, 3d ed. (Charlottesville, 1961); Buford Pickens, "Mr. Jefferson as Revolutionary Architect"; W. Adams, *Jefferson's Monticello*; Erik H. Erikson, *Dimensions of a New Identity: The 1973 Jefferson Lectures in the Humanities* (New York, 1974).

13. Randolph, *The Domestic Life of Thomas Jefferson*, 1–17, 22–23. For a plan and photo of Tuckahoe, see W. Adams, *Jefferson's Monticello*, 20–21. I am indebted to Edward Chappell for providing me with detailed plans of slave housing near the Tuckahoe big house. On Jefferson and slaves see the work of Dumas Malone, especially *Jefferson and His Time*, 6 vols. Vol. 1: *Jefferson the Virginian* (Boston, 1948), Vol. 6: *The Sage of Monticello* (Boston, 1981); and John Chester Miller, *The Wolf by the Ears: Thomas Jefferson and Slavery* (New York, 1977).

14. Randolph, *The Domestic Life of Thomas Jefferson*, 152–153.

15. Cary Carson, "Doing History with Material Culture," in *Material Culture and the Study of American Life*, ed. Ian Quimby (New York, 1978), 54.

16. See Jan Ellen Lewis Grimmelman, "This World and the Next: Religion, Death, Success and Love in Jefferson's Virginia" (Ph.D. dissertation, University of Michigan, 1977) for white reactions.

17. Letitia M. Burwell, *A Girl's Life in Virginia Before the War* (New York, 1895), 52.

18. York County, Orders, Wills, Inventories, March 20, 1726/1727, microfilm, Virginia State Library.

19. Harrower, *The Journal of John Harrower*, March 10, 1775.

20. *Virginia Gazette* (P.), April 25, 1766, in *Runaway Slave Advertisements*, ed. Windley, 40.

21. Swiss Huguenot Francis Louis Michael, "Report of the Journey of 1702," ed. W. J. Hinke, *Virginia Magazine of History and Biography* 24 (1916), 117–118;

William Hugh Grove, Diary, 1731–1733, 9, photostatic copy, Colonial Williamsburg Foundation; Woolman, *The Journal of John Woolman* (1757), 52; Cresswell, *The Journal of Nicholas Cresswell*, Sept. 13, 1774, 35–36; Hazard, "The Journal of Ebenezer Hazard," June 1777, 410; Watson, *Men and Times*, 41; Military Journal of Lt. William Feltman, June 22, 1781, Historical Society of Pennsylvania, cited in Jordan, *White Over Black*, 159; Latrobe, *The Virginia Journals*, 2:225.

22. Byrd I to Warham Horsmanden, Virginia, March 1684/1685, *Correspondence*, 1:32; Byrd, *Diary, 1709–1712*, July 15, 1710; Feb. 27, 1711; March 2, 1712.

23. Thomas Jones to Ann Cook Pratt Jones, Virginia, July 22, 1728, Roger Jones Family Papers, Library of Congress. See letter of Oct. 22, 1736, in *Virginia Magazine of History and Biography* 26 (1918), 285.

24. L. Carter, *Diary*, Dec. 13, 1757, 195.

25. Jonathan Boucher to Rev. John James, Aug. 7, 1759, "Letters of Jonathan Boucher," *Maryland Historical Magazine* 7 (1912), 6, cited by D. B. Smith, *Inside the Great House*, 37; Fithian, *Journal*, Dec. 24, 1773, reprinted in *A Documentary History of Slavery in North America*, ed. Willie Lee Rose (New York, 1976), 52; Ernest Caulfield, "Infant Feeding in Colonial America," *Journal of Pediatrics* 41 (1952), 673–687, suggests wetnursing was accepted among the elite in Massachusetts as well. See Arlene W. Scadron, "The Formative Years: Childhood and Child-Rearing in Eighteenth Century Anglo-American Culture," Ph.D. dissertation, University of California, Berkeley, 1979.

26. Jefferson, *The Family Letters*, ed. Betts and Bear, 105.

27. Hamilton Pierson, "Private Life of Thomas Jefferson," in *Jefferson at Monticello*, ed. Bear, 101. Gunderson, "The Double Bonds of Race and Sex," 351–372, notes that in the eighteenth century the black nurse was more likely to be a young woman, as in Figure 36.

28. Genovese, *Roll Jordan Roll*, 358.

29. Edward Kimber, *The London Magazine*, 1746, reprinted in "Observations in Several Voyages and Travels in America in the Year 1736," 158; Latrobe, *The Virginia Journals*, 1:125; Frances Anne Kemble, *A Journal of Residence on a Georgia Plantation* (New York, 1863), 210–211, commented on whites' "Negro mode of talking" in 1838–1839.

30. See Ernest F. Dunn, "The Black Southern White Dialect Controversy: Who Did What to Whom?" in *Black English; A Seminar*, ed. Deborah S. Harrison and Tom Trabasso (New York, 1976), 105–122; Walter Wolfram and Nona H. Clarke, eds., *Black–White Speech Relationships* (Washington, D.C., 1971); Wolfram, "The Relationship of White Southern Speech to Vernacular Black English," *Language* 50 (1974), 498–527; Dillard, *Black English*, 186–228; Ralph W. Fasold, "The Relation Between Black and White Speech in the South," *American Speech* 56 (1981), 163–189.

31. Maria Taylor Byrd to William Byrd, II, c. Feb. 1760?, *Correspondence*, 682.

32. Earl Thorpe, *The Mind of the Negro* (Baton Rouge, 1961), 81.

33. Burwell, *A Girl's Life*, 7; D. B. Smith, *Inside the Great House*, 55–81; Catherine Clinton, *The Plantation Mistress: Woman's World in the Old South* (New York, 1982); Lois Green Carr and Lorena S. Walsh, "The Planter's Wife: The Experience of White Women in Seventeenth-Century Maryland," *William and Mary Quarterly* 34 (1977), 542–571; Spruill, *Women's Life and Work in the Southern Colonies*, 65–80.

34. Harrower, *The Journal of John Harrower*, 154.
35. Fithian, *Journal*, 37.
36. Washington, *The Writings*, 35:201–202, Sept. 1, 1796. Mrs. Oney Judge Staines, interviewed by B. Chase, 1846, in Blassingame, ed., *Slave Testimony*, 248–250; James T. Flexner, *George Washington, Anguish and Farewell, 1793–1799* (Boston, [1967] 1972), 433.
37. Joel Williamson, *New People: Miscegenation and Mulattoes in the United States* (New York, 1980), 43–48; Fawn M. Brodie, *Thomas Jefferson: An Intimate History* (New York, 1974); Brodie, "Thomas Jefferson's Unknown Grandchildren A Study in Historical Silcences," *American Heritage* 27 (1976), 28–33, 94–99; Virginius Dabney, *The Jefferson Scandals: A Rebuttal* (New York, 1981); Dumas Malone and Steven H. Hochman, "A Note on Evidence: The Personal History of Madison Hemings," *Journal of Southern History* 41 (1975), 523–528.
38. Thomas Jefferson to Mary Jefferson Eppes, April 13, 1799; *Family Correspondence*, ed. Betts, 177.
39. Martha reports that Jupiter "conceived himself poisoned" and, taking "a dose" from a black doctor, went into convulsions and a coma. Martha blamed the death of Ursula, Big George, and Little George on the same doctor. Martha to Thomas Jefferson, Jan. 30, 1800, *Family Correspondence*, ed. Betts, 182–183.
40. James A. Bear, Jr., "The Hemings Family at Monticello," *Virginia Cavalcade* 29 (1979), 78–87; Genealogical table of "The Hemings Family," prepared by John Cook Wyllie, in *Jefferson at Monticello*, ed. Bear, 24; Malone, "The Hemings Family," in Malone, *Jefferson and His Time*; vol. 6: *The Sage of Monticello*, 513–514. Thomas Jefferson to Martha Randolph, July 2, 1802 and Jan. 21, 1805; Martha to Thomas Jefferson, Jan. 31, 1801; *Family Correspondence*, ed. Betts, 193, 231, 267.
41. Martha to Thomas Jefferson, Jan. 31, 1801; April 16, 1802; *Family Correspondence*, ed. Betts, 193, 222.
42. Eugène A. Vail, *De la Littérature et des Hommes de Lettres des États-Unis d'Amérique* (Paris, 1841), Ch. 5, 321–333. I am indebted to Uzi Elyada for obtaining a copy of this work in Paris, and to Professor Charlotte Vardi for translating this chapter.
43. Isaac Jefferson, "Memoir of a Monticello Slave," 9, 11; Tuckahoe, the name of the Randolph estate, was also the name of an edible fungus that grows on tree roots in the area and was eaten by Indians and poor whites. The term may well have had perjorative connotations, as it did later during the Civil War, when the poor residents of this area were called Tuckahoes.
44. Norton, Berlin, and Gutman, "The Afro-American Family in the Age of Revolution," 189. I am indebted to Ronald Hoffman for providing me with extensive information regarding Carroll's slaves at Doorhegan Manor, Maryland.
45. Washington to William Pearce, Oct. 27, 1793, *The Writings*, 33, 142. Wall's analysis of the black families' residence pattern on Washington's farms lends support to the Norton, Gutman, and Berlin thesis. Wall, "Housing and Family Life."
46. Henry St. George Tucker, to his father, Feb. 17, 1804, Winchester, Va., in *Virginia Silhouettes: Contemporary Letters Concerning Negro Slavery in the State of Virginia . . .* , ed. Mary H. Coleman (Richmond, 1934), 9.
47. Tucker, to his father, March 1, 1804, in *Virginia Silhouettes*, ed. Coleman, 10.

48. The father, St. George Tucker (1752–1827), wrote *A Dissertation on Slavery: With a Proposal for the Gradual Abolition of it in the State of Virginia* (Philadelphia, 1796). Cf. Albert, "The Protean Institution," 130. St. George Tucker's other son, Nathaniel Beverly Tucker (1784–1851), became a fervid proslavery advocate as was Henry's son, also called Nathaniel Beverly Tucker (1820–1890). Cf. Robert J. Brugger, *Beverly Tucker: Heart Over Head in the Old South* (Baltimore, 1978). Henry St. George Tucker (1780–1848), who wrote these letters, went on to serve in Congress (1815) and was a judge and law professor who was known as a moderate, opposed to secession.

49. State of Virginia, Petition 6922, Hanover, Va., Dec. 2, 1817, Virginia State Library, cited by James H. Johnston, *Race Relations in Virginia and Miscegenation in the South, 1776–1860* (Amherst, [1937] 1970), 17. The intense attachment of a nineteenth-century Louisiana slaveowner to her slaves is described in Avery Craven, *Rachel of Old Louisiana* (Baton Rouge, 1975).

50. Sally Cary Fairfax, "Diary of a Little Colonial Girl," *Virginia Magazine of History and Biography* 11 (1903–1904), 213.

51. Fairfax, "Diary of a Little Colonial Girl," 213.

52. Lucinda Lee Orr, *Journal of a Young Lady of Virginia, 1782* (Baltimore, 1871), 52–53.

53. [Blodget, The Diary of Martha Blodget, in] "Cawson's Virginia in 1795–1796," ed. Marion Tinling, *William and Mary Quarterly* 3 (1946), 281–291. Personal records indicate a wide range of concern with and consciousness of slavery. Compare the Commonplace Book of William Cabell II (1769–1770) with that of his son, William Cabel III (1787–1791). The elder writes of slaves very often, whereas the son almost never mentions any blacks.

54. Chastellux, *Travels in North America*, 442.

55. See Byrd, "To Facetia in the Bath," in *Diary, 1739–1741*, 284–286, where he writes of "tawny nymphs," who cannot be made "fair," and he openly discusses sexual games. See also his verses to "Ebonia with an Olive Skin," in *Tunbrigalia* (London, 1719), 14–15, rare copy in University of Pennsylvania Library.

56. Byrd, *Diary, 1709–1712*. Feb. 22, Oct. 6, Nov. 2, 1709; April 21, June 17, 1710; Oct. 18, Oct. 21, 1711; *Diary, 1717–1721*, Dec. 9, 1720.

57. Byrd, *Histories of the Dividing Line*, March 11, 1728, 57.

58. Byrd, Commonplace Book, 27, Virginia Historical Society.

59. Byrd, *Diary, 1709–1712*, Feb. 22, 1709.

60. Ibid., July 15, 1710; Feb. 27, 1711; March 2, 1712. Jenny and Little Jenny may be two individuals. See Jan Lewis, "Domestic Tranquillity and the Management of Emotion Among the Gentry of Pre-Revolutionary Virginia," *William and Mary Quarterly* 39 (1982), 135–149.

61. Fithian, *Journal*, 86, 187–189, 242–250; Philip J. Greven, *The Protestant Temperament: Patterns of Child-Rearing, Religious Experience, and the Self in Early America* (New York, 1977), 314–316.

62. Illegitimate mulatto children of white women appear on record throughout the colonial period. See, for example, Lunenburg County, Order Books, Oct. 1751, 474; York County, Orders, Wills, Inventories, Jan. 1721/1722, 101; June 1726, 389, microfilm, Virginia State Library; *Princess Anne County Loose Papers, Vol. 1: 1700–1789*, ed. John H. Creecy (Richmond, 1954), 106; Hartwood Baptist Church, Stafford County, Aug. 1786; the will of James Shields lists 5

adult male slaves, 3 adult female slaves, 5 slave children, and "Mary Ashby a white woman servant, Mathew and John Mulatto children of the said Mary." York County, Orders, Wills, Inventories, March 1728, 509, microfilm, Virginia State Library. See Carr and Walsh, "The Planter's Wife"; Daniel Scott Smith and Michael S. Hindus, "Premarital Pregnancy in America, 1640–1971: An Overview and Interpretation," *Journal of Interdisciplinary History* 5 (1975), 537–570; Lee A. Gladwin, "Sexual Mores in Colonial Virginia," *Virginia Social Sciences Journal* 9 (1974), 21–30; Gladwin, "Tobacco and Sex: Some Factors Affecting Non-Marital Sexual Behavior in Colonial Virginia," *Journal of Social History* 12 (1978), 57–75; Ira Berlin, "Time, Space and Evolution of Afro-American Society on British Mainland North America," *American Historical Review* 85 (1980), 69, states that in seventeenth-century Virginia, "one-quarter to one-third of the bastard children born to white women were mulattoes." Kulikoff, *Tobacco and Slaves*, 387, 395–396, maintains that the incidence of sexual relations between black men and white women had always been low and declined significantly after 1740.

63. Katherine Watkins's Case, Henrico County Deed Book, 1677–1692, 192–195, reprinted in Billings, *The Old Dominion*, 161–163. Outcome not recorded. G. Main, *Tobacco Colony*, 138–139, believes "that racial boundaries were carefully observed" by the blacks, but it seems likely that boundaries were then quite different from what they later became. Further evidence of blacks and whites socializing in seventeenth-century Virginia can be found in court testimony on other problems. For example, in a 1659 case, a witness mentions that at Thomas Blagg's house, blacks and whites were eating dinner together; Westmoreland County, Deeds and Wills, 1653–1659, folio 136; and a Mrs. Vaulx was noted to be drinking with "Negroe Frank" in her parlor; York County, Orders, Wills, Inventories, Vol. 6, folio 362; both cases cited by Neiman, "Domestic Architecture," 3122.

64. J. Davis, *Travels*, 414–415. There is no mention of any such event in the *Virginia Gazette*, but Thomas's brother John did take over the estate. The late Dr. John Sutherland's estate was advertised for sale in the *Virginia Gazette* (R.), July 28, 1774, as "A tract of Land in Spottsylvania County, 6 miles above Fredericksburg, containing 700 acres."

65. J. Davis, *Travels*, 410.

66. Williamson, *New People*, 35, 37, 42; Jordan, *White Over Black*, 136–178, 457–475. See variant view in Fogel and Engerman, *Time on the Cross*, 1:132, who believe the percentage of mulattoes was low; Paul David, in David et al., *Reckoning with Slavery: A Critical Study in the Quantitative History of American Negro Slavery* (New York, 1976), 339–357; Kulikoff, *Tobacco and Slaves*, 386–387, 395–396. Samuel Stanhope Smith, a prominent Virginia Presbyterian, advocated racial mixing as the only solution to Virginia's racial problems. See *An Essay on the Causes of the Variety of Complexion and Figure in the Human Species (1787)*, 3d ed. (New Brunswick, N.J., 1810), and *The Lectures . . . on the Subject of Moral and Political Philosophy*, 2 vols. (Trenton, N.J., 1812).

67. An Alice, age 25, was listed in the inventory of Custis's father-in-law, Daniel Parke, in 1711, and the name Alice was given to several children in the Custis black family. See Inventory 1711 (?) of real estate and personal property belonging to the estate of Daniel Parke in Virginia made by John Custis; and the

Agreement of John Custis and Francis (Parke) Custis and William Byrd II, April 15, 1712, copies in Custis Family Papers, Virginia Historical Society.

68. John Custis, Will, James City County, April 9, 1750; probated London, Nov. 19, 1753, Will-Register Books 1753, Folio 287, Public Record Office, London. On Custis see E. T. Crawson, "Col. John Custis of Arlington," *Virginia Cavalcade* 20 (1970), 14–19; D. B. Smith, *Inside the Great House*, 169–170; Custis Documents, *Virginia Magazine of History and Biography* 4 (1896), 64–66; "Agreement regulating the marriage of John and Frances Custis, Northampton County, June 1714," reprinted in *Looking for America: The People's History*, ed. Stanley I. Kutler (San Francisco, 1964), 1:45–47, notes Frances is not to call John "vile names" or interfere in his business, and John, among other requirements, is to provide Frances with a listed group of black slaves and money so that she may hire a white servant as well.

69. No formal record has been found of the manumission of John Jack other than Custis's statement in his will and a Deed of Trust, assuring freed slave Jack acreage in York County, entrusted to Mathew Moody, and dated Feb. 6, 1747/1748 which is in the Custis Family Papers, Virginia Historical Society. The land given to him was recorded in York County, Orders, Wills, Inventories, 1748, 169. "An indenture between John Custis, Esq. of the first part, Mathew Moody of the second part John, otherwise called Jack a Negro Boy of the third part and George Kendall Gent: of the fourth part and a Receipt endorsed were proved by the oaths of Benjamin Waller, George Wythe and Thomas Everard the Witnesses thereto—."

70. G. Main, *Tobacco Colony*, 250.

71. J. Power to Daniel Custis, n.d., reprinted in Wharton, *Martha Washington*, 22–23.

72. A Memorial of the Estate of Col. Custis Decest. in York County [1749], Custis Family Papers, Virginia Historical Society. Mrs. Anne Moody was left "the picture of my said Negro Boy John" as well as an annuity of 20 pounds per year. John Custis, Will, James City County, April 9, 1750; probated London, Nov. 19, 1753, Will-Register Books 1753, Folio 287, Principal Probate Registry, London.

73. "Mulatto Jack" was listed as the "jobber" or handyman in George Washington's list of servants in and about the house, an undated list presumably written soon after Mrs. Washington came to Mount Vernon in April 1759; Custis Family Papers, Virginia Historical Society. Washington refers to sending him on responsible errands in his *Diary*, 1:215, 219, 246, 250, 252, 253, 258, 266, 280. If the estate inventory item (1749) does refer to John/Jack, he would have been born in 1737 and was 23 in 1760, the last year George Washington refers to him. His name does not appear in any later diary or slave list. He may well have left to live as a free man.

74. Brodie, *Thomas Jefferson*, 389; Imogene E. Brown, *American Aristides: A Biography of George Wythe* (Rutherford, N.J., 1981), denies Wythe's fatherhood. See Julian P. Boyd, "The Murder of George Wythe," *William and Mary Quarterly* 12 (1955), 513–542. Both Brown and Wythe were murdered in 1806.

75. Inventory of Estate and Will of John Davis, Nov. 18, 1728, 543, 544, 556, 568. Petition to Void Will, Sept. 16, 1728, 544; Inventory of Anne Davis estate, Dec. 1729, 17; York County, Orders, Wills, Inventories, 1728–1729, microfilm, Virginia State Library.

76. Washington, *The Writings*, 37:276. In December 1800, a year after George Washington's death, Abigail Adams visited Martha and wrote, "She [Martha] did not feel as though her life was safe in their [the slaves'] hands, many of whom would be told that it was their interest to get rid of her. She therefore was advised to set them all free at the close of the year." Cited in Flexner, *George Washington*, 393.

77. State of Virginia, Petition 385, Northumberland County, June 3, 1777, Virginia State Library. File includes Will of John Barr, March 13, 1776; summonses to Z. Barr; Z. Barr's defense of his acts and of slavery; and restraining order of T. L. Lee.

78. The first American hospital for the mentally ill, Williamsburg, 1773, "received . . . blacks as well as whites." Elizabeth Cometti, *Social Life in Virginia During the War for Independence* (Williamsburg, 1978), 27. On this building see Whiffen, *The Public Buildings of Williamsburg*, 161–165, 193.

CHAPTER 11

1. Edwin D. Lawson, "Personal Names: 100 years of Social Science Contributions," *Names* 32 (1984), 45–73; George R. Stewart, *American Given Names: Their Origin and History in the Context of the English Language* (New York, 1979); Heinz A. Wieschhoff, "The Social Significance of Names Among the Ibo of Nigeria," *American Anthropologist* 43 (1941), 212–222; Ungina Ndoma, "Kongo Personal Names Today: A Sketch," *Names* 25 (1977), 88–98; Marion Dusser De Barenne Kilson, "The Ga Naming Rite," *Anthropos* 63–64 (1968), 904–920.

2. G. Jahoda, "A Note on Ashanti Names and their Relationship to Personality," *British Journal of Psychology* 45 (1954), 193. Jahoda reports that during World War II Asante called Hitler Kwako-Hitler or a Wednesday child. Jahoda found that contemporary Asante schoolchildren fulfilled expectations: overall, Monday children were more docile, and Wednesday children more aggressive than any others.

3. Jomo Kenyatta, "Marriage Systems," in *Peoples and Cultures of Africa: An Anthropoligical Reader*, ed. Elliott P. Skinner (Garden City, N.Y., 1973), 280.

4. Stewart, *American Given Names*, 1–27.

5. See Samuel Sewall, *Samuel Sewalls's Diary*, ed. Mark Van Doren (New York, 1963), April 3, 1677, 16; Nov. 20, 1689, 88; Aug. 17, 1690, 97; "I named my Daughter Judith for the sake of her Grandmother and Great Grandmother . . . and the Signification of it very good." Owen C. Watkins, "Biblical Prototypes," in *The Puritan Experience* (London, 1972), 210–212.

6. This pattern was retained in Virginia throughout the colonial period. The Rutmans' evidence from Middlesex expands on it for the period from 1650 to 1750, and Stewart's analysis of marriage applications from Orange County, 1772–1800, confirms that it continued through the Revolutionary period. Rutman, *A Place in Time II*, 83–107; Stewart, *American Given Names*, 18.

7. The evidence from Middlesex County in Rutman, *A Place in Time II*, 101–103, 106, n. 22; Kulikoff, *Tobacco and Slaves*, 245–250. Daniel Scott Smith has found that in this same period in Hingham, Massachusetts, parents tended to name their firstborn sons and daughters for the parent of the same sex. "Child-Naming Practices, Kinship Ties, and Change in Family Attitudes in Hingham,

Massachusetts, 1641–1880," *Journal of Social History* 18 (1985), 541–566. Although the English patterns have not yet been adequately researched, the fact that seventeenth-century Virginia and Massachusetts whites tended to name their firstborn children for the parents strongly suggests a joint English root for both. See variant interpretation in Rutman, *A Place in Time II*, 93–95.

8. Mary Beth Norton, *Liberty's Daughters: The Revolutionary Experience of American Women, 1750–1800* (Boston, 1980), 85–87, suggests 57 percent of the children of Jefferson's slaves (1774–1822) were named for grandparents and 43 percent for parents.

9. Daughters, often named for grandmothers, were far less likely to be named for their own mother. Rachel and Rachel, Jr., were noted above. See Herbert Gutman, *The Black Family in Slavery and Freedom, 1750–1925* (New York, 1976), 186–199, who believed that this was an African taboo carried into North America. See also Dillard, *Black Names*; M.D.W. Jeffreys, "Names of American Negro Slaves," *American Anthropologist* 50 (1948), 571–573; Richard Price and Sally Price, "Saramaka Onomastics: an Afro-American Naming System," *Ethnology* 11 (1972), 341–367; Newbell Niles Puckett, "American Negro Names," *Journal of Negro History* 23 (1938), 35–48; Puckett and Murry Heller, *Black Names in America, Origins and Usage* (Boston, 1975); Joseph Boskin, *Into Slavery: Racial Decisions in the Virginia Colony* (Washington, D.C., [1976] 1979), 26–37.

10. Robert Carter (1774–1804) to his children, Oct. 12, 1803, Hampton, Va., photocopy, Virginia Historical Society.

11. W. MacGaffey, *Custom and Government in the Lower-Congo* (Berkeley, 1970), 97–98, cited by Ndoma, "Kongo Personal Names," 91.

12. Wieschhoff, "The Social Significance of Names Among the Ibo of Nigeria," 212–213.

13. P. Robert Paustian, "The Evolution of Personal Naming Practices Among American Blacks," *Names* 26 (1978), 183.

14. Puckett, "American Negro Names," Rutman, *A Place in Time II*, 97–103. See variant views in Dillard, *Black Names*; Wood, *Black Majority*, 181–186; Genovese, *Roll Jordan Roll*, 447–450.

15. Orlando Patterson, *Slavery and Social Death: A Comparative Study* (Cambridge, Mass., 1982), 53.

16. Sigmund Freud, *Totem and Taboo* (London, [1912–1913], 1965), 112.

17. James Arnold in *Slave Ships and Slavery*, ed. George Dow (Port Washington, N.Y., [1927] 1969), 172, cited by Boskin, *Into Slavery*, 30.

18. Robert Carter to William Carr, March 15, 1685, Carter Papers, Duke University; Robert Carter to Robert Jones, n.d., Letterbook, University of Virginia, cited by Berlin, "Time, Space and the Evolution of Afro-American Society on British Mainland North America," 76–77, n. 62. Carter chose English names as evidenced in his "Will, probated General Court of Virginia, Oct. 16, 1732," reprinted in *Virginia Magazine of History and Biography* 5 (April 1898), 408–428, 6 (July 1898), 1–22.

19. *Virginia Gazette* (H.), Aug. 14, 1752, in Windley, *Runaway Slave Advertisements*, 1:29.

20. Rutman, *A Place in Time II*, 98–99; Gary B. Nash, "Forging Freedom: The Emancipation Experience in the Northern Seaport Cities, 1775–1820," in *Slavery and Freedom*, ed. Berlin and Hoffman, 3–48.

21. These names can be found in runaway slave advertisements, wills, inventories, and church records.

22. Thomas Jones to Ann Cook Pratt Jones, July 22, 1728, Roger Jones Family Papers, Library of Congress; Patterson, *Slaves and Social Death*, 55. Other demeaning names such as Monkey and Frogg were occasionally used. York County, Orders, Wills, Inventories, Feb. 1728/1729, 576, microfilm, Virginia State Library.

23. Inventory of Edmund Custis, dec.d, York County, Orders, Wills, Inventories, Feb. 1728/1729, March 1728/1729, 576, 591, microfilm, Virginia State Library.

24. York County, Orders, Wills, Inventories, Aug. 1723, 227, Dec. 1725, 374, microfilm, Virginia State Library, Gutman, *The Black Family*, 185–200.

25. Rutman, *A Place in Time II*, 100.

26. Francis Jerdone, Jerdone Castle, Louisa County, Slave Book, 1761–1865, in the Jerdone Family Papers, microfilm, Colonial Williamsburg Foundation.

27. Christ Church Parish Register, Middlesex County, 1653–1812, 201, Virginia State Library. For slave births 1746–1754, see 220–248, 287–297; for slave deaths 1716–1746, see 251, 254–269. The published edition, Christ Church Parish, *The Vestry Book of Christ Church Parish, Middlesex County, Virginia, 1663–1767*, ed. C. G. Chamberlayne (Richmond, 1927), does not reprint most of the slave data.

28. Lorenzo D. Turner, *Africanisms in the Gullah Dialect* (Chicago, 1949), 12.

29. Windley, *Runaway Slave Advertisements*, 1:23, 30, 42, 51, 52, 56, 71, 102.

30. Council Minutes, June 1711, PRO CO412/28, 235–236, Reel 88, Virginia Colonial Records Survey, microfilm, Colonial Williamsburg Foundation; H. R. McIllwaine, W. L. Hall, and B. J. Hillman, eds., *Executive Journals of the Council of Colonial Virginia, 1680–1775*, 6 vols. (Richmond, 1925–1966), 2 (1703), 305; 5 (1740), 200; John Carter, An Inventory of the Honorable John Carter Esq. Estate in Caroline County, c. 1750, Carter Family Papers, microfilm, Virginia Historical Society. Slaves with surnames appear in many other records. See, for example, Christ Church Parish Register, Middlesex County, 1653–1812, Virginia State Library; Bolling Family Papers, Register of Slaves, 1752–1890, Virginia Historical Society. In one case, Northumberland, Order Book, Sept. 1790, 69, two apparently white "Labourers" are referred to by first name only: William [Brown] and Elijah [Newstam alias Newsam], and in United States Bureau of the Census, *Heads of Family at the First Census of the United States Taken in the Year 1790* (Washington, D.C., 1907–1908), "State Enumeration of Virginia, 1782 to 1785," many free blacks are listed without surnames; see also John H. Gwathmey, *Historical Register of Virginians in the Revolution* (Baltimore, [1938] 1973), 579, for black men in the Navy listed as Negro Boston, Charles, Pluto, Will, and so forth.

31. Windley, *Runaway Slave Advertisements*, 1:315, 427, 429; Gutman, *The Black Family*, 244; Genovese, *Roll Jordan, Roll*, 444–449; Sobel, *Trabelin' On*, 374, n. 17; 412, n. 10.

32. Bear, Jr., *Jefferson at Monticello*, 124, n. 18, Byrd, *Correspondence*, 22. Ursula Horsemanden Rand was a "gossip" or sponsor when Ursula Byrd was baptized in 1692.

33. *Virginia Gazette* (H.), Sept. 26, 1751. Another Cain ran away from William Skipwith, *Virginia Gazette* (H.), Feb. 28, 1755; in Windley, *Runaway Slave Advertisements*, 1:23, 32.

34. F. Niyi Akinnaso, "The Sociolinguistic Basis of Yoruba Personal Names," *Anthropological Linguistics* 22 (1890), 275–304.

35. *Virginia Gazette* (P.), April 8, 1766, in Windley, *Runaway Slave Advertisements*, 1:39.

36. *Virginia Gazette* (P.D.), April 16, 1767, in Windley, *Runaway Slave Advertisements*, 1:52.

37. Peter Laslett, *Family Life and Illicit Love in Earlier Generations: Essays in Historical Sociology* (Cambridge, England, 1977); Laslett, *The World We Have Lost*; Lawrence Stone, *The Family, Sex and Marriage in England, 1500–1800* (London, 1977); A. R. Radcliffe-Brown and Daryll Forde, eds., *African Systems of Kinship and Marriage* (London, 1950); E. Thomas Lawson, *Religions of Africa: Traditions in Transformation* (San Diego, 1984), 54–55.

38. Hening, *Statutes*, 2:170; Higginbotham, *In the Matter of Color*, 40–47.

39. Raymond C. Bailey, *Popular Influence Upon Public Policy: Petitioning in Eighteenth Century Virginia* (Westport, Conn., 1979), 122.

40. Hening, *Statutes*, 3:86–88. All "mulatto bastards" born to "English" women were to be bound out until age 30.

41. Allan Kulikoff, "The Beginnings of the Afro-American Family in Maryland," in *Law, Society and Politics in Early Maryland*, ed. Aubrey C. Land et al. (Baltimore, 1977), 171–196; Kulikoff, "A 'Prolifick' People."

42. *Virginia Gazette* (P.D.) April 16, 1767, in Windley, *Runaway Slave Advertisements*, 1:52.

43. Robert "King" Carter's Will was written July 23, 1730; "Will probated General Court of Virginia, Oct. 16, 1732," reprinted in *Virginia Magazine of History and Biography* 5 (April 1898), 408–428; 6 (July 1898), 1–22. See the fine analysis of Carter's slaves in Kulikoff, "A 'Prolifick' People," where he notes that among them there were 137–140 married couples, 36 unmarried adult women, and 51 unmarried adult men. Although Carter seems to have encouraged slave marriages, and even domicile at the same farm, this does not necessarily mean that couples were living in separate homes.

44. Francis Jerdone, Jerdone Castle, Louisa Co., Slave Book 1761–1865, Jerdone Family Papers, microfilm, Colonial Williamsburg Foundation. In Spotsylvania Jerdone listed: 4 couples with 8 children; 3 mothers with 8 children; and 4 singles. At Albemarle 4 couples and 8 children; 3 mothers and 9 children; 21 not in families. See also family groups advertised for sale by lottery, *Virginia Gazette* (P.D.), Sept. 3, 1767.

45. Joshua S. Skinner, Bible Records, 1783–1835, Virginia Historical Society. For other records that occasionally note slave fathers, see Withers Family Papers, Bible Records, 1779–1853, Virginia Historical Society. Only mothers were generally listed, but some children have two names, as "Wm. Wilson Patiences child," "Green Thomas Nanny child," and "Susan Hill Nanny child." The Hankin Family Memorandum Book, 1691–1839, James City County, Hankin Family Papers, microfilm, Colonial Williamsburg Foundation, erratically list both black and white family in the same book: 1706–1719, 1758–1759, 1775, 1799; most black children's births are listed without mother or father. Paul Carrington, Account Book, 1755–1775, Virginia Historical Society, lists only "of whom born," that is, mother; but one couple, Tab and Ned, who had five children, 1775–1798, was recorded. The Christ Church Parish Register, Middlesex County, 1653–1812, Virginia State Library, lists "Birth of Negro Chil-

dren," 1702–, 70ff., 91, 220–248, 287–297, by owner or owner and mother, but four slave children born 1663–1672 are listed on page 5 with both their parents. Bolling Family Papers, Register of Slaves, 1752–1890, Virginia Historical Society, occasionally record fathers: Betsy Rawlins, daughter of Aggey, "was married to Daniel Fleming Jr."; Marry Ann Whiting and Henry had a daughter, Ellen, and four sons. Most of these Bolling records indicate nineteenth-century births, but the families begin with births in 1770 when Hannah and Ritter had Aggey. The Marshall Family Papers, Virginia Historical Society, list slave births and death, 1788–1829, generally just by child's name, occasionally with mother, but sometimes with a second name, as "Cupid Robinson" or "Susan Ann Harrison." James Cosby, Account Book, Frederick Hall plantation, Louisa County, 1746, Virginia Historical Society, lists four couples and their children, and seven singles. Names include Will Conquer (a carpenter) and Drum. The Morattico Baptist Church, Lancaster County, Minutes, 1778–1844, Virginia Baptist Historical Society, list Negro births on the last page: "Suckay Daughter of Sarah and Haynot's James was born." The Virginia Historical Society has an extensive collection of slave ledgers where only mothers and children are recorded. See, for example, Paul Carrington, Account Book, 1755–1775; Richard Corbin, A List of Negroes & Stocks at Moss Neck this 18th Day of May 1778; Boulware Family Papers, Memorandum Book, 1762–1863; Stephen Cocke, Account Book, 1772–1847; Edward Dromgoole, Memorandum Book, 1789–1819; Henry Fitzhugh, Account book, 1749–1787; Hankin Family Papers, Memorandum Book, 1691–1839; Wilkins Family Papers, Bible Records, 1769–1966; Williamson Family Papers, Bible Records, 1744–1822; Woodward-McAllester Family Papers, Bible Records, 1726–1848.

46. L. Carter, *Diary*, April 26, 1770, 396; Sept. 22, 1773, 777; June 2, 1776, 1051; July 10, 177, 1109.

47. Louis Morton, *Robert Carter of Nomini Hall: A Virginia Tobacco Planter of the Eighteenth Century*, 2d ed. (Williamsburg, [1941] 1945); Robert Carter, Day Book, 1784, 16:76, microfilm, Colonial Williamsburg Foundation.

48. Norton, Gutman and Berlin, "The Afro-American Family in the Age of the Revolution"; Wall, "Housing and Family Life of the Mt. Vernon Negro."

49. Byrd, *Correspondence*, 65, 121; Jefferson, *Farm Book*, 27.

50. See discussion of baptism of blacks in Anglican churches in Chapter 14, n. 6. A discussion of new Baptist and Methodist families can be found in Chapters 14 and 15, infra.

CHAPTER 12

1. For a variant view of the significant influences on the white attitudes toward the natural world, see T. H. Breen, "The Culture of Agriculture: The Symbolic World of the Tidewater Planter, 1760 to 1790," in *Saints and Revolutionaries: Essays on Early American History*, ed. David D. Hall (New York, 1984), 247–284.

2. Eugene Green, "Naming and Mapping the Environments of Early Massachusetts, 1620–1776," *Names* 30 (1982), 77–92. Annette Kolodny, in *The Lay of the Land: Metaphor as Experience and History in American Life and Letters* (Chapel Hill, 1975) and in *The Land Before Her: Fantasy and Experience of the American Frontiers, 1630–1860* (Chapel Hill, 1984), suggests that whereas

men saw the land as feminine waiting to be conquered and controlled, women generally viewed it as a potential domestic garden, to be enclosed and tilled. See Lowell H. Harrison, "A Virginian Moves to Kentucky, 1793," in *Essays on American Social History*, ed. John Lankford and David Reimors (New York, 1970), 100–108.

3. Dunmore to the Earl of Dartmouth, Secretary of State for the Colonies, 1774, in *Documentary History of Dunmore's War, 1774*, ed. Reuben G. Thwaites and Louise P. Kellogg (Madison, Wis., 1905), 370–371.

4. Jefferson, 1787, in W. Adams, *Jefferson's Monticello*, 188. See Erikson, *Dimensions of a New Identity*.

5. J. Davis, *Travels*, 397. See Frying Pan Baptist Church, Loudoun County, 1790–, Minutes, 1791–, photocopy, Virginia Baptist Historical Society.

6. Watson, *Men and Times*, 300. Watson had purchased a 640-acre plantation on the Chowan River, 20 miles from the cockfight site.

7. Isaac Jefferson, "Memoirs of a Monticello Slave," 22. See Dena J. Epstein, *Sinful Tunes and Spirituals: Black Folk Music to the Civil War* (Urbana, 1977). For white diversions see Edmund S. Morgan, *Virginians at Home: Family Life in the Eighteenth Century* (Williamsburg, 1952).

8. Fithian, *Journal*, Jan. 30, 1774. See also Feb. 4, 1774.

9. J. Davis, *Travels*, 414.

10. *[A] Concise Historical Account of All the British Colonies in North America* [Anonymous] (Dublin, 1776), 213.

11. John Williams, July 23, 1771, "John Williams' Journal," ed. John S. Moore, *Virginia Baptist Register* 17 (1978), 795–813. At his death, Williams owned 11 slaves. See J. Stephen Kroll-Smith, "Transmitting a Revival Culture: The Organizational Dynamic of the Baptist Movement in Colonial Virginia, 1760–1777," *Journal of Southern History* 50 (1984), 555, n. 20.

12. See Carter in Mullin, *American Negro Slavery*, 108–109; L. Carter, *Diary*, Sept. 18, 1770, Aug. 16, 1771, Sept. 2, 1777, Aug. 15, 1778. When Nassau was missing on Sept. 18, 1770, Carter suspected that a white family was harboring him. See Reginald D. Butler, "Slave Life in Eighteenth-Century Virginia: The Diary of Landon Carter," unpublished manuscript, 1980; R. Isaac, *The Transformation of Virginia*, 328–346. On father–son rivalries in Southern families, see Bertram Wyatt-Brown, *Southern Honor: Ethics and Behavior in the Old South* (New York, 1982), 149–198.

13. Burwell, *A Girl's Life*, 1, 8.

CHAPTER 13

1. Mbiti, *Introduction to African Religion*, 110; Germaine Dieterlin, "The Mande Creation Myth," in *Peoples and Cultures of Africa*, ed. Elliott P. Skinner (Garden City, N.Y., 1973), 634–653; H. Abrahamsson, *The Origin of Death: Studies in African Mythology* (New York, [1951] 1977); I. Sow, *Anthropological Structures of Madness in Black Africa* (New York, [1978] 1980), 185–223.

2. Ray, *African Religions*, 37.

3. Mbiti, *Introduction to African Religion*, 111.

4. Ibid., 111–112.

5. Ibid., 112.

6. Parrinder, *West African Religion*, 23, 106, 152; Basden, *Niger Ibos*, 275.

7. Fernandez, *Bwiti*, 281.

8. Demos, *Entertaining Satan*; Zaretsky and Shambaugh, *Spirit Possession and Spirit Mediumship in Africa and Afro-America*; Evans-Pritchard, *Witchcraft, Oracles and Magic Among the Azande*.

9. George and George, *The Protestant Mind*, 25.

10. Thomas, *Religion and the Decline of Magic*, 445, 449, 454, 508, 511; MacDonald, *Mystical Bedlam*, 32, 107–110, 155, 199, 207, 210; Macfarlane, *Witchcraft in Tudor and Stuart England*.

11. John Donne, "Death's Duel . . ." (1631), in *The English Sermon: An Anthology, Vol. 1: 1550–1650*, ed. Martin Seymour-Smith (Manchester, England, 1976), 390.

12. On African understandings of spirit, see Henderson, *The King in Every Man*, 105–125, 521; Geoffrey Parrinder, *West African Psychology: A Comparative Study of Psychological and Religious Thought* (London, 1951); Fortes, *Oedipus and Job*.

13. Mbiti, *Introduction to African Religion*, 117.

14. Basden, *Among the Ibos of Southern Nigeria*, 118, and *Niger Ibos*, 201.

15. Mbiti, *Introduction to African Religion*, 117.

16. Zahan, *The Religion, Spirituality and Thought of Traditional Africa*, 49.

17. Basden, *Niger Ibos*, 243, 275, 281.

18. Ken, *The Prose Works of the Right Reverend Thomas Ken, D.D.*, 117, 139, 141, 142.

19. Ken, in *The English Sermon, Vol. 2: 1650–1750*, ed. Sisson, 188.

20. John Dillenberger and Claude Welsh, *Protestant Christianity* (New York, 1954), 57.

21. William Perkins, *The Works* (1612–1613), 1:135, in George and George, *The Protestant Mind*, 59.

22. Zahan, *The Religion, Spirituality and Thought of Traditional Africa*, 5, 9, 10.

23. Fernandez, *Bwiti*, 281; Ray, *African Religions*, 32; Newell S. Booth, Jr., ed., *African Religions* (New York, [1977] 1979), 6–8; Zahan, *The Religion, Spirituality and Thought of Traditional Africa*, 111.

24. Cranmer in *The English Sermon. Vol. 1: 1550–1650*, ed. Seymour-Smith, 27–31, emphasis added.

25. Donne in *The English Sermon. Vol. 1: 1550–1650*, ed. Seymour-Smith, 356.

26. George and George, *The Protestant Mind*, 124–143; Dillenberger and Welsh, *Protestant Christianity*, 75.

27. Tillotson in *The English Sermon. Vol. 2: 1650–1750*, ed. Sisson, 191–204.

CHAPTER 14

1. Byrd, *Diary, 1709–1712*, Feb. 15, 1709; Feb. 20, 1709; May 7, 1709; May 21, 1709; June 18, 1709; July 2, 1709; July 30, 1709; Sept. 10, 1710. See Norman Fiering, "The First American Enlightenment: Tillotson, Leverett and Philosophical Anglicanism," *New England Quarterly* 54 (1981), 307–344.

2. George Whitefield, "To a Friend in London Concerning Archbishop Tillotson," Charleston, 1740, in Whitefield, *Three Letters from George Whitefield* (Philadelphia, 1740). Whitefield's attack, printed in Philadelphia by Benjamin Franklin, accused Tillotson of being "ignorant . . . as Mahomet" of the Biblical

doctrine of justification by faith alone and of keeping many "natural men" in America from the true faith. Arnold A. Dallimore, *George Whitefield: The Life and Times of the Great Evangelist of the Eighteenth-Century Revival*, Vol. 1 (London, 1970), 482–484.

3. Perry Miller, "The Religious Impulse in the Founding of Virginia: Religion and Society in the Early Literature," *William and Mary Quarterly* 5 (1948), 492–522, 6 (1949), 24–41; E. Clowes Chorley, "The Planting of the Church in Virginia," *William and Mary Quarterly*, 2d series, 10 (1930), 191–213.

4. George Brydon, *Virginia's Mother Church and the Political Conditions Under Which It Grew*, Vol. 1 (Richmond, 1947), Vol. 2 (Philadelphia, 1952); William H. Seiler, "The Anglican Parish in Virginia," in *Seventeenth Century America*, ed. James M. Smith (New York, 1959), 119–142; John F. Woolverton, *Colonial Anglicanism in North America* (Detroit, 1984).

5. Jarratt, "The Autobiography of the Reverend Devereux Jarratt, 1732–1763," 346–393.

6. The evidence regarding slave baptism is under investigation. A total of 157 slave baptisms was recorded by the Huguenots at Mannikan Town, 1727–1754; R. A. Brock, ed., *Documents . . . Relating to the Huguenot Emigration to Virginia* (Baltimore, [1886] 1970); William Douglas, *The Douglas Register: Births, Marriages, and Deaths . . . as Kept by Rev. William Douglas, 1750–1797*, ed. W. M. Jones (Baltimore, 1977), 347–348 (24 "colored" baptisms recorded). Parish registers indicate slave baptisms. The Bruton Parish Register, Williamsburg, 1662–1797, records some 1,122 blacks baptized; the Abington Parish Register, Gloucester County, 1678–1762, records 950 blacks; Saint Paul's Parish Register, Stafford and King George counties, 1715–1798, lists hundred of blacks; the Albemarle Parish Register, Surry and Sussex counties, 1739–1778, lists over 1,000 slave baptisms; the Kingston Parish Register, Gloucester County, 1749–1827, lists roughly 2,500 slave baptisms. The Journal of the Rev. Alexander Balmain, 1782–1821, Rector of the Episcopal Church at Winchester, includes slave births, marriages, and baptisms. (All preserved in the Virginia State Library.) *The Vestry Book and Register of Saint Peter's Parish, New Kent and James City County, Virginia, 1684–1786*, ed. C. G. Chamberlayne (Richmond, 1937), includes slave baptisms after 1733. On the extensive slave baptisms by the Associates of Dr. Bray, an organization primarily concerned with the conversion and education of blacks, see Associates of Dr. Bray, *An Account of the Designs of the Associates of the Late Dr. Bray* (London, 1769); John C. Van Horne, ed., *Religious Philanthropy and Colonial Slavery: The American Correspondence of the Associates of Dr. Bray, 1717–1777* (Urbana, 1985); John Garzia lists 341 blacks baptized 1723/1724 in the Society for the Propagation of the Gospel, Associates of Dr. Thomas Bray, microfilm, Virginia Historical Society.

7. Patricia Bonomi and Peter Eisenstadt, "Church Adherence in the Eighteenth-Century British American Colonies," *William and Mary Quarterly* 39 (1982), 258.

8. William Stevens Perry, ed., *Historical Collections Relating to the American Colonial Church*, 5 vols. (New York, [1870–1878] 1969), 1:270–272.

9. Bonomi and Eisenstadt, "Church Adherence in the Eighteenth-Century British American Colonies," 275, have argued that colonial church attendance was high, given the distances people had to travel, although they estimate that

whereas 80 percent of the Northern population went to church, only 50 percent of the South did. Kulikoff, *Tobacco and Slaves*, 233–236, provides evidence of low church attendance in the Chesapeake, estimating that in 1750
about one half of Chesapeake whites went to church. See Donald G. Mathews,
Religion in the Old South (Chicago, 1977), 47.

10. Perry, *Historical Collections*, 1:270–273, 299, 305.
11. Ibid., 1:347, 1726.
12. H. Jones, *The Present State of Virginia*, 119.
13. Gewehr, *The Great Awakening*; R. Isaac, "Evangelical Revolt: The Nature of
    the Baptists' Challenge to the Traditional Order in Virginia 1765–1775, *Wil-
    liam and Mary Quarterly* 31 (1974), 345–368. For a revisionist view of the
    Awakening see Butler, "Enthusiasm Described and Decried: The Great Awak-
    ening as Interpretive Fiction," 305–325. There is an extensive literature on the
    Great Awakening (see Butler), but the emphasis has been on New England and
    relatively little of it except for Gewehr's major work deals specifically with
    Virginia. There is an excellent analysis of events in the South in general in Ma-
    thews, *Religion in the Old South*. The classics, Carter G. Woodson, *The His-
    tory of the Negro Church*, 2d ed. (Washington, D.C., 1921) and W.E.B. DuBois,
    The Negro Church (Atlanta, 1903), should still be consulted. See also Albert J.
    Raboteau, *Slave Religion: The "Invisible Institution" in the Ante-bellum
    South* (New York, 1978); Sobel, *Trabelin' On*; Luther P. Jackson, "The Early
    Strivings of the Negro in Virginia," *Journal of Negro History* 25 (1940), 25–34;
    Milton C. Sernett, *Black Religion and American Evangelism: White Protes-
    tants, Plantation Missions, and the Flowering of Negro Christianity, 1787–
    1865* (Metuchen, N.J., 1975); Lester B. Scherer, *Slavery and the Churches in
    Early America, 1619–1819* (Grand Rapids, 1975); Robert B. Semple, *A History
    of the Rise and Progress of the Baptists in Virginia*; Garnett Ryland, *The Bap-
    tists of Virginia, 1699–1926* (Richmond, 1955); Morgan Edwards, Materials To-
    ward a History of American Baptists, American Baptist Historical Society;
    Richard Dozier, Historical Notes Concerning the Planting of Baptist Principles
    in the Northern Neck of Virginia, 1771–1811, typescript, Virginia Baptist His-
    torical Society. Mixed churches are extensively considered by Willis D. Weath-
    erford, *American Churches and the Negro: A Historical Study From Early
    Slave Days to the Present* (Boston, 1957); and Alfloyd Butler, *The Africaniza-
    tion of American Christianity* (New York, 1980), which is a fine study of the
    Awakening in South Carolina with attention to black–white interaction.
14. R. Isaac, *The Transformation of Virginia*, 58–63.
15. J. Williams, "John Williams' Journal," 795–813; Harold W. Rose, *The Colonial
    Houses of Worship in America Built in the English Colonies Before the Repub-
    lic, 1607–1789, and Still Standing* (New York, 1963), 519–525. Hulan, "Middle
    Tennessee and the Dogtrot House," 41, reprints a sketch of a log dogtrot two-
    room cabin built by Virginia migrants that served as the Samuel McAdow res-
    idence and the Cumberland Presbyterian Church, Dickson County, Tennes-
    see, 1810.
16. Samuel Davies, *Letters From the Rev. Samuel Davies, Shewing the State of
    Religion in Virginia, Particularly Among the Negroes*, 2d ed. (London, 1757),
    30.
17. Conversions of several blacks in England were important to Charles and John

Wesley. Cf. Charles Wesley, *Journal*, ed. J. Telford (London, 1909), July 12 and July 17, 1738; John Wesley, *The Works of John Wesley*, 2:433, 464.

18. George Whitefield, "A Letter to the Inhabitants of Maryland, Virginia and North and South Carolina, Concerning Their Negroes," 1740, in Whitefield, *Three Letters.*

19. Whitefield, *The Works of the Reverend George Whitefield*, 6 vols. (London, 1771–1772), 4:35–41; cited in Dallimore, *George Whitefield*, 1:494.

20. Ibid., 1:496.

21. George Whitefield, *George Whitefield's Journals: A New Edition Containing Fuller Material Than Any Hitherto Published* (London, [1738–1938] 1960), 379, 420, 422, 444, 446; Whitefield, *Works*, 1:176, 5:234, emphasis added.

22. William Seward, *Journal of a Voyage from Savannah to Philadelphia and from Philadelphia to England* (London, 1740), 7–8; cited by Dallimore, *George Whitefield*, 1:499, 501. On Whitefield in Virginia, see *Virginia Gazette*, Oct. 21, 1739; Jan. 18, 1740; Oct. 31, 1745. William H. Kenney, "George Whitefield, Dissenter Priest of the Great Awakening, 1739–41," *William and Mary Quarterly* 26 (1969), 75–93. For a variant view of Whitefield's role, see Stephen J. Stein, "George Whitefield on Slavery," *Church History* 42 (1973), 243–256. See James Albert Ukawsaw Gronnoisaw, *A Narrative of the Most Remarkable Particulars in the Life of James Albert Ukawsaw Gronnoisaw, An African Prince* (Newport, R.I., 1774), 23, 26, for a report of how Whitefield befriended this ex-slave, born in Africa in 1714.

23. John Marrant, converted 1769, "A Narrative of the Lord's Wonderful Dealings with John Marrant, a Black" (London, 1802), reprinted in full in *Early Negro Writing, 1760–1837*, ed. Dorothy Porter (Boston, 1971), 427–447.

24. Butler, *The Africanization of American Christianity*, 18, 91, 94, 108, citing Josiah Smith, "Character and Preaching of Rev. Mr. Whitefield" (1740), and Commissary Alexander Garden, "Take Heed How Ye Hear" (1742). See "A Whitefield Sermon: Marriage of Cana, 1742," in *The Great Awakening: Documents on the Revival of Religion, 1740–1745*, ed. Richard L. Bushman (New York, 1970), 33–35.

25. Davies, *Letters*, 1757, 10; George W. Pilcher, "Samuel Davies and the Instruction of the Negro in Virginia," *Virginia Magazine of History and Biography* 74 (1966), 293. On Jan. 28, 1757, Davies wrote to John Wesley with some minor hesitations, noting "some" black converts "have the art to dissemble," but he was convinced the majority were "real Christians." Cf. *Works of John Wesley*, 2:392.

26. Davies, *Letters*, 1757, 16.

27. Ibid., 12, 28, 41. See Davies, *Sermons on Important Subjects*, 3 vols., 5th ed. (New York, 1792), 2:24; Davies to Dr. Doddridge, October 2, 1750, in Perry, *Historical Collections*, 1:368–369; George W. Pilcher, *Samuel Davies: Apostle of Dissent in Colonial Virginia* (Knoxville, Tenn., 1971); Michael S. Greenberg, "Revival, Reform, Revolution: Samuel Davies and the Great Awakening in Virginia," *Marxist Perspectives* 3, no. 2 (1980), 102–119; Gewehr, *The Great Awakening*, 68–105, 235–238; Robert S. Alley, "The Rev. Mr. Samuel Davies: A Study in Religion and Politics, 1747–1759" (Ph.D. dissertation, Princeton University, 1962). In a letter to one R. C., dated April 1758, Davies did note, "I'm afraid the blessed Spirit . . . is not working so remarkably among them [the Negroes] as formerly." Davies, *Letters*, 1761, 9.

28. Davies, *Letters*, 1757, 13; 1761, 11.
29. Ibid., 1761, 15. Kenneth A. Lockridge, *Literacy in Colonial England: An Inquiry into the Social Context of Literacy in the Early Modern West* (New York, 1974), 73–87, estimates that two-thirds of the poor white men in the South (and a higher percentage of the women) were illiterate.
30. Davis, *Letters*, 1761, 15–16. Perry, *Historical Collections*, 1:384, 396. Gewehr, *The Great Awakening*, 89–90, 236.
31. Gordon, "Journal of Col. James Gordon," July 23, 1759; July 15, 1759; Sept. 24, 1759; May 26, 1760; May 15, 1761. Gordon, 1713–1768, had become a wealthy merchant by 1758 when he began this journal.
32. Gewehr, *The Great Awakening*, 94.
33. Gordon, "Journal of Col. James Gordon," Sept. 4, 1762.
34. Ibid., June 2, 1760; Feb. 24, 1762.
35. Davies, *Sermons*, Sermon Ten, "The Mediatorial Kingdom and Glories of Jesus Christ," 1:287–288.
36. Ibid., Sermon Thirty, "The Rule of Equity," 2:233.
37. Sobel, *Trabelin' On*, 84, 87, 102, 107, 188, 296; William L. Lumpkin, *Baptist Foundations in the South: Tracing Through the Separates the Influence of the Great Awakening, 1754–1787* (Nashville, 1961), 38, 147ff.; Gewehr, *The Great Awakening*, 108–109; Robert A. Baker, *The Southern Baptist Convention and Its People, 1607–1972* (Nashville, 1974), 47–57.
38. David Benedict, *Fifty Years Among the Baptists* (New York, 1860); Semple, *A History of the Rise and Progress of the Baptists in Virginia*, 79–80; Ryland, *the Baptists of Virginia, 1699–1926*; Mathews, *Religion in the Old South*, 23–24, 48, 250.
39. Morgan Edwards, "Morgan Edwards' Materials Towards a History of the Baptists in the Province of North Carolina," ed. G. W. Paschal, *North Carolina Historical Review* 7 (1930), 383–387, reprinted in *American Christianity: an Historical Interpretation with Representative Documents*, ed. H. Shelton Smith et al., 2 vols. (New York, 1960), 1:360–365.
40. Mathews, *Religion in the Old South*, 26. On ritual handclasps in Africa see Arnold van Gennep, *The Rites of Passage* (Chicago, 1960), 28.
41. David Benedict, *A General History of the Baptist Denomination in America and Other Parts of the World* (New York, 1848), 641–680; William H. Williams, *The Garden of American Methodism: The Delmarva Peninsula, 1769–1820* (Wilmington, 1984), 111–118, recognizes the high black participation but accepts the view that segregation was generally practiced from the outset.
42. Robert G. Gardner, "Eighteenth-Century Virginia and West Virginia Baptist Manuscripts," *Virginia Baptist Register* 19 (1980), 910–915, lists all known eighteenth-century Baptist church documents extant. Almost all those from Virginia were used for this study. Unless noted below, these original church records, or photocopies, are available at the Virginia Baptist Historical Society.
43. Burruss's Baptist Church, Caroline County, 1773–; Church also called Polecat, Roundabout, or Mount Carmel; minutes transcribed 1809. Buck Marsh or Berryville Baptist Church, Clarke County, 1772–; minutes 1785–1841.
44. Sobel, *Trabelin' On*, Appendix IB, 293, 296, 300, 306–308, and notes to Appendix IB: 78, 83, 87, 95–96 on 421–423.
45. Hartwood Baptist Church, Stafford County, 1771, listed blacks and whites together: the third person on their roll was Negro Edward, the twelfth, Negro

Ralph. Women too were mixed in indiscriminately. (Most churches had separate gender listings for whites.) Antioch or Dover Baptist Church, in Henrico County, 1787, which had more black members than white, nevertheless listed slaves by their owner's names. The Tussekiah Baptist Church, Lunenburg County, 1777, membership list 1798, followed the pattern that was to become fairly standard in the nineteenth century, and which reflects social distinction. "White males" and "white females" were on two separate lists followed by a list for "blacks" or "Colloured members" here noted as Smith's Bob, and so forth.

46. Minutes of the Water Lick Baptist Church, Shenandoah County, June 16, 1787.

47. Water Lick Baptist Church, July 25, 1787; Dec. 27, 1788; March 21, 1789; April 25, 1789; Jan. [?], 1793; Aug. 13, 1796.

48. Dan River Baptist Church, Pittsylvania County, 1760, recorded by Morgan Edwards and reprinted in Baker, *The Southern Baptist Convention*, 53; Hartwood Baptist Church, Stafford County, 1771; Lower Banister Baptist Church, Pittsylvania County, 1798; Morattico Baptist Church, Lancaster County, 1779–; in Boar Swamp Baptist Church, Henrico County, 1787–, there were 108 blacks and 75 whites; in Goose Creek Baptist Church, Loudoun County, 1796–, there were 45 whites and 12 blacks. In an overview of all the eighteenth-century Baptist churches we have minutes for, blacks were a majority in six, and whites were a majority in sixteen. The other records are not clear, as membership lists were often recopied or lost. Churches considered in this overview include all those in notes 43–65 and Albemarle Church, Albemarle County, 1773–; Chappawamsic Church, Stafford County, 1766–; Chesterfield Church, Chesterfield County, 1773–; Frying Pan Church, Loudoun County, 1790–; Goose Creek Church, Bedford County, 1771–; High Hills Church, Sussex County, 1787–; Ketockton Church, Loudoun County, 1751–; Lyles Church, Fluvanna County, 1774–; Lynville's Creek Church, Shenandoah County, 1756–; Mill Creek Church, Page County, 1772–; Mill Swamp Church, Isle of Wight County, 1774–; Riceville Church, Pittsylvania County, 1798–; and Thumb Run Church, Fauquier County, 1771–.

49. William Warren Sweet, "The Churches as Moral Courts of the Frontier," *Church History* 2 (1933), 3–21; Harrison W. Daniel, "Virginia Baptists and the Negro in the Early Republic," *Virginia Magazine of History and Biography* 80 (1972), 60–69.

50. Broad Run Baptist Church, Fauquier County, 1762–, June 24, 1785; July 27, 1778.

51. Upper King and Queen County Baptist Church, King and Queen County, 1774–, Sept. 16, 1780. On dress regulations, see also Meherrin Baptist Church, Lunenburg County, 1771–, Jan. 4, 1772; Buck Marsh Baptist Church, Clarke County, 1772, 1778, infra., March 2, 1793.

52. Upper King and Queen County Church, Sept. 16, 1780.

53. Waller's Baptist Church (Spotsylvania County), 1769–, July 1799, August 1800; Hartwood Church, Sept. 16, 1775; Upper King and Queen, Dec. 18, 1797; Buck March, Nov. and Dec. 1791, Jan. to March, 1792; March 2, April ?, 1793; n.d. 1799, p. 66.

54. Wallers Church, July 1799; Aug. 1800.

55. Upper King and Queen Church, Dec. 18, 1797.

56. Buck March Church, Nov.-Dec. 1791, Jan.-March 1792.

57. Occoquan Baptist Church, Prince William County, 1776–, July 25, 1795; on interracial sex see Antioch or Racoon Swamp Baptist Church, Sussex County, 1772–, May 10, 1794; the Dover Baptist Association Minutes, 1805, 6: "Q. In case a white man and black woman [slave] should live together as man and wife, are they fit subjects to be received into the church? Ans: By no means." Adultery of whites and blacks was the most widely punished offense. Blacks were more often singled out for taking a second wife. See Morattico Church, April 9, 1785, and Oct. 5, 1787.
58. Morattico Church, Oct. 1780; Broad Run Church, Aug. 24, 1782.
59. Morattico Church, Feb. 1782; Oct. 1780.
60. Meherrin Church, June, Sept., Nov. 1772; May 1773; July 1774; June 1775; January 1777. I am indebted to Richard B. Beeman for informing me of Cook's property in 1769 and 1774, citing Landon C. Bell, *Sunlight on the Southside: List of Tithes, Lunenburg County, Virginia, 1748–1783* (Philadelphia, 1931), 331; See Beeman, *The Evolution of the Southern Backcountry*, 107–110, 124, 188, 195–196, 199.
61. Broad Run Church, Feb. 12, 1803.
62. Meherrin Church, Feb. 22, 1772; May 30, 1773; June 7, 1773.
63. Meherrin Church, Sept. 1, 1775.
64. Black Creek Baptist Church, Southampton County, 1786–, August 25, 1786; May 24, 1787; Feb. 24 and June 22, 1792; South Quay Baptist Church, Suffolk County, 1775–, August [?], 1780.
65. Black Creek Church, May 13, August 26, 1786; Feb. 23, June 23, 1787. Happy Creek and Water Lick Churches raised the issue of slavery at the Ketockton Association meeting in 1796. The Virginia Baptist General Committee, antislavery in 1789, declared slavery an issue of private conscience in 1793. Cf. Sobel, *Trabelin' On*, 86–89.
66. John Poindexter (d. 1819), letter to Isaac Backus, April 3, 1797, Louisa County, Virginia Baptist Historical Society. Cf. James B. Taylor, "John Poindexter," *Virginia Baptist Ministers*, Series 1 (Philadelphia, [1837] 1859), 371. David Rice, *Slavery Inconsistent with Justice and Good Policy; Proved by a Speech Delivered in the Convention Held at Danville, Kentucky* (Philadelephia, 1792), 16, 17, 24, 25. For a variant view see James D. Essig, "A Very Wintry Season: Virginia Baptists and Slavery, 1785–1797," *Virginia Magazine of History and Biography* 88 (1980), 170–185; and Essig, *The Bonds of Wickedness: American Evangelicals Against Slavery, 1770–1808* (Philadelphia, 1982).
67. Virginia Baptists Carter Tarrant, George Smith, Donald Holmes, and Jacob Grigg all vocally opposed slaveholding. Essig, *The Bonds of Wickedness*, 147.
68. Ibid., 74–78, 146; David Barrow, *Involuntary, Unmerited, Perpetual, Absolute, Hereditary Slavery, Examined on the Principles of Nature, Reason, Justice, Policy, and Scripture* (Lexington, Ky., 1808), 38–39. In 1782 David Barrow owned two slaves. See Kroll-Smith, "Transmitting a Revival Culture," 555, n. 20.
69. Robert Carter III's (1728–1804) Day Book includes a transcription of a Leland sermon on the evils of slavery, Vol. 16, May 1784, 76; Memorandum Books, Vols. 11–12, 1777–1791; Letter Books, 1791–1793; all in Duke University Library and on microfilm, Colonial Williamsburg Foundation; Deed of Gift (Manumission), Westmoreland County, Aug. 1791, Virginia State Library. Morton, *Robert Carter of Nomini Hall*, suggested that Carter's children

thwarted some of the manumissions. Correspondence, Robert Carter and Benjamin Dawson, 1793–1800, Virginia Historical Society, indicates they wanted to.

70. L. Carter, *Diary*, 1056.

71. *Virginia Gazette* (P.D.), Oct. 1, 1767.

72. State of Virginia, Executive Papers, Sept. 5, 1789, Virginia State Library. On government action to prevent mixed religious meetings, see *Virginia Gazette*, March 26, 1772.

73. J. Williams, "John Williams' Journal," 799–813; Kroll-Smith, "Transmitting a Revival Culture," 555, n. 20.

74. William Lee, Letter Books, March 10, 1769-August 20, 1772, May 22, 1771, 24–25, Virginia Historical Society.

75. J. Williams, "John Williams' Journal," 795–813; Moore, "Writers of Early Virginia Baptist History: John Williams," 633–647; Isaac Backus, "An Eighteenth-Century Baptist Tours Virginia on Horseback," *Virginia Baptist Register* 2 (1963), 64–85. For a description of a very dramatic 1770 baptism, with thousands in attendance, see John Taylor, *A History of Ten Baptist Churches . . . in Which Will Be Seen Something of the Author's Life . . .* (Frankfort, Ky., 1823), 16.

76. Clifton H. Johnson et al., eds., *God Struck Me Dead: Religious Conversion Experiences and Autobiographies of Ex-Slaves* (Philadelphia, [1945] 1969), 14, 19, 58, 59, 61, 65, 96, 167; reprinted with additional interviews as Vol. 19 of *The American Slave*, ed. Rawick; Charles L. Perdue, Jr., et al., eds., *Weevils in the Wheat; Interviews with Virginia Ex-Slaves* (Bloomington, 1976), 320. All this evidence is from ex-slaves and recorded in the twentieth century. There is evidence that the tradition was a very old one: When slaves recounted their experience to C. C. Jones in the first half of the nineteenth century, he noted that blacks are converted through "dreams, visions, trances, voices all bearing a perfect or striking resemblance to some form or type which has been handed down for generations." Jones, *The Religious Instruction of the Negroes in the United States* (Savannah, 1842), 125. The earliest recounting of a black vision journey that I have found thus far is in the autobiography of George White, born a slave in Accomac in 1764. White had the traditional vision, however he experienced it in two parts. In his 1804 vision he (and a vision guide) went to visit hell, and in 1806, he journeyed to heaven. (White had been manumitted and had moved to New York City, where, after great trials, he became a Methodist minister.) White, *A Brief Account of the Life, Experience, Travels and Gospel Labours of George White, An African; Written by Himself and Revised by a Friend* (New York, 1811), 9–10, 14.

77. Sobel, *Trabelin' On*, 145, 234, 247; Rawick, *American Slave*, 18:149–150.

78. Bohanan, "Concepts of Time Among the Tiv," 259; Fernandez, *Bwiti*, 342.

79. Rawick, *American Slave*, 18:49.

80. Ibid., 19:55–56.

81. Perdue, *Weevils in the Wheat*, 320.

82. Rawick, *American Slave*, 19:23.

83. E. E. Evans-Pritchard, *Essays in Social Anthropology* (London, 1962), 184, cited by Zahan, *The Religion, Spirituality and Thought of Traditional Africa*, 83.

84. J. A. Tiarko Fourche and H. Morlighem, *Les communications des indigènes du*

Kasai avec les âmes des morts (Brussels, 1939), 30, cited by Zahan, *The Religion, Spirituality and Thought of Traditional Africa*, 84.

85. I. M. Lewis, *Ecstatic Religion: An Anthropological Study of Spirit Possession and Shamanism* (Harmondsworth, 1971); Bourguignon, "Ritual Dissociation and Possession Belief in Carribean Negro Religion"; Sobel, *Trabelin' On*, 371, n. 22.
86. Basden, *Niger Ibos*, 275.

CHAPTER 15

1. Thomas Rankin, The Journal of Thomas Rankin, 1773–1778, typescript transcribed by Francis H. Tees, The United Methodist Church, General Commission on Archives and History, Madison, N.J., 34, 43, 54, 62, 64.
2. Gewehr, *The Great Awakening*, 143.
3. Jarratt, to McRoberts, May 3, 1776, in *A Brief Narrative of the Revival of Religion in Virginia* (London, 1779); cited by Gewehr, *The Great Awakening*, 150, n. 66.
4. *Memoir of the Rev. Jesse Lee*, ed. Minton Thrift (New York, 1823), 16; cited by Gewehr, *The Great Awakening*, 153.
5. In Jarratt, *Narrative*, 165; cited by Gewehr, *The Great Awakening*, 153.
6. Rankin, The Journal of Thomas Rankin, 43. Rankin gave a similar description of these events in a letter to John Wesley, reprinted in Francis Asbury, *The Journal and Letters of Francis Asbury*, ed. Elmer T. Clark, 3 vols. (London, 1958), 1:219–224.
7. Rankin, in Asbury, *The Journal and Letters*, 1:222.
8. Ibid., 1:221.
9. George Eayrs, "Developments, Institutions, Helpers, Opposition," in *A New History of Methodism*, ed. W. J. Townsend et al., 2 vols. (Nashville, 1909), 1:285, citing *The Nature, Design and General Rules of the United Societies, in London, Bristol, King's Wood and Newcastle-Upon–Tyne*, 1743. Classes separated the sexes and the married from the unmarried. Although evidence as to the racial composition of these Virginia classes has not yet been found, by 1776 blacks were sitting in the gallery at Boisseau's Chapel, and it is likely that blacks and whites had separate classes. But at informal sessions the races were mixed, as at Brother White's house, the evening of June 30, 1776, where Rankin "spent an hour in exhortation and prayer with some hundreds white and black." Rankin, Journal, 43. At Roanoke Chapel, July 21, 1776, "the white people were within the chapel, and the black people without." Rankin, in Asbury, *The Journal and Letters*, 1:226.
10. James Meacham, "A Journal and Travels of James Meacham, Part 1, May 19 to Aug. 31, 1789," *Trinity College Historical Papers* 9 (1912), 79, 88, July 23, 1789, August 15, 1789; cited by Epstein, *Sinful Tunes*, 110.
11. Asbury, *The Journal and Letters*, 1:655, Oct. 30, 1790. The spelling of Accomac (or Accawmack) County was formally changed to Accomack in 1940.
12. Ibid., 3:15, Jan. 24, 1773; 1:351, 355. In other areas Asbury also preached to blacks, both separately and together with whites: 1:9, 43, 56, 57, 89, 2:41, 44.
13. Philip Cox to Bishop Coke, July, 1787, *Arminian Magazine* (American) 2 (1790), 91–92; R. Garrettson, "An Account of the Revival of the Work of God at Petersburg in Virginia, Feb. 1799," *Arminian Magazine* (England) 13 (1790),

300–307; both cited by Gewehr, *The Great Awakening*, 169–170. See Mederic Moreau de Saint-Méry's description of blacks in the Methodist church in Norfolk, 1794, from *Voyage aux États-Unis de l'Amérique, 1793–1798*, ed. S. J. Mims (New Haven, 1913), reprinted in "The Bitter Thoughts of President Moreau," *This Was America*, ed. Oscar Handlin (New York, 1949), 89.

14. *Maryland Journal and Baltimore Advertiser*, June 14, 1793, reprinted in "Eighteenth-Century Slaves As Advertised By Their Masters," *Journal of Negro History* 1 (1916), 202. Advertisements mentioning slave preachers can be found in the *Virginia Gazette* (P.D.) Oct. 1, 1767; April 18, 1771; Feb. 27, 1772; in (R.), Oct. 27, 1768, Feb. 16, 1769, Feb. 27, 1772; in (P.) Sept. 8, 1775.

15. See Beeman, *The Evolution of the Southern Backcountry*, 114–115, 188–189, for an excellent analysis of the change in the Baptists' economic status and its implications in the Southside; see also Beeman and Rhys Isaac, "Cultural Conflict and Social Change in the Revolutionary South: Lunenberg County, Virginia," *Journal of Southern History* 46 (1980), 525–550.

16. See the minutes of the Morattico and Upper King and Queen Churches, Virginia Baptist Historical Society; Sobel, *Trabelin' On*, 137–218.

17. Water Lick Church, Dec. 27, 1788; March 21, 1789; Jan. 5, 1793. To my knowledge Water Lick was the only eighteenth-century Virginia church that explicitly gave women the vote (in 1787), but even there a husband had to approve a wife's joining.

18. Buck Marsh Church, Jan. 1791.

19. Ibid., Jan. 1792; March, 1793; Jan. 1799.

20. Ibid., Dec. 1789.

21. Ira Berlin, *Slaves Without Masters: The Free Negro in the Antebellum South* (New York, 1974), 46.

22. Dover Association Minutes, 1801, 9.

23. Emmaus Baptist Church, Charles City County, 1790, Virginia Baptist Historical Society, cited by Berlin, *Slaves Without Masters*, 68, voted to allow all "free male members" a vote in 1792. Evidence that blacks elected black deacons can be found in the minutes of Beulah Baptist Church, July 22, 1815; Wallers Baptist Church, August 3, 1811. See Luther P. Jackson, "Religious Development of the Negroes in Virginia from 1760 to 1860," *Journal of Negro History* 16 (1931), 175; Harrison W. Daniel, "Virginia Baptists, 1861–1865," *Virginia Magazine of History and Biography* 72 (1964), 110.

24. James O'Kelly, *Essay on Negro Slavery* (Philadelphia, 1789), 7–8, 13, 17–20, reprinted in *American Christianity*, ed. Smith, et al., 466–469; Essig, *The Bonds of Wickedness*, 62–63, 78–83; Donald G. Mathews, "Religion and Slavery—The Case of the American South," in *Anti-Slavery, Religion and Reform: Essays in Memory of Roger Anstey*, ed. Christién Bolt and Seymour Drescher (Folkstone, England, 1980), 207–232.

25. The Baptist General Committee, Minutes, Richmond (1789), 7; (1791), 5; (1793), 4. David Barrow, *Circular Letter of David Barrow, Southampton County, Feb. 14, 1798* (Norfolk, 1798). Daniel, "Virginia Baptists and the Negro in the Early Republic," 60–69. Kirk Mariner, *Revival's Children: A Religious History of Virginia's Eastern Shore* (Salisbury, Md., 1979), 95–97, records Methodist manumissions; Dwight Culver, *Negro Segregation in the Methodist Church* (New Haven, 1953), 41–46; Donald G. Mathews, *Slavery and Methodism: A Chapter in American Morality, 1780–1845* (Princeton, 1965); Robert

W. Todd's *Methodism of the Peninsula, or, Sketches of Notable Characters and Events in the History of Methodism in the Maryland and Delaware Peninsula* (Philadelphia, 1886), concentrates primarily on the nineteenth century but devotes much attention to slave preachers and interracial influence, essentially of whites on blacks.

26. Ketockton Baptist Association (1796), 4; (1797), 6.
27. Smith's Creek Baptist Church (Shenandoah County), 1774–1794, Virginia Baptist Historical Society.
28. Richard Dozier, Historical Notes Concerning the Planting of Baptist Principles in the Northern Neck of Virginia, 1771–1811, 24, 26, 32, 35, typescript, Virginia Baptist Historical Society.
29. Sobel, *Trabelin' On*, 192–193, 404, notes 15 and 16; George J. Hobday, "Historical Sketch of the Court Street Baptist Church, Portsmouth, Virginia," in *The Centennial of the Court Street Baptist Church, 1889* (Philadelphia, 1889), 30; Semple, *History of the Rise of the Baptists in Virginia*, 170.
30. Sobel, *Trabelin' On*, 194–196, 405, n. 18; William Spottswood White, *The African Preacher* (Philadelphia, 1849). Jack was freed by a subscription raised by white supporters.
31. John Early (1786–1873), Diary, 1808–1814, Aug. 7, 1808, 26, typescript, Virginia Baptist Historical Society; Early, "Diary of Bishop John Early," *Virginia Magazine of History and Biography* 30 (1926), 303; Beeman, *The Evolution of the Southern Backcountry*, 192–194, notes that Early was raised as a Baptist.
32. Early, Diary, Aug. 7, 1808, 26.
33. Ibid., July 22, 1808, 24.
34. Ibid., Aug. 7, 1808, 26.
35. See Anne C. Loveland, *Southern Evangelicals and the Social Order, 1800–1860* (Baton Rouge, 1980); Lawrence Levine, *Black Culture and Black Consciousness: Afro-American Folk Thought from Slavery to Freedom* (New York, 1977). In 1819, James F. Watson attacked white Methodists for participating in slave singing, religious dancing (shouts), and all-night devotions, which had "visibly affected the religious manner of some whites." Watson, *Methodist Error or Friendly Christian Advise to Those Methodists Who Indulge in Extravagant Religious Emotions and Bodily Exercises* (Trenton, N.J., 1819), in Eileen Southern, ed., *Readings in Black American Music* (New York, 1971), 62–64. When J. Milton Emerson visited both black and white Methodist meetings in Accomac County in 1841, he found they both made sounds he had never heard before: "They exhorted, prayed, sung, shouted, cryed, grunted and growled." Emerson concluded that the blacks must have learned this behavior from the local whites. Journal of J. Milton Emerson, Sept. 26, 1841, cited by Kenneth M. Stampp, "The Daily Life of the Southern Slave," in *Key Issues*, ed. Huggins, 134.

CHAPTER 16

1. Ralph Roberts, "A Slave's Story," *Putnam's Monthly* 9, no. 54 (June 1857), 614–620.
2. L. Alex Swan, *Survival and Progress: The Afro-American Experience* (Westport, Conn., 1981); Sobel, *Trabelin' On*.
3. Benjamin Rush to his wife, Julia, Philadelphia, Aug. 22, 1793, in George A. Sin-

gleton, *The Romance of African Methodism: A Study of the African Methodist Episcopal Church* (New York, 1952), 199.

4. Banna, in Blassingame, ed., *Slave Testimony*, 38.

5. Hannah to Thomas Jefferson, Poplar Forest, 1818, Massachusetts Historical Society, reprinted in Blassingame, ed., *Slave Testimony*, 14–15. Born in 1770, Hannah, daughter of Thomas Jefferson's slave Kate, was then 48 years old and the mother of six of Thomas Jefferson's slaves, born 1791–1805.

6. David George, in a letter from Rev. Joseph Cook of Euhaw, S.C., Sept. 15, 1790, *The Baptist Annual Register*, ed. John Rippon (London, 1790–1793), 474–475, reprinted in "Letters Showing the Rise and Progress of the Early Negro Churches of Georgia and the West Indies," *Journal of Negro History* 1 (1916), 69; Sobel, *Trabelin' On*, 110.

7. "Mighty Day," in Hymns of the Slave and the Freedman," ed. William E. Barton, *New England Magazine* (1899); "Who's dat a callin?" in "Negro Camp Meeting Melodies," ed. Henry C. Wood, *New England Magazine* (1892); reprinted in *The Social Implications of Early Negro Music in the United States*, ed. Bernard Katz (New York, 1969), 73, 93.

8. Burnaby, *Travels through the Middle Settlements*, 66–67.

9. Langston Hughes and Arna Bontemps, eds., *The Book of Negro Folklore* (New York, 1958), 195. Puckett, *Folk Beliefs of the Southern Negro*, 151, 313, 411, 415.

10. Puckett, *Folk Beliefs of the Southern Negro*, 152. For persistence of these beliefs into the twentieth century see Hyatt, *Hoodoo, Conjuration, Witchcraft, Rootwork*; and Charles L. Perdue, Jr., et al., eds., *An Annotated Listings of Folklore, Collected by the W.P.A.* (Norwood, Penn., 1979).

11. See the fine compilation and analysis of folkways in Olli Alho, *The Religion of the Slaves: A Study of the Religious Tradition and Behaviour of Plantation Slaves in the United States, 1830–1865* (Helsinki, 1976), 111, citing Thomas Wentworth Higginson, "Negro Spirituals," *Atlantic Monthly* 19 (June 1867), 685–694.

12. Alho, *The Religion of the Slaves*, 80, citing Higginson, "Negro Spirituals," 685–694.

13. Alho, *The Religion of the Slaves*, 159–162; Raboteau, *Slave Religion*, 230–231, Puckett, *Folk Beliefs of the Southern Negro*, 92–94.

14. George Pullen Jackson, *White and Negro Spirituals; Their Life Span and Kinship* (Locust Valley, N.Y., 1943), 63, n. 9.

15. John Leland, *Some Events in the Life of John Leland* (Richmond, 1836), 22.

16. Robert Hunter, *Quebec to Carolina in 1785–1786; Being the Travel Diary and Observations of Robert Hunter Jr., a Young Merchant of London*, ed. Louis B. Wright and Marion Tinling (San Marino, Calif., 1943), 214.

17. Donald Gregory Jeane, "The Traditional Upland South Cemetery," *Landscape* 18, no. 2 (1969), 39–41; Jeane, "The Upland South Cemetery: An American Type," *Journal of Popular Culture* 11 (1977–1978), 895–903; Jeane, "Combining Age-Old Religious and Cultural Customs in Cemetery Traditions," *American Cemetery* 54 (June 1982), 18–22; Jeane, personal correspondence, February 1984; Henry Miller has located mounded graves at two Virginia cemeteries, one at Old St. Luke's graveyard, Route 10, Smithfield, and the second on Route 17, south of Tappahanick, in Essex County. At this second site there is at least one mounded grave with broken-glass decorations. Mrs.

U. Hux, recordkeeper of the Old Brick Church Cemetery, Surry (in use since the seventeenth century), reports that in the relatively recent past the graveyard had raised or mounded graves, but that in order to facilitate the mowing of grass they were flattened. This apparently happened at other Virginia sites, as is confirmed by Richard Austen of Smithfield, who brought existing mounds at Cedar Hill Cemetery, Suffolk, to my attention. Elliott Stonehill has located both black and white graves with some of these "Upland South" elements. He found scraped grave sites, randomly placed under trees, in the cemetery of the black Providence Baptist Church, Hanover County, Route 662 off Route 54. The nearby Abrams family graveyard has scraped and mounded graves on a wooded hillside. Scraped graves can be found at the cemetery of White Oak Primitive Baptist Church, Stafford County (organized 1789). The Methodist Fletcher's Chapel graveyard has mounded and scraped graves in orderly rows, with standard headstones. I want to thank Henry Miller, Mark Witkofski, Anne M. Hogg, Charles L. Perdue, Jr., Jeffrey O'Dell, and Elliott Stonehill, all of whom helped me in a search for Virginia graveyards. See Anne M. Hogg and Dennis A. Tosh, eds., *Virginia Cemeteries: A Guide to Resources* (Charlottesville, 1986). See also R. Thompson and Cornet, *The Four Moments of the Sun*, 183, 198, 200.

18. Jeane, "The Upland South Cemetery," 900.
19. Vlach, *The Afro-American Tradition in Decorative Arts*, 139–150.
20. John D. Combes, "Ethnography, Archaeology, and Burial Practices Among Coastal South Carolina Blacks," in *Conference on Historic Site Archaeology Papers* 7 (Columbia, S.C., 1972), 52–61.
21. Communication from Fred Anderson, Executive Director, The Virginia Baptist Historical Society, April 25, 1984, confirms his having seen shells on white graves and knowing of toys having been placed on white children's graves.
22. Forde, *African Worlds*, 118; R. Thompson, *Flash of the Spirit*, 132–157; Puckett, *Fold Beliefs of the Southern Negro*, 48ff., 98ff., 223–245, 432–445; Anita Pitchford, "The Material Culture of the Traditional East Texas Graveyard," *Southern Folklore Quarterly* 43 (1979), 277–290; Fred A. Tarpley, "Southern Cemeteries: Neglected Archives for the Folklorist," *Southern Folklore Quarterly* 27 (1963), 323–333; John S. Otto and Nain E. Anderson, "The Diffusion of Upland South Folk Culture, 1790–1840," *South Eastern Geographer* 22 (1982), 89–98; John R. Stilgoe, "Folklore and Graveyard Design," *Landscape* 22, no. 3 (1978), 22–28; Wilbur Zelinsky, "Unearthly Delights; Cemetery Names and the Map of the Changing American Afterworld," in *Geographies of the Mind: Essays in Historical Geosophy*, ed. David Lowenthal and Martyn J. Bowden (New York, 1975), 171–195. See also Richard Francaviglia, "The Cemetery as an Evolving Cultural Lanscape," *Annals of the American Association of Geographers* 61 (1971), 501–509; Edwin S. Dethlefsen, "The Cemetery and Culture Change; Archaeological Focus and Ethnographic Perspective," in *Modern Material Culture: The Archaeology of Us*, ed. Richard M. Gould and Michael B. Schiffer (New York, 1981), 137–160; Fred Kniffen, "Necrogeography in the United States," *Geographical Review* 57 (1967), 426–427. A "Plantation Graveyard" with gravesheds can be seen in a sketch by A. B. Ward titled "Scenes on a Cotton Plantation," published in *Harper's Weekly*, in 1867, and reprinted in Sam Hillard, "Plantations Created the South," *Geographical Magazine* (London) 52, no. 6 (1979–1980), 410. White gravesheds, c. 1900, can be

seen in a photograph in Charles E. Martin, *Hollybush: Folk Building and Social Change in an Appalachian Community* (Knoxville, Tenn., 1984), 66.

23. Neiman, *The "Manner House" Before Stratford*, Figure 5.

24. Jefferson, 1771, in W. Adams, *Jefferson's Monticello*, 67.

25. Rawick, *The American Slave*, 12:2, 286. W.P.A. Virginia interviewer, Mary S. Venable, referred to " 'slave graveyards' within the enclosure of 'family graveyards.' " Perdue, *Weevils in the Wheat*, 8.

26. Perdue, *Weevils in the Wheat*, 23; Foster T. Craggett, "A Form Critical Approach to the Oral Traditions of the Black Church as They Relate to the Celebration of Death" (Ph.D. dissertation, School of Theology at Claremont, 1980); David R. Roediger, " 'And Die in Dixie': Funerals, Death and Heaven in the Slave Community, 1700–1865," *Massachusetts Review* 22 (1981), 163–183.

27. [Lewis] Grimmelman, "This World and the Next," 61, 101, 116–118, 129. See the published version of this study, Jan Lewis, *The Pursuit of Happiness: Family and Values in Jefferson's Virginia* (Cambridge, England, 1983); D. B. Smith, *Inside the Great House*, 286; Zuckerman, "William Byrd's Family," 255–257; L. Carter, *Diary*, April 25, 1758, 221.

28. See Philippe Ariès, *Western Attitudes Toward Death, From the Middle Ages to the Present* (Baltimore, 1974); Ariès, *The Hour of Our Death* (New York, 1981); Philip Alexander Bruce, *Social Life of Virginia in the Seventeenth Century*, 2d ed., rev. (Lynchburg, Va., 1927), 98–105, 186–189; Charles O. Jackson, *Passing: The Vision of Death in America* (Westport, Conn., 1977); David E. Stannard, ed., *Death in America* (Philadelphia, 1975); Stannard, *The Puritan Way of Death: A Study in Religion, Culture and Social Change* (New York, 1977); Gordon E. Geddes, *Welcome Joy: Death in Puritan New England* (Ann Arbor, 1981); Robert Habenstein and William M. Lamers, "American Colonial Funeral Behavior," in *The History of American Funeral Directing*, 2d ed. (Milwaukee, 1962), 195–223; compare with Gittings, *Death, Burial and the Individual in Early Modern England*.

29. Watts, b. 1674, published his first edition of *Hymns and Spiritual Songs* in London in 1707. (See hymn no. 6 on death.) Vastly expanded versions were printed in 1709 (see nos. 26, 31, 56, 61, and 156) and in 1719. See Louis F. Benson, *The English Hymn: Its Development and Use in Worship* (Richmond, [1915] 1962); Clayton McNearney, "Ah, Lovely Appearance of Death," *Soundings* 65 (1982), 57–77.

30. Martha Winburn England, "Emily Dickinson and Isaac Watts," in *Hymns Unbidden: Donne, Herbert, Blake, Emily Dickinson, and the Hymnographers*, M. England and John Sparrow (New York, 1966), 116, referring to Emily Dickinson.

31. Watts, *Hymns and Spiritual Songs* (1707), no. 66.

32. Charles Wesley, in McNearney, "Ah, Lovely Appearance of Death," 57.

33. Reprinted in Jackson, *White and Negro Spirituals*, 57. In 1805 this song appeared in both a Northern and a Southern Methodist collection, suggesting that it was "commonly" known among Methodists. See David B. Mintz, *Spiritual Song Book* (Halifax, N.C., 1805), and Elias Smith and Abner Jones, *Hymns, Original and Selected, for the Use of Christians* (Boston, 1805), cited by Jackson, *White and Negro Spirituals*, 63, notes 8, 10.

34. Grimmelman, "This World and the Next," 129; Ann Douglas, "Heaven Our

Home: Consolation Literature in the Northern United States, 1830–1880," in *Death in America*, ed. David E. Stannard (Philadelphia, 1975), 49–68.

35. James Maury in James Fontaine, *Memoirs of a Huguenot Family*, 398–399.

36. L. Hubbard Diary, Sept. 14, 1831, cited by Grimmelman, "This World and the Next," 101. White Southerners were also migrating to the North in significant numbers. See McClelland and Zeckhauser, *Demographic Dimensions of the New Republic*, 7, 18, 51–52.

37. John and Rachel Rickets to brother, Dec. 23, 1838, Kentucky Historical Society, cited by Lewis O. Saum, "Death in the Popular Mind of Pre-Civil War America," in *Death in America*, ed. Stannard, 45.

38. Jackson, *White and Negro Spirituals*, 57, emphasis added.

39. Dickson D. Bruce, Jr., "Death as Testimony in the Old South," *Southern Humanities Review* 12 (1978), 123–132; Christopher Crocker, "The Southern Way of Death," in *The Not So Solid South*, ed. Kenneth Moreland (Athens, 1971), 114–129.

40. [Anonymous,] Peedee River, S.C., April 25–Aug. 24, 1790, *Rippons Journal*, 1790–1793, 104–105. James Maury wrote, "The grand business of life is to prepare for death, as that is preparing for eternity. Of all the acts of that piece, the last is the most important, as well as the most difficult, and therefore requires spiritual succor to perform it well." James Fontaine, *Memoirs of a Huguenot Family*, 398.

41. Samuel Davies, *Sermons*, Sermon Twenty, "The Universal Judgment," 2:24. See also S. Davies, *The Duty of Christians to Propagate their Religion Among the Heathens, Ernestly Recommended to the Masters of Negro Slaves in Virginia. A Sermon Preached in Hanover, Jan. 8, 1757* (London, 1758), 8.

42. Uncle John Spencer in Perdue, *Weevils in the Wheat*, 278. See Matthew, 25:32–33; Davies, *Sermons*, Sermon Twenty, "The Universal Judgment," 2:15.

CHAPTER 17

1. Stith Mead, Letterbook, 1792–1795, June 12, 1793, 24, Virginia Historical Society; *[An] Authentic Account of the Conversion and Experience of a Negro* [Anonymous] (n.p., 1812), 3.

2. Black Creek Church Minutes, May 27, 1786, Virginia State Library.

3. Fithian, *Journal*, Sept. 1, 1774 (Harry was the young man who was spending all his free time with the black workers). Davies, *Sermons*, 2:24; J. Williams, "John Williams' Journal," 799; Leventhal, *In the Shadow of the Enlightenment*, 192–217; Byrd, *Diary, 1709–1712*, June 21, 1711, 290; "Read Some English about the Soul Being a Spirit."

4. Martha Zeigler, born ca. 1852, in Perdue, *Weevils in the Wheat*, 345.

5. Edward Baptist, Diary, Virginia Historical Society. Born in 1790, in Mecklenburg County, Edward Baptist became a Baptist preacher; however, he rejected the search for visions as a false goal. Monroe Conway, born 1832, on a Falmouth, Virginia, plantation with some 50–60 slaves, remembered that "Our own kitchen-fireside was nightly the scene of religious exercises and conversations which were very fascinating to me, and from which I had to be dragged with each returning bedtime." He reported hearing "dreams, visions and ecstasies" of the New Jerusalem that he found "gorgeous." Conway, *Testimonies*

Concerning Slavery (London, 1864), 1–8, in A Documentary History of Slavery in North America, ed. Rose, 406–410.

6. Charles Wesley Andrews, Memoir of Mrs. Ann R. Page, 2d ed. (New York, [1844] 1856), 17–18.

7. Ibid., 18–19.

8. Ibid., 86, 88. In 1832 Ann Page manumitted and sent many of her former slaves to Africa.

9. Byrd, Commonplace Book, 99; Diary, 1709–1712, Jan. 24, 1710, 133.

10. Rev. Peter Fontaine, Jr., to John Fontaine, Rock Castle, Hanover County, July 5, 1765, in James Fontaine, Memoirs of a Huguenot Family, 374.

11. Epstein, Sinful Tunes, 227.

12. Mbiti, Introduction to African Religion, 111–112.

13. Kagame, "The Empirical Apperception of Time and Conception of History in Bantu Thought," 113; See Horton and Finnegan, Modes of Thought: Essays on Thinking in Western and Non-Western Societies. Bohanan notes that "Instead of saying, 'We cut the guinea corn when the first harmattan comes,' as we would in English, Tiv just as often say, 'The first harmattan comes when we cut the guinea corn.' " Bohanan believes that "this reversibility is indicative of the fact that neither event is considered primary or basic to the other. Instead of an implied causal relationship, there is mere association of two events." Bohanan, "Concepts of Time Among the Tiv," 254–255.

CHAPTER 18

1. See Winthrop D. Jordan, "Planter and Slave Identity Formation: Some Problems in the Comparative Approach," in Comparative Perspectives on Slavery in New World Plantation Societies, ed. Vera Rubin and Arthur Tuden (New York, 1977), 35–40; Jack P. Greene, "Search for Identity: An Interpretation of the Meaning of Selected Patterns of Social Response in Eighteenth-Century America," Journal of Southern History 3 (1970), 189–224; Erik H. Erikson, "Race and the Wider Identity," in Identity Youth and Crisis (New York, 1968), 304; Michael Zuckerman, "The Fabrication of Identity in Early America," William and Mary Quarterly 34 (1977), 183–214. For a variant view of Southern identity, see Carl Degler, Place Over Time: The Continuity of Southern Distinctiveness (Baton Rouge, 1977).

2. Joseph Priestly, Socrates and Jesus Compared (London, 1803); Jefferson, Philosophy of Jesus of Nazareth. Jefferson's Extracts from the Gospels: "The Philosophy of Jesus," and "The Life and Morals of Jesus," ed. Dickinson W. Adams and Ruth W. Lester (Princeton, 1983), 38, 41. For a variant view, also emphasizing Jefferson's interest in Jesus, see Charles B. Sanford, The Religious Life of Thomas Jefferson (Charlottesville, 1984). An important book on this Southern elite, which suggests that blacks had virtually no effect, is Richard Beale Davis, Intellectual Life in the Colonial South, 1585–1763, 3 vols. (Knoxville, Tenn. 1978).

3. Jefferson, in Randolph, The Domestic Life of Thomas Jefferson, 429.

4. W. Adams, Jefferson's Monticello, 231; Gittings, Death, Burial and the Individual in Early Modern England, 139, 171, 172; R. Thompson, Flash of the Spirit, 134, 258; Jack Goody, Death, Property and the Ancestors; A Study of the Mortuary Customs of the Lodagaa of West Africa (London, 1962), 58, 96,

184–196, 220–225. Benjamin Henry Latrobe, *The Journals of Benjamin Henry Latrobe, 1799–1820: From Philadelphia to New Orleans*, ed. Edward C. Carter, II et al., Series 1, vol. 3 (New Haven, 1981), 302. In parts of West Africa other colors, brown, black and red among them, signify death, whereas white stands for goodness and life. Cf. Victor W. Turner, "Colour Classification in Ndembu Ritual: A Problem in Primitive Classification," in *Anthropological Approaches to the Study of Religion*, ed. Michael Banton (London, 1966), 47–82.

5. Louis B. Wright, "The Classical Tradition in Colonial Virginia," *Papers of the Bibliographical Society of America* 33 (1939), 85–97; Bruce, *Institutional History of Virginia in the Seventeenth Century*, 1:316–330, 350–449.

6. Jane Carson, *James Innes and His Brothers of the F.H.C.* (Charlottesville, 1965), 61, 73; James McLachlin, "Classical Names, American Identities," in *Classical Traditions in Early America*, ed. John W. Eadie (Ann Arbor, 1976), 81–98.

7. See Thomas Jones to his wife, Ann Cook Pratt Jones, then in England, July 22, 1728, asking her to get his proper coat of arms as well as livery for his servants. Roger Jones Family Papers, Library of Congress.

8. William A. Crozier, ed., *Virginia Heraldica: Being a Registry of Virginia Gentry Entitled to Coat Armor* (Baltimore, 1930), 87–88, 97, 109–110; Charles K. Bolton, *Bolton's American Armory* (Baltimore, 1964), 322; Eugene Zieber, *Heraldry in America*, 2d ed. (New York, 1969), 30, 174; "Jefferson Family," *Tyler's Quarterly Historical and Genealogical Magazine* 6 (1935), 199. I am indebted to John E. Ingram for bringing these sources to my attention.

9. Byrd, Commonplace Book, Virginia Historical Society. The Christian volume analyzed is Rev. Mr. William Wollaston's *Religion of Nature Delineated* (1722). An example of one of Byrd's collected wisdom sayings can be found on page 9: "Cato used to say that for his part he had rather go without his Reward for doing well, than without his punishment for doing ill because a man's never in so bad a way as when he may transgress with impunity."

10. Jefferson, *Papers*, 1:494–495.

11. F. Nwabueze Okoye, "Chattel Slavery as the Nightmare of the American Revolutionaries," *William and Mary Quarterly* 37 (1980), 28. Okoye's references are primarily from New England, but Southerners too spoke of being "enslaved" by England.

12. Samuel Whitcomb, Jr. [notes on an] Interview with Thomas Jefferson, Charlottesville, Va., 31 May 1824; in manuscript at the Massachusetts Historical Society and reprinted as "A Book Peddler Invades Monticello," ed. William Peden, *William and Mary Quarterly* 6 (1949), 631–636. (Comments cited, 633.)

13. Burwell, *A Girl's Life in Virginia*, 8.

14. Kelso, *Kingsmill Plantations*, 42, 44. Lewis Burwell I immigrated to Virginia in 1635. By 1700 the family had extensive landholdings and by 1720, the Kingsmill property. In 1775 Lewis Burwell IV moved to Mecklenburg, and by 1782 he had 62 of his 172 slaves housed there. See Jackson Turner Main, "The One Hundred," *William and Mary Quarterly* 11 (1954), 355–384. Letitia Burwell's grandfather, presumably Aunt Christian's "Ole Marster," was William A. Burwell (1780–1821) and Letitia's father was William M. Burwell. See Lyon G. Tyler, *Encyclopedia of Virginia Biography* (New York, 1915), 2:102. I am indebted to L. Eileen Parris for bringing this source to my attention.

15. David Brian Davis, *The Problem of Slavery in Western Culture* (Ithaca, 1966),

526–527; Thomas E. Drake, *Quakers and Slavery in America* (Gloucester, Mass., [1950] 1965), 51–64, 68–71.

16. John Woolman, *Some Considerations on the Keeping of Negroes: Recommended to the Professors of Christianity, of Every Denomination* (Northampton, Mass., [1754] 1970); Society of Friends, London, Epistles Received, Vols. 4–5, 1758–1801, microfilm, Virginia State Library.

17. Jean R. Soderlund, *Quakers & Slavery: A Divided Spirit* (Princeton, 1985), 26–31; Jack D. Marietta, *The Reformation of American Quakerism, 1748–1783* (Philadelphia, 1984), 115–120.

18. John Woolman, *The Journal of John Woolman* and *A Plea for the Poor* (New York, [1774] 1961), 214–215, emphasis added.

19. Woolman, *The Journal of John Woolman*, 216.

20. Ibid., 185–186.

21. Jacques Le Goff, "The Learned and Popular Dimensions of Journeys in the Otherworld in the Middle Ages," in *Understanding Popular Culture: Europe from the Middle Ages to the Nineteenth Century*, ed. Steven L. Kaplan (Berlin, 1984), 19–38.

22. John Bunyan, *The Pilgrim's Progress* (London, [1678] 1964); Bunyan, *Grace Abounding* (London, [1666] 1966). For extensive examples of sudden rebirths see Jon Alexander, *American Personal Religious Accounts, 1600–1980; Toward an Inner History of America's Faiths* (New York, 1983); Hambrick-Stowe, *The Practice of Piety*; Paul Delany, "Quaker Autobiography," in *British Autobiography in the Seventeenth Century*, 97–106; Watkins, *The Puritan Experience*. A traditional vision journey to hell and heaven was experienced by John Benson (1744–1818), a white sailor on a slave ship calling at Sierra Leone c. 1764. (He was ill and being cared for by a slave who spoke broken English.) John Benson, *A Short Account of the Voyages, Travels, And Adventures of John Benson . . .* (N.p., 182?), 79–98.

23. Whitefield, Journal, in Cameron, *The Rise of Methodism*, 85; W. B. FitzGerald, "George Whitefield," in *A New History of Methodism*, ed. W. J. Townsend et al., 2 vols. (Nashville, 1909), 1:259–260.

24. J. Wesley, *The Works*, 1:103. Wesley himself had been dubious of the possibility of instantaneous rebirth. It was only after contact with the Moravians, and after his mission to Georgia, that he came to have a personal experience of this nature. See Stuart Andrews, *Methodism and Society* (London, 1970), 31, 34, 99.

25. An unexplored influence is the fact that blacks heard about and read Bunyan's *The Pilgrim's Progress*. See, for example, John Jea, *The Life, History, and Unparalleled Sufferings of John Jea, The African Preacher* (Portsmouth, N.H., 1815), 15.

26. The Journal of Bishop Richard Whatcoat, Sept. 4, 1789, in *Religion on the American Frontier*, ed. William Warren Sweet, Vol. 4: *The Methodists* (Chicago, 1946), 77.

27. C. Jones, *The Religious Instruction of the Negroes in the United States*, 125.

28. Perdue, *Weevils in the Wheat*, 170, 320. On the transitional Revolutionary period see Ira Berlin and Ronald Hoffman, eds., *Slavery and Freedom in the Age of the American Revolution* (Charlottesville, 1983). For analyses of nineteenth-century master–slave relationships, see Genovese, *Roll Jordan Roll*, in-

fra.; and James Oakes, *The Ruling Race: A History of American Slaveholders* (New York, 1982), 52–55, 171–179, 155–169, 218–219.

29. Jane C. Beck, "The West Indian Supernatural World: Belief Integration in a Pluralistic Society," *Journal of American Folklore* 88 (1975), 235–244, suggests "one supernatural world" exists for both black and white West Indians, even though they remain socially separated.

30. Rankin Journal, see also July 20, 1775, 27; April 16, 1776, 39.

31. Henry Glassie, *Pattern in the Material Folk Culture of the Eastern United States* (Philadelphia, 1968), 17–18. Compare the Virginia doll in Figure 46 with Kongo cloth mannequins, *niombo*, in R. Thompson and Cornet, *The Four Moments of the Sun*, 18, 26, 28, 59–68.

Bibliography

PRIMARY SOURCES

Manuscript Materials

Abington Parish Register, Gloucester County, 1678–1762. Virginia State Library, Richmond.

Albemarle, or Garrison's, Lewis's, Buck Mountain, or Chestnut Grove Baptist Church, Albemarle County, 1773–. Minutes 1773–1779, 1792–1811. Photocopy, Virginia Baptist Historical Society, Richmond.

Albemarle Parish Register, Surry and Sussex County, 1739–1778. Virginia State Library, Richmond.

Antioch or Dover Baptist Church, Henrico County, 1787–. Minutes, 1787–1828. Virginia Baptist Historical Society, Richmond.

Antioch Baptist Church or Raccoon Swamp, Sussex County, 1772–. Minutes, 1772–1892. Virginia State Library, Richmond.

Balmain, Alexander, 1740–1821. Journal, 1782–1821. Virginia State Library, Richmond.

Banks, Henry, 1761–1833. Papers, 1781–1817. Virginia Historical Society, Richmond.

Baptist, Edward, 1790–1863. Diary, n.d.–1861. Virginia Historical Society, Richmond.

Baptist General Committee. Minutes. Richmond, 1789–1799. Virginia Baptist Historical Society, Richmond.

Black Creek Baptist Church, Southampton County, 1786–. Minutes, 1774–1889. Virginia Baptist Historical Society, Richmond.

Boar Swamp, or Antioch Baptist Church, Henrico County, 1777–. Minutes, 1787–1828. Virginia Baptist Historical Society, Richmond.

Bolling Family Papers. Register of Slaves, 1752–1890 [sic]. Virginia Historical Society, Richmond.

Boulware Family Papers. Memorandum Book, 1762–1863. Virginia State Library, Richmond.

Broad Run or Pignut Ridge Baptist Church, Fauquier County, 1762–. Minutes, 1762–1872. Microfilm, Virginia Baptist Historical Society, Richmond.

Bruton Parish Register, Williamsburg, 1662–1797. Virginia State Library, Richmond.

Buck Marsh, or Berryville Baptist Church, Clarke County, 1772–. Minutes, 1785–1841. Virginia Baptist Historical Society, Richmond.

Burruss's or Polecat, Roundabout, or Mount Carmel Baptist Church, Caroline County, 1773–. Minutes, 1799–1935. (Transcribed 1809.) Virginia Baptist Historical Society, Richmond.

Byrd, William, 1674–1744. Commonplace Book, c. 1722–1732. Virginia Historical Society, Richmond.

————. Inventory of the Estate of William Byrd . . . In the County of Henrico at the Falls of the James River, June 1746. Huntington Library, San Marino.

Byrd Family Papers. Virginia Historical Society, Richmond.

Cabell, William, II, 1730–1798. Commonplace Book, 1769–1770. Virginia Historical Society, Richmond.

Cabell, William, III, 1759–1822. Commonplace Book, 1787–1791. Virginia Historical Society, Richmond.

Carrington, Paul, 1733–1818. Account Book, 1755–1775. Virginia Historical Society, Richmond.

Carter, John. An Inventory of the Honorable John Carter, Esq. Estate in Caroline County, c. 1750. Microfilm, Virginia Historical Society, Richmond.

Carter, Landon, 1710–1778. An Inventory of the Estate of Landon Carter, Esq. Dec'd, Taken Feb. 1779. Landon Carter Papers, University of Virginia, Charlottesville.

Carter, Robert, 1705–1732. Diary, 1722–1727. Microfilm, University of Haifa, Haifa.

Carter, Robert, III, 1728–1804. Day Book, Vol. 16, 1784. Microfilm, Colonial Williamsburg Foundation, Williamsburg.

———. Letter Books, 1791–1793. Microfilm, Colonial Williamsburg Foundation, Williamsburg.

———. Memorandum Book, Vols. 11–12: 1777–1791. Microfilm, Colonial Williamsburg Foundation, Williamsburg.

———. Correspondence with Benjamin Dawson, 1793–1800. Virginia Historical Society, Richmond.

Carter, Robert, 1774–1804. Letter to his children, Oct. 12, 1803, Hampton, Va. Photocopy, Virginia Historical Association, Richmond.

Carter, Robert Wormley, 1734–1797. Diary in *Virginia Almanac for 1776*. Colonial Williamsburg Foundation, Williamsburg.

Carter Family Papers. Virginia Historical Society, Richmond.

Chappawamsic Baptist Church, Stafford County, 1766 – c. 1955. Minutes, 1766–1860. Photocopy, Virginia State Library, Richmond.

Chesterfield, or Lower End, Clay's or Rehoboth Baptist Church, Chesterfield County, 1773 – c. 1909. Minutes, 1773–1788. Virginia Baptist Historical Society, Richmond.

Christ Church Parish Register, Middlesex County, 1653–1812. Virginia State Library, Richmond.

Cocke, Stephen, 1754–1794. Account Book, 1772–1847. Virginia Historical Society, Richmond.

Colonial Papers. Virginia State Library, Richmond.

Corbin, Richard, 1708–1790. A list of Negroes & Stocks at Moss Neck this 18th Day of May 1778. Virginia Historical Society, Richmond.

Cosby, James. Account Book, 1746. Virginia Historical Society, Richmond.

Croom-Hatcher-Dement. Family Bible Records, 1742–1893. Virginia Historical Society, Richmond.

Custis, John. Will, James City County, April 9, 1750. Probated London, Nov. 19, 1753: Will-Register Books 1753, Folio 287. Public Record Office, London.

Custis Family Papers. Virginia Historical Society, Richmond.

Dover Baptist Association. Minutes, 1801–1805. Virginia Baptist Historical Society, Richmond.

Dozier, Richard. Historical Notes Concerning the Planting of Baptist Principles in the Northern Neck of Virginia, 1771–1811. Typescript, Virginia Baptist Historical Society, Richmond.

Dromgoole, Edward, 1751–1835. Memorandum Book, 1789–1819. Virginia Historical Society, Richmond.

314

Early, John, 1786–1873. Diary, 1808–1814. Typescript, Virginia Baptist Historical Society, Richmond.

Edwards, Morgan, 1722–1795. Materials Toward a History of American Baptists. American Baptist Historical Society, Rochester, New York.

Essex County. Orders, 1699–1702. Microfilm, Virginia State Library, Richmond.

Fitzhugh, Henry, 1723–1783. Account Book, 1749–1787. Photocopy, Virginia Historical Society, Richmond.

Fontaine, Peter, 1691–1757. Sermon Preached at Westover, May 10, 1727. Transcript, Colonial Williamsburg Foundation, Williamsburg.

Frying Pan Baptist Church, Loudoun County, 1790–. Minutes, 1791. Photocopy, Virginia Baptist Historical Society, Richmond.

Gooch, William, 1681–1751. Records of Lt. Gov. Gooch, 1727–1749. 3 vols. Typescript, Virginia Historical Society, Richmond.

Goose Creek or Bedford, Turner's, or Morgan's Baptist Church, Bedford County, 1771–. Minutes, 1787–1821. Virginia Baptist Historical Society, Richmond.

Goose Creek, or Pleasant Valley Baptist Church, Loudoun County, 1775–. Minutes, 1775–1860. Photocopy, Virginia Baptist Historical Society, Richmond.

Grove, William Hugh. Diary, 1731–1733. Photostatic copy, Colonial Williamsburg Foundation, Williamsburg.

Hankin Family Papers. Memorandum Book, 1691–1839. Colonial Williamsburg Foundation, Williamsburg.

Hartwood or Potomac Baptist Church, Stafford County, 1771 – c. 1861. Minutes, 1775–1861. Virginia Baptist Historical Society, Richmond.

Henrico County. Order Books, 1694–1701, 1707–1709, 1710–1714. Court Minute Book, 1719–1724. Microfilm, Virginia State Library, Richmond.

High Hills Baptist Church, Sussex County, 1787–. Minutes, 1787–1845. Virginia Baptist Historical Society, Richmond.

Hite, Isaac, 1758–1836. Commonplace Book, 1776–1859 [*sic*]. Virginia Historical Society, Richmond.

Historic American Building Survey. Photographs and loose papers. Library of Congress, Washington, D.C.

Hunter, Dangerfield, 1781?–1856. (Slave of Louis Abraham Pauly.) Will, June 18, 1856, Augusta County. Typed copy, Virginia Historical Society, Richmond.

Jerdone Family Papers. Slave Book, 1761–1865. Microfilm, Colonial Williamsburg Foundation, Williamsburg.

Jones, Thomas. Letter to Ann Cook Pratt Jones. July 22, 1728. Roger Jones Family Papers. Library of Congress, Washington, D.C.

Ketockton Baptist Association, Loudoun County. Minutes, 1795, 1797, 1801–1803. Virginia Baptist Historical Society, Richmond.

Kingston Parish Register, Gloucester County, 1749–1827. Virginia State Library, Richmond.

Lee, Richard Henry, 1750–1794. Memorandum Book, 1776–1794. Microfilm, Colonial Williamsburg Foundation, Williamsburg.

Lee, William, 1739–1795. Letterbooks, March 10, 1769 – Aug. 20, 1772; May 22, 1777 – June 24, 1778; Aug. 5, 1783 – April 11, 1787; Sept. 26, 1787 – Aug. 17, 1788; May ?, 1792 – May 30, 1793. Virginia Historical Society, Richmond.

Lee Family Papers, 1742–1795. Microfilm, University of Haifa, Haifa.

Lower Banister, or Riceville Baptist Church, Pittsylvania County, 1798–. Minutes, 1798–1845. Virginia Baptist Historical Society, Richmond.

Lunenburg County. Order Books Nos. 1–5, 1746–1759. Microfilm, Virginia State Library, Richmond.

Lyles Baptist Church, Fluvanna County, 1774–. Minutes, 1770–? Virginia Baptist Historical Society, Richmond.

Lynville's Creek, or Smith's Creek, North River of Shenandoah, or Brock's Gap Baptist Church, Shenandoah County, 1756–. Minutes, 1756–1777, 1787–1844. Microfilm, Virginia Baptist Historical Society, Richmond.

Marshall Family Papers. Virginia Historical Society, Richmond.

Mason, Lewis E. Lists of Negroes, c. 1851–1854. Virginia Historical Society, Richmond.

Mead, Stith, 1767–1834. Letterbook, 1792–1795. Virginia Historical Society, Richmond.

Meherrin, or Williams Baptist Church, Lunenburg County, 1771–1842. Minutes, 1771–1784, 1793–1837. Virginia Baptist Historical Society, Richmond.

Meherrin Baptist Association, Lunenburg County. Minutes, 1804–1825. Virginia Baptist Historical Society, Richmond.

Mill Creek, or Ebenezer, or White House Baptist Church, Page County, 1772 – c. 1824. Minutes, 1798–1824. Photocopy, Virginia Baptist Historical Society, Richmond.

Mill Swamp, or Isle of Wight, Jones', or Barrows' Baptist Church, Isle of Wight County, 1774–. Minutes, 1774–1811. Microfilm, Virginia Baptist Historical Society, Richmond.

Monroe, James, 1758–1831. Executive Papers of Gov. James Monroe, Aug.–Dec. 1800, Jan.–June 1801. Virginia State Library, Richmond.

Morattico Baptist Church, Lancaster County, 1778–. Minutes, 1778–1844. Virginia Baptist Historical Society, Richmond.

Occoquon Baptist Church, Prince William County, 1776–. Minutes, 1794–1831. Photocopy, Virginia Baptist Historical Society, Richmond.

Poindexter, John, d. 1819. Letter to Isaac Backus, April 3, 1797. Virginia Baptist Historical Society, Richmond.

Rankin, Thomas, 1738–1810. The Journal of Thomas Rankin, 1773–1778. Typescript, transcribed by Francis H. Tees. The United Methodist Church, General Commission on Archives and History, Madison, N.J.

Riceville or Lower Banister Baptist Church, Pittsylvania County, 1798–. Minutes, 1798–. Virginia Baptist Historical Society, Richmond.

Roanoke District Baptist Association, Pittsylvania and Surrounding Counties. Minute Book, 1789 – Oct. 1831. Photocopy, Virginia State Library, Richmond.

Saint Paul's Parish Register, Stafford and King George Counties, 1715–1798. Virginia State Library, Richmond.

Skinner, Joshua S., 1752–1829. Bible Records, 1783–1835. Virginia Historical Society, Richmond.

Smith's Creek Baptist Church, Shenandoah County, 1774–. Minutes, 1779–1805. Virginia Baptist Historical Society, Richmond.

Society for the Propagation of the Gospel Associates of Dr. Thomas Bray. American Papers, 1735–1774. Microfilm (on Misc. Reel 3), Virginia State Library, Richmond.

Society for the Propagation of the Gospel, Associates of Dr. Thomas Bray. Microfilm, Virginia Historical Society, Richmond.

Society of Friends, London. Epistles Received, Vol. 4: 1758–1778, Vol. 5: 1778–1801, Vol. 6: 1800–1829. Microfilm, Virginia State Library, Richmond.

South Quay Baptist Church, Suffolk County, 1785–. Minutes, 1775–1827. Photocopy, Virginia Baptist Historical Society, Richmond.

Sussex County. Court of Oyer and Terminer, 1754–1798. Microfilm (on reel with Order Books, 1754–1798), Virginia State Library, Richmond.

Thumb Run, or Manor Baptist Church, Fauquier County, 1771–. Minutes, 1771–1778. Microfilm, Virginia Baptist Historical Society, Richmond.

Tussekiah Baptist Church, Lunenburg County, 1777–. Minutes, 1784–1826. Virginia Baptist Historical Society, Richmond.

Upper King and Queen Baptist Church, King and Queen County, 1774–. Minutes, 1774–1816. Virginia Baptist Historical Society, Richmond.

Virginia, Auditor of Public Records. Condemned, Executed, and Transported Slaves, 1783–1865. Virginia State Library, Richmond.

Virginia Colonial Records Project. Microfilm, Colonial Williamsburg Foundation, Williamsburg.

Virginia Historic Landmarks Commission. Photographs and Loose Papers, Richmond.

Virginia, State of. Calendar of State Papers, 1790–1792. Virginia State Library, Richmond.

———. Executive Papers, 1789–1805. Virginia State Library, Richmond.

———. Petitions. Filed in order of county and date. Virginia State Library, Richmond.

Wallers, or Lower Spotsylvania or Lower End Baptist Church, Spotsylvania County, 1769–. Minutes, 1799–1818. Virginia Baptist Historical Society, Richmond.

Water Lick Baptist Church, Shenandoah County, 1787–. Minutes, 1787–1817. Typescript, Virginia Baptist Historical Society, Richmond.

Westmoreland County. Order Book, 1791. Virginia State Library, Richmond.

Wilkins Family Papers. Bible Records, 1769–1966. Virginia Historical Society, Richmond.

Williamson Family Papers. Bible Records, 1744–1822. Photocopy, Virginia Historical Society, Richmond.

Withers Family Papers. Bible Records, 1779–1853. Virginia Historical Society, Richmond.

Woodward-McAllester Family Papers. Bible Records, 1726–1848. Virginia Historical Society, Richmond.

York County. Orders, Wills, Inventories, 1720–1759. Judgments and Orders, 1759–1765. Microfilm, Virginia State Library, Richmond.

Published Works

A.S.S. "Sketches of the South Santee." *American Monthly Magazine* 8 (Oct./Nov. 1836). Reprinted in *Travels in the Old South: Selected from Periodicals of the Times*. Ed. Eugene L. Schwabb. 2 vols. Lexington, 1973.

Ainsworth, Henry. *Solomon's Song of Songs in English Metre with Annotations and References to Other Scriptures*. London, 1623.

Anburey, Thomas. *Travels Through the Interior Parts of America*. 2 vols. Boston, [1789] 1923.

Andrews, Charles Wesley. *Memoir of Mrs. Ann R. Page.* 2d ed. New York, [1844] 1856.

Asbury, Francis. *The Journal and Letters of Francis Asbury.* Ed. Elmer T. Clark. 3 vols. London, 1958.

Associates of Dr. Thomas Bray. *An Account of the Designs of the Associates of the Late Dr. Bray.* London, 1769.

Aubrey, John. *Remaines of Gentilisme and Judaisme.* Nendeln, Lichtenstein, [1881] 1967.

[An] Authentic Account of the Conversion and Experience of a Negro [Anonymous]. N.p., 1812.

Backus, Isaac. "An Eighteenth-Century Baptist Tours Virginia on Horseback," *Virginia Baptist Register* 2 (1963), 64–85.

Barrow, David. *Circular Letter of David Barrow, Southampton County, Feb. 14, 1798.* Norfolk, 1798.

———. *Involuntary, Unmerited, Perpetual, Absolute, Hereditary Slavery, Examined on the Principles of Nature, Reason, Justice, Policy, and Scripture.* Lexington, Ky., 1808.

Bartram, Benjamin. "A Memoir Concerning the Fascinating Faculty Which Has Been Ascribed to the Rattle-Snake and Other American Serpents." In *Transactions of the American Philosophical Society* 4 (1799), 74–113.

Bear, James A., Jr. *Jefferson at Monticello.* Charlottesville, 1967.

Beaver Creek Baptist Church Minutes, Henry County, Virginia, 1786–. Ed. J. F. Thompson. Columbia, Mo., 1933.

Benson, John. *A Short Account of the Voyages, Travels and Adventures of John Benson . . .* N.p., 182?.

Beverly, Robert. *The History and Present State of Virginia.* London, 1705.

Bibb, Henry. *Narrative of the Life and Adventures of Henry Bibb, An American Slave.* New York, 1849.

Blassingame, John W., ed. *Slave Testimony: Two Centuries of Letters, Speeches, Interviews, and Autobiographies.* Baton Rouge, 1977.

[Blodget, Martha.] [The Diary of Martha Blodget.] "Cawson's Virginia in 1795–1796." Ed. Marion Tinling, *William and Mary Quarterly,* 3d series, 3 (1946), 281–291.

Brock, R. A., ed. *Documents . . . Relating to the Huguenot Emigration to Virginia.* Baltimore, [1886] 1970.

Bunyan, John. *Grace Abounding.* London, [1666] 1966.

———. *The Pilgrim's Progress.* London, [1678] 1964.

Burnaby, Andrew. *Travels Through the Middle Settlements in North-America in the Years 1759 and 1760.* 3d ed. New York, [1798] 1904.

Burwell, Letitia M. *A Girl's Life in Virginia Before the War.* New York, 1895.

Bushman, Richard L., ed. *The Great Awakening: Documents on the Revival of Religion, 1740–1745.* New York, 1970.

Byrd, William. *Another Secret Diary of William Byrd of Westover, 1739–1741; with Letters and Literary Exercises, 1696–1726.* Ed. Maude A. Woodfin and Marion Tinling. Richmond, 1942.

———. *The Correspondence of the Three William Byrds of Westover, Virginia, 1684–1776.* Ed. Marion Tinling. 2 vols. Charlottesville, 1977.

———. *History of the Dividing Line and Other Notes, from the Papers of William*

Byrd of Westover in Virginia, Esquire. Ed. Thomas Wynne. 2 vols. Richmond, 1866.

————. *William Byrd's Histories of the Dividing Line Betwixt Virginia and North Carolina.* Ed. William K. Boyd. Raleigh, 1929.

————. *The London Diary (1717–1721), and Other Writings of William Byrd of Virginia.* Ed. Louis B. Wright and Marion Tinling. New York, 1958.

————. *The Prose Works of William Byrd of Westover: Narratives of a Colonial Gentleman.* Ed. Louis B. Wright. Cambridge, Mass., 1966.

————. *The Secret Diary of William Byrd of Westover, 1709–1712.* Ed. Louis B. Wright and Marion Tinling. Richmond, 1941.

————. *Tunbrigalia.* London, 1719.

————. *The Writings of Colonel William Byrd of Westover in Virginia, Esquire.* Ed. John S. Bassett. New York, 1901.

Cameron, R. M., ed. *The Rise of Methodism: A Source Book.* New York, 1954.

Carter, Landon. *The Diary of Colonel Landon Carter of Sabine Hall, 1752–1778.* Ed. Jack P. Greene. 2 vols. Charlottesville, 1965.

Carter, Robert ["King"]. "Will, probated General Court of Virginia, Oct. 16, 1732." In *Virginia Magazine of History and Biography* 5 (April 1898), 408–428; 6 (July 1898), 1–22.

Catterall, Helen T., ed. *Judicial Cases Concerning American Slavery and the Negro.* Vol. 1: *Cases from the Courts of England, Virginia, West Virginia and Kentucky.* New York, 1968.

Chamberlayne, C. G., ed. *The Vestry Book and Register of St. Peter's Parish, New Kent and James City County, Virginia, 1684–1786.* Richmond, 1937.

Chastellux, François Jean, Marquis de. *Travels in North America in the Years 1780, 1781, and 1782.* Trans. and ed. Howard C. Rice. 2 vols. Chapel Hill, 1963.

Christ Church Parish. *The Vestry Book of Christ Church Parish, Middlesex County, Virginia, 1663–1767.* Ed. C. G. Chamberlayne. Richmond, 1927.

Coleman, Mary H., ed. *Virginia Silhouettes: Contemporary Letters Concerning Negro Slavery in the State of Virginia, to Which is Appended, A Dissertation on Slavery with a Proposal for the Gradual Abolition of it in the State of Virginia.* Richmond, 1934.

Commons, John R. et al., eds. *A Documentary History of American Industrial Society.* 10 vols. New York, [1910–1911] 1958.

[A] Concise Historical Account of All the British Colonies in North America [Anonymous]. Dublin, 1776.

Cook, George Smith et al., eds. *Shadows in Silver: A Record of Virginia, 1850–1900 in Contemporary Photographs Taken by George and Huestis Cook.* New York, 1954.

Cott, Nancy F., ed. *Root of Bitterness: Documents of the Social History of American Women.* New York, 1972.

Cresswell, Nicholas. *The Journal of Nicholas Cresswell, 1774–1777.* New York, 1924.

Cumberland Parish. Lunenburg County. *Vestry Book, 1746–1816.* Ed. Landon C. Bell. Richmond, 1930.

Custis, John, and Frances Custis. "Agreement regulating the marriage of John and Frances Custis. Northampton County, June 1714." In *Looking for America: The People's History.* Ed. Stanley I. Kutler. San Francisco, 1964.

Dauphiné, Durand de. *A Huguenot Exile in Virginia, or Voyages of a Frenchman Exiled for His Religion, with a Description of Virginia and Maryland*. Trans. and ed. Gilbert Chinard. New York, [1687] 1934.

Davies, Samuel. *The Duty of Christians to Propagate their Religion Among Heathens, Ernestly Recommended to the Masters of Negro Slaves in Virginia. A Sermon Preached in Hanover, Jan. 8, 1757*. London, 1758.

———. *Letters From the Rev. Samuel Davies, Shewing the State of Religion in Virginia, Particularly Among the Negroes*. 2d ed. London, 1757; 3d ed. London, 1761.

———. *Sermons on Important Subjects*. 3 vols. 5th ed. New York, 1792.

Davis, John. *Personal Adventures and Travels of Four Years and a Half in the United States of America*. London, 1817.

———. *Travels of Four Years and a Half in the United States of America During 1798, 1799, 1800, 1801, and 1802*. New York, [1803] 1909.

Donnan, Elizabeth. *Documents Illustrative of the History of the Slave Trade to America*. 4 vols. New York, [1930–1935] 1969.

Douglas, William. *The Douglas Register: Births, Marriages, and Deaths . . . as Kept by Rev. William Douglas, 1750–1797*. Ed. W. M. Jones. Baltimore, 1977.

Douglass, Frederick. *Narrative of the Life of Frederick Douglass, An American Slave*. Ed. Benjamin Quarles. Cambridge, Mass., 1973.

Drayton, Michael. *The Works of Michael Drayton*. Ed. J. W. Hebel. 5 vols. Oxford, 1961.

Early, John. "Diary of Bishop John Early." *Virginia Magazine of History and Biography* 30 (1926), 303–314.

Eddis, William. *Letters from America, Historical and Descriptive: Comprising Occurrences from 1769 to 1777 Inclusive*. London, 1792.

Edwards, Morgan. "Morgan Edwards' Materials Towards a History of the Baptists in the Province of North Carolina." Ed. G. W. Paschal. *North Carolina Historical Review* 7 (1930), 383–387. Reprinted in *American Christianity: An Historical Interpretation with Representative Documents*. Ed. H. Shelton Smith et al. 2 vols. New York, 1960.

"Eighteenth-Century Slaves as Advertised by their Masters." *Journal of Negro History* 1 (1916), 163–216.

Equiano, Olaudah. "The Life of Olaudah Equiano, or Gustavus Vassa, the African" (1784). In *Great Slave Narratives*, ed. Arna Bontemps. Boston, 1969.

Fairfax, Sally Cary. "Diary of a Little Colonial Girl." *Virginia Magazine of History and Biography* 11 (1903–1904), 212–214.

Fithian, Philip Vickers. *Journal and Letters of Philip Vickers Fithian, 1773–1774: A Plantation Tutor of the Old Dominion*. Ed. Hunter D. Farish. Williamsburg, 1943.

Foner, Philip S., and Ronald L. Lewis, eds. *The Black Worker: A Documentary History from Colonial Times to the Present*. Vol. 1: *The Black Worker to 1869*. Philadelphia, 1978.

Fontaine, James. *Memoirs of a Huguenot Family*. Ed. Ann Maury. Baltimore, 1973.

Fontaine, John. *The Journal of John Fontaine, An Irish Huguenot Son in Spain and Virginia, 1710–1719*. Ed. Edward P. Alexander. Williamsburg, 1972.

Franklin, Benjamin. *The Writings of Benjamin Franklin*. Ed. Albert Smyth. 10 vols. New York, 1970.

Gooch, William. "Governor Gooch's Letters to the Bishop of London, 1727–1749."

Virginia Magazine of History and Biography 32 (1924), 209–237, 321–334; 34 (1925), 51–64.

Gordon, James. "Journal of Col. James Gordon of Lancaster County, Virginia." *William and Mary Quarterly*, 1st series, 11 (1902–1903), 98–112, 195–205, 217–236; 12 (1903–1904), 1–12.

Grimes, William. *The Life of William Grimes, The Runaway Slave, Brought Down to the Present Time.* New Haven, 1855.

Gronnoisaw, James Albert Ukawsaw. *A Narrative of the Most Remarkable Particulars in the Life of James Albert Ukawsaw Gronnoisaw, An African Prince.* Newport, R.I., 1774.

Harrower, John. *The Journal of John Harrower: An Indentured Servant in the Colony of Virginia, 1773–1776.* Ed. Edward M. Riley. Williamsburg, 1963.

Hartwell, Henry, James Blair, and Edward Chilton. *The Present State of Virginia and the College.* Ed. H. D. Farish. Williamsburg, [1697] 1940.

Hazard, Ebenezer. "The Journal of Ebenezer Hazard in Virginia, 1777." Ed. Fred Shelly. *Virginia Magazine of History and Biography* 62 (1954), 400–423.

Hening, William W., ed. *The Statutes at Large, Being a Collection of all the Laws of Virginia, from the First Session of the Legislature in the Year 1619.* 13 vols. Richmond, 1809–1823.

Hunter, Robert. *Quebec to Carolina in 1785–1786; Being the Travel Diary and Observatons of Robert Hunter Jr., a Young Merchant of London.* Ed. Louis B. Wright and Marion Tinling. San Marino, Calif., 1943.

Jarratt, Devereux. "The Autobiography of the Reverend Devereux Jarratt, 1732–1763." Ed. Douglas Adair. *William and Mary Quarterly*, 3d series, 9 (1952), 346–393.

Jea, John. *The Life, History, and Unparalleled Sufferings of John Jea, The African Preacher.* Portsmouth, 1815.

Jefferson, Isaac. "Memoirs of a Monticello Slave as Dictated to Charles Campbell by Isaac Jefferson at Monticello." In *Jefferson at Monticello.* Ed. James A. Bear, Jr. Charlottesvile, 1967.

Jefferson, Thomas. *The Complete Jefferson.* Ed. Saul K. Padover. Freeport, N.Y., [1943] 1968.

———. *The Family Letters of Thomas Jefferson.* Ed. Edwin M. Betts and James A. Bear, Jr. Columbia, Mo., 1966.

———. *Philosophy of Jesus of Nazareth. Jefferson's Extracts from the Gospels: "The Philosophy of Jesus" and "The Life and Morals of Jesus."* Ed. Dickinson W. Adams and Ruth W. Lester. Princeton, 1983.

———. *Notes on the State of Virginia.* New York, [1787] 1964.

———. *The Papers of Thomas Jefferson.* Ed. Julian P. Boyd. 21 vols. Princeton, 1950–1982.

———. *Thomas Jefferson's Farm Book.* Ed. Edwin M. Betts. Charlottesville, 1976.

———. *Thomas Jefferson's Garden Book, 1766–1824.* Ed. Edwin M. Betts. Philadelpia, 1981.

Johnson, Clifton H. et al., eds. *God Struck Me Dead: Religious Conversion Experiences and Autobiographies of Ex-Slaves.* Philadelphia, [1945] 1969.

Jones, Hugh. *The Present State of Virginia.* Ed. Richard L. Morton. Chapel Hill, [1724] 1956.

Kemble, Frances Anne. *A Journal of Residence on a Georgia Plantation.* New York, 1863.

Ken, Thomas. *The Prose Works of the Right Reverend Thomas Ken, D.D.* Ed. W. Benham. London, 188?.

[Kimber, Edward]. "Observations in Several Voyages and Travels in America in the Year 1736; from the *London Magazine,* July 1746." *William and Mary Quarterly,* 1st series, 15 (1907), 1–17, 143–159, 215–224, pagination irregular.

Latrobe, Benjamin H. *The Virginia Journals of Benjamin Henry Latrobe, 1795–1798.* Ed. Edward C. Carter, II, and Angeline Polites. 2 vols. New Haven, 1977.

———. *The Journals of Benjamin Henry Latrobe, 1799–1820: From Philadelphia to New Orleans.* Ed. Edward C. Carter, II, et al. Series 1, Vol. 3. New Haven, 1981.

Lederer, John. *The Discoveries of John Lederer.* Charlottesville, 1958.

Leland, John. *Some Events in the Life of John Leland.* Richmond, 1836.

"Letters Showing the Rise and Progress of the Early Negro Churches of Georgia and the West Indies." *Journal of Negro History* 1 (1916), 69–92.

McIllwaine, H. R., W. L. Hall, and B. J. Hillman, eds. *Executive Journals of the Council of Colonial Virginia, 1680–1775.* 6 vols. Richmond, 1925–1966.

Marrant, John. "A Narrative of the Lord's Wonderful Dealings with John Marrant, a Black." London, 1802. In *Early Negro Writing, 1760–1837.* Ed. Dorothy Porter. Boston, 1971.

Michael, Francis Louis. "Report of the Journey of 1702." Ed. W. J. Hinke. *Virginia Magazine of History and Biography* 24 (1916), 1–43, 113–141, 275–288.

Minter, Jeremy. *Scripture Proofs of Sorcery and Warning Against Sorcerers.* Richmond, 1814.

Moreau de Saint-Méry, Mederic. "The Bitter Thoughts of President Moreau." In *This Was America.* Ed. Oscar Handlin. New York, 1949.

Morrison, A. J., ed. *Travels in Virginia in Revolutionary Times.* Lynchburg, 1922.

Morse, Jedidiah. *American Geography.* London, 1792.

Mullin, Michael, ed. *American Negro Slavery: A Documentary History.* Columbia, S.C., 1976.

Olmstead, Frederick Law. *The Cotton Kingdom.* 2 vols. New York, [1861] 1966.

———. *A Journey in the Back Country.* New York, 1860.

———. *A Journey in the Seaboard States.* New York, 1856.

Orr, Lucinda Lee. *Journal of a Young Lady of Virginia, 1782.* Baltimore, 1871.

Perry, William Stevens, ed. *Historical Collections Relating to the American Colonial Church.* 5 vols. New York, [1870–1878] 1969.

Princess Anne County Loose Papers. Vol. 1: *1700–1789.* Ed. John H. Creecy. Richmond, 1954.

Rawick, George P., ed. *The American Slave: A Composite Autobiography.* Series 1 and 2. 19 vols. Westport, Conn., [1941] 1972.

"Record of the Trial of Grace Sherwood, in 1705, Princess Anne County, for Witchcraft." *Collections of Virginia Historical and Philosophical Society* 1 (1833), 69–78.

Revel, James. "The Poor Unhappy Transported Felon's Sorrowful Account of his Fourteen Years Transportation at Virginia in America" [c. 1680]. Ed. John M. Jennings. *Virginia Magazine of History and Biography* 56 (1948), 180–186. Reprinted in *The Old Dominion in the Seventeenth Century: A Documentary History of Virginia, 1606–1689.* Ed. Warren M. Billings. Chapel Hill, 1975.

Rice, David. *Slavery Inconsistent with Justice and Good Policy; Proved by a Speech Delivered in the Convention Held at Danville, Kentucky.* Philadelphia, 1792.

Roberts, Ralph. "A Slave's Story." *Putnam's Monthly* 9, no. 54 (June 1857), 614–620.

Rose, Robert. *The Diary of Robert Rose: A View of Virginia by a Scottish Colonial Parson, 1746–1751*. Ed. Ralph E. Fall. Verona, Va., 1977.

Rose, Willie Lee, ed. *A Documentary History of Slavery in North America*. New York, 1976.

Semple, Robert B. *A History of the Rise and Progress of the Baptists in Virginia*. Richmond, 1810.

Sewall, Samuel. *Samuel Sewall's Diary*. Ed. Mark Van Doren. New York, 1963.

Seymour-Smith, Martin, ed. *The English Sermon: An Anthology. Vol. 1: 1550–1650*. Manchester, England, 1976.

Sisson, Charles Hubert, ed. *The English Sermon: An Anthology. Vol. 2: 1650–1750*. Manchester, England, 1976.

Smith, H. Shelton, et al., eds. *American Christianity: An Historical Interpretation with Representative Documents*. 2 vols. New York, 1960.

Smith, John. *A Map of Virginia*. Oxford, 1612.

Smith, Samuel Stanhope. *An Essay on the Causes of the Variety of Complexion and Figure in the Human Species (1787)*. 3d ed. New Brunswick, N.J., 1810.

———. *The Lectures . . . on the Subject of Moral and Political Philosopy*. 2 vols. Trenton, N.J., 1812.

Smyth, John F. D. *A Tour in the United States of America*. 2 vols. London, 1784.

Southern, Eileen. *Readings in Black American Music*. New York, 1971.

Symonds, William. *Virginia: A Sermon Preached at White-Chapel, London 1609*. Amsterdam, [1609] 1968.

Taylor, John. *A History of Ten Baptist Churches . . . in Which Will Be Seen Something of the Author's Life*. Frankfort, Ky., 1823.

Thwaites, Reuben G., and Louise P. Kellogg, eds. *Documentary History of Dunmore's War, 1774*. Madison, Wis., 1905.

Tucker, St. George. *A Dissertation on Slavery: With a Proposal for the Gradual Abolition of it in the State of Virginia*. Philadelphia, 1796.

Turner, Nat. *The Confessions of Nat Turner*. Transcribed by Thomas R. Gray. Baltimore, 1831. Reprinted in *The Southern Slave Revolt of 1831: A Compilation of Source Material*. Ed. Henry I. Tragle. Amherst, 1971.

United States Bureau of the Census. *Heads of Families at the First Census of the United States Taken in the Year 1790*. Washington, D.C., 1907–1908.

Vail, Eugène A. *De la Littérature et des Hommes de Lettres des États-Unis d'Amérique*. Paris, 1841.

Van Horne, John C., ed. *Religious Philanthropy and Colonial Slavery: The American Correspondence of the Associates of Dr. Bray, 1717–1777*. Urbana, 1985.

Virginia Gazette. Williamsburg, 1736–1780.

Walduck, Thomas. "Account of the Rattlesnake, Read Before the Royal Society, Jan. 7th, 1713/14." In "Colonial Rattlesnake Lore, 1714," Ed. James R. Masterson. *Zoologica* 23 (1938), 213–216.

Washington, George. *The Diaries of George Washington*. Ed. Donald Johnson et al. 6 vols. Charlottesville, 1976–1979.

———. *The Writings of George Washington, From the Original Manuscript Sources, 1745–1799*. Ed. John C. Fitzpatrick. 39 vols. Washington, D.C., 1931–1944.

Watson, Elkanah. *Men and Times of the Revolution; or, Memoirs of Elkanah Watson, Including His Journals of Travels in Europe and America . . . 1777–1842.* 2d ed. New York, [1857] 1861.

Watson, James F. *Methodist Error or Friendly Christian Advise to Those Methodists Who Indulge in Extravagent Religious Emotions and Bodily Exercises.* Trenton, N.J., 1819. Excerpts reprinted in *Readings in Black American Music.* Ed. Eileen Southern. New York, 1971.

Webb, George. *The Office and Authority of a Justice of the Peace.* Williamsburg, 1736.

Weld, Isaac. *Travels Through the States of North America, and the Provinces of Upper and Lower Canada, During the Years 1795, 1796, and 1797.* London, 1799.

Wesley, Charles. *Journal.* Ed. J. Telford. London, 1909.

Wesley, John. *The Journal of the Rev. John Wesley.* Ed. N. Curnock. 8 vols. London, 1909–1916.

———. *The Works of John Wesley.* 3d ed. 14 vols. Grand Rapids, 1984.

[Whitcomb, Samuel, Jr.]. "A Book Peddler Invades Monticello." Ed. William Peden. *William and Mary Quarterly* 6 (1949), 631–636.

White, George. *A Brief Account of the Life, Experience, Travels and Gospel Labours of George White, An African; Written by Himself and Revised by a Friend.* New York, 1810.

Whitefield, George. *George Whitefield's Journals. A New Edition Containing Fuller Material Than Any Hitherto Published.* London, [1738–1938] 1960.

———. "A Letter to the Inhabitants of Maryland, Virginia, North and South Carolina, Concerning Their Negroes." In George Whitefield, *Three Letters from George Whitefield.* Philadelphia, 1740.

———. "To a Friend in London Concerning Archbishop Tillotson." In George Whitefield, *Three Letters from George Whitefield.* Philadelphia, 1740.

———. *The Works of the Reverend George Whitefield.* 6 vols. London, 1771–1772.

———. *Three Letters from George Whitefield.* Philadelphia, 1740.

Williams, John. "John Williams' Journal." Ed. John S. Moore. *Virginia Baptist Register* 17 (1978), 795–813.

Windley, Lathan A., ed. *Runaway Slave Advertisements: A Documentary History from the 1730s to 1790.* Vol. 1: *Virginia and North Carolina.* Westport, Conn., 1983.

Woolman, John. *The Journal of John Woolman and A Plea for the Poor.* New York, [1774] 1961.

———. *Some Considerations on the Keeping of Negroes: Recommended to the Professors of Christianity, of Every Denomination.* Northampton, Mass., [1754] 1970.

Yetman, Norman R. *Life Under the "Peculiar Institution": Selections from the Slave Narrative Collection.* New York, 1970.

SECONDARY SOURCES
(All references to the *William and Mary Quarterly* are to the third series, unless otherwise noted.)

Abrahams, Roger D. "The Shaping of Folklore Traditions in the British West Indies." *Journal of Inter-American Studies* 9 (1967), 456–480.

Abrahamsson, H. *The Origin of Death: Studies in African Mythology*. New York, [1951] 1977.

Adams, Marie Jeanne. "The Harriet Powers Pictorial Quilts." In *Afro-American Folk Art and Crafts*. Ed. William Ferris. Boston, 1983.

Adams, Percy G. "The Real Author of William Byrd's Natural History of Virginia." *American Literature* 28 (1956–1957), 211–220.

Adams, William Howard. *Jefferson's Monticello*. New York, 1983.

Afigbo, A. E. "Prolegomena to the Study of the Culture History of the Igbo-speaking Peoples of Nigeria." In *West African Cultural Dynamics: Archeological and Historical Perspectives*. Ed. B. K. Swartz, Jr., and R. E. Dumett. The Hague, 1980.

Akiga. *Akiga's Story: The Tiv Tribe as Seen by One of Its Members*. Trans. Rupert East. 2d ed. London, 1965.

Akinnaso, F. Niyi. "The Sociolinguistic Basis of Yoruba Personal Names." *Anthropological Linguistics* 22 (1980), 275–304.

Albert, Peter Joseph. "The Protean Institution: The Geography, Economy and Ideology of Slavery in Post-Revolutionary Virginia." Ph.D. dissertation, University of Maryland, 1976.

Alexander, Jon. *American Personal Religious Accounts, 1600–1980; Toward an Inner History of America's Faiths*. New York, 1983.

Alho, Olli. *The Religion of the Slaves: A Study of the Religious Tradition and Behaviour of Plantation Slaves in the United States, 1830–1865*. Helsinki, 1976.

Alley, Robert S. "The Rev. Mr. Samuel Davies: A Study in Religion and Politics, 1747–1759." Ph.D. dissertation, Princeton University, 1962.

Andrews, Stuart. *Methodism and Society*. London, 1970.

Anthony, Carl. "The Big House and the Slave Quarters." *Landscape* 20, no. 3 (1976), 8–19; 21, no. 1 (1976), 9–15.

Appleby, Joyce. "Value and Society." In *Colonial British America; Essays in the New History of the Early Modern Era*. Ed. Jack P. Greene and J. R. Pole. Baltimore, 1984.

Ariès, Philippe. *The Hour of Our Death*. New York, 1981.

———. *Western Attitudes Toward Death, From the Middle Ages to the Present*. Baltimore, 1974.

Bailey, Raymond C. *Popular Influence Upon Public Policy: Petitioning in Eighteenth Century Virginia*. Westport, Conn., 1979.

Baker, Robert A. *The Southern Baptist Convention and Its People, 1607–1972*. Nashville, 1974.

Ballagh, James C. *A History of Slavery in Virginia*. Baltimore, [1902] 1968.

———. *White Servitude in the Colony of Virginia: A Study of the System of Indentured Labor in the American Colonies*. Baltimore, 1895.

Barley, Nigel. *Adventures in a Mud Hut: An Innocent Anthropologist Abroad*. New York, [1983] 1984.

Bascom, William R. *Ifa Divination*. Bloomington, 1969.

———, and Melville J. Herskovits, eds. *Continuity and Change in African Cultures*. Chicago, [1959] 1962.

Basden, G. T. *Among the Ibos of Southern Nigeria*. London, 1921.

———. *Niger Ibos*. London, 1938.

Bassett, Fletcher S., ed. *Legends and Superstitions of the Sea and of Sailors*. London, 1885.

Bear, James A., Jr. "The Hemings Family at Monticello." *Virginia Cavalcade* 29 (1979), 78–87.

Beattie, John, and John Middleton, eds. *Spirit Mediumship and Society in Africa.* London, 1969.

Beck, Jane C. "The West Indian Supernatural World: Belief Integration in a Pluralistic Society." *Journal of American Folklore* 88 (1975), 235–244.

Bedini, Silvio A. "Thomas Jefferson, Clock Designer." *Proceedings of the American Philosophical Society* 108 (1964), 163–180.

Beeman, Richard R. *The Evolution of the Southern Backcountry: A Case Study of Lunenburg County Virginia, 1746–1832.* Philadelphia, 1984.

———, and Rhys Isaac. "Cultural Conflict and Social Change in the Revolutionary South: Lunenburg County, Virginia." *Journal of Southern History* 46 (1980), 525–550.

Beidelman, T. O. "Kaguro Time Reckoning: An Aspect of the Cosmology of an East African People." *Southwestern Journal of Anthropology* 19 (1963), 9–20.

Benedict, David. *A General History of the Baptist Denomination in America and Other Parts of the World.* New York, 1848.

———. *Fifty Years Among the Baptists.* New York, 1860.

Benson, Louis F. *The English Hymn: Its Development and Use in Worship.* Richmond, [1915] 1962.

Berger, Peter. *The Sacred Canopy.* Garden City, N.Y., 1969.

Berlin, Ira. *Slaves Without Masters: The Free Negro in the Antebellum South.* New York, 1974.

———. "Time, Space and the Evolution of Afro-American Society on British Mainland North America." *American Historical Review* 85 (1980), 44–78.

———, and Ronald Hoffman, eds. *Slavery and Freedom in the Age of the American Revolution.* Charlottesville, 1983.

Bertelson, David. *The Lazy South.* New York, 1967.

Billings, Warren M., ed. *The Old Dominion in the Seventeenth Century: A Documentary History of Virginia, 1606–1689.* Chapel Hill, 1975.

Bishir, Catherine W. "Black Builders in Antebellum North Carolina." *North Carolina Historical Review* 61 (1984), 423–461.

Blake, Russell L. "Ties of Intimacy: Social Values and Personal Relationships of Ante-Bellum Slaveholders." Ph.D. dissertation, University of Michigan, 1978.

Blanton, Wyndham B. *Medicine in Virginia in the Eighteenth Century.* Richmond, 1931.

———. "Washington's Medical Knowledge and Its Sources." *Annals of Medical History* 5 (1933), 52–61.

Blassingame, John W. "Using the Testimony of Ex-Slaves: Approaches and Problems." *Journal of Southern History* 41 (1975), 473–492.

Bohanan, Paul. "Concepts of Time Among the Tiv of Nigeria." *Southwestern Journal of Anthropology* 9 (1953), 251–262.

Bonomi, Patricia, and Peter Eisenstadt. "Church Adherence in the Eighteenth-Century British American Colonies." *William and Mary Quarterly* 39 (1982), 245–286.

Booth, Newell S., Jr., ed. *African Religions.* New York, [1977] 1979.

———. "Time and Change in African Traditional Thought." *Journal of Religion in Africa* 7 (1975), 81–91.

Borgen, Ole E., ed. *John Wesley: The Man and his Thought.* Leiden, 1966.

Boskin, Joseph. *Into Slavery: Racial Decisions in the Virginia Colony.* Washington, D.C., [1976] 1979.

Bourguignon, Erika. "Ritual Dissociation and Possession Belief in Caribbean Negro Religion." In *Afro-American Anthropology: Contemporary Perspectives.* Ed. Norman E. Whitten, Jr., and John F. Szwed. New York, 1970.

Bowman, Larry G. "Virginia's Use of Blacks in the French and Indian War." *Western Pennsylvania Historical Magazine* 53 (1970), 57–63.

Boyd, Julian P. "The Murder of George Wythe." *William and Mary Quarterly* 12 (1955), 513–542.

Braun, Hugh. *Elements of English Architecture.* Newton Abbot, England, 1973.

Brearley, H. C. "Are Southerners Really Lazy?" *American Scholar* 18 (1948–1949), 68–75.

Breen, T. H. "A Changing Labor Force and Race Relations in Virginia, 1660–1710." *Journal of Social History* 7 (1973), 3–25.

———. "The Culture of Agriculture: The Symbolic World of the Tidewater Planter, 1760 to 1790." In *Saints and Revolutionaries: Essays on Early American History,* ed. David D. Hall. New York, 1984.

———. "Of Time and Nature: A Study of Persistent Values in Colonial Virginia." In his *Puritans and Adventurers: Change and Persistence in Early America.* New York, 1980.

———. *Tobacco Culture: The Mentality of the Great Tidewater Planters on the Eve of Revolution.* Princeton, 1985.

———, and Stephen Innes. *"Myne Owne Ground": Race and Freedom on Virginia's Eastern Shore, 1640–1676.* New York, 1980.

———, James H. Lewis, and Keith Schlesinger. "Motive for Murder: Servant's Life in Virginia, 1678." *William and Mary Quarterly* 40 (1982), 106–120.

Bridenbaugh, Carl. *Vexed and Troubled Englishmen, 1590–1642.* New York, 1968.

Brodie, Fawn M. *Thomas Jefferson: An Intimate History.* New York, 1974.

———. "Thomas Jefferson's Unknown Grandchildren: A Study in Historical Silences." *American Heritage* 27 (1976), 28–33, 94–99.

Brown, Imogene E. *American Aristides: A Biography of George Wythe.* Rutherford, N.J., 1981.

Brown, Robert E., and B. Katherine Brown. *Virginia, 1705–1786: Democracy or Aristocracy?* East Lansing, 1964.

Bruce, Dickson D., Jr. "Death as Testimony in the Old South." *Southern Humanities Review* 12 (1978), 123–132.

Bruce, Philip Alexander. *Economic History of Virginia in the Seventeenth Century.* 2 vols. New York, [1895] 1935.

———. *Institutional History of Virginia in the Seventeenth Century.* 2 vols. Gloucester, Mass., [1910] 1964.

———. *Social Life of Virginia in the Seventeenth Century.* 2d ed., rev. Lynchburg, Va., 1927.

Brugger, Robert J. *Beverly Tucker: Heart Over Head in the Old South.* Baltimore, 1978.

Brydon, George. *Virginia's Mother Church And the Political Conditions Under Which It Grew.* Vol. 1. Richmond, 1947; Vol. 2. Philadelphia, 1952.

Buchanan, Paul E. "The Eighteenth-Century Frame Houses of Tidewater Virginia." In *Building Early America: Contributions Toward the History of a Great Industry*. Ed. Charles E. Peterson. Radnor, Penn., 1976.

Buchanan, William T., Jr., and Edward F. Heite. "The Hallowes Site: A Seventeenth-Century Yeoman's Cottage in Virginia." *Historical Archeology* 5 (1971), 38–48.

Bushman, Richard C. "American High-Style and Vernacular Cultures." In *Colonial British America: Essays in the New History of the Early Modern Era*. Ed. Jack P. Greene and J. R. Pole. Baltimore, 1984.

Butler, Alfloyd. *The Africanization of American Christianity*. New York, 1980.

Butler, Jon. "Enthusiasm Described and Decried: The Great Awakening as Interpretive Fiction." *Journal of American History* 69 (1982), 305–325.

———. "The Dark Ages of American Occultism, 1760–1848." In *The Occult in America: New Historical Perspectives*. Ed. Howard Kerr and Charles L. Crow. Urbana, 1983.

———. "Magic, Astrology and the Early American Religious Heritage, 1600–1760." *American Historical Review* 84 (1979), 317–346.

Butler, Reginald D. "Slave Life in Eighteenth-Century Virginia: The Diary of Landon Carter." Unpublished manuscript, 1980.

Campbell, Mildred. "Social Origins of Some Early Americans." In *Seventeenth-Century America: Essays in Colonial History*. Ed. James Morton Smith. New York, 1959.

Capp, Bernard. *English Almanacs, 1500–1800: Astrology and the Popular Press*. Ithaca, 1979.

Cappon, Lester J., and Stella F. Duff. *Virginia Gazette Index, 1736–1780*. 2 vols. Williamsburg, 1950.

Carr, Lois Green, and Russell R. Menard. "Immigration and Opportunity: The Freedman in Early Colonial Maryland." In *The Chesapeake in the Seventeenth Century: Essays on Anglo-American Society*. Ed. Thad W. Tate and David L. Ammerman. New York, 1979.

———, and Lorena S. Walsh. "Inventories and Analysis of Wealth and Consumption Patterns in St. Mary's County, Maryland, 1658–1777." *Historical Methods* 13 (1980), 81–104.

———. "The Planter's Wife: The Experience of White Women in Seventeenth-Century Maryland." *William and Mary Quarterly* 34 (1977), 542–571.

Carson, Cary. "Doing History with Material Culture." In *Material Culture and the Study of American Life*. Ed. Ian Quimby. New York. 1978.

———, Norman F. Barka, William M. Kelso, Gary Wheeler Stone, and Dell Upton. "Impermanent Architecture in the Southern American Colonies." *Winterthur Portfolio* 16 (1981), 135–196.

Carson, Jane. *James Innes and His Brothers of the F.H.C.* Charlottesville, 1965.

Caulfield, Ernest. "Infant Feeding in Colonial America." *Journal of Pediatrics* 41 (1952), 673–687.

Chappell, Edward. "Slave Housing." *Fresh Advices* (Nov. 1982), 1–4.

Chase, Judith W. "American Heritage from Ante-Bellum Black Craftsmen." *Southern Folklore Quarterly* 42 (1978), 135–158.

Chorley, E. Clowes. "The Planting of the Church in Virginia." *William and Mary Quarterly*, 2d series, 10 (1930), 191–213.

328

———. "The Rev. Devereux Jarratt, 1732–1801." *Historical Magazine of the Protestant Episcopal Church* 5 (1936), 47–64.

Cipolla, Carlo. *Clocks and Culture, 1300–1700.* New York, 1967.

Clinton, Catherine. *The Plantation Mistress: Woman's World in the Old South.* New York, 1982.

Coleman, D. C. "Labour in the English Economy of the Seventeenth Century." In *Seventeenth Century England: Society in an Age of Revolution.* Ed. Paul S. Seaver. New York, 1976.

Collinson, Patrick. *The Religion of Protestants: The Church in English Society, 1559 1625.* Oxford, 1982.

Combes, John D. "Ethnography, Archaeology, and Burial Practices Among Coastal South Carolina Blacks." In *Conference on Historic Site Archaeology Papers,* 7. Columbia, S.C., 1972.

Cometti, Elizabeth. *Social Life in Virginia During the War for Independence.* Williamsburg, 1978.

Conlin, Joseph R. "Another Side to William Byrd of Westover: An Explanation of the Food in His Secret Diaries." *Virginia Cavalcade* 26 (1977), 125–132.

Cooper, Clare. "The House as Symbol of the Self." In *Designing for Human Behavior: Architecture and the Behavioral Sciences.* Ed. J. Lang et al. Stroudsburg, Penn., 1974.

Cottle, Thomas J., and Stephen L. Klineberg. *The Present of Things Future: Explorations of Time in Human Experience.* New York, 1974.

Cragg, Gerald R. *Puritanism in the Period of the Great Persecution, 1660–1688.* Cambridge, England, 1957.

Craggett, Foster T. "A Form Critical Approach to the Oral Traditions of the Black Church as They Relate to the Celebration of Death." Ph.D. dissertation, School of Theology at Claremont, 1980.

Craton, Michael, ed. "Roots and Branches; Current Directions in Slave Studies." *Historical Reflections* 6, no. 2 (Summer 1979), entire issue.

Craven, Avery. "Poor Whites and Negroes in the Ante-bellum South." *Journal of Negro History* 15 (1930), 14–25.

———. *Rachel of Old Louisiana.* Baton Rouge, 1975.

Craven, Wesley Frank. *White, Red and Black: The Seventeenth-Century Virginian.* Charlottesville, 1971.

Crawson, E. T. "Col. John Custis of Arlington." *Virginia Cavalcade* 20 (1970), 14–19.

Crocker, Christopher. "The Southern Way of Death." In *The Not So Solid South.* Ed. Kenneth Moreland. Athens, Ga., 1971.

Culver, Dwight. *Negro Segregation in the Methodist Church.* New Haven, 1953.

Cuming, G. J. *A History of Anglican Liturgy.* 2d ed. London, [1969] 1982.

Cumming, William P. "Early Maps of the Chesapeake Bay Area: Their Relation to Settlement and Society." In *Early Maryland in a Wider World.* Ed. David B. Quinn. Detroit, 1982.

Curtin, Philip D. *The Atlantic Slave Trade: A Census.* Madison, Wis., 1969.

———, ed. *Africa Remembered: Narratives by West Africans from the Era of the Slave Trade.* Madison, Wis., 1967.

Dabney, Virginius. *The Jefferson Scandals: A Rebuttal.* New York, 1981.

Dallimore, Arnold A. *George Whitefield: The Life and Times of the Great Evangelist of the Eighteenth-Century Revival.* Vol. 1. London, 1970.

Daniel, Harrison W. "Virginia Baptists, 1861–1865." *Virginia Magazine of History and Biography* 72 (1964), 94–130.

———. "Virginia Baptists and the Negro in the Early Republic." *Virginia Magazine of History and Biography* 80 (1972), 60–69.

Danquah, J. B. *The Akan Doctrine of God: A Fragment of Gold Coast Ethics and Religion.* London, 1968.

David, Paul A. et al. *Reckoning with Slavery: A Critical Study in Quantitative History of American Negro Slavery.* New York, 1976.

Davies, Horton. *Worship and Theology in England; From Andrewes to Baxter and Fox, 1603–1690.* Princeton, 1975.

Davis, David Brian. *The Problem of Slavery in Western Culture.* Ithaca, 1966.

Davis, Richard Beale. *Intellectual Life in the Colonial South, 1585–1763.* 3 vols. Knoxville, Tenn., 1978.

———. *Literature and Society in Early Virginia, 1608–1840.* Baton Rouge, 1973.

Dawson, Roger R. "Greenway Court and White Post: Virginia Home of Thomas, Lord Fairfax." *Pioneer America* 1 (1969), 33–39.

Deetz, James. *In Small Things Forgotten: The Archeology of Early American Life.* Garden City, N.Y., 1977.

Degler, Carl N. *Place Over Time: The Continuity of Southern Distinctiveness.* Baton Rouge, 1977.

Delany, Paul. *British Autobiography in the Seventeenth Century.* London, 1969.

Demos, John. *Entertaining Satan: Witchcraft and the Culture of Early New England.* New York, 1982.

Denyer, Susan. *African Traditional Architecture: An Historical and Geographical Perspective.* London, 1978.

Dethlefsen, Edwin S. "The Cemetery and Culture Change: Archaeological Focus and Ethnographic Perspective." In *Modern Material Culture: The Archaeology of Us.* Ed. Richard A. Gould and Michael B. Schiffer. New York, 1981.

Devisse, Jean. *The Image of the Black in Western Art.* 2 vols. New York, 1979.

Dillard, J. L. *Black English: Its History and Usage in the United States.* New York, 1972.

———. *Black Names.* The Hague, 1976.

———. *Perspectives on Black English.* The Hague, 1975.

Dillenberger, John, and Claude Welsh. *Protestant Christianity.* New York, 1954.

Dorson, Richard. *American Folklore.* Chicago, [1959] 1964.

———, ed. *America Begins: Early American Writings.* Greenwich, Conn., 1950.

Douglas, Ann. "Heaven Our Home: Consolation Literature in the Northern United States, 1830–1880." In *Death in America.* Ed. David E. Stannard. Philadelphia, 1975.

Douglas, Mary. "The Lele of Kasai." In *African Worlds.* Ed. Daryll Forde. London, [1954] 1960.

Drake, Fred. "Witchcraft in the American Colonies, 1647–62." *American Quarterly* 20 (1968), 694–725.

Drake, Thomas E. *Quakers and Slavery in America.* Gloucester, Mass., [1950] 1965.

DuBois, W.E.B. *The Negro Church.* Atlanta, 1903.

Dunn, Ernest F. "The Black Southern White Dialect Controversy: Who Did What to Whom?" In *Black English: A Seminar*. Ed. Deborah S. Harrison and Tom Trabasso. New York, 1976.

Dunn, Richard S. "Black Society in the Chesapeake, 1776–1810." In *Slavery and Freedom in the Age of the American Revolution*. Ed. Ira Berlin and Ronald Hoffman. Charlottesville, 1983.

———. "Servants and Slaves: The Recruitment and Employment of Labor." In *Colonial British America: Essays in the New History of the Early Modern Era*. Ed. Jack P. Greene and J. R. Pole. Baltimore, 1984.

———. "Masters, Servants and Slaves in the Colonial Chesapeake and the Caribbean." In *Early Maryland in a Wider World*. Ed. David B. Quinn. Detroit, 1982.

———. "A Tale of Two Plantations: Slave Life at Mesopotamia in Jamaica and Mount Airy in Virginia, 1799 to 1828." *William and Mary Quarterly* 34 (1977), 32–65.

Earle, Carville V. *The Evolution of a Tidewater Settlement System: All Hallow's Parish, Maryland, 1650–1783*. Chicago, 1975.

Eayrs, George. "Developments, Institutions, Helpers, Opposition." In *A New History of Methodism*. Ed. W. J. Townsend et al. 2 vols. Nashville, 1909.

Elkins, Stanley. *Slavery: A Problem in American Institutional and Intellectual Life*. Chicago, 1959.

Ellenberger, Henri F. "A Clinical Introduction to Psychiatric Phenomenology and Existential Analysis." In *Existence: A New Dimension in Psychiatry and Psychology*. Ed. Rollo May et al. New York, 1958.

Elton, G. R. "Contentment and Discontent on the Eve of Colonization." In *Early Maryland in a Wider World*. Ed. David B. Quinn. Detroit, 1982.

England, Martha Winburn. "Emily Dickinson and Isaac Watts." In *Hymns Unbidden: Donne, Herbert, Blake, Emily Dickinson, and the Hymnographers*. M. England and John Sparrow. New York, 1966.

Epstein, Dena J. *Sinful Tunes and Spirituals: Black Folk Music to the Civil War*. Urbana, 1977.

Erikson, Erik H. "Race and the Wider Identity." In *Identity Youth and Crisis*. New York, 1968.

———. *Dimensions of a New Identity: The 1973 Jefferson Lectures in the Humanities*. New York, 1974.

Essig, James D. *The Bonds of Wickedness: American Evangelicals Against Slavery, 1770–1808*. Philadelphia, 1982.

———. "A Very Wintry Season: Virginia Baptists and Slavery, 1785–1797." *Virginia Magazine of History and Biography* 88 (1980), 170–185.

Evans, David L. *I Sought My Brother: An Afro-American Reunion*. Boston, 1981.

Evans-Pritchard, E. E. *Essays in Social Anthropology*. London, 1962.

———. *The Nuer: A Description of the Modes of Livelihood and Political Institutions of a Nilotic People*. Oxford, 1968.

———. "Nuer Time Reckoning." *Africa* 12 (1939), 189–216.

———. *Witchcraft, Oracles and Magic Among the Azande*. Oxford, 1937.

Fasold, Ralph W. "The Relation Between Black and White Speech in the South." *American Speech* 56 (1981), 163–189.

Faust, Joan Lee. "The Gardens at Monticello." *America* 1 (1973), 6–8.

Feest, Christian F. "The Virginia Indian in Pictures, 1612–1624." *The Smithsonian Journal of History* 2, no. 1 (Spring 1967), 1–30.

Fernandez, James W. *Bwiti: An Ethnology of the Religious Imagination in Africa.* Princeton, 1982.

Ferris, William R., ed. *Afro-American Folk Art and Crafts.* Boston, 1983.

Fiering, Norman. "The First American Enlightenment: Tillotson, Leverett and Philosophical Anglicanism." *New England Quarterly* 54 (1981), 307–344.

Fischer, David Hackett. *Growing Old in America.* New York, 1977.

Fisher, Miles Mark. *Negro Slave Songs in the United States.* Ithaca, 1953.

Fishwick, Marshall. "The Pepys of the Old Dominion." *American Heritage* 11 (1959), 5–7, 117–119.

FitzGerald, W. B. "George Whitefield." In *A New History of Methodism.* Ed. W. J. Townsend et al. 2 vols. Nashville, 1909.

Flaherty, David H. "A Select Guide to the Manuscript Court Records of Colonial Virginia." *American Journal of Legal History* 19 (1975), 112–137.

Flexner, James T. *George Washington: Anguish and Farewell, 1793–1799.* Boston, [1967] 1972.

Flynt, J. Wayne. *Dixie's Forgotten People: The South's Poor Whites.* Bloomington, 1979.

———, and Dorothy S. Flynt. *Southern Poor Whites: A Selected Annotated Bibliography of Published Sources.* New York, 1981.

Fogel, Robert W., and Stanley L. Engerman. *Time on the Cross: The Economics of American Negro Slavery.* 2 vols. Boston, 1974.

Forde, Daryll. *African Worlds: Studies in the Cosmological Ideas and Social Values of African Peoples.* London, [1954] 1970.

———, and G. I. Jones. *The Ibo and Ibibio-Speaking Peoples of Southeastern Nigeria.* London, 1962.

Fortes, Meyer. *Oedipus and Job in West African Religion.* Cambridge, England, 1959.

———. *The Web of Kinship Among the Tallensi.* London, [1949] 1957.

Francaviglia, Richard. "The Cemetery as an Evolving Cultural Landscape." *Annals of the American Association of Geographers* 61 (1971), 501–509.

Fry, Gladys-Marie. "Harriet Powers: Portrait of a Black Quilter." In *Missing Pieces: Georgia Folk Art 1770–1976.* Ed. Anna Wadsworth. Atlanta, 1976.

Fussell, G. E. *The English Rural Labourer.* London, 1949.

Galenson, David W. "British Servants and the Colonial Indenture System in the Eighteenth Century." *Journal of Southern History* 44 (1978), 41–66.

———. *White Servitude in Colonial America: An Economic Analysis.* Cambridge, England, 1981.

Gardet, L. et al. *Cultures and Time.* Paris, 1976.

Gardner, Robert G. "Eighteenth-Century Virginia and West Virginia Baptist Manuscripts." *Virginia Baptist Register* 19 (1980), 910–915.

Gay, Peter. *Art and Act: On Causes in History—Manet, Gropius, Mondrian.* New York, 1976.

———. *Freud for Historians.* New York, 1985.

Geddes, Gordon E. *Welcome Joy: Death in Puritan New England.* Ann Arbor, 1981.

Gemery, Henry A., and Jan S. Hogendorn, eds. *The Uncommon Market: Essays in the Economic History of the Atlantic Slave Trade.* New York, 1979.

Genovese, Eugene D. " 'Rather be a Nigger than a Poor White Man': Slave Perceptions of Southern Yeoman and Poor Whites." In *Toward a New View of America, Essays in Honor of Arthur C. Cole.* Ed. Hans L. Trefousse. New York, 1977.

———. *Roll, Jordan, Roll: The World the Slaves Made.* New York, 1974.

George, Charles H., and Katherine George. *The Protestant Mind of the English Reformation, 1570–1640.* Princeton, 1961.

Georgia Writers Project. *Drums and Shadows: Survival Studies Among the Georgia Coastal Negroes.* Athens, Ga., 1940.

Gerrard, Nathaniel. "Serpent-Handling Religions of West Virginia." *Tennessee Folklore Society Bulletin* 36 (1970), 22–28.

Gewehr, Wesley M. *The Great Awakening in Virginia, 1740–1790.* Chapel Hill, 1930.

Gillis, John R. *Youth and History: Tradition and Change in European Age Relations, 1770–Present.* New York, 1981.

Gittings, Clare. *Death, Burial and the Individual in Early Modern England.* London, 1984.

Gladwin, Lee A. "Sexual Mores in Colonial Virginia." *Virginia Social Sciences Journal* 9 (1974), 21–30.

———. "Tobacco and Sex: Some Factors Affecting Non-Marital Sexual Behavior in Colonial Virginia." *Journal of Social History* 12 (1978), 57–75.

Glasgow, Ellen. *The Woman Within.* New York, 1954.

Glassie, Henry. "Eighteenth-Century Cultural Process in Delaware Valley Folk Building." *Winterthur Portfolio* 7 (1972), 29–57.

———. *Folk Housing in Middle Virginia: A Structural Analysis of Historic Artifacts.* Knoxville, Tenn., 1975.

———. *Pattern in the Material Folk Culture of the Eastern United States.* Philadelphia, 1968.

———. "The Types of the Southern Mountain Cabin." In *The Study of American Folklore: An Introduction.* By Jan Harold Brunvand. New York, 1968.

Glück, Julius F. "African Architecture." In *Peoples and Cultures of Africa—An Anthropological Reader.* Ed. E. P. Skinner. Garden City, N.Y., 1973.

Gockerell, Nina. "Telling Time Without a Clock." In *The Clockwork Universe: German Clocks and Automata 1550–1650.* Ed. Klaus Maurice and Otto Mayr. New York, 1980.

Gold, J. R., and J. Burgess, eds. *Valued Environments.* London, 1982.

Goldin, Claudia. *Urban Slavery in the American South, 1820–1860: A Quantitative History.* Chicago, 1976.

Goody, Jack. *Death, Property and the Ancestors; A Study of the Mortuary Customs of the Lodagaa of West Africa.* London, 1962.

Gough, Isabel. "Witchcraft—Northumberland Style." *Northumberland County Historical Bulletin* 5 (1968), 52–57.

Grant, Douglas. *The Fortunate Slave: An Illustration of African Slavery in the Early Eighteenth Century.* London, 1968.

Grattan, J.H.G., and Charles Singer. *Anglo-Saxon Magic and Medicine.* London, [1952] 1977.

Green, Eugene. "Naming and Mapping the Environments of Early Massachusetts, 1620–1776." *Names* 30 (1982), 77–92.

Green, H. B. "Temporal Attitudes in Four Negro Subcultures." In *The Study of Time,* ed. J. T. Fraser et al. Berlin, 1972.

333

Greenberg, Michael S. "Gentlemen Slaveholders: The Social Outlook of the Virginia Planter Class." Ph.D. dissertation, Rutgers University, 1972.

———. "Revival, Reform, Revolution: Samuel Davies and the Great Awakening in Virginia." *Marxist Perspectives* 3, no. 2 (1980), 102–119.

Greene, E. B., and V. D. Harrington. *American Population Before the Federal Census of 1790*. New York, 1932.

Greene, Jack P. *Landon Carter: An Inquiry Into the Personal Values and Social Imperatives of the Eighteenth-Century Virginia Gentry*. Charlottesville, 1967.

———. "Search for Identity: An Interpretation of the Meaning of Selected Patterns of Social Response in Eighteenth-Century America." *Journal of Southern History* 3 (1970), 189–224.

———, and J. R. Pole, eds. *Colonial British America: Essays in the New History of the Early Modern Era*. Baltimore, 1984.

Greven, Philip J. *The Protestant Temperament: Patterns of Child-Rearing, Religious Experience, and the Self in Early America*. New York, 1977.

Griaule, Marcel, and Germaine Dieterlen. "The Dogon of the French Sudan." In *African Worlds: Studies in the Cosmological Ideas and Social Values of African Peoples*. Ed. Daryll Forde. London, [1954] 1970.

Grider, Sylvia. "The Shotgun House." *Pioneer America* 7 (1975), 47–55.

Grimmelman, Jan Ellen Lewis. [See also Jan Lewis.] "This World and the Next: Religion, Death, Success and Love in Jefferson's Virginia." Ph.D. dissertation, University of Michigan, 1977.

Gundersen, Joan Rezner. "The Double Bonds of Race and Sex: Black and White Women in a Colonial Virginia Parish." *Journal of Southern History* 52 (1986), 351–372.

Gurevich, A. J. "Time as a Problem of Cultural History." In *Cultures and Time*. Ed. L. Gardet et al. Paris, 1976.

Gurvitch, Georges. *The Spectrum of Social Time*. Dordrecht, Holland, 1964.

Gutman, Herbert. *The Black Family in Slavery and Freedom, 1750–1925*. New York, 1976.

Habenstein, Robert, and William M. Lamers. *The History of American Funeral Directing*. 2d ed. Milwaukee, 1962.

Hall, David D. "Introduction." In *Understanding Popular Culture: Europe from the Middle Ages to the Nineteenth Century*. Ed. Steven L. Kaplan. Berlin, 1984.

———. "The Mental World of Samuel Sewall." In *Saints and Revolutionaries: Essays on Early American History*. Ed. David D. Hall et al. New York, 1984.

———. "The World of Print and Collective Mentality in Seventeenth-Century New England." In *New Directions in American Intellectual History*. Ed. John Highan and Paul K. Conkin. Baltimore, 1979.

Hall, Edward T. *Beyond Culture*. Garden City, N.Y., 1976.

———. *The Dance of Life: The Other Dimension of Time*. Garden City, N.Y., 1983.

———. *The Hidden Dimension*. Garden City, N.Y., 1966.

———. *The Silent Language*. Garden City, N.Y., 1959.

Hambly, Wilfred D. *Serpent Worship in Africa*. In Publications of Field Museum of Natural History, Anthropological Series, 21. New York, [1931] 1968.

Hambrick-Stowe, Charles E. *The Practice of Piety: Puritan Devotional Disciplines in Seventeenth Century New England*. Chapel Hill, 1982.

Hammond, J. L., and Barbara Hammon. *The Village Laborer, 1760–1832: A Study in the Government of England Before the Reform Bill*. New York, [1920] 1970.

Harder, Kelsie B. *Illustrated Dictionary of Place Names, United States and Canada.* New York, 1976.

Harrison, Lowell H. "A Virginian Moves to Kentucky, 1793." In *Essays on American Social History.* Ed. John Lankford and David Reimors. New York, 1970.

Hast, Adele. "The Legal Status of the Negro in Virginia, 1705–1765." *Journal of Negro History* 54 (1969), 217–239.

———. *Loyalism in Revolutionary Virginia: The Norfolk Area and the Eastern Shore.* Ann Arbor, 1982.

Hatch, Charles E., Jr. *Popes Creek Plantation; Birthplace of George Washington.* Wakefield, Va., 1979.

Hecht, J. Jean. *The Domestic Servant Class in Eighteenth-Century England.* London, 1956.

Henderson, Richard N. *The King in Every Man: Evolutionary Trends in Onitsha Ibo Society and Culture.* New Haven, 1972.

Henretta, James A. "Families and Farms: *Mentalité* in Pre-Industrial America." *William and Mary Quarterly* 35 (1978), 3–32.

Herskovits, Melville J. *The Myth of the Negro Past.* Boston, [1941] 1958.

———. *The New World Negro: Selected Papers in Afroamerican Studies.* Bloomington, 1966.

———, and William R. Bascom. "The Problem of Stability and Change in African Cultures." In *Continuity and Change in African Cultures.* Ed. W. R. Bascom and M. J. Herskovits. Chicago, [1959] 1962.

Higginbotham, A. Leon, Jr. *In the Matter of Color; Race and the American Legal Process: The Colonial Period.* New York, 1978.

Hill, Christopher. *Change and Continuity in Seventeenth-Century England.* London, 1974.

———. *Reformation to Industrial Revolution: The Making of Modern English Society. Vol. 1: 1530–1780.* New York, 1968.

———. "Science and Magic in Seventeenth-Century England." In *Culture, Ideology and Politics: Essays for Eric Hobsbawn.* Ed. Raphael Samuel and Gareth S. Jones. London, 1982.

———. *Society and Puritanism in Pre-Revolutionary England.* New York, 1964.

———. *The World Turned Upside Down: Radical Ideas During the English Revolution.* London, 1972.

Hillard, Sam. "Plantations Created the South." *Geographical Magazine* (London) 52, no. 6 (1979–1980), 409–416.

Historic American Building Survey. *Virginia Catalog: A List of Measured Drawings, Photographs, and Written Documentation in the Survey.* Charlottesville, 1976.

Hobday, George J. "Historical Sketch of the Court Street Baptist Church, Portsmouth, Virginia." In *The Centennial of the Court Street Baptist Church, 1889.* Philadelphia, 1889.

Hodges, Robert A. "Some Madstones of Virginia." *Pioneer America* 4 (1972), 1–8.

Hogg, Anne M., and Dennis A. Tosh, eds. *Virginia Cemeteries: A Guide to Resources.* Charlottesville, 1986.

Holmes, David. "Devereux Jarratt: A Letter and a Reevaluation." *Historical Magazine of the Protestant Episcopal Church* 47 (1978), 37–49.

Holmes, Ronald. *Witchcraft in British History.* London, 1974.

Hooks, Bell. *Ain't I A Woman: Black Women and Feminism.* Boston, 1981.

Horn, James. "Servant Emigration to the Chesapeake in the Seventeenth Century." In *The Chesapeake in the Seventeenth Century*. Ed. Thad W. Tate and David L. Ammerman. New York, 1979.

Horton, Robin, and Ruth Finnegan. *Modes of Thought: Essays on Thinking in Western and Non-Western Societies*. London, 1973.

Howarth-Williams, Martin. *R. D. Laing: His Work and Its Relevance for Sociology*. London, 1977.

Howells, John Mead. *Lost Examples of Colonial Architecture: Buildings That Have Disappeared or Been So Altered as to be Denatured*. New York, [1931] 1963.

Hudgins, Carter. "Exactly as the Gentry do in England: Culture, Aspirations, and Material Things in the Eighteenth Century Chesapeake." Conference on "The Colonial Experience: The Eighteenth Century Chesapeake." Baltimore, September 1984, mimeographed.

Hughes, Langston, and Arna Bontemps, eds. *The Book of Negro Folklore*. New York, 1958.

Hughes, Sarah S. "Slaves for Hire: The Allocation of Black Labor in Elizabeth City County, Virginia, 1782 to 1810." *William and Mary Quarterly* 35 (1978), 260–286.

Hulan, Richard H. "Middle Tennessee and the Dogtrot House." *Pioneer America* 7 (1975), 37–46.

Hummel, Ray O., Jr. *A List of Places Included in Nineteenth Century Virginia Directories*. Richmond, 1960.

Hyatt, Harry. *Hoodoo, Conjuration, Witchcraft, Rootwork: Beliefs Accepted by Many Negroes and White Persons, These Being Orally Recorded Among Blacks and Whites*. 5 vols. Hannibal, Mo., 1970.

Ingle, Edward. "A Virginia Witch." *Magazine of American History* 10 (1883), 425–427.

Isaac, Erick. "Religion, Landscape and Space." *Landscape* 9, no. 2 (1959–1960), 14–18.

Isaac, Rhys. "Ethnographic Method in History: An Action Approach." *Historical Methodology* 12 (1980), 43–61.

———. "Evangelical Revolt: The Nature of the Baptists' Challenge to the Traditional Order in Virginia, 1765–1775." *William and Mary Quarterly* 31 (1974), 345–368.

———. "Idleness Ethic and the Liberty of Anglo-Americans." *Reviews in American History* 4 (1976), 47–52.

———. *The Transformation of Virginia, 1740–1790: Community, Religion, and Authority*. Chapel Hill, 1982.

Jackson, Charles O. *Passing: The Vision of Death in America*. Westport, Conn., 1977.

Jackson, George Pullen. *White and Negro Spirituals: Their Life Span and Kinship*. Locust Valley, N.Y., 1943.

Jackson, Luther P. "Religious Development of the Negroes in Virginia from 1760 to 1860." *Journal of Negro History* 16 (1931), 168–189.

———. "The Early Strivings of the Negro in Virginia." *Journal of Negro History* 25 (1940), 25–34.

Jahoda, G. "A Note on Ashanti Names and their Relationship to Personality." *British Journal of Psychology* 45 (1954), 192–195.

336

James, Edward W. "Grace Sherwood, the Virginia Witch." *William and Mary Quarterly*, 1st series, 3 (1894–1895), 96–101, 190–192, 242–244; 4 (1895–1896), 18–22.

Jeane, Donald Gregory. "Combining Age-Old Religious and Cultural Customs in Cemetery Traditions." *American Cemetery* 54 (June 1982), 18–22.

———. "The Upland South Cemetery: An American Type." *Journal of Popular Culture* 11 (1977–1978), 895–903.

———. "The Traditional Upland South Cemetery." *Landscape* 18, no. 2 (1969), 39–41.

Jeffreys, M.D.W. "Names of American Negro Slaves." *American Anthropologist* 50 (1948), 571–573.

Jernegan, Marcus W. *Laboring and Dependent Classes in Colonial America, 1607–1783*. New York, 1931.

Johnson, Whittington B. "Black Patterns of Employment, 1750–1820." In *From Freedom to Freedom: African Roots in American Soil*. Ed. Mildred Bain and Ervin Lewis. New York, 1977.

Johnston, James H. "The Participation of White Men in Virginia Negro Insurrections." *Journal of Negro History* 16 (1931), 158–167.

———. *Race Relations in Virginia and Miscegenation in the South, 1776–1860*. Amherst, [1937] 1970.

Jones, Alice Hanson. *American Colonial Wealth: Documents and Methods*. 3 vols. New York, 1978.

Jones, C. C. *The Religious Instruction of the Negroes in the United States*. Savannah, 1842.

Jones, Gwilym I. "Ibo Age Organization with Special Reference to the Cross River and North-Eastern Ibo." *Journal of the Royal Anthropological Institute of Great Britain and Ireland* 92 (1962), 191–221.

Jones, Jacqueline. *Labor of Love, Labor of Sorrow: Black Women, Work, and the Family from Slavery to the Present*. New York, 1985.

Jones, Steven L. "The African-American Tradition in Vernacular Architecture." In *The Archaeology of Slavery and Plantation Life*. Ed. Theresa A. Singleton. Orlando, 1985.

Jones, W. T. "World Views: Their Nature and Function." *Current Anthropology* 13 (1972), 79–109.

Jordan, Terry G. *American Log Buildings: An Old World Heritage*. Chapel Hill, 1985.

Jordan, Winthrop D. "Planter and Slave Identity Formation: Some Problems in the Comparative Approach." In *Comparative Perspectives on Slavery in the New World Plantation Societies*. Ed. Vera Rubin and Arthur Tuden. New York, 1977.

———. *White Over Black: American Attitudes Toward the Negro, 1550–1812*. Chapel Hill, 1968.

Kagame, Alexis. "The Empirical Apperception of Time and the Concepton of History in Bantu Thought." In *Cultures and Time*. Ed. L. Gardet et al. Paris, 1976.

Katz, Bernard, ed. *The Social Implications of Early Negro Music in the United States*. New York, 1969.

Kaufman, William. *The Overseer: Plantation Management in the Old South*. Baton Rouge, 1966.

Kelly, Kevin P. " 'In Dispers'd Plantations': Settlement Patterns in Seventeenth-Century Surry County, Virginia." In *The Chesapeake in the Seventeenth Cen-*

tury: Essays on Anglo-American Society. Ed. Thad W. Tate and David L. Ammerman. New York, 1979.

Kelso, William M. *Kingsmill Plantations, 1619–1800: Archaeology of Country Life in Colonial Virginia*. Orlando, 1984.

Kenney, William H. "George Whitefield, Dissenter Priest of the Great Awakening, 1739–41." *William and Mary Quarterly* 26 (1969), 75–93.

Kenyatta, Jomo. "Marriage Systems." In *Peoples and Cultures of Africa: An Anthropological Reader*. Ed. Elliott P. Skinner. Garden City, N.Y., 1973.

Kerridge, Eric. *The Farmers of Old England*. London, 1973.

Kilson, Marion Dusser De Barenne. "West African Society and the Atlantic Slave Trade, 1441–1865." In *Key Issues in the Afro-American Experience*. Ed. Nathan I. Huggins et al. New York, 1971.

———. "The Ga Naming Rite." *Anthropos* 63–64 (1968), 904–920.

Kimball, Fiske. *Thomas Jefferson, Architect*. New York, [1916] 1968.

Klein, Herbert S. *The Middle Passage: Comparative Studies in the Atlantic Slave Trade*. Princeton, 1978.

———. "Slaves and Shipping in Eighteenth Century Virginia." *Journal of Interdisciplinary History* 3 (1975), 383–412.

Klein, Martin, and Paul E. Lovejoy. "Domestic Slavery in West Africa." In *The Uncommon Market: Essays in the Economic History of the Trans-Atlantic Slave Trade*. Ed. H. Gemery and J. S. Hogendorn. New York, 1979.

Klemp, Egon, ed. *America in Maps: Dating from 1500 to 1856*. New York, 1976.

Kniffen, Fred. "Folk Housing: Key to Diffusion." *Annals of the Association of American Geographers* 55 (1965), 549–577.

———. "Louisiana House Types." In *Readings in Cultural Geography*. Ed. P. Wagner. Chicago, 1962.

———. "Necrogeography in the United States." *Geographical Review* 57 (1967), 426–427.

———, and Henry Glassie. "Building in Wood in the Eastern United States: A Time–Place Perspective." *Geographical Review* 56 (1966), 40–66.

Kolodny, Annette. *The Land Before Her: Fantasy and Experience of the American Frontiers, 1630–1860*. Chapel Hill, 1984.

———. *The Lay of the Land: Metaphor as Experience and History in American Life and Letters*. Chapel Hill, 1975.

Kroll-Smith, J. Stephen. "Transmitting a Revival Culture: The Organizational Dynamic of the Baptist Movement in Colonial Virginia, 1760–1777." *Journal of Southern History* 50 (1984), 551–568.

Kulikoff, Allan. "The Beginnings of the Afro-American Family in Maryland." In *Law, Society and Politics in Early Maryland*. Ed. Aubrey C. Land et al. Baltimore, 1977.

———. "The Origins of Afro-American Society in Tidewater Maryland and Virginia, 1700 to 1790." *William and Mary Quarterly* 35 (1978), 226–259.

———. "A 'Prolifick' People: Black Population Growth in the Chesapeake Colonies, 1700–1790." *Southern Studies* 16 (1977), 391–428.

———. *Tobacco and Slaves: The Development of Southern Cultures in the Chesapeake, 1680–1800*. Chapel Hill, 1986.

———. "Uprooted Peoples: Black Migrants in the Age of the American Revolution, 1790–1820." In *Slavery and Freedom in the Age of the American Revolution*. Ed. Ira Berlin and Ronald Hoffman. Charlottesville, 1983.

Kuna, Ralph. "Hoodoo: The Indigenous Medicine and Psychiatry of the Black American." *Mankind Quarterly* 18 (1977), 137–151.

Kussmaul, Ann. *Servants in Husbandry in Early Modern England*. Cambridge, England, 1981.

Laing, R. D. *The Politics of the Family, and Other Essays*. London, 1971.

Land, Aubrey C. "Economic Base and Social Structure: The Northern Chesapeake in the Eighteenth Century." *Journal of Economic History* 25 (1965), 639–654.

——— et al., eds. *Law, Society and Politics in Early Maryland*. Baltimore, 1977.

Landes, David S. *Revolution in Time: Clocks and the Making of the Modern World*. Cambridge, Mass., 1983.

Lane, Ann J., ed. *The Debate Over Slavery: Stanley Elkins and His Critics*. Urbana, 1971.

Laslett, Peter. *Family Life and Illicit Love in Earlier Generations: Essays in Historical Sociology*. Cambridge, England, 1977.

———. *The World We Have Lost: England Before the Industrial Age*. 2d ed. London, 1971.

Lasne, Sophie, and André P. Gaultier. *A Dictionary of Superstitions*. Englewood Cliffs, N.J., 1984.

Lawson, E. Thomas. *Religions of Africa: Traditions in Transformation*. San Diego, 1984.

Lawson, Edwin D. "Personal Names: 100 years of Social Science Contributions." *Names* 32 (1984), 45–73.

Lee, Susan Ann. "The Value of the Local Area." In *Valued Environments*. Ed. J. R. Gold and J. Burgess. London, 1982.

Lee, Umphrey. *The Historical Background of Early Methodist Enthusiasm*. New York, 1967.

Le Goff, Jacques. "The Learned and Popular Dimensions of Journeys in the Otherworld in the Middle Ages." In *Understanding Popular Culture: Europe from the Middle Ages to the Nineteenth Century*. Ed. Steven L. Kaplan. Berlin, 1984.

———. *Time, Work, and Culture in the Middle Ages*. Chicago, 1980.

Leone, Mark P. "Material Culture of the Georgian World." Conference on "The Colonial Experience: The Eighteenth Century Chesapeake." Baltimore, September 1984, mimeographed.

Leventhal, Herbert. *In the Shadow of the Enlightenment: Occultism and Renaissance Science in Eighteenth-Century America*. New York, 1976.

LeVine, Robert A. *Dreams and Deeds: Achievement Motivation in Nigeria*. Chicago, 1966.

Levine, Lawrence. *Black Culture and Black Consciousness; Afro-American Folk Thought from Slavery to Freedom*. New York, 1977.

Levy, Babette M. "Early Puritans in the Southern and Island Colonies." *American Antiquarian Society Proceedings* 70 (1960), pt. 1, 69–348.

Levy-Bruhl, Lucien. *Primitives and the Supernatural*. New York, [1935] 1973.

Lewis, I. M. *Ecstatic Religion: An Anthropological Study of Spirit Possession and Shamanism*. Harmondsworth, England, 1971.

Lewis, Jan. [See also Jan Ellen Lewis Grimmelman.] "Domestic Tranquillity and the Management of Emotion Among the Gentry of Pre-Revolutionary Virginia." *William and Mary Quarterly* 39 (1982), 135–149.

———. *The Pursuit of Happiness: Family and Values in Jefferson's Virginia*. Cambridge, England, 1983.

Lewis, Peirce. "Common Houses, Cultural Spoor." *Landscape* 19, no. 2 (1975), 1–22.

———. "Learning from Looking: Geographic and Other Writing about the American Cultural Landscape." *American Quarterly* 35 (1983), 242–261.

Littlefield, Daniel C. *Rice and Slaves: Ethnicity and the Slave Trade in Colonial South Carolina*. Baton Rouge, 1981.

Litwack, Leon F. *Been in the Storm So Long: The Aftermath of Slavery*. New York, 1980.

Lockridge, Kenneth A. *Literacy in Colonial New England: An Enquiry into the Social Context of Literacy in the Early Modern West*. New York, 1974.

Lomax, Alan. "The Homogeneity of African-Afro-American Musical Style." In *Afro-American Anthropology: Contemporary Perspectives*. Ed. Norman E. Whitten, Jr., and John F. Szwed. New York, 1970.

Lovejoy, Paul E. *Transformations in Slavery: A History of Slavery in Africa*. Cambridge, England, 1983.

Loveland, Anne C. *Southern Evangelicals and the Social Order, 1800–1860*. Baton Rouge, 1980.

Luccketti, Nicholas. "17th-Century Planters in 'New Pocosin': Excavations at Bennett Farm and River Creek." *Notes on Virginia* 23 (1983), 26–29.

Luckman, Thomas. *The Invisible Religion: The Problem of Religion in Modern Society*. New York, 1967.

———, and Peter L. Berger. *The Social Construction of Reality: A Treatise in the Sociology of Knowledge*. London, 1966.

Lumpkin, William L. *Baptist Foundations in the South: Tracing Through the Separates the Influence of the Great Awakening, 1754–1787*. Nashville, 1961.

Luraghi, Raimondo. *The Rise and Fall of the Plantation South*. New York, 1978.

Luxton, Imogen. "The Reformation and Popular Culture." In *Church and Society in England: Henry* VIII *to James* I. Ed. Felicity Heal and Rosemary O'Day. London, 1977.

McCabe, Carol. "Mr. Jefferson's Garden." *Early American Life* 14, no. 3 (1983), 44–49.

McClelland, Peter D., and Richard J. Zeckhauser. *Demographic Dimensions of the New Republic; American Interregional Migration, Vital Statistics, and Manumissions, 1800–1860*. Cambridge, England, 1982.

McDaniel, George W. *Hearth and Home: Preserving a People's Culture*. Philadelphia, 1982.

McDonald, Forrest, and Ellen Shapiro McDonald. "The Ethnic Origins of the American People, 1790." *William and Mary Quarterly* 37 (1980), 179–199.

MacDonald, Michael. *Mystical Bedlam: Madness, Anxiety and Healing in Seventeenth-Century England*. Cambridge, England, 1981.

Macfarlane, Alan. *Witchcraft in Tudor and Stuart England: A Regional and Comparative Study*. London, 1970.

McGee, James Sears. *The Godly Man in Stuart England: Anglicans, Puritans, and the Two Tables, 1620–1670*. New Haven, 1976.

McJimsey, George D. "Topographic Terms in Virginia." *American Speech* 15 (1940), 3–39, 149–180, 262–301, 381–420.

McLachlin, James. "Classical Names, American Identities." In *Classical Traditions in Early America*. Ed. John W. Eadie. Ann Arbor, 1976.

340

McNearney, Clayton. "Ah, Lovely Appearance of Death." *Soundings* 65 (1982), 57–77.

Main, Gloria L. *Tobacco Colony: Life in Early Maryland, 1650–1720.* Princeton, 1982.

Main, Jackson Turner. "The Distribution of Property in Post-Revolutionary Virginia." *Mississippi Valley Historical Review* 41 (1954–1955), 241–258.

———. "The One Hundred." *William and Mary Quarterly* 11 (1954), 355–384.

———. *The Social Structure of Revolutionary America.* Princeton, 1965.

Malcolmson, R. W. *Life and Labour in England, 1700–1780.* New York, 1981.

Malone, Dumas. *Jefferson and His Time.* 6 vols. Vol. 1: *Jefferson the Virginian.* Boston, 1948. Vol. 6: *The Sage of Monticello.* Boston, 1981.

———, and Steven H. Hochman. "A Note on Evidence: The Personal History of Madison Hemings." *Journal of Southern History* 41 (1975), 523–528.

Mandelbaum, Maurice. *The Anatomy of Historical Knowledge.* Baltimore, 1977.

Manning, Patrick. "The Slave Trade in the Bight of Benin, 1640–1890." In *The Uncommon Market: Essays in the Economic History of the Atlantic Slave Trade.* Ed. Henry A. Gemery and Jan S. Hogendorn. New York, 1979.

Marambaud, Pierre, *William Byrd of Westover, 1674–1744.* Charlottesville, 1971.

Marietta, Jack D. *The Reformation of American Quakerism, 1748–1783.* Philadelphia, 1984.

Mariner, Kirk. *Revival's Children: A Religious History of Virginia's Eastern Shore.* Salisbury, Md., 1979.

Marshall, Dorothy. *The English Domestic Servant in History.* London, 1949.

———. *The English Poor in the Eighteenth Century.* London, 1926.

Marx, Leo. *The Machine in the Garden: Technology and the Pastoral Ideal in America.* London, 1964.

Mathews, Donald G. *Religion in the Old South.* Chicago, 1977.

———. *Slavery and Methodism: A Chapter in American Morality, 1780–1845.* Princeton, 1965.

———, "Religion and Slavery—The Case of the American South." In *Anti-Slavery, Religion and Reform: Essays in Memory of Roger Anstey.* Ed. Christien Bolt and Seymour Drescher. Folkestone, England, 1980.

May, Rollo. "Contributions of Existential Psychotherapy." In *Existence: A New Dimension in Psychiatry and Psychology.* Ed. Rollo May et al. New York, 1958.

Mbiti, John S. *Introduction to African Religion.* London, 1975.

Mekkawi, Mod. *Bibliography on Traditional Architecture in Africa.* Washington, D.C., 1978.

Menard, Russell R. "From Servants to Slaves: The Transformation of the Chesapeake Labor System." *Southern Studies* 16 (1977), 355–390.

———, Lois Green Carr, and Lorena S. Walsh. "A Small Planter's Profits: The Cole Estate and the Growth of the Early Chesapeake Economy." *William and Mary Quarterly* 40 (1983), 171–196.

Mercer, Eric. *English Vernacular Houses: A Study of Traditional Farmhouses and Cottages.* London, 1975.

Merriam, Alan P. "African Music." In *Continuity and Change in African Cultures.* Ed. William R. Bascom and Melville J. Herskovits. Chicago, 1959.

Metraux, A. *Voodoo in Haiti.* New York, 1959.

Miers, Suzanne, and Igor Kopytoff, eds. *Slavery in Africa; Historical and Anthropological Perspectives.* Madison, Wis., 1977.

Miller, John Chester. *The Wolf by the Ears: Thomas Jefferson and Slavery*. New York, 1977.

Miller, Mary R. *Place Names of the Northern Neck of Virginia: From John Smith's 1606 Map to the Present*. Richmond, 1983.

Miller, Perry. *Errand Into the Wilderness*. New York, 1956.

——. "The Religious Impulse in the Founding of Virginia: Religion and Society in the Early Literature." *William and Mary Quarterly* 5 (1948), 492–522; 6 (1949), 24–41.

Minchinton, Walter, Celia King, and Peter Waite, eds. *Virginia Slave Trade Statistics, 1698–1775*. Richmond, 1984.

Mintz, Sidney W., and Richard Price. *An Anthropological Approach to the Afro-American Past: A Caribbean Perspective*. Philadelphia, 1976.

Mitchell, Henry H. *Black Belief: Folk Beliefs in America and West Africa*. New York, 1975.

Moore, John S. "Writers of Early Virginia Baptist History: John Williams." *Virginia Baptist Register* 14 (1975), 633–647.

Morgan, Edmund S. *American Slavery, American Freedom: The Ordeal of Colonial Virginia*. New York, 1975.

——. *Virginians at Home: Family Life in the Eighteenth Century*. Williamsburg, 1952.

Morgan, Philip D. "Slave Life in the Virginia Piedmont, 1720–1790: A Demographic Report." Conference on "The Colonial Experience: The Eighteenth Century Chesapeake." Baltimore, September 1984, mimeographed.

——. "Work and Culture: The Task System and the World of Low-country Blacks, 1700 to 1800." *William and Mary Quarterly* 39 (1982), 563–599.

Morton, Louis. *Robert Carter of Nomini Hall: A Virginia Tobacco Planter of the Eighteenth Century*. 2d ed. Williamsburg, [1941] 1945.

——. "Robert Wormley Carter of Sabine Hall: Notes on the Life of a Virginia Planter." *Journal of Southern History* 12 (1946), 345–365.

Mullin, Gerald W. *Flight and Rebellion: Slave Resistance in Eighteenth-Century Virginia*. New York, 1972.

Nash, Gary B. "Forging Freedom: The Emancipation Experience in the Northern Seaport Cities, 1775–1820." In *Slavery and Freedom in the Age of the American Revolution*. Ed. Ira Berlin and Ronald Hoffman. Charlottesville, 1983.

——. *Red, White and Black: The Peoples of Early America*. Englewood Cliffs, N.J., 1974.

Ndoma, Ungina. "Kongo Personal Names Today: A Sketch." *Names* 25 (1977), 88–98.

Neiman, Fraser D. "Domestic Architecture at the Clifts Plantation: The Social Context of Early Virginia Building." *Northern Neck of Virginia Historical Magazine* 28 (1978), 3096–3128.

——. *The "Manner House" Before Stratford: Discovering the Clifts Plantation*. Stratford, Va., 1980.

Newton, James E. "Slave Artisans and Craftsmen: The Roots of Afro-American Art." *Black Scholar* 9 (1977), 35–44.

——, and Ronald L. Lewis, eds. *The Other Slaves: Mechanics, Artisans and Craftsmen*. Boston, 1978.

Nichols, Frederick D. *Thomas Jefferson's Architectural Drawings.* 3d ed. Charlottesville, 1961.

———, and James A. Bear, Jr. *Monticello.* Monticello, 1982.

Nicholls, Michael L. "Building the Virginia Southside: A Note on Architecture and Society in the Eighteenth Century." Typescript.

———. "Origins of the Virginia Southside, 1703–1750: A Social and Economic Study." Ph.D. dissertation, College of William and Mary, 1972.

Norton, Mary Beth. *Liberty's Daughters: The Revolutionary Experience of American Women, 1750–1800.* Boston, 1980.

———, Herbert Gutman, and Ira Berlin. "The Afro-American Family in the Age of the Revolution." In *Slavery and Freedom in the Age of the American Revolution.* Ed. Ira Berlin and Ronald Hoffman. Charlottesville, 1983.

Notestein, Wallace. *The English People on the Eve of Colonization, 1603–1630.* New York, 1962.

Nsugbe, Philip O. *Ohaffia: A Matrilineal Ibo People.* Oxford, 1974.

Oakes, James. *The Ruling Race: A History of American Slaveholders.* New York, 1982.

Ofori, Patrick E. *Black African Traditional Religions and Philosophy: A Select Bibliographic Survey of the Sources from the Earliest Times to 1974.* Nendeln, Lichtenstein, 1977.

Okoye, F. Nwabueze. "Chattel Slavery as the Nightmare of the American Revolutionaries." *William and Mary Quarterly* 37 (1980), 3–28.

Oliver, Paul, ed. *Shelter in Africa.* London, 1971.

Oliver, Roland, and Michael Crowder, eds. *The Cambridge Encyclopedia of Africa.* Cambridge, England, 1981.

O'Malley, James R., and John B. Rehder. "The Two-Story Log House in the Upland South." *Journal of Popular Culture* 11 (1977–1978), 904–915.

Opie, John. "A Sense of Place: The World We Have Lost." In *An Appalachian Symposium: Essays Written in Honor of Cratis D. Williams.* Ed. J. W. Williamson. Boone, N.C., 1977.

Ottenberg, Simon. "Ibo Receptivity to Change." In *Continuity and Change in African Cultures.* Ed. William R. Bascom and Melville J. Herskovits. Chicago, [1959] 1962.

Otto, John S. "Artifacts and Status Differences—A Comparison of Ceramics from Planter, Overseer, and Slave Sites on an Antebellum Plantation." In *Research Strategies in Historical Archeology.* Ed. Stanley South. New York, 1977.

———. *Cannon's Point Plantation, 1794–1860: Living Conditions and Status Patterns in the Old South.* Orlando, 1984.

———. "A New Look at Slave Life." *Natural History* 88 (1979), 8–30.

———, and Nain E. Anderson. "The Diffusion of Upland South Folk Culture, 1790–1840." *South Eastern Geographer* 22 (1982), 89–98.

———, and Augustus M. Burns, III. "Black Folks and Poor Buckras: Archeological Evidence of Slave and Overseer Living Conditions on an Antebellum Plantation." *Journal of Black Studies* 14 (1983), 185–200.

Owens, Leslie H. *"This Species of Property": Slave Life and Culture in the Old South.* New York, 1976.

Painter, Floyd. "An Early Eighteenth Century Witch Bottle: A Legacy of the

Wicked Witch of Pongo." *The Chesopiean: A Journal of North American Archeology* 18 (1980), 62–71.

Parrinder, Geoffrey. *African Traditional Religion*. London, 1954.

———. *West African Psychology: A Comparative Study of Psychological and Religious Thought*. London, 1951.

———. *West African Religion: A Study of the Beliefs and Practices of Akan, Ewe, Yoruba, Ibo and Kindred Peoples*. 2d rev ed. London, [1949] 1969.

Patterson, Orlando. *Slavery and Social Death: A Comparative Study*. Cambridge, Mass., 1982.

Paustian, P. Robert. "The Evolution of Personal Naming Practices Among American Blacks." *Names* 26 (1978), 177–191.

Peek, Phil. "Afro-American Material Culture and the Afro-American Craftsman." *Southern Folklore Quarterly* 42 (1978), 109–134.

Perdue, Charles L., Jr., et al., eds. *Weevils in the Wheat; Interviews with Virginia Ex-Slaves*. Bloomington, 1976.

———. *An Annotated Listings of Folklore, Collected by the W.P.A.* Norwood, Penn., 1979.

Perdue, Robert E. *Black Laborers and Black Professionals in Early America, 1750–1830*. New York, 1975.

Pickens, Buford. "Mr. Jefferson as Revolutionary Architect." *Journal of the Society of Architectural Historians* 34 (1975), 257–279.

Pilcher, George W. *Samuel Davies: Apostle of Dissent in Colonial Virginia*. Knoxville, Tenn., 1971.

———. "Samuel Davies and the Instruction of the Negro in Virginia." *Virginia Magazine of History and Biography* 74 (1966), 293–300.

Pinchbeck, Ivy, and Margaret Hewitt. *Children in English Society*. 2 vols. London, 1969–1973.

Pinchbeck, Raymond. *The Virginia Negro Artisan and Tradesman*. Richmond, 1926.

Pitchford, Anita. "The Material Culture of the Traditional East Texas Graveyard." *Southern Folklore Quarterly* 43 (1979), 277–290.

Portman, Derek. "Vernacular Building in the Oxford Region in the Sixteenth and Seventeenth Centuries." In *Rural Change and Urban Growth, 1500–1800*. Ed. C. W. Chalkin and M. A. Havindin. London, 1974.

Potter, Jim. "Demographic Development and Family Structure." In *Colonial British America: Essays in the New History of the Early Modern Era*. Ed. Jack P. Greene and J. R. Pole. Baltimore, 1984.

Poulsen, Richard C. *The Pure Experience of Order: Essays on the Symbolic in the Folk Material Culture of Western America*. Albuquerque, 1982.

Prest, John. *The Garden of Eden: The Botanic Garden and the Re-Creation of Paradise*. New Haven, 1981.

Price, Derek de Sola. "Clockwork Before the Clock and Timekeepers Before Timekeeping." In *The Study of Time* II. Ed. J. T. Fraser and N. Lawrence. Berlin, 1975.

Price, Richard, and Sally Price. "Saramaka Onomastics: an Afro-American Naming System." *Ethnology* 11 (1972), 341–367.

Prussin, Labelle. "An Introduction to Indigenous African Architecture." *Journal of the Society of Architectural Historians* 33 (1974), 183–205.

————, and David Lee. "Architecture in Africa: An Annotated Bibliography." *Africana Library Journal* 4 (1973), 2–32.

Puckett, Newbell Niles. "American Negro Names." *Journal of Negro History* 23 (1938), 35–48.

————. *Folk Beliefs of the Southern Negro*. New York, [1926] 1968.

————, and Murry Heller. *Black Names in America, Origins and Usage*. Boston, 1975.

Puckrein, Gary A. *Little England: Plantation Society and Anglo-Barbadian Politics, 1627–1700*. New York, 1984.

Quaife, G. R. *Wanton Wenches and Wayward Wives: Peasants and Illicit Sex in Early Seventeenth Century England*. London, 1979.

Quarles, Benjamin. "Lord Dunmore as Liberator." *William and Mary Quarterly* 15 (1958), 494–507.

Quinn, David B., ed. *Early Maryland in a Wider World*. Detroit, 1982.

Raboteau, Albert J. *Slave Religion: The "Invisible Institution" in the Ante-bellum South*. New York, 1978.

Radcliffe-Brown, A. R., and Daryll Forde, eds. *African Systems of Kinship and Marriage*. London, 1950.

Randolph, Sarah N. *The Domestic Life of Thomas Jefferson*. Charlottesville, [1871] 1978.

Rasmussen, William. "Sabine Hall, A Classical Villa in Virginia." *Journal of the Society of Architectural Historians* 39 (1980), 286–296.

Rattenbury, Arnold. "Methodism and the Tatterdemalions." In *Popular Culture and Class Conflict, 1590–1914: Explorations in the History of Labour and Leisure*. Ed. E. Yeo and S. Yeo. Sussex, 1981.

Rawley, James A. *The Transatlantic Slave Trade: A History*. New York, 1981.

Ray, Benjamin C. *African Religions: Symbol, Ritual, and Community*. Englewood Cliffs, N.J., 1976.

Robertson, Claire, and Martin A. Klein, eds. *Women and Slavery in Africa*. Madison, Wis., 1983.

Robinson, Jean W. "Black Healers During the Colonial Period and Early Nineteenth Century America." Ph.D. dissertation, Southern Illinois University, 1979.

Roediger, David R. " 'And Die in Dixie': Funerals, Death and Heaven in the Slave Community, 1700–1865." *Massachusetts Review* 22 (1981), 163–183.

Rose, Harold W. *The Colonial Houses of Worship in America Built in the English Colonies Before the Republic, 1607–1789, and Still Standing*. New York, 1963.

Rose, Willie Lee. *Slavery and Freedom*. New York, 1982.

Rutman, Darrett B. "The Evolution of Religious Life in Early Virginia." *Lex et Scientia* 14 (1978), 190–214.

————, and Anita H. Rutman. *A Place in Time: Middlesex County, Virginia, 1650–1750 [I]*. New York, 1984.

————, *A Place in Time: Explicatus [II]*. New York, 1984.

————, Charles Wetherell, and Anita H. Rutman. "Rhythms of Life: Black and White Seasonality in the Early Chesapeake." *Journal of Interdisciplinary History* 11 (1980–1981), 29–53.

Ryland, Garnett. *The Baptists of Virginia, 1699–1926*. Richmond, 1955.

Salusbury-Jones, G. T. *Street Life in Medieval England*. 2d ed. Hassocks, Sussex, [1948] 1975.

Sanchez-Saavedra, E. M. *A Description of the Country: Virginia's Cartographers and Their Maps, 1607–1881*. Richmond, 1975.

Sanford, Charles B. *The Religious Life of Thomas Jefferson*. Charlottesville, 1984.

Sauer, Carl O. *Sixteenth Century North America: The Land and the People as Seen by the Europeans*. Berkeley, 1971.

Saum, Lewis O. "Death in the Popular Mind of Pre-Civil War America." In *Death in America*. Ed. David E. Stannard. Philadelphia, 1975.

Savitt, Todd L. *Medicine and Slavery: The Diseases and Health Care of Blacks in Antebellum Virginia*. Urbana, 1978.

Scadron, Arlene W. "The Formative Years: Childhood and Child-Rearing in Eighteenth Century Anglo-American Culture." Ph.D. dissertation, University of California, Berkeley, 1979.

Scarisbrick, J. J. *The Reformation and the English People*. Oxford, 1984.

Scheper, George L. "Reformation Attitudes Toward Allegory and the Song of Songs." *PMLA* 89 (1974), 551–562.

Scherer, Lester B. *Slavery and the Churches in Early America, 1619–1819*. Grand Rapids, 1975.

Schuyler, Robert, ed. *Archaeological Perspectives on Ethnicity in America*. New York, 1980.

Seiler, William H. "The Anglican Parish in Virginia." In *Seventeenth Century America*. Ed. James M. Smith. New York, 1959.

———. "Land Processioning in Colonial Virginia." *William and Mary Quarterly* 6 (1949), 416–436.

Sernett, Milton C. *Black Religion and American Evangelism: White Protestants, Plantation Missions, and the Flowering of Negro Christianity, 1787–1865*. Metuchen, N.J., 1975.

Shammas, Carole. "English-Born and Creole Elites in Turn-of-the-Century Virginia." In *The Chesapeake in the Seventeenth Century: Essays on Anglo-American Society*. Ed. Thad W. Tate and David L. Ammerman. New York, 1979.

Shea, William L. *The Virginia Militia in the Seventeenth Century*. Baton Rouge, 1983.

Sheldon, Marianne B. "Black–White Relations in Richmond, Virginia, 1782–1820." *Journal of Southern History* 45 (1979), 27–44.

Simpson, Lewis P. *The Dispossessed Garden: Pastoral and History in Southern Literature*. Athens, Ga., 1975.

———. "William Byrd and the South." *Early American Literature* 7 (1972), 187–195.

Singleton, George A. *The Romance of African Methodism: A Study of the African Methodist Episcopal Church*. New York, 1952.

Singleton, Theresa A., ed. *The Archaeology of Slavery and Plantation Life*. Orlando, 1985.

Skinner, Elliott P., ed. *Peoples and Cultures of Africa*. Garden City, N.Y., 1973.

Skolle, John. "Adobe in Africa: Varieties of Anonymous Architecture." *Landscape* 12, no. 2 (1962), 15–17.

Smith, Abbot Emerson. *Colonists in Bondage: White Servitude and Convict Labor in America, 1607–1776*. Chapel Hill, 1947.

Smith, Alan. *The Established Church and Popular Religion, 1750–1850*. London, 1970.

Smith, Daniel Blake. "Autonomy and Affection: Parents and Children in Eighteenth-Century Chesapeake Families." *Psychohistory Review* 6 (1977–1978), 32–51.

———. *Inside the Great House: Planter Family Life In Eighteenth-Century Chesapeake Society*. Ithaca, 1980.

———. "Mortality and Family in the Colonial Chesapeake." *Journal of Interdisciplinary History* 8 (1978), 403–427.

Smith, Daniel Scott. "Child-Naming Practices, Kinship Ties, and Change in Family Attitudes in Hingham, Massachusetts, 1641–1880." *Journal of Social History* 18 (1985), 541–566.

———, and Michael S. Hindus. "Premarital Pregnancy in America, 1640–1971: An Overview and Interpretation." *Journal of Interdisciplinary History* 5 (1975), 537–570.

Smith, David. "William Byrd Surveys America." *Early American Literature* 11 (1976), 296–310.

Smith, George Cook, et al., eds. *Shadows in Silver: A Record of Virginia, 1850–1900 in Contemporary Photographs Taken by George and Huestic Cook*. New York, 1954.

Smith, J. T. "The Evolution of the English Peasant House to the Late Seventeenth Century: The Evidence of Buildings." *Journal of the British Archaeological Association* 33 (1970), 122–147.

Smith, James Morton, ed. *Seventeenth-Century America: Essays in Colonial History*. New York, [1959] 1972.

Sobel, Mechal. *Trabelin' On: The Slave Journey to an Afro-Baptist Faith*. Westport, Conn., 1979.

Soderlund, Jean R. *Quakers & Slavery: A Divided Spirit*. Princeton, 1985.

Sow, I. *Anthropological Structures of Madness in Black Africa*. New York, [1978] 1980.

Spruill, Julia Cherry. *Women's Life and Work in the Southern Colonies*. New York, [1938] 1972.

Stampp, Kenneth M. "The Daily Life of the Southern Slave." In *Key Issues in the Afro-American Experience*. Ed. Nathan I. Huggins et al. New York, 1971.

———. *The Peculiar Institution: Slavery in the Ante-Bellum South*. New York, 1956.

Stannard, David E., ed. *Death in America*. Philadelphia, 1975.

———. *The Puritan Way of Death: A Study in Religion, Culture and Social Change*. New York, 1977.

Stavisky, Leonard P. "The Origins of Negro Craftsmanship in Colonial America." *Journal of Negro History* 32 (1947), 417–429.

Stearns, Raymond P. *Science in the British Colonies of America*. Urbana, 1970.

Stein, Stephen J. "George Whitefield on Slavery." *Church History* 42 (1973), 243–256.

Stewart, George R. *American Given Names: Their Origin and History in the Context of the English Language*. New York, 1979.

Stilgoe, John R. *Common Landscape of America, 1580 to 1845*. New Haven, 1982.

———. "Folklore and Graveyard Design." *Landscape* 22, no. 3 (1978), 22–28.

Stone, Lawrence. *The Family, Sex and Marriage in England, 1500–1800*. London, 1977.

Stowell, Marion B. *Early American Almanacs: The Colonial Weekday Bible*. New York, 1977.

Swan, L. Alex. *Survival and Progress: The Afro-American Experience*. Westport, Conn., 1981.

Sweet, William Warren. "The Churches as Moral Courts of the Frontier." *Church History* 2 (1933), 3–21.

———, ed. *Religion on the American Frontier*. Vol 4: *The Methodists*. Chicago, 1946.

Tarpley, Fred A. "Southern Cemeteries: Neglected Archives for the Folklorist." *Southern Folklore Quarterly* 27 (1963), 323–333.

Tate, Thad W. "The Discovery and Development of the Southern Colonial Landscape: Six Commentators." *Procedings of the American Antiquarian Society* 93 (1983), 289–311.

———. *The Negro in Eighteenth-Century Williamsburg*. Williamsburg, 1965.

———, and David L. Ammerman, eds. *The Chesapeake in the Seventeenth Century: Essays on Anglo-American Society*. New York, 1979.

Taylor, James B. *Virginia Baptist Ministers*. Series 1. Philadelphia, [1837] 1859.

Thomas, Keith. "Age and Authority in Early Modern England." *Procedings of the British Academy* 62 (1976), 205–248.

———. *Man and the Natural World: Changing Attitudes in England, 1500–1800*. London, 1983.

———. *Religion and the Decline of Magic: Studies in Popular Beliefs in Sixteenth and Seventeenth Century England*. London, 1971.

———. "Work and Leisure in Pre-Industrial Society." *Past and Present* 29 (1964), 50–62.

Thompson, Denys, ed. *Change and Tradition in Rural England: An Anthology of Writings on Country Life*. Cambridge, England, 1980.

Thompson, E. P. *The Making of the English Working Class*. London, 1963.

———. "Time, Work-Discipline and Industrial Capitalism." *Past and Present* 38 (1967), 56–97.

Thompson, Robert Farris. "African Influence on the Art of the United States." In *Black Studies in the University: A Symposium*. Ed. Armstead L. Robinson et al. New Haven, 1969.

———. "An Aesthetic of the Cool: West African Dance." *American Forum* 2 (1966), 85–102.

———. *Flash of the Spirit: African and Afro-American Art and Philosophy*. New York, 1983.

———, and Joseph Cornet. *The Four Moments of the Sun: Kongo Art in Two Worlds*. Washington, D.C., 1982.

Thorpe, Earl. *The Mind of the Negro*. Baton Rouge, 1961.

Tipps, Dean C. "Modernization Theory and the Comparative Study of Societies: A Critical Perspective." *Comparative Studies in Society and History* 15 (1973), 199–226.

Todd, Robert W. *Methodism of the Peninsula, or Sketches of Notable Characters and Events in the History of Methodism in the Maryland and Delaware Peninsula*. Philadelphia, 1886.

Tuan, Yi-Fu. "Rootedness Versus Sense of Place." *Landscape* 24, no. 1 (1980), 3–8.

———. "Space, Time, Place: A Humanistic Frame." In *Making Sense of Time*. Vol. 1. Ed. T. Carlstein et al. London, 1978.

——. *Topophilia: A Study of Environmental Perception, Attitudes and Values.* Englewood Cliffs, N.J., 1974.

Turner, Lorenzo D. *Africanisms in the Gullah Dialect.* Chicago, 1949.

Turner, Victor W. "Colour Classification in Ndembu Ritual: A Problem in Primitive Classification." In *Anthropological Approaches to the Study of Religion.* Ed. Michael Banton. London, 1966.

Uchendu. Victor C. *The Igbo of Southeast Nigeria.* New York, 1965.

——. "Slaves and Society in Igboland, Nigeria." In *Slavery in Africa; Historical and Anthropological Perspectives.* Ed. Suzanne Miers and Igor Kopytoff. Madison, Wis., 1977.

——. "Social Determinants of Agricultural Change." In *Agricultural Change in Tropical Africa.* Ed. Kenneth R. M. Anthony et al. Ithaca, 1979.

United States Bureau of the Census. *Historical Statistics of the United States. Colonial Times to 1970.* 2 vols. Washington, D.C., 1975.

Upton, Dell. "The Origins of Chesapeake Architecture." In *Three Centuries of Maryland Architecture: A Selection of Presentations Made at the Eleventh Annual Conference of the Maryland Historic Trust.* Mimeographed. Annapolis, 1982.

——. "Ordinary Buildings: A Bibliographical Essay on American Vernacular Architecture." *American Studies International* 19, no. 2 (Winter 1981), 57–75.

——. "The Power of Things: Recent Studies in American Vernacular Architecture." *American Quarterly* 35 (1983), 262–279.

——. "Slave Housing in 18th-Century Virginia: A Report to the Department of Social and Cultural History, National Museum of American History, Smithsonian Institution." Washington, D.C., 1982, typescript.

——. "Toward a Performance Theory of Vernacular Architecture: Early Tidewater Virginia as a Case Study." *Folklore Forum* 12 (1979), 173–196.

——. "Traditional Timber Framing: An Interpretive Essay." In *The Material Culture of the Wooden Age.* Ed. Brooke Hindle. Tarrytown, N.Y., 1981.

——. "Vernacular Domestic Architecture in Eighteenth-Century Virginia." *Winterthur Portfolio* 17 (1982), 95–119.

Vansina, Jan. *Oral Tradition: A Study in Historical Methodology.* Chicago, 1965.

Verner, Coolie. "The Fry and Jefferson Map." *Imago Mundi* 21 (1967), 70–94.

Viering, Norman. "The First American Enlightenment: Tillotson, Leverett and Philosophical Anglicanism." *New England Quarterly* 54 (1981), 307–344.

Virginia Historic Landmarks Commission. *The Virginia Landmarks Register.* Richmond, 1976.

Vlach, John Michael. *The Afro-American Tradition in Decorative Arts.* Cleveland, 1979.

——. "Shotgun Houses." *Natural History* 87 (1977), 50–57.

——. "The Shotgun House: An African Architectural Legacy." *Pioneer America* 8 (1976), 47–70.

Wahlman, Maude S., and John Scully. "Aesthetic Principles in Afro-American Quilts." In *Afro-American Folk Art and Crafts.* Ed. William Ferris. Boston, 1983.

Walker, Sheila S. *Ceremonial Spirit Possession in Africa and Afro-America: Forms, Meanings and Functional Significance for Individuals and Social Groups.* Leiden, 1972.

Wall, Charles C. "Housing and Family Life of the Mount Vernon Negro." Mt. Vernon, [1954] 1962, typescript.

Walsh, James P. "Holy Time and Sacred Space in Puritan New England." *American Quarterly* 32 (1980), 79–95.

Walsh, Lorena S. "Changing Work Roles for Slave Labor in Chesapeake Agriculture, 1620–1820." Conference on "The Colonial Experience: The Eighteenth Century Chesapeake." Baltimore, September 1984, mimeographed.

———, and Russell R. Menard. "Death in the Chesapeake: Two Life Tables for Men in Early Colonial Maryland." *Maryland Historical Magazine* 69 (1974), 211–227.

Waterman, Thomas Tileston. *The Mansions of Virginia, 1706–1776.* Chapel Hill, 1946.

———, and John A. Barrows. *Domestic Colonial Architecture of Tidewater Virginia.* New York, [1932] 1969.

Watkins, Owen C. *The Puritan Experience.* London, 1972.

Wax, Darold D. "Preferences for Slaves in Colonial America." *Journal of Negro History* 58 (1973), 371–401.

Wearmouth, Robert F. *Methodism and the Common People of the Eighteenth Century.* London, 1945.

Weatherford, Willis D. *American Churches and the Negro: A Historical Study From Early Slave Days to the Present.* Boston, 1957.

Webb, Stephen Saunders. *1676, The End of American Independence.* Cambridge, Mass., 1985.

Weisberger, Bernard A. *They Gathered at the River: The Story of the Great Revivalists and their Impact Upon Religion in America.* Boston, 1958.

Weisman, Richard. *Witchcraft, Magic and Religion in 17th-Century Massachusetts.* Amherst, 1984.

Wells, Robert V. *The Population of the British Colonies in America Before 1776: A Survey of Census Data.* Princeton, 1975.

Wertenbaker, Thomas J. *The Golden Age of Colonial Culture.* 2d ed. rev. New York, [1942] 1949.

Westbury, Susan A. "Colonial Virginia and the Atlantic Slave Trade." Ph.D. dissertation, University of Illinois, 1981.

Wharton, Anne Hollingsworth. *Martha Washington.* New York, 1897.

Wheeler, Douglas L. "Toward a History of Angola: Problems and Sources." In *Western African History.* Ed. D. F. McCall et al. New York, 1969.

Whiffen, Marcus. *The Public Buildings of Williamsburg; Colonial Capital of America.* Williamsburg, 1958.

White, William Spottswood. *The African Preacher.* Philadelphia, 1849.

Whitten, Norman E., Jr. "Contemporary Patterns of Malign Occultism Among Negroes in North Carolina." *Journal of American Folklore* 65 (1962), 311–325.

Wieschhoff, Heinz A. "The Social Significance of Names Among the Ibo of Nigeria." *American Anthropologist* 43 (1941), 212–222.

Williams, Arnold. *The Common Expositor: An Account of the Commentaries on Genesis, 1527–1633.* Chapel Hill, 1948.

Williams, William H. *The Garden of American Methodism: The Delmarva Peninsula, 1769–1820.* Wilmington, 1984.

Williamson, Joel. *New People: Miscegenation and Mulattoes in the United States.* New York, 1980.

Wilson, Eugene M. "The Single Pen Log House in the South." *Pioneer America* 2 (1970), 21–28.

———. "Some Similarities Between American and European Folk Houses." *Pioneer America* 3 (1971), 8–14.

Windley, Lathan A. "A Profile of Runaway Slaves in Virginia and South Carolina from 1730 through 1787." Ph.D. dissertation, University of Iowa, 1974.

Wolfram, Walt. "The Relationship of White Southern Speech to Vernacular Black English." *Language* 50 (1974), 498–527.

———, and Nona H. Clarke, eds. *Black–White Speech Relationships.* Washington, D.C., 1971.

Wood, Peter H. *Black Majority: Negroes in Colonial South Carolina from 1670 through the Stono Rebellion.* New York, 1974.

———. " 'I Did the Best I Could For My Day': The Study of Early Black History During the Second Reconstruction, 1960 to 1976." *William and Mary Quarterly* 35 (1978), 185–225.

———. "People's Medicine in the Early South." *Southern Exposure* 6 (1978), 50–53.

———. "Whetting, Setting and Laying Timbers: Black Builders in the Early South," *Southern Exposure* 8 (1980), 3–8.

Woodson, Carter G. *The History of the Negro Church.* 2d ed. Washington, D.C., 1921.

Woodward, C. Vann. "The Southern Ethic in a Puritan World." *William and Mary Quarterly* 25 (1968), 343–370.

———. "Clio with Soul." *Journal of American History* 56 (1969), 5–20.

———. "History from Slave Sources." *American Historical Review* 79 (1974), 470–481.

Woolverton, John F. *Colonial Anglicanism in North America.* Detroit, 1984.

Wright, Louis B. "The Classical Tradition in Colonial Virginia." *Papers of the Bibliographical Society of America* 33 (1939), 85–97.

———. *The Colonial Search for a Southern Eden.* University, Ala., 1953.

———. "William Byrd of Westover: An American Pepys." *South Atlantic Quarterly* 39 (1940), 259–274.

Wright, Martin, "Antecedents of the Double-Pen House Type." *Annals of the Association of American Geographers* 48 (1958), 109–117.

Wrightson, Keith. *English Society: 1580–1680.* New Brunswick, N.J., 1982.

———, and David Levine. *Poverty and Piety in an English Village; Terling, 1525–1700.* New York, 1979.

Wyatt-Brown, Bertram. *Southern Honor: Ethics and Behavior in the Old South.* New York, 1982.

Yeomans, D. T. "A Preliminary Study of 'English' Roofs in Colonial America." *APT Bulletin* 13 (1981), 9–18.

Yetman, Norman. "Ex-Slave Interviews and the Historiography of Slavery." *American Quarterly* 36 (1984), 181–210.

Zahan, Dominique. *The Religion, Spirituality and Thought of Traditional Africa.* Chicago, [1970] 1979.

Zaretsky, Irving I., and Cynthia Shambaugh. *Spirit Possession and Spirit Mediumship in Africa and Afro-America: An Annotated Bibliography.* New York, 1978.

Zelinsky, Wilbur. "Unearthly Delights: Cemetery Names and the Map of the Changing American Afterworld." In *Geographies of the Mind: Essays in Historical Geosophy.* Ed. David Lowenthal and Martyn J. Bowden. New York, 1975.

BIBLIOGRAPHY

Zuckerman, Michael. "Dreams That Men Dare to Dream: The Role of Ideas in Western Modernization." *Social Science History* 2 (1978), 332–345.

———. "The Fabrication of Identity of Early America." *William and Mary Quarterly* 34 (1977), 183–214.

———. "William Byrd's Family." *Perspectives in American History* 12 (1979), 255–311.

Index

A bracketed name indicates the surname of a slave's owner when it is not known if this name was used by the slave.

LIBRARY OF CONGRESS CATALOGING-IN-PUBLICATION DATA

Sobel, Mechal.
The world they made together.

Bibliography: p.
Includes index.
1. Afro-Americans—Virginia—History—18th century. 2. Virginia—Race
relations. 3. Virginia—Race relations. 3. Virginia—History—Colonial
period, ca. 1600-1775. 4. United States—Civilization—
Afro-American influences. I. Title.

E185.93.V8S64 1987   975.5'00496073   87-3536
ISBN 0-691-04747-2 (alk. paper)